IBM Cognos TM1 Cookbook

Build real world planning, budgeting, and forecasting solutions with a collection of over 60 simple but incredibly effective recipes

Ankit Garg

PUBLISHING

BIRMINGHAM - MUMBAI

IBM Cognos TM1 Cookbook

First published: December 2011

Production Reference: 1081211

Published by Packt Publishing Ltd.
Livery Place
35 Livery Street
Birmingham B3 2PB, UK.

ISBN 978-1-84968-210-7

www.packtpub.com

Cover Image by Sandeep Babu (sandyjb@gmail.com)

Credits

Author

Ankit Garg

Reviewers

Wim Gielis

Abhishek Sanghani

Acquisition Editor

Amey Kanse

Development Editor

Hyacintha D'Souza

Technical Editors

Kedar Bhat

Kavita Iyer

Project Coordinator

Jovita Pinto

Proofreaders

Mario Cecere

Kelly Hutchinson

Indexer

Hemangini Bari

Graphics

Manu Joseph

Production Coordinator

Alwin Roy

Cover Work

Alwin Roy

About the Author

Ankit Garg is a software professional having over seven and a half years of experience in implementing, designing, and managing data warehousing and BI solutions for industry leaders. He has catered to multiple clients, spanning various geographies and industry domains. His core skills include a full set of BI and DW skills, which includes ETL, BI, Data Warehousing, and Predictive Analysis.

Currently, he is involved in product R&D and is employed by a software major.

The book is the result of his technical experience acquired, while implementing planning and budgeting solutions for the industry.

I would like to thank the PACKT team and Editors for their full faith on my authoring and technical skills. They played a pivotal role in bringing the book to the current shape.

Dedicated to my mother and special thanks to my friend Abhishek for the initiative he has taken, for me to get started.

All the best to dear readers, really hope they find the stuff useful and worth reading.

About the Reviewers

Wim Gielis, is currently a Business Intelligence consultant at Aexis Belgium. He is responsible for implementing custom IBM Cognos TM1 applications as well as providing (custom) TM1 training sessions.

He regularly posts articles written in English on IBM Cognos TM1 on his blog: http://www.wimgielis.be. He is also very active on several online message boards regarding TM1 (such as http://www.tm1forum.com), and Excel VBA (such as www.mrexcel.com, www.ozgrid.com, and various others).

Wim Gielis was awarded the Microsoft Excel MVP award in 2011 for exceptional contributions to the Excel community.

He can be contacted at wim.gielis@gmail.com.

Abhishek Sanghani was born in India and attended Mumbai University where he majored in Computer Engineering. He began his career in 2004 as a Business Intelligence and Cognos Consultant, and has worked with leading IT and Finance Services companies since then.

He pursued Finance Management degree along with his work in the field of Cognos and BI, successfully progressing and winning awards and certifications year after year. Presently, he is working in the United Kingdom, utilizing his skills in Cognos, SQL, BI and Data Warehousing. In his free time, he writes technical blogs and also provides training/seminars on demand.

He wrote his first book *IBM Cognos 8 Report Studio Cookbook* with Packt Publishing that covers many basic to advanced features of Report Authoring. It begins by bringing readers on the same platform and introducing the fundamental features useful across any level of reporting. Then it ascends to advanced techniques and tricks to overcome Report Studio 8 limitations.

He thinks that this book is "a wonderful compilation of knowledge and techniques to work on TM1 which will prove very useful to the readers."

It was a great pleasure to review this book. Thanks to Ankit for producing such useful literature and to Packt for giving me this opportunity to review. I hope my feedback proved useful.

I would also like to thank my lovely wife Dolly for all her support.

www.PacktPub.com

Support files, eBooks, discount offers and more

You might want to visit www.PacktPub.com for support files and downloads related to your book.

Did you know that Packt offers eBook versions of every book published, with PDF and ePub files available? You can upgrade to the eBook version at www.PacktPub.com and as a print book customer, you are entitled to a discount on the eBook copy. Get in touch with us at service@packtpub.com for more details.

At www.PacktPub.com, you can also read a collection of free technical articles, sign up for a range of free newsletters and receive exclusive discounts and offers on Packt books and eBooks.

 PACKTLiB®

http://PacktLib.PacktPub.com

Do you need instant solutions to your IT questions? PacktLib is Packt's online digital book library. Here, you can access, read and search across Packt's entire library of books.

Why Subscribe?

- ▶ Fully searchable across every book published by Packt
- ▶ Copy and paste, print and bookmark content
- ▶ On demand and accessible via web browser

Free Access for Packt account holders

If you have an account with Packt at www.PacktPub.com, you can use this to access PacktLib today and view nine entirely free books. Simply use your login credentials for immediate access.

Instant Updates on New Packt Books

Get notified! Find out when new books are published by following @PacktEnterprise on Twitter, or the *Packt Enterprise* Facebook page.

Table of Contents

Preface

IBM Cognos TM1 is one of the most popular multidimensional analysis tools used to build collaborative planning, budgeting, and forecasting solutions, as well as analytical and reporting applications. This cube-based technology does fast number crunching at the server end and helps end customers move away from manual and tedious planning, budgeting, and analytics processes.

IBM Cognos TM1 Cookbook is a complete manual to building and managing applications with IBM Cognos TM1.

Every important aspect of TM1 is covered with the help of practical recipes, which will make you well acquainted with the tool and ready to take on TM1 projects in the real world. Existing TM1 users and developers will also benefit from the practical recipes covered in the book.

The book will start with a chapter focusing on fundamentals of MOLAP and dimensional modelling, which forms the foundation on which IBM Cognos TM1 is based. Thereafter, chapters will be more TM1-specific, starting with an introduction on dimensions and cubes and how to create and manage them. Further chapters will dig deeper into TM1 objects and rules.

Then we will learn the more advanced features of TM1 such as automating common processes using scripts, customizing drill paths, using rules for advanced modelling, converting currencies, modelling for different fiscal requirements, and more.

At the end of the book, we will cover how to present data and reports, workflows, and TM1 application security.

What this book covers

Chapter 1, Getting Started with TM1, introduces multidimensional concept, IBM Cognos Suite of tools, and concepts such as Enterprise Planning, BI, and OLAP. It introduces the idea of IBM Cognos TM1 being a strong OLAP tool. It also familiarizes you with the architecture and installation of IBM Cognos TM1 and setting up example planning application for the first time.

Chapter 2, Creating dimensions in TM1, introduces dimensions in IBM Cognos TM1 and working with them. It extends sample planning application introduced in *Chapter 1* to demonstrate use cases around TM1 dimensions.

Chapter 3, Building Cubes and Views, introduces cubes in IBM Cognos TM1 and working with them. It extends the example planning application to demonstrate use cases around TM1 cubes and views.

Chapter 4, Loading and Maintaining Data, familiarizes the readers with loading and maintaining data (ETL) in TM1. It introduces you to Turbo Integrator module. It extends the example planning application to demonstrate ETL processes using Turbo Integrator module.

Chapter 5, Adding Business Rules, introduces the readers to IBM Cognos TM1 rules editor to write business rules. It presents you the syntax and semantics of major business rules and demonstrates how business logic can be implemented using TM1 Business Rules.

Chapter 6, Automating Data Load Processes using Scripts, guides readers in writing scripts for some of the most useful and common use cases which a TM1 developer may need to write in a real-life planning implementation.

Chapter 7, Customizing Drill Paths, guides readers in implementing drill paths. Recipes are included for drill implementations across cubes and to an ODBC data source.

Chapter 8, Using Rules for Advanced Modelling, extends the idea of writing business rules to implement some of the complex business use cases for instance, virtual cubes, lookup cubes, and spread profile cubes.

Chapter 9, Converting Currencies, introduces the challenges of business being carried out in multiple currencies. Creating a currency dimension and cube in TM1 helps in keeping a single reporting currency and hence consistency while reporting the business results. The chapter has various recipes to demonstrate the concept.

Chapter 10, Modelling for Different Fiscal Requirements, introduces the readers to the time-related aspect and includes recipes to implement a time dimension and continuous time model.

Chapter 11, Optimizing Rules Performance, talks about tuning rules performance. Recipes are included to demonstrate how FEEDERS and SKIPCHECK are written to improve rules performance in a typical TM1 planning application.

Chapter 12, Working with Managed Planning Applications, covers IBM Cognos TM1 Contributor components in a comprehensive manner. It includes the recipes on installation, configuration, usage, and integration of IBM Cognos TM1 Contributor components with IBM Cognos TM1.

Chapter 13, Defining Workflow, introduces IBM Cognos TM1 Workflow component, its installation, configuration, usage, and integration with other IBM Cognos TM1 Components.

Chapter 14, Integration with IBM Cognos BI, deals with integration of the planning application and reporting layer. Recipes are included to demonstrate how IBM Cognos BI components can be interfaced with IBM Cognos TM1 planning application.

What you need for this book

IBM Cognos TM1 (9.5.2) Server, Web Client, and Perspectives for Microsoft Excel

IBM Cognos TM1 (9.5.2) Workflow

IBM Cognos TM1 (9.5.2) Contributor and Contributor Web Client

Microsoft Excel

Microsoft Internet Information Server

Apache Tomcat

Java and .NET framework installed and working

IBM Cognos 8.X BI Server and Framework Manager

Who this book is for

The book is intended for prospective TM1 developers or analysts who want to successfully build and manage a complete planning, budgeting, and forecasting solution with IBM Cognos TM1. No previous knowledge of TM1 is expected.

Existing TM1 users and developers will also benefit from the practical recipes covered in the book.

Conventions

In this book, you will find a number of styles of text that distinguish between different kinds of information. Here are some examples of these styles, and an explanation of their meaning.

Code words in text are shown as follows: "Each TM1 data server as shown must have `tm1s.cfg` (configuration file) and `tm1s.lic` file in the TM1 data server directory."

A line of code is set as follows:

```
static:value1:value2:value3:value4.
```

When we wish to draw your attention to a particular part of a code block, the relevant lines or items are set in bold:

```
Profit = Unit Sales Price - Unit Cost
```

New terms and **important words** are shown in bold. Words that you see on the screen, in menus or dialog boxes for example, appear in the text like this: "First dimension in column is **Time (Years)** and second dimension in column is **Product (Product Line)**".

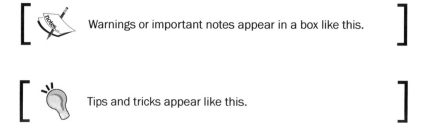

[Warnings or important notes appear in a box like this.   ]

[Tips and tricks appear like this.   ]

Reader feedback

Feedback from our readers is always welcome. Let us know what you think about this book—what you liked or may have disliked. Reader feedback is important for us to develop titles that you really get the most out of.

To send us general feedback, simply send an e-mail to `feedback@packtpub.com`, and mention the book title via the subject of your message.

If there is a book that you need and would like to see us publish, please send us a note in the **SUGGEST A TITLE** form on `www.packtpub.com` or e-mail `suggest@packtpub.com`.

If there is a topic that you have expertise in and you are interested in either writing or contributing to a book, see our author guide on `www.packtpub.com/authors`.

Customer support

Now that you are the proud owner of a Packt book, we have a number of things to help you to get the most from your purchase.

Errata

Although we have taken every care to ensure the accuracy of our content, mistakes do happen. If you find a mistake in one of our books—maybe a mistake in the text or the code—we would be grateful if you would report this to us. By doing so, you can save other readers from frustration and help us improve subsequent versions of this book. If you find any errata, please report them by visiting `http://www.packtpub.com/support`, selecting your book, clicking on the **errata submission form** link, and entering the details of your errata. Once your errata are verified, your submission will be accepted and the errata will be uploaded on our website, or added to any list of existing errata, under the Errata section of that title. Any existing errata can be viewed by selecting your title from `http://www.packtpub.com/support`.

Piracy

Piracy of copyright material on the Internet is an ongoing problem across all media. At Packt, we take the protection of our copyright and licenses very seriously. If you come across any illegal copies of our works, in any form, on the Internet, please provide us with the location address or website name immediately so that we can pursue a remedy.

Please contact us at copyright@packtpub.com with a link to the suspected pirated material.

We appreciate your help in protecting our authors, and our ability to bring you valuable content.

Questions

You can contact us at questions@packtpub.com if you are having a problem with any aspect of the book, and we will do our best to address it.

1
Getting Started with TM1

IBM Cognos TM1 integrates business planning, performance measurement, and operational data to enable companies to optimize business effectiveness and customer interaction, regardless of geography or structure.

TM1 provides immediate visibility into data, accountability within a collaborative process, and a consistent view of information, allowing managers to quickly stabilize operational fluctuations and take advantage of new opportunities.

TM1 has a distinctive advantage over other analytical tools in the market in the following major points:

- ▶ TM1 is based on multi-dimensional database in the form of cubes with write-back functionality to the source databases
- ▶ The TM1 engine performs complex calculations in memory on the client side, resulting infast processing and scalability
- ▶ Only non-null data cells are transferred to the client machine which generally forms no more than 20 percent of the overall data set; hence, network bandwidth related issues are nonexistent

The forthcoming chapter will introduce TM1 as a solution along with general performance management concepts to start with.

IBM Cognos Performance Management Solution consists of the following major components:

- ▶ Enterprise Planning
- ▶ Enterprise Business Intelligence

TM1 would be covered under Enterprise Planning and will remain the focal point in this book. Please note that TM1 cubes can serve as a data source for Business Intelligence (BI) applications. The basics of this integration will be dealt with in last chapter of this book. However, BI will not be covered in full detail with respect to authoring reports, charts, ad hoc query generation, and other specific authoring practices adopted in Cognos BI suite. These are best explained on other offerings by Packt Publishing such as *Cognos Cookbook*.

The book will focus on creating and managing planning applications using TM1 offerings. It will also discuss the contributor component and its applications in detail. Lastly, it will touch upon integration points between the planning application and BI infrastructure which may or may not be useful to all readers.

Enterprise Planning

Tools under this category are meant for planning, budgeting, forecasting, modelling, consolidation, and financial reporting. A primary use case is to create managed planning applications that can be used by business users to contribute planning data to a central repository. Business data once submitted can be reviewed by stakeholders and can be approved or rejected. The whole workflow is controlled by applying different levels of security. Data, once finalized, can be viewed in different templates and users can perform a slice and dice as applicable.

An example would be a central budgeting application in which business users are spread across different geographical locations and contribute data according to the subsidiaries they are responsible for. Once submitted, data are reviewed by associated managers and if approved final numbers are written back to the source databases. Top-level management can be provided with reports and templates to view and manipulate data as they want.

Enterprise Business Intelligence

Tools under this category serve to model and analyze business data and discover hidden business trends. It enables users to define key performance indicators and track the critical business metrics against business-specific parameters and criterions. This would typically include reporting, dashboarding, scorecarding, and so on, and would each be covered by different tools under Cognos BI Suite such as Report Studio, Metric Studio, Event Studio, Analysis Studio, and so on.

Major Cognos tools for Enterprise Planning and Business Intelligence are
shown below:

Category	Tool	Description
Enterprise Planning	Cognos Planning Suite	Planning and budgeting solution.
Enterprise Planning	Cognos TM1	Planning and budgeting solution.
Enterprise Business Intelligence	Cognos BI	Scorecarding, event management, analysis, and reporting.
Enterprise Business Intelligence	Cognos GO	Extended BI (Office integration, mobile portability, and flash-based dashboarding).
Enterprise Business Intelligence	Cognos NOW	Transactional and runtime BI solution.

In the following chapters we will focus on Cognos TM1 as a planning and budgeting tool,
based on OLAP technology as explained in the following section.

Online Analytic Processing (OLAP)

In computing, OLAP is an approach to swiftly answer multi-dimensional
analytical queries.

Typically, OLAP uses a multi-dimensional data model to build a relational database (ROLAP) or
is directly based on a multi-dimensional cube (MOLAP).

The OLAP tool refers to the category of software tools that provides analysis of data and can
include either a ROLAP or MOLAP. In this book we refer to TM1, which performs MOLAP as it
is directly based on multi-dimensional cubes. A ROLAP tool would have a multi-dimensional
Model/View on top of a relational database, allowing multi-dimensional queries. However, a
relational database is still referred to in the backend.

When we say that data is stored in a multi-dimensional database we mean that data is stored
in a cube data structure, a single point of data to be measured can be viewed and analyzed
from different perspectives at the same time.

This single point of data (mostly numerical in nature) is analogous to a measure (which needs
to be measured) and a perspective (descriptive in nature) is analogous to a dimension, which
again can be hierarchical in nature.

Imagine an N-coordinate system with an axis referring to dimensions and a data tuple referring to a measure. The dimensions can again be flat or hierarchical in nature.

A hierarchical dimension refers to functionally similar data, arranged in different levels of detail.

For example, year, month, and day data refers to similar time-related data, but can be arranged in different levels as Years | Month | Day. This structure enables the user to navigate from a higher level of detail (Year) to a lower level of detail (Month | Day).Navigating from higher level details to lower level details is called drilling down, .Navigating from lower level details to higher level details is called drilling up. Hence, in the preceding example, the hierarchical nature of the time dimension enables the user to drill up (for example, from month to year) and drill down (for example, from year to month).

A similar analogy would be a region dimension, with different levels such as World | Country | Region | City.

As has been just explained, there can be multiple hierarchical dimensions and measures which can together be arranged as cubes. An example of such a cube can be a Sales cube which has Sales Revenue and Sales Target as two measures.Time (Year | Month | Day) and Product (Product Line | Product Type | Product) can be two hierarchical dimensions in such a cube. Please note it is not absolutely necessary for a dimension to be hierarchical in nature. The exact nature may depend on the business use cases that an analyst is trying to achieve.

As a logical conclusion to the explanation above, once such Sales cube is ready, a user can view Sales Revenue and Sales Target from different dimensions (Time or Product) and at a different level of details (drill up, drill down) and all this can be done at the same time, even when user is in offline mode.

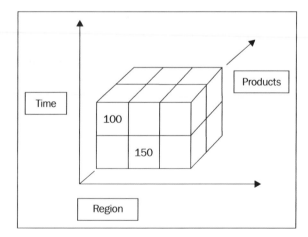

The preceding figure depicts the multi-dimensional Sales cube with three axes signifying the three dimensions. A cube cell represents data value or tuples that have a numerical value such as Sales Target.

 Please note that there are NULLS in the cube for some combinations. These NULLS will be skipped while processing is done in client side memory; the processing is much faster and more efficient.

A few possible dimensional analysis scenarios based on the above Sales cube setup would be worth showing as simple crosstabs created manually in Excel:

		Region = 'Asia Pacific'		
Sales ('Millions)		Product (Product Lir		
		FMCG	Vehicles	Elec
	1996	100	200	
	1997	340	200	
Time (Year)	1998	1000	340	
	1999	1500	400	

The preceding figure illustrates a dimensional modelling scenario where the measure, for example, Sales volume which is in millions is being viewed from more than one perspective and is represented as dimension (level) in rows, columns, and filters. The first dimension in column is **Time (Years)** and second dimension in the row is **Product (Product Line)**.

The data shown is only for the Asia Pacific region as stated in the filter for Region.

So, we are using three dimensions in the preceding analysis: **Region, Time,** and **Product Line** while measure being analyzed is Sales Revenue.

Year and Product Line are levels of Time and Product dimensions, respectively. Asia Pacific is a member of the topmost level of the Region dimension.

		Time = 2010, Region = 'Asia Pacific'		
Sales ('Millions)		Product (Product Line)		
		FMCG	Vehicles	Electronics
	Jan	50	100	150
	Feb	30	200	100
Time (Months)	Mar	40	200	120
	Apr	100	400	100
	May	200	300	250

Similarly, the preceding figure illustrates analysis with three dimensions again: **Time (Months)**, **Product (Product Line)**, and **Region**.

Months, displayed in rows, is second level of **Time** dimension. In this case we drill down on 2010, to view monthly level of details along the **Time** dimension.

Ideally, monthly level of details should add up to give yearly figures as a default behavior; the year, being the consolidated element, is the sum of the individual monthly figures.

Time = 2010, Product Line = 'Vehicles', Region = 'Asia Pacific'				
Sales ('Millions)			Product (Product Type)	
		2 Wheel	4 Wheel	Trucks
	Jan	50	40	10
	Feb	150	25	25
Time(Months)	Mar	125	15	60
	Apr	100	250	50
	May	150	150	0

The preceding figure extends the same example, but the **Product** dimension is further drilled down to the **Product Type** level to find details for the **Vehicles Product Line** as shown. Please note that detailed figures for each month add up to the **Vehicles** figures for the respective months.

Time = 2010, Product Line = 'Vehicles', Region = 'Asia Pacific'				
Profit Booked ('000 USD)			Product (Product Type)	
		2 Wheel	4 Wheel	Trucks
	Jan	100	40	10
	Feb	150	25	25
Time(Months)	Mar	125	120	45
	Apr	20	140	50
	May	150	150	100

As shown in the above figure, measures can also be changed (Profit Booked instead of Sales Volume) according to the business use cases. The case shown in the above figure is similar, where figures now represent Profit Booked in '000 USD instead of Sales Volume in Millions.

OLAP data structures terminology

This topic intends to introduce the data structure terminology generally used when it comes to OLAP. These terms are quite liberally used throughout this book and in the data warehousing/ BI world in general.

Please refer to the following table for the terminology:

Terminology	Description	Example
Dimensions	Perspectives through which users want to slice and dice data.	Product Time
Hierarchies	Group of functionally similar descriptive data arranged in levels, One or more hierarchies form a dimension.	Product Line | Product Type Year | Month | Day
Levels	Individual building blocks of a hierarchy.	Product Line Day
Measures	Values which can be measured for various dimensional members.	Sales Revenue Sales Target
Cubes	Collection of dimensions and measures. Functionally similar data which can be analyzed in an OLAP tool.	Sales Cube
Members	Individual data values.	FMCG, 4 Wheelers 2010, JAN
Attributes	Provide additional details for member values.	Color Number of Hours

OLAP (Online Analytical Processing) versus OLTP (Online Transactional)

As we move further, it's worth understanding the difference between an OLTP)-based and an OLAP-based system. This is just for the sake of knowing, as TM1 is based on OLAP technology which is the primary focus of this book.

[In a nut shell, all the day-to-day processing of databases support daily transactional processing, do not focus on historical data analysis, and are based on OLTP technology.]

OLAP-based systems are more historical databases, intended to support MIS or DSS with fast read operations and large volumes of aggregated data. **Denormalization** is the key to such databases as opposed to OLTP systems which follow a **Normalization** approach.

Denormalization refers to the process of attempting to optimize the read performance of a database by adding redundant data or by grouping data. Hence, different but related pieces of information are still duplicated across tables, avoiding joins while read operations are performed.

Normalization would try to avoid this duplication by storing different pieces of related information in different tables, making data manipulation statements (inserts/updates) fast, but read-only queries now have to use more joins and the performance is slower.

Refer to the following table to compare the OLAP and OLTP approaches:

	OLAP	OLTP
Definition	Multi-dimensional analysis of data arranged in cube format and modeled in a dimensional structure.	Analysis of data arranged in a relational database. Dimensional structuring of data is not necessary.
Schema	Star Schema, Snow Flake Schema.	Flat Schema.
Normalization	Renormalized.	Normalized.
Limitations	Inserts and updates are slow.	Read operations are slow.
Advantages	Fast read operations.	Fast updates and inserts.
Portability	Cubes can be created and accessed in an offline mode.	OLTP processing typically requires users to be online if they need to do any data analysis.
Use	Typically used where quick and efficient analysis is the primary use case.	Typically used where insertions and updates are to be performed frequently as part of day-to-day operations.
Data volumes	Typically involves large data volumes and historical data.	Typically data volumes are less and historical data is generally not maintained.
Pre-aggregated values	Computed at cube creation time itself for fast analysis, for example, total sales revenue for each quarter.	Computed at runtime, saving a lot of disk space but slower at the time of retrieval.

Introduction to TM1

TM1 is an OLAP tool with one or more powerful TM1 data servers running remotely or on a single server. TM1 data servers provide access to shared data in an organization. These data servers are controlled by one or more admin servers. Users can work on shared data and objects across the organization through intuitive client interfaces, which interact and send requests to admin servers. Admin servers then pass on the request to one of the TM1 data servers.The data server then provides access to the shared objects to the clients.

Client interfaces provided with TM1 are:

- Excel add-on (TM1 Perspectives)
- Web browser (TM1 Web)
- TM1 Architect

The interface users want to use depends on the role they play in the organization as well as the comfort level they have with the particular interface.

In addition, clients have to install TM1 Perspectives for Excel as a separate add-in. While installing TM1, though this gets installed automatically, clients who just need to access the data need not have a full blown TM1 setup, but only have the Excel plugin if they want to use TM1 Perspectives for Microsoft Excel.

TM1 Web does not require any installation on the client side and can be accessed through the Web.

 In subsequent chapters we will be using TM1 Architect as the interface to create and view sample applications.

TM1 has a built-in ETL (Extraction Transform and Load) tool to perform data transfers from source databases to target multi-dimensional cubes, in the required format. In TM1 terminology the ETL module is called Turbo Integrator and ETL processes are called Turbo Integrator (TI) processes.

TI processes can also be written to write-back data in source databases, as and when the user modifies business data and decides to save that back to the backend databases.

In a nut shell, business-specific multi-dimensional models are created using one of the client interfaces stated above. Inbuilt TI processes enable users to pull data from the backend source databases and populate cubes on top of the models. TI processes can also be custom written and modified for specific ETL requirements. Business-specific reporting templates are then created, again using one of the client interfaces on top of the relevant cubes. Users are given access to the cubes and templates to view, analyze, and modify data. Data can also be saved to cubes to source databases using inbuilt TI processes.

Examine TM1 user roles

Users can be given access to client interfaces and tools in TM1 depending on the role they play in the organization. Some might be interested in defining business logic, while others may assume a role to model multi-dimensional cubes by defining dimensions and facts.

Admin roles also need to be clearly defined to perform housekeeping activities such as defining users, security policies, backup and recovery.

Contributors are end users who want to fill in business-specific data in already designed templates and play a role in final analysis and consolidation.

Please find the summary of the users and generic roles which are generally followed. The exact nature of user distribution and their respective responsibilities can differ from organization to organization.

User	Roles and responsibilities
Modeler/Analyst/Application Developer	Designs and builds multi-dimensional models and cubes, applies business logic, maps data flows, and creates custom templates and reports.
Administrator	Manages technical deployment of the application as a whole. Reviews hardware and software requirements. Keeps track of all the housekeeping activities such as security, replication, backup and recovery.
Contributor	Input data in templates. Views reports and answers business-specific queries.

Subsequent chapters will introduce different set of activities carried out by each of these in detail. Although the preceding table should be taken as a general guideline, there is no clear line of demarcation between duties performed by these users as roles often overlap among users.

TM1 architecture

TM1 is based on client server architecture and different components that interact with each other in a seamless manner to achieve the desired functionality. The following figure depicts the development process in a broad manner:

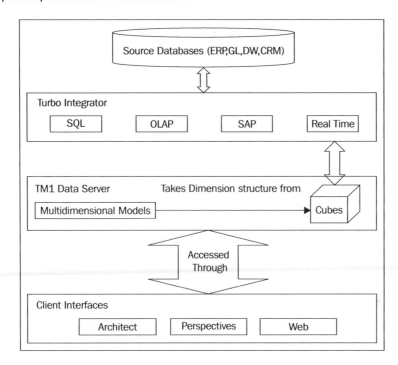

As depicted in the preceding figure, multi-dimensional cubes reside on TM1 data servers. These cubes in turn take their dimensional structure from multi-dimensional models, created by the modeler. Data is fed to these cubes from one of the backend data sources through inbuilt turbo integrator processes. Please note that these ETL processes can be modified as per the user requirements.

Turbo integrator processes can be written to fetch data from a variety of data sources including SAP, OLAP, relational (using SQL queries), and real time systems.

Import from text and Excel files is also possible.

Therefore, backend data sources can be of any type and turbo integrator handles all the database-specific complexities. Users don't have to worry about disparate multiple data sources.

Data can be modified through client interfaces and transferred to cubes. Therefore, changed data in cubes can then be saved back to backend databases, usually through inbuilt or customized TI processes as per the business-specific requirements.

The TM1 cubes are nothing but business data in a multi-dimensional format. Though dimensions and facts in the cubes are decided by the multi-dimensional model created by the analyst/modeler, the data in the cubes are usually viewed and analyzed using one of the client interfaces given by TM1.

TM1 cubes, along with its dimensions and other components, are referred to as TM1 objects and are hosted on one of the TM1 data servers. Different TM1 data servers can host different TM1 objects depending on the semantics of the organization. For example, there may be a separate data server to host financial-related cubes and processes, with only the finance department, CFO, and CEO having access to it. Similarly, a sales-related data server hosts sales plan, sales revenue, and expenses-related cubes shares only with the sales department and higher management.

TM1 Admin Server is a process that keeps track of all TM1 Data Servers running on a network and registered to it. An Admin Server runs on a computer known as an Admin Host.

The TM1 Data Server needs to have the associated Admin Host specified in the configurations file which is specific to each TM1 Data Server. In future sections we will discuss this in detail.

When a TM1 Data Server starts, the server registers itself with the Admin Server process that is running on the specified Admin Host. TM1 clients reference the Admin Server process to determine which TM1 Data Server are available on the network.

A user, depending on his role, can issue a request to access shared TM1 objects (cubes, dimensions, and subsets) through one of the client interfaces. These requests are routed to TM1 Data Server by one of the TM1 Admin Server processes.

The users, through client interfaces (Excel, web, or Architect), are given access to Server Explorer which is the interface provided by the TM1 Admin Server process. A Server Explorer lists all the TM1 Data Servers registered with the TM1 Admin Server process on the network, depending on the access rights a user may have.

TM1 Perspectives and TM1 Architect can connect to a local TM1 server, which acts as a repository for private TM1 data. With proper authority, we can copy data from a remote server to the local server by replicating that data, and then synchronize the updates back to the remote server.

The TM1 Data Server then exposes the shared TM1 objects it hosts to the user, depending on the security policies set by admin. This is how a user can create and access the TM1 objects using one of the client interfaces, again depending on the security policies already defined.

In the backend, turbo integrator processes come into play. ETL jobs related to these processes are then executed and can be customized.

Turbo integrator processes are executed from within Architect or Perspectives and hide from the users the complexity involved in querying multiple databases of different types.

Please refer to the following figure to get an idea of a typical deployment scenario of a TM1-based application, different components, and how they interact with each other.

All the TM1 Data Servers can reside on a single server or on multiple servers. Each TM1 Data Server as shown must have a `tm1s.cfg` (configuration file) and `tm1s.lic` file in the TM1 Data Server directory.

As we hinted previously, the `tm1s.cfg` file is the configuration file which is specific for every TM1 Data Server. This file is continuously polled at the interval of 60 seconds by the TM1 Data Server to detect any changes to the dynamic parameters. If a dynamic parameter is changed while the TM1 Data Server is running, the changed value is applied immediately and a restart is not needed.

Most parameters in the `Tm1s.cfg` file are static. These parameter values are read from the `Tm1s.cfg` file only when the TM1 Data Server starts. If we want to change a static parameter value, we must shut down the TM1 Data Server, edit the value in the `Tm1s.cfg` file, and then restart the TM1 Data Server.

If a parameter value contains spaces, you must enclose the parameter values within double quotes.

Now, in the following section we will discuss another very important concept which is specific to each TM1 Data Server installed. We will return to the `Tm1s.cfg` file after that.

Data directory

The data directory, which is again specific to a TM1 Data Server contains the cubes, dimensions, and system information that are loaded into memory when a TM1 Data Server is started. When we access a TM1 Data Server from any of the TM1 clients, TM1 reads not null data from that server's data directory and loads that in the memory.

Any changes we make to cube data values are immediately stored in the memory and in the transaction log (Tm1s.log). Calculations and consolidations are done on demand in the memory. Hence, all the TM1 data files, that is cubes, dimensions, and so on are maintained in the memory and all the manipulations on that are performed in the memory, making the processing really fast. This in-memory processing of data along with the feature that only not null data is loaded gives the tool a distinctive advantage in terms of processing speed.

TM1 saves the data back to the data directory on disk when any of the following occur:

- The TM1 Data Server is shut down.
- A user, depending on the privileges, right-clicks a server icon in **Server Explorer** and chooses **Save Data** from the pop-up menu. This directs TM1 to save the changes to the selected server.
- An administrator chooses **File | Save Data All** in **Server Explorer**. This directs the TM1 admin process to save the changes to all the connected TM1 Data Server, if he has the proper authority.
- A user saves the batch updates.

Therefore, until the data is saved either manually or through TI processes all operations are done in the memory, causing fast processing.

We need to choose the path for the data directory when TM1 is installed. Please note that we need to specify different locations of the data directory for local and remote servers.

- For a local server, we need to specify the location of the data directory by naming this directory in the DataBaseDirectory parameter of the Tm1p.ini file. We can change the .ini file by using the **TM1 Options** menu in **Server Explorer**. By default, the path of the data directory for the local server is <install_dir>\custom\ tm1data\PData.
- For a remote server, we need to specify the location of the data directory by using the DataBaseDirectory parameter in the Tm1s.cfg.

 When TM1 is installed the planning sample TM1 Data Server is installed by default with the data directory as <install_dir>\custom\tm1data\ PlanSamp. The password for an admin user is apple and the default user ID and password is admin/apple. Readers are encouraged to install TM1 and play around with the sample data server.

Please refer to the following table which describes each of the mandatory parameter values in the `Tm1s.cfg` file, described in the previous section. Both parameter values are static in nature.

Sr No	Parameter name	Description
1	AdminHost	Specifies the computer name or IP address of the Admin Host on which an Admin Server is running. We can specify multiple Admin Hosts by separating each host name with a semicolon on a Windows TM1 Server, or a colon on a UNIX TM1 Server.
		The string specifying the Admin Host(s) is limited to 1020 characters or bytes.
2	DataBaseDirectory	Specifies the data directory from which the server loads cubes, dimensions, and other objects. You can list multiple data directories by separating them with semicolons.

Now we will give a quick brief of another important file in TM1 called the `Tm1p.ini` file. The `Tm1p.ini` file specifies the environment information for a TM1 client (TM1 Perspectives, TM1 Architect) and is specific to each user logging in to the TM1 Data Server through one of the clients stated above. `Tm1p.ini` has the `AdminHost` parameter which has the TM1 Admin Host referenced by the client.

When we install TM1, the installation location for the system default version of the `Tm1p.ini` file is `%ALLUSERSPROFILES%\Application Data\Applix\TM1\Tm1p.ini`.

In most cases, the full path to the `Tm1p.ini` file is:

```
C:\Documents and Settings\All Users\Application Data\Applix\TM1\Tm1p.
ini
```

The system default version of `Tm1p.ini` allows multiple users to use TM1 on a given computer. `Tm1p.ini` must be present the first time a user starts TM1 on the computer, the parameters in the system's default version govern the behavior of the initial startup of the TM1 client for each user.

After a user starts TM1 on the computer, a user-specific copy of `Tm1p.ini` is created in `%APPDATA%\Applix\TM1\Tm1p.ini`.

In most cases, the full path to the `Tm1p.ini` file is:

```
C:\Documents and Settings\<user name>\Application Data\Applix\TM1\
Tm1p.ini
```

The user-specific copy of `Tm1p.ini` accepts all parameter settings and changes for the user and governs the behavior of the TM1 client for all subsequent user sessions of the TM1 client.

`DataBaseDirectory` is one of the important parameters specified in the file which is used to specify the full path to the local server data directory. We can specify multiple data directories by separating the directory names with semicolons. A detailed description of these setting can be referenced in TM1 Administer and Deploy guide.

Please take a note of the important parameters in the `Tm1p.ini` file.

Sr No	Parameter name	Description
1	AdminHost	Displays the Admin Host name on which an Admin Server is running. On TM1 Options, use Login Parameters Admin Host.
2	DataBaseDirectory	Uses the full path to the local server data directory. We can specify multiple data directories by separating the directory names with semicolons.

The **TM1 Options** dialog box also stores many of the settings available in `Tm1p.ini`. The **TM1 Options** menu is available in **Server Explorer**. We can change these settings using either the TM1 Options dialog box or by editing the `Tm1p.ini` file.

In a nut shell we can specify the location of the Admin Host differently for clients and remote servers.

> ▸ Specify the Admin Host referenced by clients in the AdminHost parameter of the `Tm1p.ini` file. You can change the `Tm1p.ini` file by using the **TM1 Options** menu in **Server Explorer**.

> ▸ Specify the Admin Host and the remote servers they are registered with by using the AdminHost parameter in the `Tm1s.cfg` file.

TM1 Perspectives and TM1 Architect can connect to a local TM1 server, which acts as a repository for private TM1 data. With proper authority, we can copy data from a remote server to the local server by replicating that data, and then synchronize the updates back to the remote server.

Now we will look at the whole workflow summary in the following diagram:

```
  ┌──────────┐      ┌──────────┐      ┌──────────┐
  │ TM1 Data │      │ TM1 Data │      │ TM1 Data │
  │  Server  │      │  Server  │      │  Server  │
  └────┬─────┘      └────┬─────┘      └────┬─────┘
       │         Registered With          │
       ▼        ◄───────     ───────►      ▼
  ┌──────────────────┐   ┌──────────────────┐
  │  TM1 Admin Host  │   │  TM1 Admin Host  │
  │ ┌──────────────┐ │   │ ┌──────────────┐ │
  │ │TM1 Server Exp│ │   │ │TM1 Server Exp│ │
  └─┴──────────────┴─┘   └─┴──────────────┴─┘

            Access TM1 Data
            Servers through
            server explorer

  ┌────────────────────────────────────────┐
  │ TM1 Clients                             │
  │ ┌────────────┐ ┌─────────┐ ┌──────────┐ │
  │ │Perspectives│ │ TM1 Web │ │Architect │ │
  │ └────────────┘ └─────────┘ └──────────┘ │
  └────────────────────────────────────────┘
```

Installing TM1 server and clients on a machine

This section will demonstrate the installation of a typical TM1 single machine setup which we will use for subsequent examples to be followed in the book.

Please note that it is assumed that users have the necessary licenses in place to use the TM1V9.5.2 server and its components, which forms the infrastructure backbone of all the following practical applications.

Let's begin with the installation:

1. Copy TM1 setup on the local drive and click on `setup.exe`.

2. Click on **Next** and accept the default options in subsequent prompts and wizards. Only the important screens will be captured in subsequent steps, for the rest just accept the default values and click on the **OK** or **Next** button, whichever is applicable.

3. In the following screenshot you can select:

   ❑ **TM1 Perspectives** to install the server and perspectives for Microsoft Excel for clients with an Excel interface.

   ❑ **TM1** to install the TM1 Server, TM1 Architect, and TM1 Perspectives.

   ❑ **TM1 Web** to install the TM1 Server, TM1 Architect, TM1 Web, and TM1 Perspectives.

   ❑ **TM1 Contributor** to install TM1 Server, TM1 Architect, TM1 Web, TM1 Perspectives, and TM1 Contributor.

4. In the following screenshot **TM1** has been selected, but ideally readers should select **TM1 Contributor** if they are interested in TM1 Web and Contributor as well, which will be covered in detail later. The installation steps shown next will be the same for all of the preceding options.

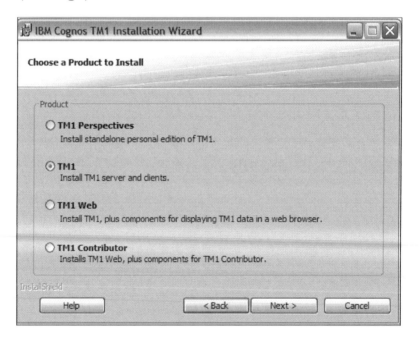

5. Review and change the required installation directory, as shown in the first pane in the following screenshot. Select **Standard** as the installation type, it will install all the components of TM1 and TM1 Contributor on the single machine. The second option is useful if multi-server installation is required where components are distributed across multiple machines.

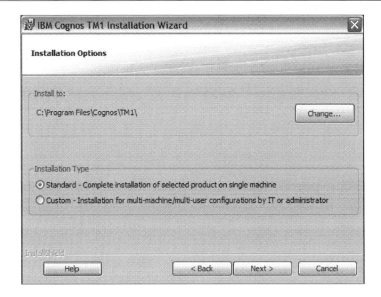

6. All the TM1 components communicate with TM1 Admin Server using SSL. The admin server also supports older TM1 clients which cannot use SSL by listening on two ports, one secured and the other unsecured. For TM1 clients that can use SSL, connect to the TM1 Admin Server using a secured port (otherwise they connect using unsecured port). If the secured port number is already in use in Admin Host, a different port can be specified for the secured port. In general this is not required and can be used as it is.

7. Please note down the port number that the TM1 Server will use during the course of action, as shown in the following screenshot:

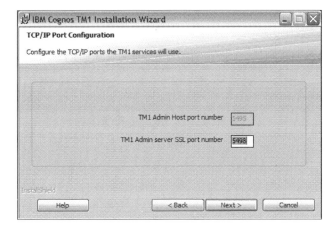

8. Type a valid Administrator username and password of the machine on which the TM1 components are being installed. Please ensure that the correct user credentials are given in the boxes, otherwise the installation will not proceed.

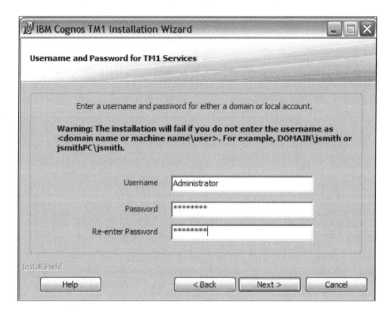

9. Click on **Install** button to start the installation.

10. Click on **Finish** to complete the installation and restart the machine.

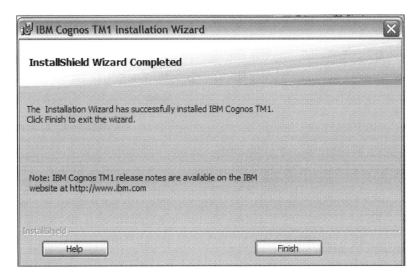

The preceding steps will install the TM1 Server and components on the same server. Components installed depend on which option is selected at the beginning. As explained earlier, **TM1 Contributor** will install TM1 Server, its clients (including TM1 Web), and TM1 Contributor on the same server.

Also the **Planning Sample** TM1 Data Server is installed by default.

Please refer to the two new services, under Windows services explorer, which will become visible after the successful installation, as shown in the following screenshot.

The first service is **TM1 Admin** Server and the second is the default **Planning Sample** TM1 Server, which is installed by default but is not necessarily required.

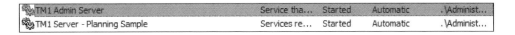

Please note that old models, cubes, and TM1 objects can now be ported on the fresh installation and used as before.

All subsequent recipes will assume this local single server installation scenario on a Windows box.

After successful installation, **Architect** and **Perspectives for MS Excel** will be shown in the **Start Menu**, as shown in the following screenshot:

At the end of this section we have successfully installed TM1 V 9.5.2 on a Windows box as a single server installation. TM1 components are installed on the single server and we will be able to follow subsequent practical scenarios as required.

Creating a new TM1 Data Server

We will now create a new TM1 Data Server called DemoData and set up the connection.

1. From the **Start** menu, click on **Control Panel | Administrative Tools | Services** as shown in the following screenshot. Alternatively, press *Windows + R* and then type **Services.msc** to directly open Windows services.

2. Ensure that the **TM1 Admin Server** service is started.

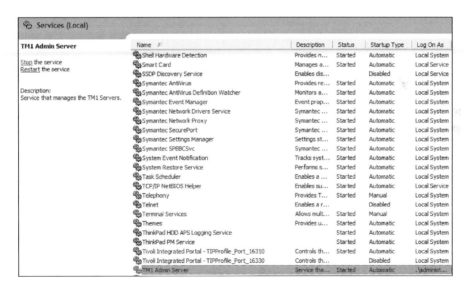

3. Browse to `C:\Program Files\Cognos\TM1\Custom\TM1Data\PlanSamp` and copy the `tm1s.cfg` file.

4. Browse to `C:\Program Files\Cognos\TM1\Custom\TM1Data` and create a subfolder called `DemoData`.

5. Create subfolders called `Logfiles` and `Data` in `C:\Program Files\Cognos\TM1\Custom\TM1Data\DemoData`.

6. Paste the `tm1s.cfg` file copied in step 3 and paste in to `C:\Program Files\Cognos\TM1\Custom\TM1Data\DemoData\Data`.

7. Open `tm1s.cfg` in Notepad.

8. Change `ServerName` to `DemoData`.

9. Change `DataBaseDirectory` to `C:\Program Files\Cognos\TM1\Custom\TM1Data\DemoData\Data`.

10. Change the `PortNumber` to `11111`.

11. Change `AdminHost` to `localhost`.

12. Add a return after `DataBaseDirectory` = and then type the following `LoggingDirectory=C:\Program Files\Cognos\TM1\Custom\TM1Data\DemoData\Logfiles`.

13. Save and close the file.

14. Browse to `C:\Program Files\Cognos\TM1\bin` and create a shortcut for `tm1s.exe` on the desktop.

15. Rename the shortcut to **DemoData**.

16. Right-click on the folder and then click on **Properties**.

17. In the **Target** box at the end of the given expression type `-z "C:\Program Files\Cognos\TM1\Custom\TM1Data\DemoData\Data"`. The complete expression should now look like `"C:\Program Files\Cognos\TM1\bin\tm1s.exe" -z "C:\Program Files\Cognos\TM1\Custom\TM1Data\DemoData\Data"`.

18. Click on **OK**.

19. Double-click the **DemoData** icon to start the data server just created.

20. The following window pops up to display the status of the server, which has started and the taskbar status will change from **Loading** to **Running**.

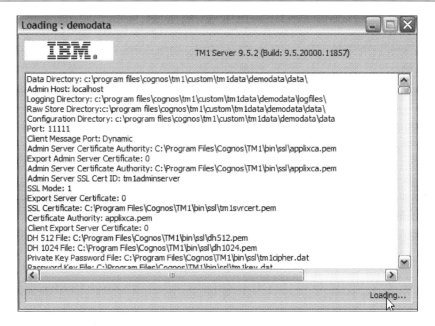

21. The server is now ready for usage.

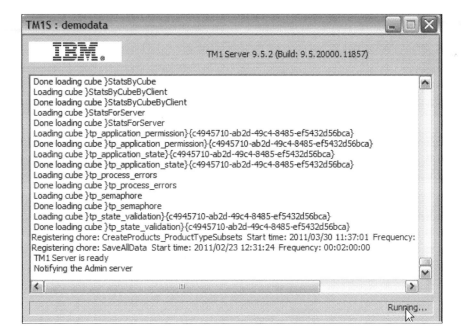

22. Close the preceding window to shutdown the server. Don't save anything as we haven't changed any configuration parameters for the server.

23. No two TM1 Data Servers running on the same machine can have same port number and data server name.

24. In our demo scenario we have just created a TM1 Data Server called **DemoData** on the machine. Another data server called **Planning Sample** is already created and shipped with the installation.

25. These data servers can be made visible as a Windows service, as in the case of **Planning Sample,** or they can be accessed as a desktop shortcut as in the case of **DemoData**.

26. Now these data servers can be accessed through Admin Server and any of the clients we installed in the preceding steps.

Connecting to an existing TM1 Server

We will now set up a connection to the existing TM1 Server called **Planning Sample**.

1. As explained in previous recipe, please open Windows services by pressing *Windows + R* and then typing **Services.msc**.

2. Ensure that the **TM1 Admin Server** service is started.

3. Ensure that **TM1 Server – Planning Sample** is started, as shown in the following screenshot:

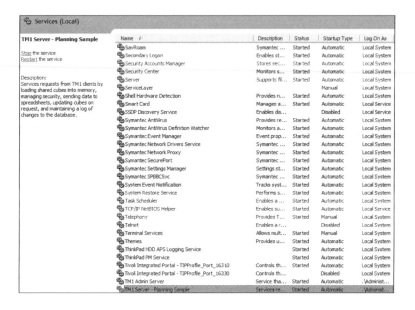

4. Double-click on the **DemoData** icon on the desktop to start the data server we created in the preceding steps.

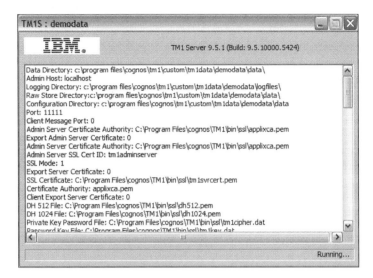

5. Open the **Architect** tool from the **Start** menu as shown in the following screenshot:

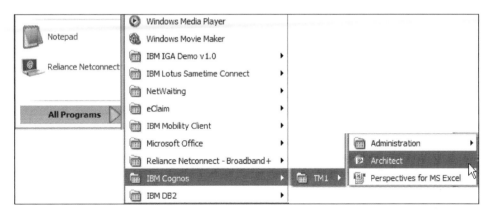

6. In the **Architect** our two data servers are visible.

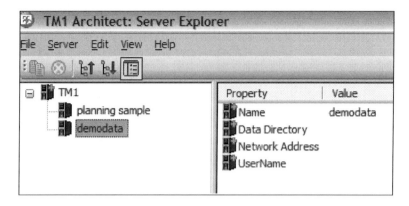

7. Double-click on **planning sample** and provide the login credentials as `admin`/`apple`. Please note that TM1 is not case sensitive, while typing the user credentials lower/ uppercase is irrelevant.

8. Various sample applications, cubes, and dimensions created on **planning sample** are visible:

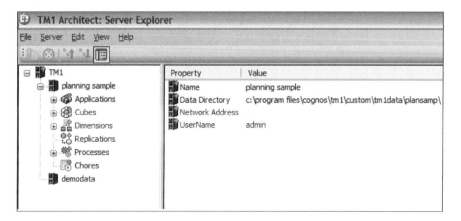

9. Similarly, log in to **DemoData** using `admin` as the user and no password. It doesn't have any objects created (as we have created the TM1 Data Server from scratch) yet the different nodes are visible.

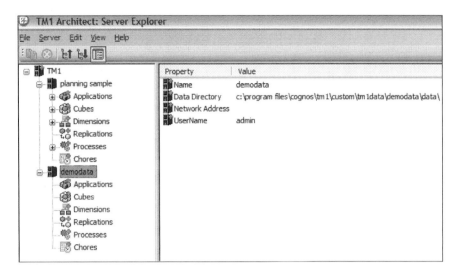

10. The servers are ready for business now and can be accessed through one of the client interfaces as per user preferences. In subsequent modules, we will always access the server explorer using the **Architect**.

11. **TM1 Admin Server** keeps track of all the TM1 Data Servers running on a network. When a TM1 Data Server starts, it registers itself with the Admin Server that runs on a specified Admin Host. Single or multiple Admin Hosts need to be specified as comma separated values in the Admin Host field for every TM1 Data Server in the `tm1s.cfg` file for the Data Server.

12. In our case Admin Server (localhost) and TM1 Data Servers/Application Servers (Planning Sample) are installed on the same server along with the clients. We have created one more TM1 Data Server as part of the demo scenario above (DemoData).

Setting up TM1 Data Server to run as a Windows service

1. Open a DOS box/command prompt: **Start | Run | cmd** and navigate to the TM1 `bin` directory using the `cd` command and go to the TM1 bin directory.

2. Please note that the default installation path is `C:\Program Files\Cognos\TM1\bin`. Type the following command:

```
tm1sd.exe -install -n"NameOfTM1Server" -z"PathtoTm1s.cfgFile"
```

3. In the preceding command `NameOfTM1Server` (after the `-n`) is the name we want to give to this TM1 Server service. If the name we are going to use contains any spaces, this value must be specified in double quotes. `PathtoTm1s.cfgFile` (after the `-z`) is the path to the `tm1s.cfg` file for the TM1 Server we are setting up. For example:

```
tm1sd.exe -install -n"DemoData" -z"C:\Program Files\Cognos\TM1\Custom\TM1Data\DemoData"
```

4. If the preceding command is successful, it will return the following message: **TM1 Server / tm1 production server installed**. We can then go into the services listing, and see the new TM1 Server service you set up. Following the preceding example, the service would be listed as: **TM1 Server / DemoData.** We can then configure the service to run automatically and to run under a specific domain user.

If we are setting up a completely new TM1 Server for which we don't already have a `tm1s.cfg` file, you can copy the `tm1s.cfg` from the **Planning Sample** TM1 Server and modify it accordingly. As a minimum, we will need to modify the `ServerName`, `DataBaseDirectory`, and `PortNumber` parameter values. If the service does not start (error message stating the service cannot be started), starting the same TM1 Logical Server as a desktop application will usually provide more detailed information on the error.

Removal of the TM1 service

1. To remove a TM1 Server service (again, following the preceding example), follow steps 1 and 2, then type the following command:

```
tm1sd.exe -remove -n"NameOfTM1Server"
```

2. Where the `NameOfTM1Server` (after the `-n`) is the name of the TM1 Server service we wish to remove. For example:

```
tm1sd.exe -remove -n"DemoData"
```

Summary

In this chapter, we started with an introduction to Performance Management Solutions by IBM and gradually moved to IBM Cognos TM1 as an Enterprise Planning solution. We learnt the concept of OLAP; TM1 uses OLAP technology.

The modules that followed took us through the basic workflow and architecture of TM1.

Subsequent modules demonstrated how to install TM1 as a single server setup and access servers through Architect.

The following chapters will be more specific to TM1 and will extend the idea of creating and working with dimensions which were introduced in this chapter.

2
Creating dimensions in TM1

In this chapter, we will cover:

- ▶ Creating dimensions manually
- ▶ Creating a Months dimension
- ▶ Adding additional levels in Months dimension
- ▶ Adding "Next" and "Previous" attributes to the "Months" dimension
- ▶ Creating dimensions using turbo integrator
- ▶ Execution of scripts for a TM1 process

Introduction

In this chapter we are going to cover dimensions which are basic building blocks of TM1 cubes. In general, a dimension is a data element that categorizes each item in a data set into non-overlapping regions. It provides structured labeling information to otherwise unordered numeric measures and provide the means to "slice and dice" data.

Here we will discuss the concept of dimensions specific to TM1 and will gradually refine the subject.

As just stated dimensions are fundamental building blocks of TM1 Cubes. Therefore, in accounting domain if we are dealing with simple numeric measures like profit booked and total revenue then region, time, and products can be a few of the possible dimensions. Hence profit booked can change for different regions, time period and products. Again time dimension can be structured in a year, month, and day format, which form a hierarchy for time dimension. Year, month, and day can be different levels of the time dimension. Other dimensions can also be structured into multiple levels; however, it's not necessary for a dimension to have more than one level.

Similarly, total revenue can be another measure or a measure dimension, both imply the same thing in TM1 terminology. It is interesting to note that in TM1 a measure dimension may not be always different from a regular analysis dimension. Hence, we can have both numeric and string values in a measure dimension. The only difference lies in what needs to be viewed and what acts as perspective to view that. For example, product type can be a measure dimension in one case where we want to know the most popular product for different region and time period combinations. Otherwise, it would be a regular dimension when we want to measure total booked revenue for region and time period combinations.

Such structure once defined leads to creation of cubes and hence analysis of our measures (booked profit) from different perspectives (dimensions like time, region, product types). Imagine an analysis needs to be performed for total revenue year 2010 (time) for Asia Pacific region (Region). Now that we know the figure, say 200 million USD, we want to further drill down to see how the figure is distributed among different products. So how much, from 200 million USD was contributed by FMCG and how much by VEHICLES. Since time dimension has different levels (year as the first level), we can also know the monthly breakup of these figures, and to do that we just need to drill down from 2010 (year level) to month level (Jan' 2010, Feb' 2010, Dec' 2010). Drilling up from month level to year level should also be possible in such a case (say from Jan' 2010 to 2010).

In a nut shell, depending on the organizations needs and availability of data, dimensions and measures are defined. Dimensions are then structured in different levels to form a hierarchy. Once such structure is in place (multi-dimensional model is ready). A cube can be created that is the same as organizational data, but in the multi-dimensional format, the structure of which is defined by the model. Cubes are then shared among the users, who can analyze data as per business needs.

Therefore, in the preceding example products, time and region are dimensions (regular dimension). Out of these time is a multi-level dimension and structured in a hierarchy, where days are rolled up into months and months are rolled up in a year (year | month | day). Total revenue and booked profit are measures (measure dimension).

Each of such dimensions (a regular dimension or a measure dimension) is made up of elements, which are actual data in the cube and are structured lists of related items. Elements are actual data which comprises the dimensions and hence cubes. For example, time dimension is made up of elements like 2010, January, 21 December 2010, which are again structured in a hierarchy as just explained. Product dimension is made up of elements such as vehicles, FMCG, and so on. Total revenue and total booked profit are measure dimensions and are elements in themselves.

As just explained, elements are used to define data in the cubes. These act as coordinates that identify a certain numeric value or a text string in a cube. Elements are basic building blocks of cubes and define what data is actually stored in a cube.

Every element has a type associated with it in TM1 as shown in the following table:

Symbol	Element type	Description	Example
n	Simple	Element at lowest level of hierarchy. It doesn't have any child elements.	Sales Revenue, 21 Dec 2011 (assuming time dimension has day as the last level)
s	String	Elements which define those cells that have string data.	"Life Insurance" (Policy Type),"Asia Pacific" (Region)
Σ	Consolidated	Elements that define aggregated data in a cube. One or more children elements roll up to a consolidated element.	Net Profit (=Total revenue - Total cost), 2010 (Day rolled up in months and months rolled up in years)

Weights are used in context with elements and aggregations. Hence, weight defines contribution of an element in an aggregation. For example, if we consider a consolidated element, Total Sale Price, for a product which we intend to calculate as summation of Base Price and Tax, then each simple element that is Base Price and Tax contributes equally with a factor 1. Hence:

Total Sales Price = Base Price (1) +Tax (1).

Here 1 can be called as weights of respective simple elements Base Price and Tax.

If we have another aggregation such that Total Perimeter of rectangle = 2 * length +2 * width, then my individual weights would be 2 for both the simple elements which are length and width in this case.

Similarly different simple elements can contribute differently to aggregated elements. Negative weights are also possible for a case that requires subtraction, for example:

Actual Sales Price = Marked Price – Discount.

Hence, here Marked Price has weight as 1 while Discount has -1 as its weight.

Similarly, we assign 0 as weight to certain elements as we do not want to consider them in the consolidation.

The same results can be achieved using rules, but using weights and consolidations in the preceding manner to achieve the output is much faster than rules.

 Please note that all the aggregations are performed at run time in RAM. Cube only sores leaf level, simple, not null elements.

As we just learned elements identify data in a cube. Element attributes describe the elements themselves. Attributes are used to describe elements. These are used to describe features of an element, aliases or alternative names, format, and precision. We can select elements by attribute values in the subset editor, which we will see in later sections. We can also display element names in the TM1 window using their aliases.

To create attributes and assign attribute values, we use attributes editor and will be described in later sections.

- ▸ Types of Attributes
  - ❑ Descriptive Attributes, for example, an element January may have a descriptive attribute such as number of days, short name, month number, and so on.
  - ❑ Alias Attributes, for example an element January may be called differently in German, French, and Chinese are different aliases of the same element.
  - ❑ Display Format Attributes, for example a numeric measure element may be formatted by applying different format attributes such as currency, precision, percentage, and so on.

Please note that attributes just contribute and provide supporting data for an element.

It is recommended to apply display formats to measure dimension (the measures we track) in the cube using either attributes editor or cube viewer window. TM1 determines which display format to use in the cube viewer window, as follows:

- ▸ TM1 first checks the elements in the column dimension for display formats. If dimensions are stacked, then TM1 checks from the bottom upward.
- ▸ If no format is found, TM1 checks the elements in the row dimension for display formats. If dimensions are stacked, then TM1 checks from right to left.
- ▸ If no format is found, then TM1 checks the title elements for display formats. The elements are inspected from right to left.
- ▸ If no format is found, then TM1 applies the format for the current view.

To ensure that TM1 applies the format for the cube measures, position the dimension containing the measures as the bottommost column dimension.

When we want to list multiple attribute values for a single element, additional elements or dimensions should be created, otherwise we might lose valuable detail. For example, if a car is available in multiple colors then we should consider creating additional elements for each color in a separate dimension. That way we can determine car sales for a particular color. However, if a car is available in a single color, then color of the car say red, should be an attribute rather than an additional element in a separate dimension.

Dimension can be created manually or using turbo integrator processes. TM1 does support spaces and some special characters as names. Utmost care should be taken while defining names to the dimension as these define where exactly a data cell is located in the cube. Hence, renaming a dimension will change how data points are aligned in the cube. If we need to rename a dimension, it is advisable that we destroy and recreate the cube.

Business-specific names with proper naming conventions across the organization should be used while naming and defining dimensions and elements. Dimensions can be created:

▶ Manually

▶ Using turbo integrator

▶ Using dimension worksheets

Creating dimensions manually

As we have seen earlier, dimensions form an integral part of TM1 cubes. We can create dimensions either manually or by using rules.

Getting ready

We will use the demodata TM1 server we created in the previous chapter.

How to do it...

1. From the **Start** menu, click on **Control Panel | Administrative Tools | Services** as shown in the following screenshot. Alternatively, press *Windows +R* and then type **Services.msc** to directly open Windows services.

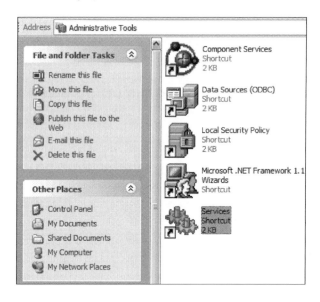

2. Ensure that **TM1 Admin Server** service is started.

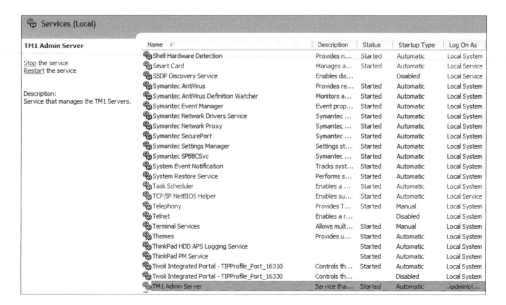

3. Double-click on the **demodata** icon on desktop to start the data server, created as part of *Chapter 1*.

4. Open the **Architect** tool from the **Start** menu.

5. In the **Architect** our two Application Servers/Data Servers are visible as shown in the following screenshot.

6. Double-click on **demodata**. For username enter "admin" and for password, do not enter anything.

7. Click on the **OK** button to view expended **demodata** object.

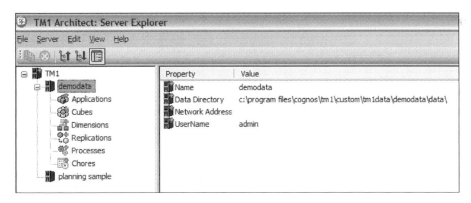

8. Right-click on **Dimensions** and then click on **Create New Dimension**.

9. It will open **Dimensions Editor** window. The same can be done by clicking on **Dimensions** and then clicking on **Create New Dimension** from the **Dimensions** menu on the toolbar.

10. In the **Dimension Editor** right-click and choose **Insert Element** from the menu. The same functionality can be achieved by clicking on **Edit menu** and choosing **Insert Element**.

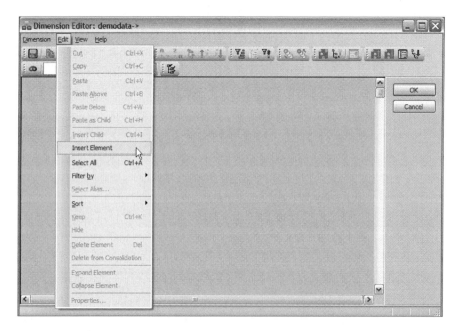

11. In the **Dimension Element Insert** window, for **Insert Element Name** type **Unit Sales Price**. Keep the rest to default and click on **Add** button. Other available options in **Element Type** drop-down list are worth noting in context to element types explained in the previous section.

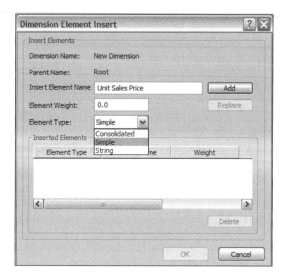

12. Similarly add **Unit Cost**, **Margin**, and **Margin%**, and click on **OK**.

13. Click on **Display Properties Window** as shown in the following screenshot:

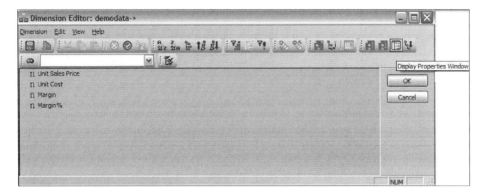

14. After clicking on the ▤ icon, you will see the next window. It shows properties such as the **Name**, **Security owner**, **Type**, **Level**, and more.

15. Click on **Save** button.

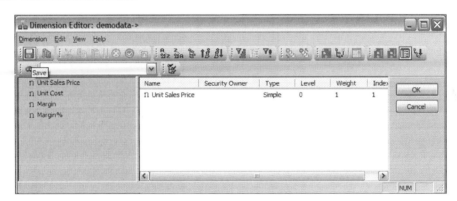

16. Type name of the dimension as **Price_Cost_Measures** and click on **OK**.

17. Please note change in the title bar.

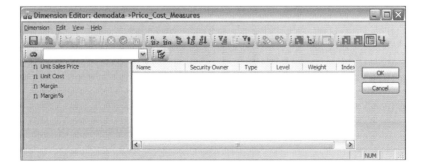

18. Now we will be adding a consolidated calculated item **Profit** as shown in the following screenshot. On the same window right-click to open the menu and select **Insert Element** as shown.

19. Insert a consolidated element by name of **Profit** and select **Consolidated** from the **Element Type** drop down. Click on **Add** and then **OK**.

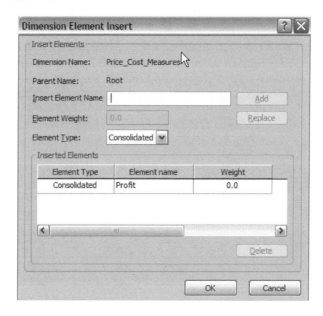

20. It will add a new element **Profit**. Please note that it is a consolidated item hence displayed differently.

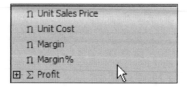

21. Drag-and-drop **Unit Sales Price** and **Unit Cost** under **Profit** as shown in the following screenshot:

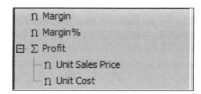

22. Change the element weight of **Unit Cost** to **-1** as shown so that while Profit is being calculated as consolidation of Unit Sales Price and Unit Cost the actual formula applied is

```
Profit = Unit Sales Price - Unit Cost
```

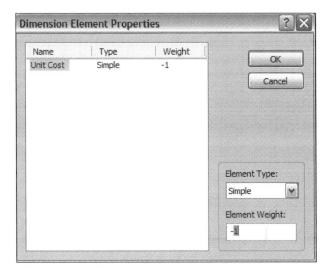

23. Click on **OK** to close the **Dimension Element Properties** window. Now when cube values are calculated, **Profit** will be calculated as consolidation of **Unit Sales Price** and **Unit Cost**, by subtraction of **Unit Cost** from **Unit Sales Price** as weight of **Unit Cost** is **-1**. Now click on **OK** to close the **Dimension Editor** without saving the latest addition of **Profit** element, which we have added just to give an idea towards adding consolidated and calculated elements. We will use more such elements in later recipes.

How it works...

In the preceding steps we have created a measure dimension **Price_Cost_Measures**, manually using **Architect**. This measure dimension can now be included in a cube and data can be populated for its elements. Calculated and consolidated elements are calculated as and when required and as defined in the measure dimension.

See also

We have already seen creating a measure dimension manually. In the same chapter we will be *Creating a Months dimension,* which we will use as a time dimension in the following section. We will also be *Creating dimensions using the turbo integrator.*

Creating a Months dimension

Now we will create a **Months** dimension which will act like a time dimension for our model. A Months dimension, when included in the cube will give time perspective to the data populated in the cube.

Time dimension is desirable in almost all the use cases, in a practical scenario, to view and analyze data from time aspect.

Getting ready

Please ensure that as explained above TM1 Admin server service is started and demodata TM1 server is running.

How to do it...

1. Keep the **Server Explorer** window for demodata server open as shown in the following screenshot:

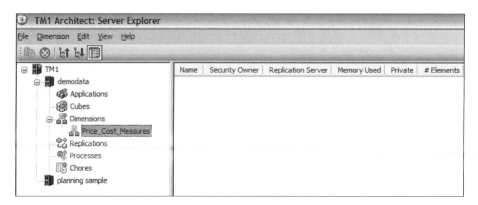

2. Right-click **Dimensions** and click on **Create New Dimension**.

3. Open Excel and type **Jan** in **A1** cell as shown in the following screenshot:

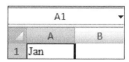

4. Place the cursor on lower right corner of A1 until it becomes "+" sign.

5. Drag the cursor vertically till **A12** until all 12 months appear as shown.

6. Copy the 12 months from Excel and paste them in the grey pane of **Dimensional Editor**.

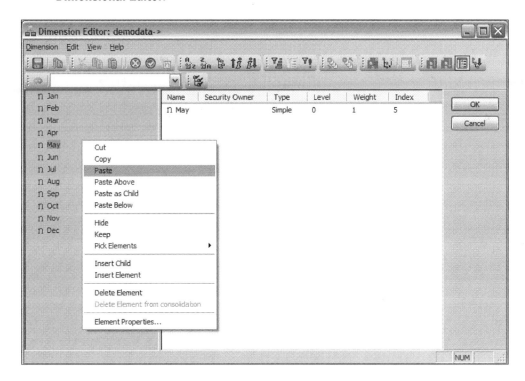

7. Save the dimension with the name **Months** and click on **OK**.

Please note that [n] symbol besides the elements denotes that these are leaf level numeric elements. These act as pointers to map data in cubes and maps to a numeric data value and not a text.

Now we will create another dimension by the name of **Versions** dimension as shown in the following screenshot. Please keep the **Server Explorer** window from the preceding recipe open as shown in the following screenshot:

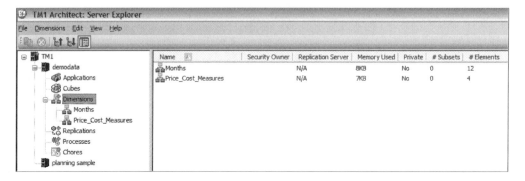

1. Right-click on **Dimensions** and click on **Create New Dimension**.

2. In the **Dimension Editor** insert **Budget Version 1** and **Budget Version 2** as elements.

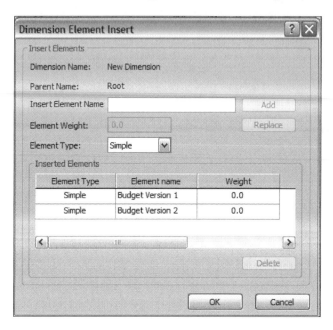

3. Click on **OK** and save the dimension as **Versions**.

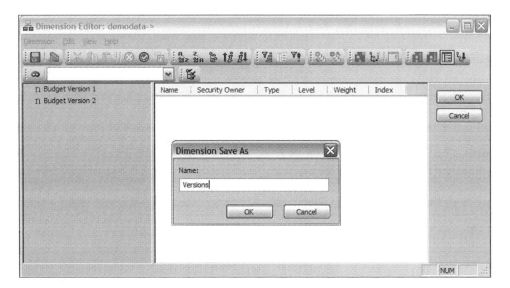

How it works...

Now the demodata server has two regular dimension which are Months, Versions, and a measure dimension called Price_Cost_Measures.

Please note that Price_Cost_Measures contains numeric measures and hence it is a measure dimension. It is just a grouping of measures and should not be confused with regular dimensions which have descriptive data to define where each data point is mapped in the cube. Each data point described above can be termed as a measure.

There's more...

Elements in a regular dimension which maps string data instead of numeric measures are called as string elements. An example of such a string element is "Comments". We will create string elements later in the book. A dimension having at least one string element is called as string dimension.

 As a general practice string dimensions are created last. Measure dimensions are created after regular dimensions as an accepted practice. Hence, it is advisable to create measure dimension first followed by regular dimensions and string dimension at last.

Adding additional levels in Months dimension

In this section we will be creating additional levels in Months dimension. We will be adding these levels manually using **Dimension Editor**.

How to do it...

1. In **Server Explorer** for demodata right-click on **Months** dimension and click on **Edit Dimension Structure**.

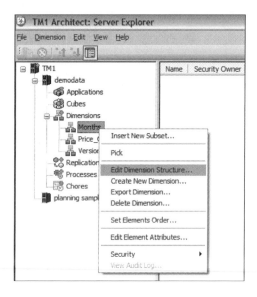

2. From the **Edit** menu click on **Insert Element** and add the following with default options.

    - ❑ **Q1**
    - ❑ **Q2**
    - ❑ **Q3**
    - ❑ **Q4**
    - ❑ **Total Year**

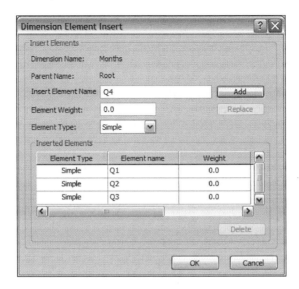

3. In the preceding screenshot please note that though the weights are 0 they will be 1 when children are created in the dimension.

4. The resulting dimensional structure should look like as shown in the following screenshot:

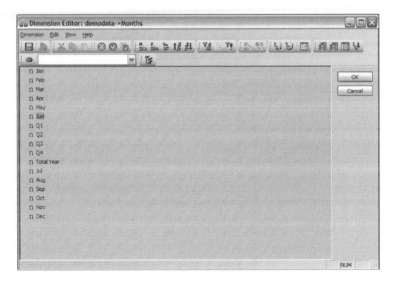

Press *Ctrl* key and select Jan, Feb, and Mar and drag it besides **Q1.Release** when 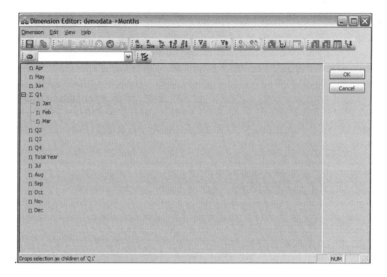 icon appears to move Jan, Feb, and Mar as child elements to Q1. This denotes values which are mapped to Jan, Feb, and Mar are rolled up to Q1 (Quarter 1). Σ sign denotes Q1 being a consolidated element. Its value will be aggregation of child values which are Jan, Feb, and Mar. Similar is the case for other consolidated elements.

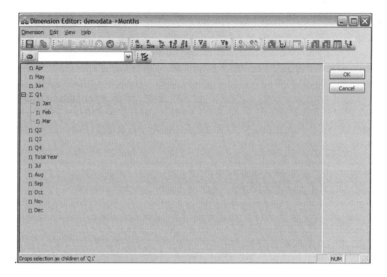

5. Same results can be achieved by creating **Total Year**. Right-click on **Total Year** and insert Q1, Q2, Q3, and Q4 as its children. Again right-click on Q1 and insert Jan, Feb, Mar as its children, and so on.

6. Right-click on Q1 and click on **Element Properties** to verify that.

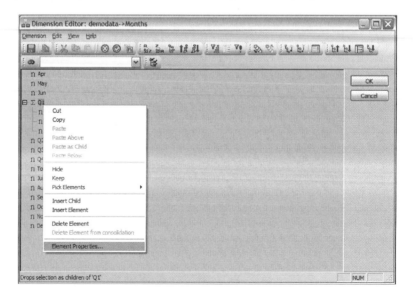

7. Please note that **Element Type** is set to **Consolidated**.

8. Other **Element Types** are **Simple** and **String** as explained in previous sections.

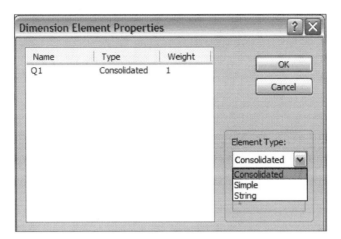

9. Similarly, click on **Jan** to view its element properties which will be **Simple**.

10. As explained in the preceding steps, repeat to make the hierarchy as shown in the following screenshot. Hence, other consolidated elements Q2, Q3, Q4 and Total Year are created in the same fashion.

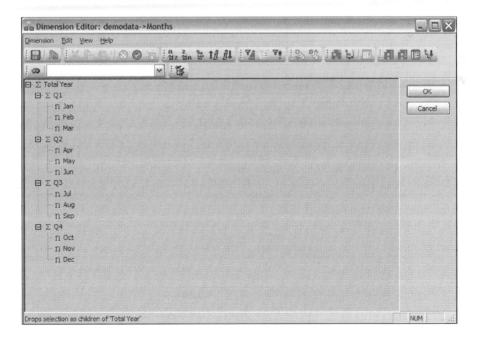

11. Click on **Set Dimension Order** as shown in the following screenshot. **Save** the resulting dimension and close the **Dimension Editor**.

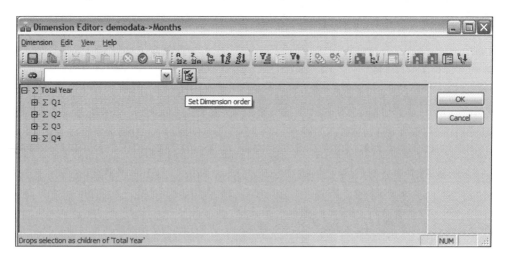

How it works...

Each element is assigned a unique index in a dimension. This is used to order the elements in a dimension. When we change the order of elements in a dimension we need to explicitly tell TM1 to assign new index numbers to each element by clicking on **Set Dimension Order**. Next time when the dimension is opened, the same order is maintained.

Adding Next and Previous attributes to the Months dimension

In this section we will be adding text attributes to the existing **Months** dimension using **Attribute Editor**. Then we will demonstrate adding an alias attribute. Lastly, we will apply formatting to **Price_Cost_Measures** using **Format** attribute.

Getting ready

Make sure that TM1 Admin server service is started. We will be using demodata TM1 server to demonstrate the recipe hence make sure that the TM1 server is also started.

Keep IBM Cognos TM1 Architect open from the **Start Menu**.

How to do it...

We will start with the **Server Explorer** window as seen before.

1. Open **Server Explorer**, right-click on Months dimension and select **Edit Element Attributes** as shown in the following screenshot.

2. From the **Edit** menu select **Add New Attribute**.

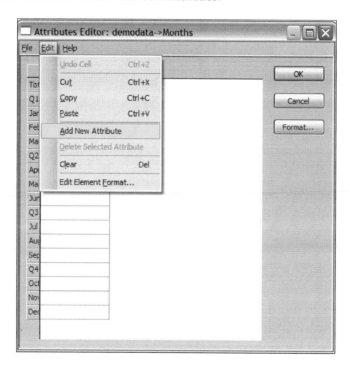

3. In the **New Attribute** dialog box type **Name** of the new attribute as **Next** with default options.

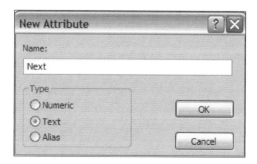

4. Similarly, add another **Text** attribute called **Previous**.

5. Now enter the values for attribute values as shown in the following screenshot. Add another attribute with name **Full Name** and of type **Alias**. By default TM1 assigns default values to **Alias** attribute. These values can be changed as shown in **Attribute Editor**.

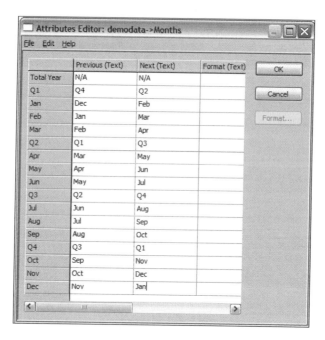

6. Click on **OK** and close.

7. Hence, we have added text attributes (Next, Previous) and alias attribute (Full Name) for Months dimension. Next we will add formatting attribute to **Price_Cost_Measures** to format elements in the measure dimension.

8. In **Server Explorer** right-click **Price_Cost_Measures** and click on **Edit Element Attributes**.

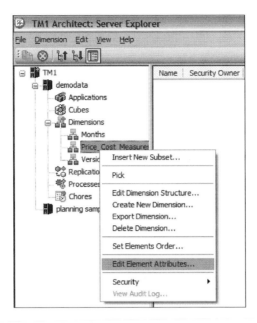

9. Click on **Unit Sales Price** and drag till **Margin** without releasing the mouse button to select three cells as shown. Then click on **Format** button.

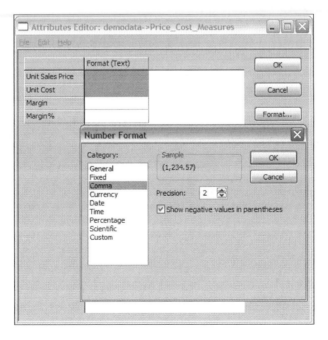

10. Click on **Currency** option and then click on **OK**. Similarly for **Margin%** click on **percentage** and then click **OK**.

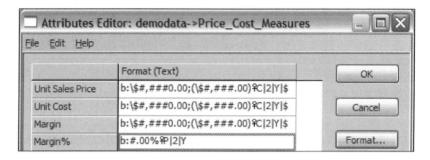

11. Click on **OK** to close.
12. Hence, we have done formatting of measure elements using **Format** attribute.

How it works...

In the preceding section, we demonstrated functionality related to attributes and have used them as text attributes for a dimension. We also used the alias attribute and applied formatting to elements using format attributes.

See also

So far we have created dimensions manually and added attributes. In the next section we will be *Creating dimensions using the Turbo Integrator*.

Creating dimensions using the Turbo Integrator

Next, we will introduce another important TM1 concept, Turbo Integrator, which is an ETL tool built-in in TM1. Turbo Scripts generated in the module, and data from the variety of sources can be Extracted, Transformed and Loaded in TM1 cubes.

Turbo Integrator is an ETL (Extraction Transform and Load) tool which is shipped with TM1. Turbo Integrator's basic object is the Turbo Integrator process which can be created to:

▸ Create and maintain dimensions
▸ Load Data into the cubes

These processes can be run manually or can be scheduled to run at fixed intervals. A Turbo Integrator process can load data from a variety of sources including CSV, ODBC, other TM1 objects, and so on.

In the next section, we will create dimensions using the TI process. Further details will follow in later sections.

Getting ready

Make sure that TM1 Admin server service is started. We will be using demodata TM1 server to demonstrate the recipe so make sure that the TM1 server is also started.

Keep IBM Cognos TM1 Architect open from the **Start Menu**.

How to do it...

Now we will create a new **Products** dimension using TI processes.

1. Create `Products.csv` which will act as the data source for the demo. Open and empty Excel sheet and enter data as shown in the following screenshot. Save the file as `Products.csv` at `C:\Program Files\cognos\TM1\Custom\TM1Data\ TI_Data`. Please note the path may differ according to the location where TM1 is installed. The path where the CSV is kept can be according to user preferences. The preceding path is just an example and may be changed according to the specific preferences.

	A	B	C
1	Cooking Gear	CAMPING EQUIPMENT	TOTAL PRODUCTS
2	Lanterns	CAMPING EQUIPMENT	TOTAL PRODUCTS
3	Packs	CAMPING EQUIPMENT	TOTAL PRODUCTS
4	Sleeping Bags	CAMPING EQUIPMENT	TOTAL PRODUCTS
5	Tents	CAMPING EQUIPMENT	TOTAL PRODUCTS
6	Golf Accessories	GOLF EQUIPMENT	TOTAL PRODUCTS
7	Irons	GOLF EQUIPMENT	TOTAL PRODUCTS
8	Putters	GOLF EQUIPMENT	TOTAL PRODUCTS
9	Woods	GOLF EQUIPMENT	TOTAL PRODUCTS
10	Climbing Accessories	MOUNTAINEERING EQUIPMENT	TOTAL PRODUCTS
11	Rope	MOUNTAINEERING EQUIPMENT	TOTAL PRODUCTS
12	Saftey	MOUNTAINEERING EQUIPMENT	TOTAL PRODUCTS
13	Tools	MOUNTAINEERING EQUIPMENT	TOTAL PRODUCTS
14	First Aid	OUTDOOR PROTECTION	TOTAL PRODUCTS
15	Insect Repellents	OUTDOOR PROTECTION	TOTAL PRODUCTS
16	Sunscreen	OUTDOOR PROTECTION	TOTAL PRODUCTS
17	Binoculars	PERSONAL ACCESSORIES	TOTAL PRODUCTS
18	Eyewear	PERSONAL ACCESSORIES	TOTAL PRODUCTS
19	Knives	PERSONAL ACCESSORIES	TOTAL PRODUCTS
20	Navigation	PERSONAL ACCESSORIES	TOTAL PRODUCTS
21	Watches	PERSONAL ACCESSORIES	TOTAL PRODUCTS

2. Open **Server Explorer** and right-click on **Processes** as shown in the following screenshot. Select **Create New Process**.

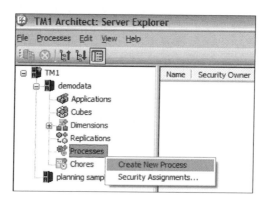

3. In the Turbo Integrator dialog box, select **Text** as **Data Source Type**. Browse to the Products.csv. **Delimiter Type** should be selected as **Delimited** and **Delimiter** should be selected as **Comma**. Click on **Preview** to view first 10 rows in the data source.

4. Click on **OK** to dismiss the following warning, which is only relevant when working on a remote server. When working on remote server Universal Naming Convention (UNC) path should be used for files.

5. Please note that this is just an informative warning stating that in case data source is on the remote computer then the text file must be named according to UNC naming conventions. In the demo we are following, text file is placed on local server; hence, the warning does not apply to us. Example of such an UNC naming path is stated as follows: \\ComputerName\SharedFolder\Resource.

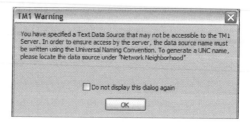

6. After we dismiss the warning by clicking on **OK** and follow the preceding steps **Turbo Integrator** dialog should look as shown in the following screenshot:

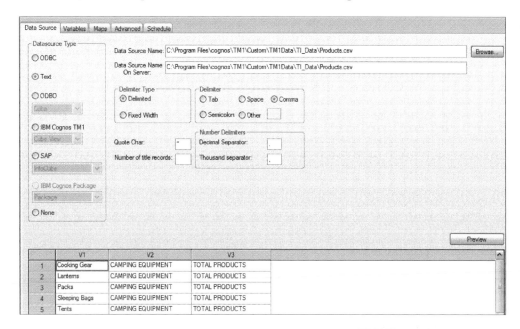

7. Click on **Variables** tab and modify **Variable Name** and **Contents** as shown in the following screenshot:

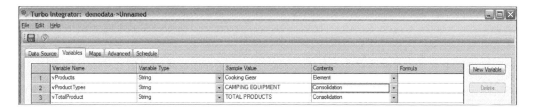

First row with variable name "v1" signifies leaf level element. Hence, **Contents** column for this row should be set to "Element". The column indicates how the incoming data will be used, transformed, and mapped in the TI process. Other values which this column can have are as shown in the following table, with a description. Hence, for more clarification on these please refer to the following table.

Contents	Description
Ignore	Ignore the contents of the column
Element	Column is converted to leaf level elements
Consolidation	Column is converted to consolidated elements, and parent to other elements
Data	Column has data values for the cube
Attribute	Column contains element attributes
Other	Values do not fall in any of the above categories. It is used by custom variables or formulas

String values from first column in `Products.csv` will be read in **vProducts** variable; hence, the **Variable Type for this variable has been specified as String**. Values read from the variable will be directly mapped to the leaf level elements in the **Products** dimension. Formulas can also be specified to transform the data and read into the variables so that The TM1 object is created/updated accordingly, with the modified data.

Second and third columns in the CSV are associated to **vProductTypes** and **vTotalProduct** variables respectively. These will be mapped to consolidated elements. `Products.csv` populates these with string values, which will be represented as consolidated elements in the **Products** dimension. No formula is required as the string values read from the CSV are directly mapped to the elements of the **Products** dimension.

8. Click on **Maps** tab and then on **Dimensions** tab. This tab specifies mapping from source to target dimension for leaf elements only.

As shown the parent dimension is **Products** for leaf level element **vProducts**. We are creating this dimension for the first time; hence, we let TI take **Create** action rather than **Update** or **Recreate**.

Target element to be created will be of Numeric type as selected in the **Element Type** drop down.

Another option here for **Element Type** is **String**, which as explained in the previous section will map to string descriptions in the cube, for example, **Comments** element can have strings, which are stored in the cube.

Above setting is directly mapped to "N" or "S" symbols, visible in dimensional or subset editor, as already explained in previous sections. Hence **Element Type** for **vProducts** is set as **Numeric** as elements created will serve as coordinates to a numerical measure instead of some string description.

The **Element Order** specifies the sort order by which elements will be arranged in the final dimension. Internally, elements in the dimension are sorted according to the indices assigned to each of the elements. The setting will determine what indices are assigned to which elements and hence the sort orders in the resulting dimension.

The **Element Order** can be set to **Automatic** or **Manual**: The former setting enables users to sort elements according to the **Hierarchy** (sorted by upper levels first and then within a level), **Level** (sorted within the same level), or by **Name in alphabetical order**. The latter setting allows users to arrange elements manually in the dimensional editor itself.

Click on **By Input** button. In the **Dimension Element Ordering** dialog click on **Automatic** sort and sort by **Hierarchy**. Click on **OK**.

9. Resulting **Dimensions** tab should look as shown in the following screenshot:

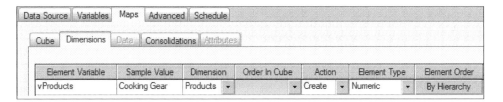

Element Variable	Sample Value	Dimension	Order In Cube	Action	Element Type	Element Order
vProducts	Cooking Gear	Products		Create	Numeric	By Hierarchy

10. Click on **Consolidations** tab. This tab specifies mapping from source to target dimension for consolidated elements.

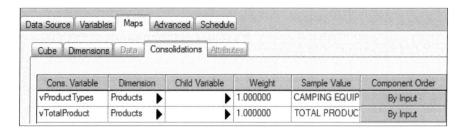

11. For **vProductTypes** row, click on **Child Variable** column and select **vProducts** as shown in the following screenshot:

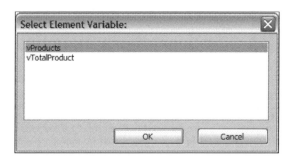

12. Similarly, for **vTotalProduct** row select **Child Variable** as **vProductTypes**.

13. Under **Component Order** for **vProductTypes**, click on **By Input** button. Click on **Automatic** for **Select one of the sort**.

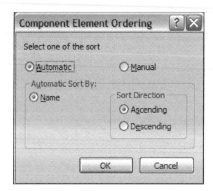

14. Similarly, for **vTotalProducts** row, click on **By Input** button and click on **Automatic**. Resulting screen should look as shown in the following screenshot:

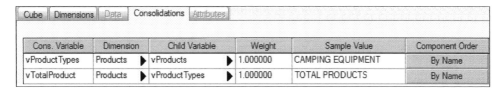

Cons. Variable	Dimension	Child Variable	Weight	Sample Value	Component Order
vProductTypes	Products ▶	vProducts ▶	1.000000	CAMPING EQUIPMENT	By Name
vTotalProduct	Products ▶	vProductTypes ▶	1.000000	TOTAL PRODUCTS	By Name

 As seen in the preceding screenshot the dimension under which these elements will be created is **Products** which is specified for **Dimension column**.

15. As these are consolidated elements, child variables are specified for **Child Variable** column as shown in the preceding screenshot. **Weight** in the above figure signifies by how much the specified child element contributes while rolling up to parent consolidated element. Click on the **Advanced** tab and then click on **Prolog**, **Metadata**, **Data**, and **Epilog** tabs so that underlying scripts are updated, reviewed, and compiled.

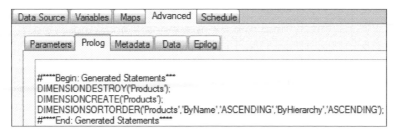

See also

We have just created dimensions manually and using Turbo Integrator processes. Cubes can now be created using the dimensions and arranging them in a specific order. We will see more about creating cubes in *Chapter 3* when we discuss *Creating cubes*.

Execution of scripts for a TM1 process

There are four scripts which are executed while a TI process is kicked off. Each of the tabs shown in the preceding screenshot displays the code executed with each script. It is important to click on each tab so that the scripts are updated, compiled, and saved after creation/ modification of the associated TI process is done. These scripts can also be modified manually if absolutely required. More details about the scripts will be shared in later chapters.

Getting ready

Make sure that TM1 Admin server service is started. We will be using demodata TM1 server to demonstrate the recipe; hence, make sure that the TM1 server is also started.

Keep IBM Cognos TM1 Architect open from the **Start Menu**.

How to do it...

1. Click on save 🖫 and type **CreateProductCSV** as name of the process. It is recommended to save the process immediately when a new empty process is created. Using the TI wizard a process cannot be executed until all fields and tabs are completed without (syntax) errors. So saving in advance is very useful in many cases.

2. Click on run 🕘 to execute the process.

3. Click on **OK** button and close the **Turbo Integrator** dialog box.

4. In the **Server Explorer** window note a new dimension called **Products** has been created. Double-click on the **Products** dimension to view the elements and associated hierarchy.

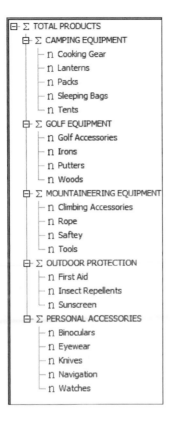

5. These are the same elements which are in the `Products.csv`. We have already ordered these according to the hierarchy in TI process; otherwise it would have been possible to order them in the **Dimensional Editor** window.

6. Similarly, we can create a dimension based on `Channels.csv` with the help of the TI process called **CreateChannelCSV**. Please take a note of the sample CSV as shown in the following screenshot:

7. Resulting dimension should look as shown in the following screenshot:

8. The preceding created dimension will be used for further recipes.

How it works...

In the preceding steps we have created the **Products** and **Channels** dimension through Turbo Integrator process. Elements are created directly from corresponding CSVs.

Therefore, in a similar fashion we can create dimensions out of data spread across a variety of data sources using Turbo Integrator processes.

See also

Chapter 3 will focus on *Creating cubes* and we will see *Loading data using Turbo Integrator processes* in *Chapter 4*, which will enable us to load data in the cubes.

3

Building Cubes and Views

In this chapter, we will cover:

- ▶ Re-ordering dimensions in a cube
- ▶ Creating a multi-dimensional Cube
- ▶ Creating a static pick list
- ▶ Creating the Sales_Plan Cube
- ▶ Creating a subset pick list

Introduction

In the previous chapter we have seen dimensions in detail which are basic building blocks of the TM1 cubes. We also created and used attributes as an alias to the elements and to format measure dimension.

In this chapter, we will extend the same concepts and use these to create TM1 cubes.

Multi-dimensional cubes are a data structure which allows manipulation and analysis of data from multiple perspectives.

A TM1 cube stores data for reports, analysis, and staging data for further calculations. Source data can come from multiple sources and be arranged in a multi-dimensional format called cube. There can be multiple cubes based on a model. Each cube contains data and business logic clubbed together, and the structure is defined by the underlying model, which again is composed of multiple dimensions, measures rules, and calculations.

Generally as per semantics, a TM1 cube should have at least one measure dimension and two or more regular dimensions, which in turn are made up of one or more elements. Though in practical scenarios there can be cubes without a measure dimension.

Elements from each dimension identify a single tuple or data point inside a cube. It's like a three dimensional axis system (x, y, z) each coordinate tuple identifies a specific data point in space. Cube can be thought of as an extension of the same three axis system, but with n number of dimensions instead of three as in the preceding example.

Additionally, as best coding practice please ensure the dimension order keeping in mind the following mentioned rule:

- ▶ Include measure dimension in last.
- ▶ String elements must reside in the last dimension in a cube. If string element is not defined in the last dimension, it is ignored by the cube.
- ▶ Order dimensions from smallest sparse to largest sparse and then from smallest dense to largest dense.

A sparse dimension will have relatively lesser percentage of filled data points then a dense dimension. **Memory Used** is a measure available in the properties pane for cubes and dimensions and can serve as a pointer to decide sparsity.

In this chapter, you will also learn about pick lists which are a list of valid values that appear when a user wants to select valid values for a cell in the cube. These values are predefined and offer valid values which a specific element or a cube cell can have.

When an administrator defines a pick list for an element or a cell, a drop-down menu containing predefined values appear for data entry, into the specified cell, when user is browsing a cube in one of the clients. The user, while entering values for such elements and cube cells, can only select from predefined values defined in the pick list, and that is the way to provide validation checks to ensure the user cannot enter any ad hoc wrong values in the cube.

Data type and format for the pick list and element must match, for administrator to define the pick list on the element or cell. Please note that string pick list, which can only be applied to string elements, must also reside in last dimension in the cube, otherwise they won't appear.

The data entered via Turbo Integrator processes or using Spreading, after pick list is defined, will not be validated by pick lists. So it is possible to see values in the cells that do not match with the ones in the pick list.

For example, if we have gender as a dimension, then it makes sense to provide users with only two valid options while they enter data for gender which are male and female. Anything other than that cannot be entered and TM1 will throw error if a user tries to enter anything other than what is defined in the pick list.

There are two ways to create a pick list:

- ▶ Simple pick list, by creating a new attribute called pick list. This appears in every cube containing that dimension.

- ▶ Advanced pick list, using rules to determine when the pick list should appear.

There are three types of pick list:

- ▶ Static pick list is composed of colon—delimited list of values using the syntax,

  ```
  static:value1:value2:value3:value4
  ```

- ▶ Subset pick list contains values corresponding to all elements in a named subset. If the elements of the subset change, value in the pick list changes correspondingly. A subset pick list is defined using the syntax:

  ```
  subset:dimension_name:subset_name
  ```

- ▶ Dimension pick list contains values corresponding to all elements in a dimension. If the elements of the dimension change, values in the pick list changes same as before correspondingly. It is defined using the syntax:

  ```
  dimension:dimension_name
  ```

As an accepted coding practice first item in the static pick list is always left blank, which allows the user to clear the existing selection. For MS Excel a space needs to be defined for blank.

Re-ordering dimensions in a cube

It's not always possible to be completely familiar with the business data; hence, sparsity of dimensions in a cube is not always predictable.

Cube data and the distribution also changes with time; therefore, order of dimensions based on sparsity may shift from ideal to less than ideal. This results in less than optimal performance. It is important to note that it is not advisable to reorder dimensions frequently as the reorder operation is a very expensive operation in terms of memory consumption.

To address the above issue TM1 includes a feature that lets the user optimize the order of dimensions in a cube, thereby consuming less memory and improving performance.

How to do it...

1. In the **Tree** pane of the **Server Explorer**, select the cube to be optimized.
2. Click on **Cube**, **Re-order Dimensions**.

3. The **Cube Optimizer** dialog box opens as shown in the following screenshot:

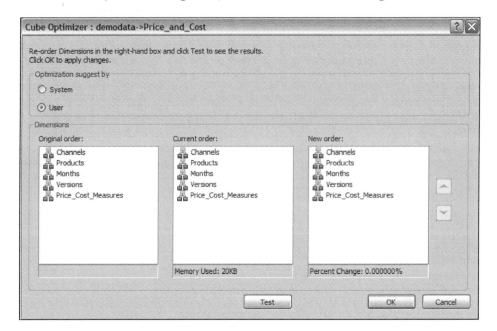

4. Select a dimension in the **New Order of Dimensions** list box.

5. Click the up or down arrows to change the order of the dimension in the cube.

6. Click on **Test**.

7. Note the value next to the **Percent Change** label. If this value is negative, the new order of dimensions consumes less memory and is therefore more efficient.

8. Repeat steps 3 through 5 until the most efficient ordering of dimensions is achieved.

9. Click on **OK**.

There's more...

Views are created on top of existing cubes to focus on a specific layout of dimensions in the cube. These can be saved for future references and signify a useful snapshot of dimensions and data, which can be updated with the latest data on a click of **Recalculate** button, while keeping the underlying arrangements of dimensions and filter the same.

Views can then be saved as **Public** or **Private** views depending on the business requirements and users can be given access to these, selectively based on the security model applied. The functionality of **Recalculate** button is similar to refresh and used to load the view with the latest data every time the user clicks on that. Unlike **Public** views, **Private** views are only accessible to the user who has created the view. **Public** views are available to all users based on security applied.

Generally, an Administrator controls the creation and access to such views. View is functionally similar to database views which are quite well-known. These do not have data but just store definition and provide a pigeon hole view inside the cubes, very specific to business requirements.

We will be creating a default view on a multi-dimensional cube in the next recipe, *Creating a multi-dimensional cube*.

Creating a multi-dimensional cube

Now we will be creating a cube and using demodata TM1 server. The cube will be called Price_and_Cost cube and detailed steps are shown in the following sections.

Getting ready

Ensure that TM1 Admin service is started. The demodata TM1 server must be running and ready for business. Keep IBM Cognos TM1 Architect open from the Start Menu and log on to the demodata server to expose TM1 objects in Server Explorer.

How to do it...

1. Open **Server Explorer** window.
2. Right-click on **Cubes** and click on **Create new cube** as shown in the following screenshot:

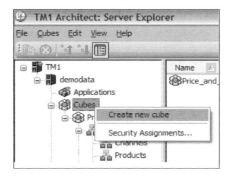

3. In the **Creating Cube** dialog, type **Price_and_Cost** as the name of the cube. Select the entire available dimension in left pane; double-click to move all dimensions to **Dimensions in new cube** in right pane as shown in the following screenshot.

 We have used underscores for names in the example, but that is not absolutely required as spaces are allowed in TM1. Users are free to use spaces in TM1 object names as required.

4. Change order of the dimensions using the **Up** and **Down** arrow, as shown. Please note that the order is complied with the already stated ordering rule in the previous section. Click on the **Create Cube** button.

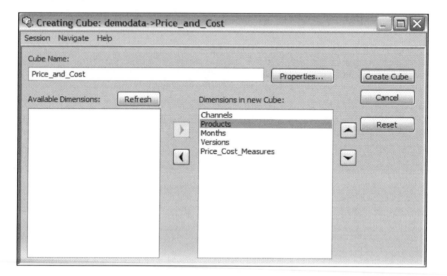

5. The new cube called **Price_and_Cost** cube appears in the **Server Explorer** window. At this point of time cube is an empty box without any data. Nevertheless, the structure given by dimensions and elements is there.

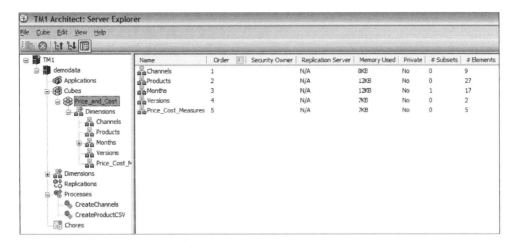

6   Double-click on **Price_and_Cost** cube. The cube viewer window opens up to display dimensions in the title, row, and column areas.

7. Drag-and-drop **Price_and_Cost_Measures** on top of **Months** dimension (**Total Year**) in the title area to swap them as shown in the following screenshot:

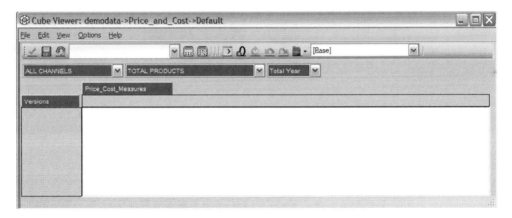

8. Click on **Months** dimension once to open the **Subset Editor** as shown in the following screenshot:

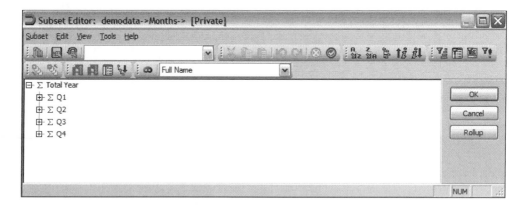

9. Click on **All** icon to expand the dimension to the lowest level.

10. Now, click on **Filter by Level** 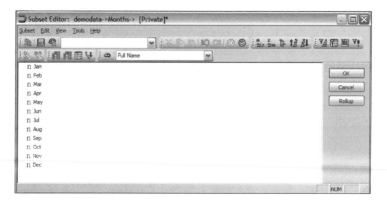, select lowest level that is 0 and click on **OK**.

11. From the **Subset** menu click on **Save As,** for name type **Months** and select options as shown in the following screenshot:

12. Hence, a subset called **Months** has been saved which can be used in other cubes and views as time dimension. Click on **OK** to close the **Subset Editor**.

13. Here in the preceding step we have just created a public subset which is available to all users who have at least read access to the associated dimension. Admin privilege to the parent dimension is needed to create a public subset. A private subset on the other hand is available only to the user who creates them.

14. Click-and-drag **Versions** on to **Products** (**TOTAL PRODUCTS**) dimension to swap them. Click on **Recalculate** button to populate latest data.

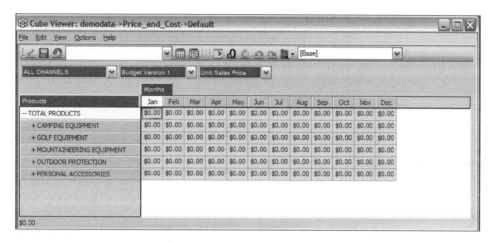

15. Click on down arrow next to **ALL CHANNELS** and select **Golf Shop** from the drop down. Click on **Recalculate** button to load the latest data.

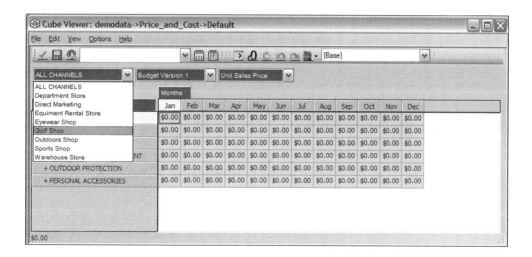

16. Click on **Save As** from **File Menu** and select **Default**.

17. This will save current view as default view which is automatically opened when the cube name is double-clicked. A view also can be saved either as a **Public** or a **Private** view by clicking on the checkbox. Similar to subsets, public views are available to all users who at least have read privileges on the cube containing the view data. Only TM1 administrators and users having admin privileges on the associated cube can create a public view on the cube. Private views on the other hand are available only to users.

 A cube view cannot be saved as a public view if it contains a private subset.

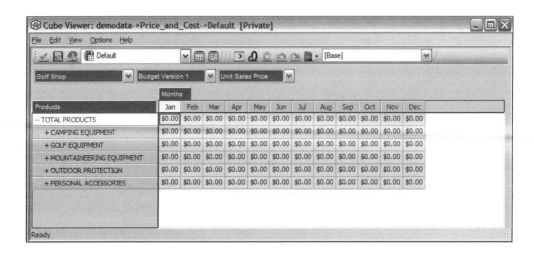

18. Close the cube viewer. The data for this cube will be loaded in subsequent chapters.

How it works...

In the preceding steps we have created **Price_and_Cost** cube from an interface provided by IBM Cognos TM1 Architect. We have also defined subsets which can be reused while designing other TM1 objects. Default view on Price_and_Cost cube also has been created which enables users to access just the information they are entitled to view.

See also

The following recipes *Creating a static pick list*, *Creating the Sales_Plan cube*, and *Creating a subset pick list* will focus on pick lists.

Creating a static pick list

We will be creating a static pick list and exploring different types of pick list in subsequent sections.

Getting ready

Ensure that TM1 Admin service is started. DemoData TM1 server must be running and ready for business. Keep IBM Cognos TM1 Architect open from the **Start Menu** and log on to the DemoData server to expose TM1 objects in **Server Explorer**.

How to do it...

1. Open the **Server Explorer** window and click on **Dimensions** to expand.

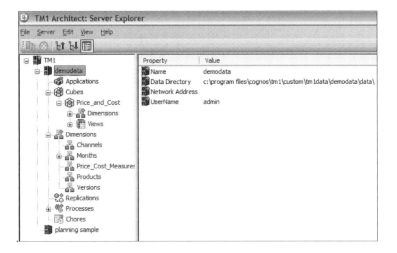

2. Right-click on **Price_Cost_Measures** and click on **Edit Dimension Structure**.

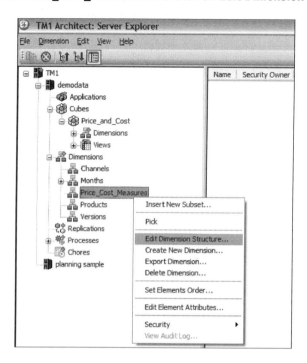

3. Click on last element, click on **Edit** and click on **Insert Element**.

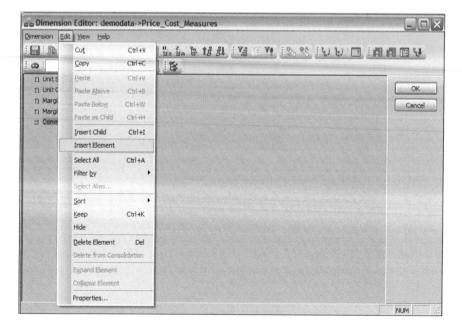

4. Add a new **String** element with element name as **Comment** and **Element Type** as **String**.

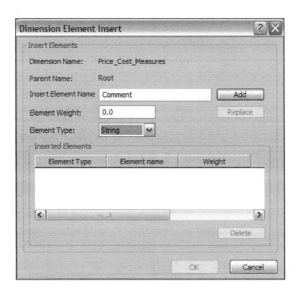

5. Save the resulting dimension.
6. Click on **OK** and close the **Dimension Editor**.
7. In **Server Explorer**, right-click **Price_Cost_Measures** and click on **Edit Element Attributes**.
8. This will open **Attribute Editor** as show in the following screenshot:

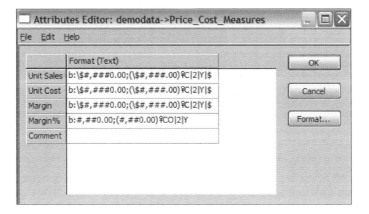

9. Click on **Edit** menu in **Attribute Editor** and select **Add New Attribute**.

10. Enter **Picklist** for **Name** and ensure **Text** is selected as shown in the following screenshot:

11. This will add an additional attribute called **Picklist** as shown in the following screenshot:

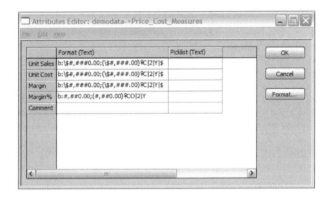

12. In the cell next to **Comment** and user **Picklist** enter following:

```
Static::High:Medium:Low
```

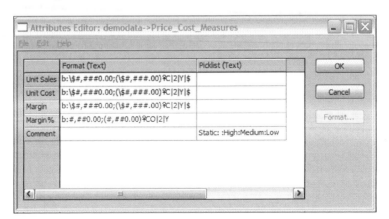

13. This will add a pick list for element **Comment** and the resulting pick list will have values as **High**, **Medium**, and **Low**.

14. Click on **OK** to close the **Attribute Editor**.

The preceding steps have added a text element called **Comment** to hold values entered through the pick list. String element always has to be created in the last dimension of the cube; otherwise it will be ignored by the cube. If **Dimension** for **Price_and_Cost** cube, is expended, **Price_Cost_Measures** is the last dimension, where exactly the string element **Comments** have been added.

15. Double-click **Price_and_Cost** cube in **Server Explorer** to open it in the **Cube Viewer**.

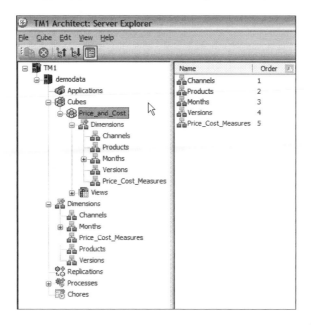

16. The cube viewer shows the default view created in the previous sections.

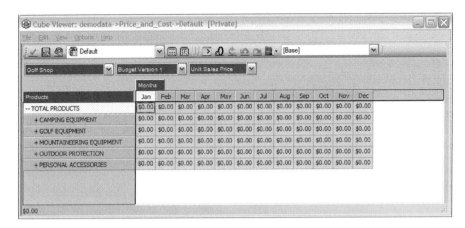

17. Double-click **Price_Cost_Measures** to open in the subset editor. In the subset editor double-click on **All** icon and click on **OK** to close the **Subset Editor**.

18. In the **Cube Viewer** window click on **Price_Cost_Measures** drop down and select **Comment**. Click on **Racalculate** icon.

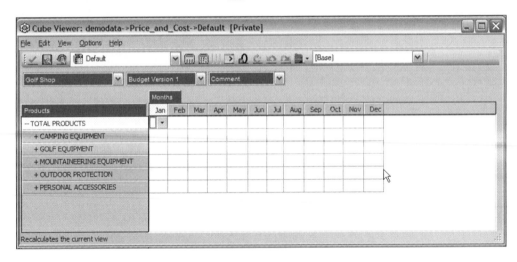

19. In the **Cube Viewer**, click on **Months** to open the dimension in **Subset Viewer** as shown in the following screenshot:

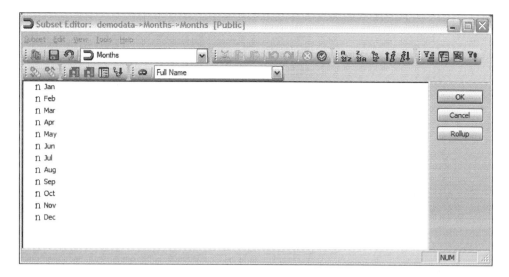

20. Click on **Use Alias icon** 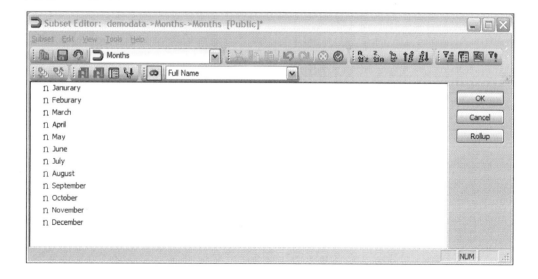 on **Subset Editor** and ensure the drop down besides the icon is selected to **Full Name** as shown. Click on **OK** to close the window.

21. Click on the **Recalculate** icon in the **Cube Viewer** window.

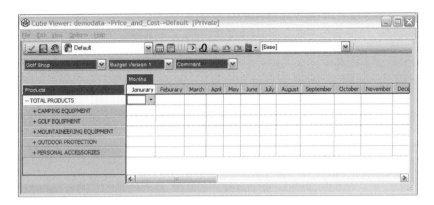

22. From **File Menu**, in the **Cube Viewer** window, save the view as **Private** view called as **Price Comment** as shown in the following screenshot:

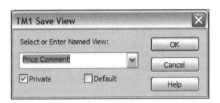

23. On **Cube Viewer** window, click to expand **TOTAL PRODUCTS** and **CAMPING EQUIPMENT** and click in the first cell under **January**. It will show the **Picklist** defined in the previous section. Click on any of the values appearing in the pick list to populate the cell.

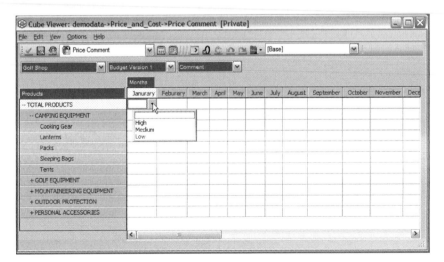

24. Select **High** value and the view changes as shown in the following screenshot:

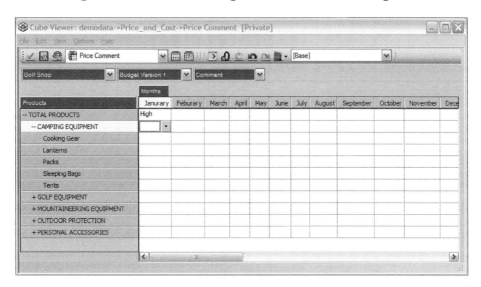

25. The cell will not take any value other than what is defined for the **Picklist**. Any attempt to assign the **Comment** element with any other value will throw an error. Hence, only those values which are defined for the **Picklist** that is **High**, **Medium**, and **Low** can be saved. Any other arbitrary value for example, **A** will not be saved in the cell as shown in the following screenshot:

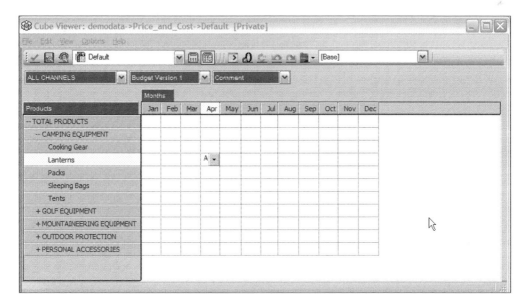

26. Close the cube viewer.

In the preceding steps we have added **Comment** element which can take any of the three values among **High**, **Medium**, and **Low** depending on the price value of a particular product in a given month.

See also

Subset pick list will be discussed in the subsequent recipe, *Creating a subset pick list*, but before that we will be looking at *Creating the Sales_Plan cube* in the next recipe.

Creating the Sales_Plan cube

In this recipe we are going to create the Sales_Plan cube which will help us build on our demodata example. We will be going through subsequent recipes, which will be based on the Sales_Plan cube.

Getting ready

Ensure that TM1 Admin service is started. DemoData TM1 server must be running and ready for business. Keep IBM Cognos TM1 Architect open from the **Start Menu** and log on to the DemoData server to expose TM1 objects in **Server Explorer**.

How to do it...

1. Create the **Subsidiaries.csv** with data as shown in the following screenshot:

GO Americas	GO AMERICAS REGION	TOTAL COMPANY
GO Asia Pacific	GO ASIA PACIFIC REGION	TOTAL COMPANY
GO Accessories GmbH	GO EUROPE GMBH	TOTAL COMPANY
GO Central Europe	GO EUROPE GMBH	TOTAL COMPANY
GO Northern Europe	GO EUROPE GMBH	TOTAL COMPANY
GO Southern Europe	GO EUROPE GMBH	TOTAL COMPANY

2. In the **Server Explorer** window, right-click on **processes and create a new process** called **CreateSubsidiariesDim** as shown:

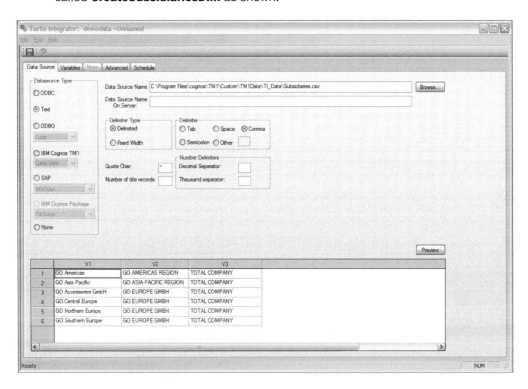

3. Click on the **Variables** tab and define variables to read data from the source as shown. Take a note of the **Contents** column which specifies intended usage of the variable. For example, data read in **vSubsidiary** will form elements of the Subsidiary dimension, while data read in **vTotal** will form consolidated elements of the dimension.

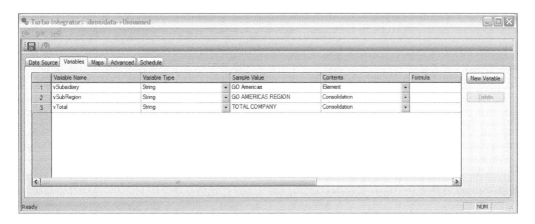

4. Click on **Maps** tab and click on **Dimensions** tab to define mapping to lowest level elements in the dimension.

5. Click on **Consolidations** tab under **Dimensions** to define mapping for consolidated elements.

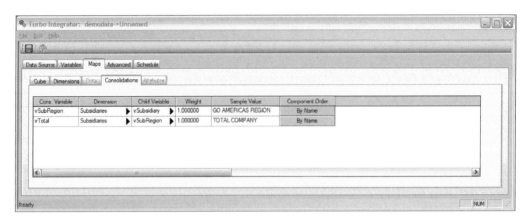

6. Click on **Advanced** tab and then on **Prolog**, **Metadata**, **Data**, and **Epilog** to generate metadata and required scripts.

7. Save the process and execute.

8. Take a note of the **Subsidiaries** dimension hence created.

9. Create another dimension called **Sales_Plan_Measures**, manually through the excel sheet. The elements to be included in the dimension are shown in the following screenshot:

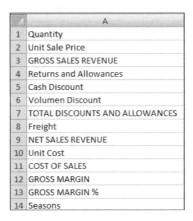

	A
1	Quantity
2	Unit Sale Price
3	GROSS SALES REVENUE
4	Returns and Allowances
5	Cash Discount
6	Volumen Discount
7	TOTAL DISCOUNTS AND ALLOWANCES
8	Freight
9	NET SALES REVENUE
10	Unit Cost
11	COST OF SALES
12	GROSS MARGIN
13	GROSS MARGIN %
14	Seasons

10. The last element that is **Seasons** is a String element and remaining 13 elements from A1:A13 are numeric elements.

11. Right-click on `Dimension` folder in **Server Explorer** and click on **Create New Dimension**.

12. Copy cells A1:A13 in the CSV shown above and paste them in the **Dimension Editor** as shown in the following screenshot:

13. Click on the last element that is **GROSS MARGIN** %, go to the **Edit** menu and click on **Insert Element** to create **Seasons** element as a String element, as shown. Sibling element like that we have added above can be done by clicking on the 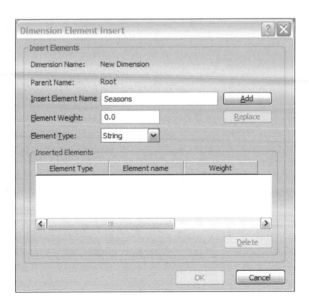 icon in the bar.

14. Save the dimension as **Sales_Plan_Measures** as shown in the following screenshot:

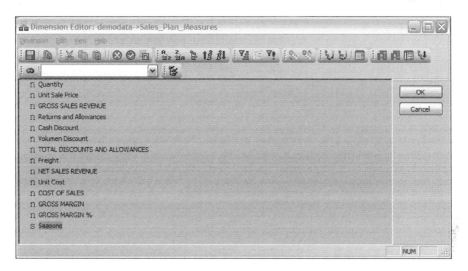

15. In the **Server Explorer** window right-click on the **Cubes** and click on **Create New Cube**. Take a note of the dimensions to be included and the most optimum order for them to be included in. As described in *Chapter 2*, to optimize performance of the cube we should order dimensions accordingly.

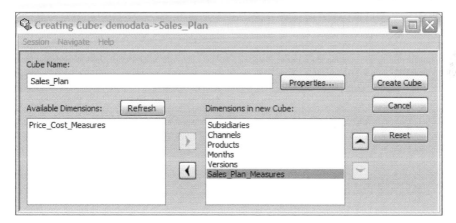

16. Click on **Create Cube** and now the new cube is visible in **Server Explorer** window under Cubes folder.

See also

In the next recipe, *Creating a subset pick list* we will be using the **Sales_Plan** cube created in this recipe.

Creating a subset pick list

A subset pick list contains values corresponding to all elements of a named subset. If the members of the subset change, the values available in the pick list change correspondingly. Similarly, a **Dimension Pick List** contains values corresponding to all elements of a dimension. If the members of the dimension change, the values available in the pick list change correspondingly.

This recipe will be based on a subset pick list. A dimension Pick List is created in a similar fashion and the basic concept remains the same.

Getting ready

Ensure that TM1 Admin service is started. DemoData TM1 server must be running and ready for business. Keep IBM Cognos TM1 Architect open from the Start Menu and log on to the DemoData server to expose TM1 objects in Server Explorer.

How to do it...

1. In the **Server Explorer** window double-click the **sales_plan** cube to open **Cube Viewer**.

2. Swap **Sales_Plan_Measures** with **Versions** and then **Versions** with **Months** to get the following screenshot:

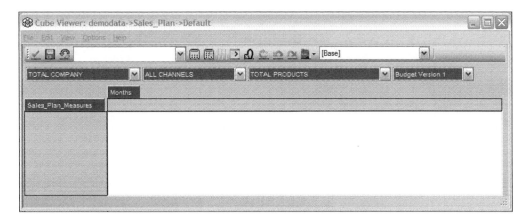

3. Click on **Months** dimension, click to open the **Subset Editor**. Click on **Months** from the select subset drop down shown in the following screenshot:

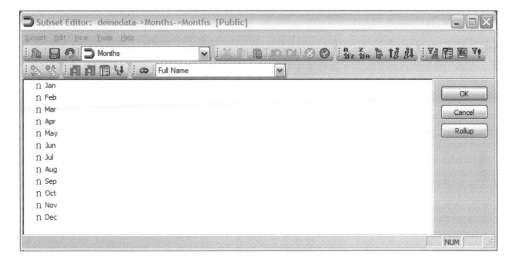

4. Click on **OK** button to close the editor and continue. Click on **Recalculate** button 🔳 to load the data, as shown in the following screenshot:

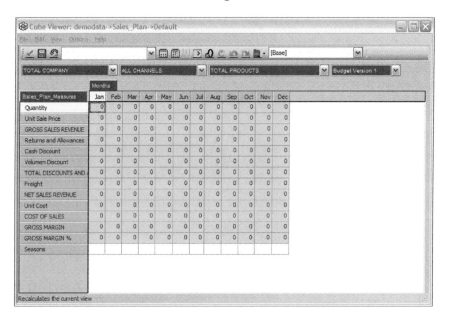

5. Double-click on **TOTAL PRODUCTS** and open the **Subset Editor**. In **Subset Editor** expand **CAMPING EQUIPMENT**, select **Lanterns** and click on **OK**, as shown in the following screenshot:

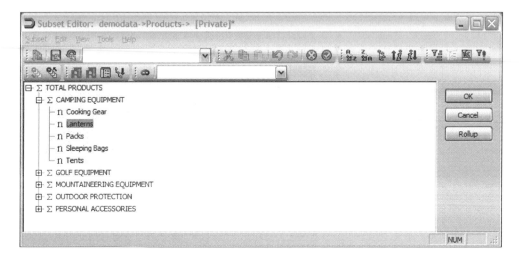

6. In **Cube Viewer** window click on **Recalculate** button to display the cube in current configuration.

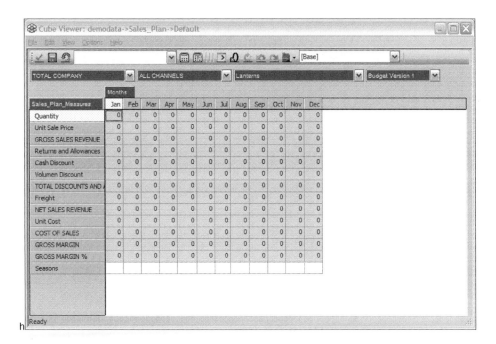

7. From the **File** menu save the view as **Default** view as shown in the following screenshot:

8. Open the **Server Explorer** window, right-click on **Sales_Plan_Measures** and click on **Edit Element Attributes** to open **Attribute Editor**.

9. In the **Attribute Editor** click on **Add New Attribute** from **Edit** menu. Name the attribute as **Picklist**.

10. In the **Picklist** column next to seasons element type Subset:Months:Months.

11. The preceding code will add a subset pick list based on **Months** subset in **Months Dimension**.

12. Select **Unit Sales Price** cell under **Format** and drag it till **Gross Margin** to select all the cells below **Format** and between the two elements. Please refer to the following screenshot:

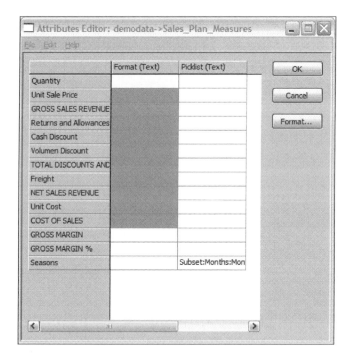

13. Click on **Format** button, click on **Currency**, and then click on **OK**.

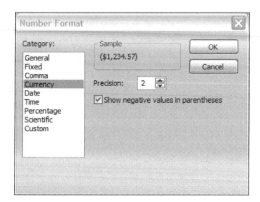

14. Click on **OK** to close.

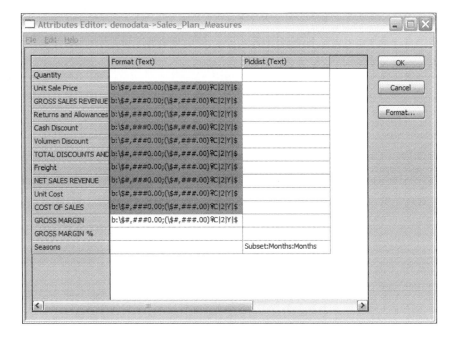

15. For Quantity values, apply a **Comma** format.

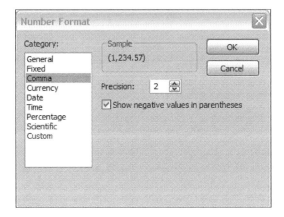

16. Click on **OK** to close the **Attribute Editor**.

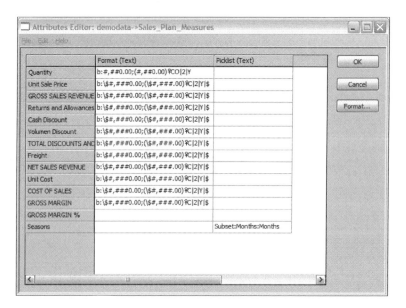

17. In the **Server Explorer** window open the default view of **Sales_Plan** cube. Note list of **Months** appear when drop down in cells for **Seasons** element are clicked.

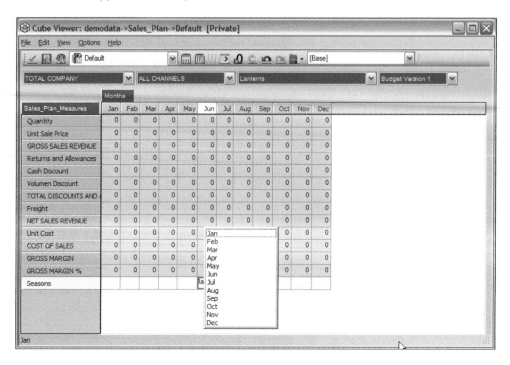

18. Hence, a subset pick list has been created in **Seasons** element which sources itself from a subset called **Months**. This subset belongs to **Months** dimension. Close all the windows saving the work done so far.

How it works...

We have added a pick list defining all the possible values a cube cell can take. Defining a pick list serves as a guideline to the user while entering data as well as it makes sure that cube only contains valid values.

See also

Now we have learned how to create dimensions and cubes, we will look at *Loading data using Turbo Integrator processes* in *Chapter 4*. We will also learn more about Turbo Integrator processes and how they are useful in maintaining data in cubes.

4
Loading and Maintaining Data

In this chapter, we will cover:

- ▶ Loading data using Turbo Integrator processes
- ▶ Using formulas in variables
- ▶ Clearing data from a cube using a process
- ▶ Accumulating data using a process
- ▶ Saving data using a process

Introduction

Now, as we have already covered how to create dimensions, cubes, and views in previous chapters, we will be focusing on loading data in this chapter.

As explained in previous chapter, Turbo Integrator is an ETL module provided with TM1, which enables application developers to **extract**, **transform**, and **load** data in cubes which can be deleted or updated as per the requirements, again using Turbo Integrator processes.

In this chapter we will cover how TM1 is compatible with different types of databases. We will also learn how to create Turbo Integrator processes (TI processes), to load, delete, and maintain business-specific data in cubes and models.

We will use the same demodata example and extend the various objects we have created so far.

We will first take a look at the types of data sources which can feed TM1 models and cubes.

Turbo Integrator can load data from:

- ODBC sources
- Text files
- TM1 views and dimensions
- ODBO (Used with Microsoft Analysis Services)
- SAP source tables via RFC function module

 RFC (**Remote Function Call**) is the proprietary SAP AG interface for communication between a SAP system and other SAP or third-party compatible system over TCP/IP or CPI-C connections. Remote function calls may be associated with SAP software and ABAP programming and provide a way for an external program (written in languages such as PHP, ASP, Java, or C, C++) to use data returned from the server. Data transactions are not limited to getting data from the server, but can insert data into server records as well. SAP can act as the client or server in an RFC call.

Data can also be entered manually through:

- Direct type in cells, copy–paste
- Data spreading

Data can also be entered through processing worksheet DBSS functions. Processing worksheets are specially formatted Microsoft Excel sheets used to load data in the cube.

TM1 worksheet functions return a numeric or string value, and can be used anywhere in an Excel worksheet.

To access these functions in Excel, choose **Insert | Function** from the Excel menu bar, or click on ![fx] in the Excel toolbar.

Data in numeric cells can be entered at leaf level only, which ultimately rolls up to form higher level data points for aggregated elements. For string cells, data can be entered at all levels.

Loading data using Turbo Integrator processes

In the recipe we will see exactly how data is loaded in a cube through a TI process.

> TI processes are neither case sensitive nor space sensitive.

The steps involved in loading data using TI processes are:

- ▶ Connecting to the source and preview data
- ▶ Creating and mapping variable content
- ▶ Identifying cube, dimensions, and measures
- ▶ Saving and executing the TI process

In this recipe we will see how data from an ASCII file can be loaded into a cube. We will follow our previously-created data server called DemoData and will be loading price and cost data from an ASCII file to the price and cost cube.

Getting ready

Ensure that the TM1 Admin service is started. demodata TM1 Server should be running and **Server Explorer** open in TM1 Architect.

Create the `Price and Cost.csv` in Microsoft Excel and save as `.csv`.

	A	B	C	D	E	F
1	Product	Month	Cost	Price	Version	Channel
2	Cooking Gear	Jan	1500	1200	Budget Version 1	Department Store
3	Cooking Gear	Feb	2500	1100	Budget Version 1	Department Store
4	Cooking Gear	Mar	1200	1200	Budget Version 1	Department Store
5	Cooking Gear	Apr	1100	1500	Budget Version 1	Department Store
6	Cooking Gear	May	1300	1500	Budget Version 1	Department Store
7	Cooking Gear	Jun	2500	1500	Budget Version 1	Department Store
8	Cooking Gear	Jul	2000	1500	Budget Version 1	Warehouse Store
9	Cooking Gear	Aug	4000	2000	Budget Version 1	Warehouse Store
10	Cooking Gear	Sep	2000	2000	Budget Version 1	Warehouse Store
11	Cooking Gear	Oct	3000	3000	Budget Version 1	Warehouse Store
12	Cooking Gear	Nov	3500	3000	Budget Version 1	Warehouse Store
13	Cooking Gear	Dec	6000	3000	Budget Version 1	Warehouse Store
14	First Aid	Jan	2000	1500	Budget Version 1	Outdoors Shop
15	First Aid	Feb	3000	2000	Budget Version 1	Outdoors Shop
16	First Aid	Mar	2500	2000	Budget Version 1	Outdoors Shop
17	First Aid	Apr	2000	2000	Budget Version 2	Sports Shop
18	First Aid	May	4000	4000	Budget Version 2	Sports Shop
19	First Aid	Jun	2000	2000	Budget Version 1	Sports Shop
20	Tents	Jan	1200	4000	Budget Version 1	Sports Shop
21	Tents	Feb	1100	2100	Budget Version 1	Sports Shop
22	Tents	Mar	3200	1000	Budget Version 1	Direct marketing
23	Tools	Dec	1200	1250	Budget Version 2	Sports Shop
24	Tools	Feb	1000	3400	Budget Version 2	Sports Shop
25	Tools	Mar	3400	4350	Budget Version 1	Outdoors Shop
26						

How to do it...

1. Start the **demodata** server and open a **Server Explorer** window as shown in the following screenshot:

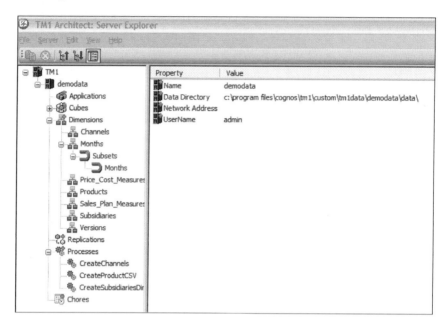

2. In the **Server Explorer** window right-click **Processes**, click on **Create New Process** and click on **Text** to open a **Turbo Integrator** window.

3. In the **Turbo Integrator** window, in the **Data Source Name** dialog box click on **Browse** and point to the `Price and Cost.csv` to open the file. In the **Number of title records** field type **1** to indicate that the first row in the text file contains descriptive information about the data. Click on **Preview** to see the first 10 rows in the source.

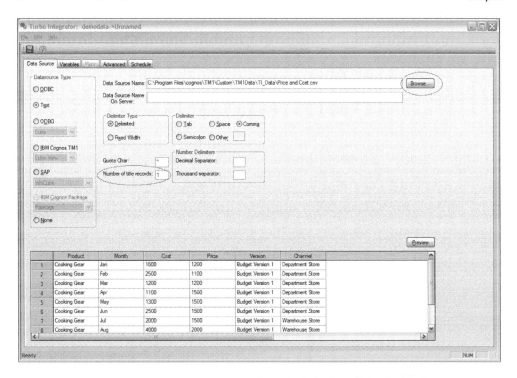

4. Click on the **Variables** tab. Here, variables need to be defined to read from the source. Define the variables corresponding to different fields in the data source as shown in the following screenshot:

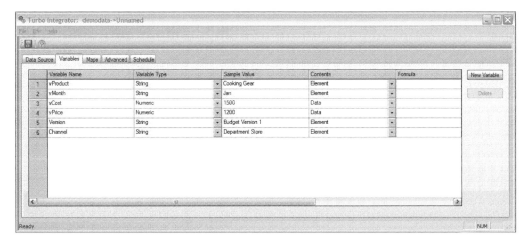

In the preceding context, if a column name is reserved to TM1 or contains a space then it will be replaced by Vx. Also, take a note of the **Contents** for each variable, which determines if a particular variable contains data corresponding to an element or a data point in the cube. In other words, contents property is set to **Element** when the values are used to identify an element from a dimension, and set to **Data** if the values are the actual data to be stored in the intersection. In this example, Cost and Price are Data and everything else is Element. Take a note of other options which further define non-leaf consolidated elements or attributes.

Therefore, in the preceding steps we have defined a variable for each dimension. Measure dimensions are mapped to Data while other leaf level dimensions are mapped to Element.

5. Click on the **Maps** tab to map the source data to a target cube and select **Update Cube** for **Cube Action**. Other cube actions are:

Create Cube	Create a new cube
Recreate Cube	Destroy and recreate the cube
No Action	No action

6. As we already have a **Price_and_Cost** cube, we will just select the existing cube from the drop down and update the cube as shown in the following screenshot:

7. Click on the **Dimensions** tab to map variables to dimensions in the cube, as shown in the following screenshot:

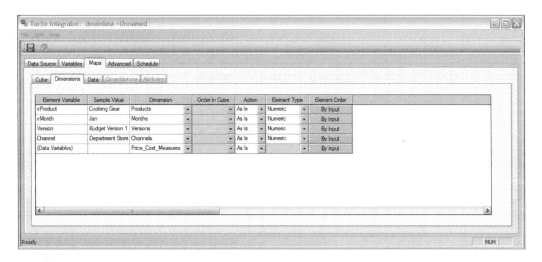

In the preceding steps, **Element Variables** are being mapped to existing dimensions in the cube. No new dimension elements will be created, hence, **Action** is set to **As Is**.

8. The **Element Type** for the **Data Variables** row which corresponds to **Price_Cost_ Measures** is left as **Numeric** as it contains a numeric element. In case we plan to load string data in the cube we should have selected **String**. In our case, we select **Numeric** as we are loading numeric data only in the cube. For example, if we had another string element in **Price_Cost_Measures** called **Comments**, defined as part of the cube, then we would have specified **Element Type** as **String**.

We use the **Dimensions** sub-tab to map element variables to dimension elements. **Element Type** directly corresponds to the element type of the dimension elements. For example, **vProduct** corresponds to the elements of the **Products** dimension which has Numeric elements (each product element can have a numeric value at an intersection in the cube), hence **Element Type** is set to **Numeric**.

9. Click on the **Data** tab to map data values to the **Price_Cost_Measures** dimension. For **vPrice** click on the arrow under **Element** to open the **Subset Editor**. Select **Unit Cost** to map data from the **vCost** variable to the **Unit Cost** measure element.

10. Similarly, map **vPrice** to **Unit Sales Price** in the **Subset Editor**.

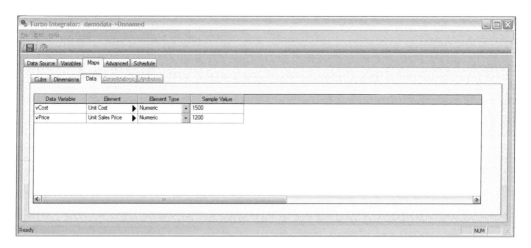

11. Click on the **Advanced** tab and click on **Prolog**, **Metadata**, **Data**, and **Epilog** to generate scripts.

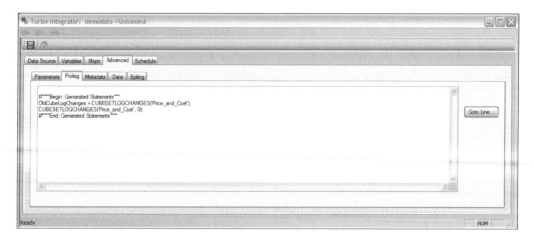

The scripts generated are a direct result of the options the user has chosen in the Turbo Integrator wizard. These scripts run at the backend to transform and transfer data. These scripts can also be edited and handwritten as required, according to the functions provided in the TI module. Documentation for the TI functions which can be used to author such scripts is available in the **Help** menu. We will be introducing such manual scenarios, involving handwritten scripts, later in the book.

12. Click on **Save** and in the **Name** box type name as **LoadPriceAndCostCSV** and click on **OK**.

13. Click on **Run** and once the process is completed close the **Turbo Integrator**.

14. In the **Server Explorer** window double-click on **Price_and_Cost** cube to open **Cube Viewer** as shown in the following screenshot. Select **Default** view from the drop-down and click on **Recalculate** to view data in the default view. Alternatively, as the view is the default view, it should be automatically loaded if you double-click the cube in the **Server Explorer**.

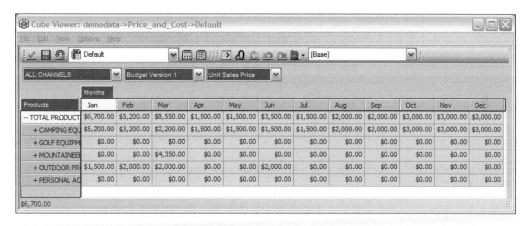

Using formulae in variables

Formulae are used in variables:

- ▶ To do data-type conversions
- ▶ For placeholders for data not present in the source
- ▶ To combine elements
- ▶ To extract only portions of data for an element

There is a variety of functions available to be used in TI. Refer to the TM1 Function reference guide to understand a list of functions.

Getting ready

Ensure that the TM1 Admin service is started. The demodata TM1 Server should be running and **Server Explorer** should be open in TM1 Architect.

Create an Excel file called `SalesPlan2.xls` to be used as an ODBC data source for loading Sales Plan Measures. Take a note of the number of columns and sample data.

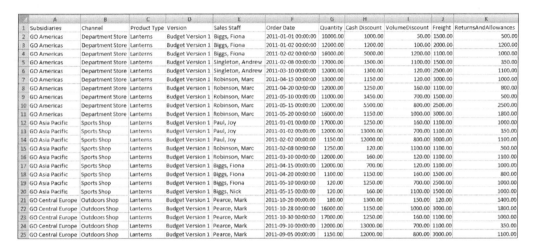

There are 11 columns in the Excel file. The column names and data types are shown below:

Column name	Data type
Subsidiaries	Text
Channel	Text
Product Type	Text
Version	Text
Sales Staff	Text
Order Date	Number
Quantity	Number
Cash Discount	Number
Volume Discount	Number
Freight	Number
ReturnsAndAllowances	Number

We will be loading **Order Date** which has month numbers in it. In our **Months** dimension we have month names; we will be adding month number aliases to the months dimension.

Create the Excel file as discussed with sample data, as shown in the preceding screenshot, in the Microsoft Excel interface.

Select the whole of the data content in the Excel, right-click and select **Name a Range**.

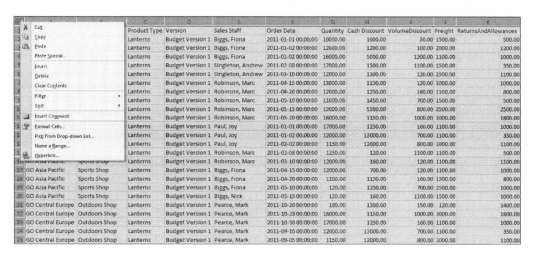

Type **Sales** for **Name**, select **Workbook** for **Scope**, and click on **OK**. Save and close the Excel sheet.

This will define a range in Microsoft Excel which will be used as the database named in the TI process.

How to do it...

1. In the **Server Explorer** window in **TM1 Architect** right-click on **Months** dimension and click on **Edit Element Attributes**.

We will create an attribute for the number of each month, which will allow us to use a TI function to map month numbers from the **Order Date** column to the alias instead of the element names. We can use an element name or an alias as they are fully equivalent.

2. From the **Edit** Menu in the **Attributes Editor,** click on **Add New Attribute**.

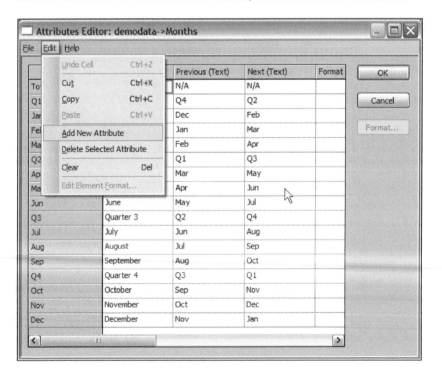

3. In the **Name** box, type **MonthNumber** and click on **Alias**. Click on **OK** and ignore the warning.

4. Type month numbers from 1 to 12 in the **MonthNumber (Alias)** column, as shown in the following screenshot. Overwrite cell entries if needed.

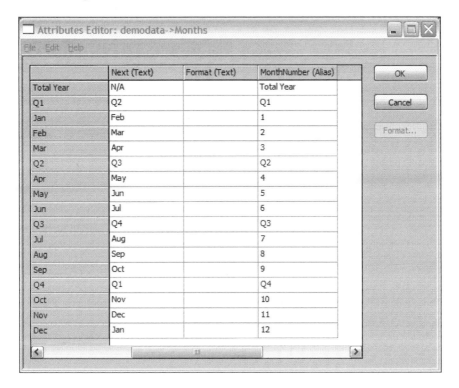

5. Click on **OK** and close.

6. Now from the Start Menu, click on **Run** and type `odbccp32.cpl`, as shown, to add a DSN to the existing `SalesPlan2.xls`. The exact steps could differ if the user is in a different environment.

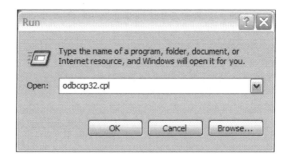

7. Click on the **Add** button in the **ODBC Data Source Administrator** to add a **System DSN** and select **Microsoft Excel** Driver, as shown in the following screenshot:

8. Click on **Finish** to open **ODBC Microsoft Excel Setup**.

9. Select the `SalesPlan2.xls` and for the data source name type **Sales_Plan**. Select the appropriate version and click on **OK** to add the ODBC.

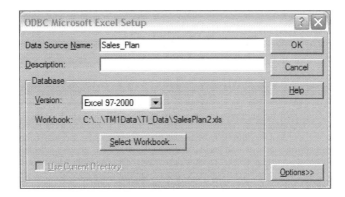

10. In the **ODBC Data Source Administrator** the newly added system DSN will become visible, as shown in the following screenshot:

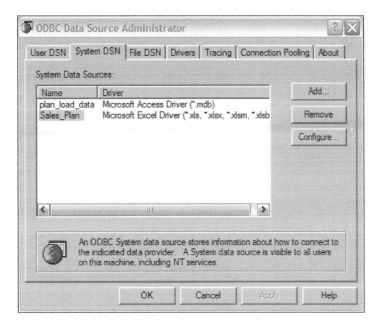

11. In the **Server Explorer** window in TM1 Architect, right-click on **Processes** and select **Create New Process** to open the **Turbo Integrator** window. Click on **ODBC**, for **Data Source Name**, click on **Browse** and select **Sales_Plan** DSN from the available list of DSN, and for the query type `select *from sales`. Click on **Preview** to display a sample of the first 10 rows from Excel.

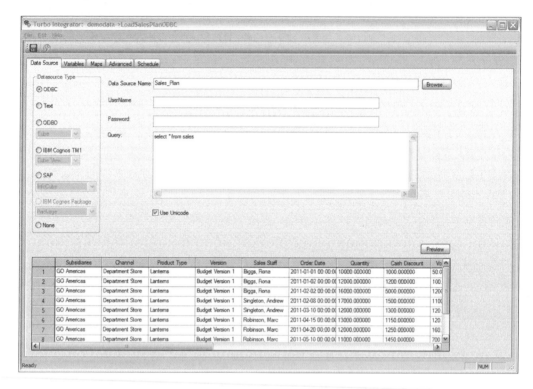

12. Click on the **Variables** tab. Change the **Variable Names** so that they relate to the dimensions they are associated with. Define the **Contents** for each variable according to the following table:

Contents	Description
Other	Available to TI process (even if the user decides to write the code manually), but not mapped to Element, Attribute, or Consolidation.
Ignore	Not available to TI process and not mapped to Element, Attribute, or Consolidation.

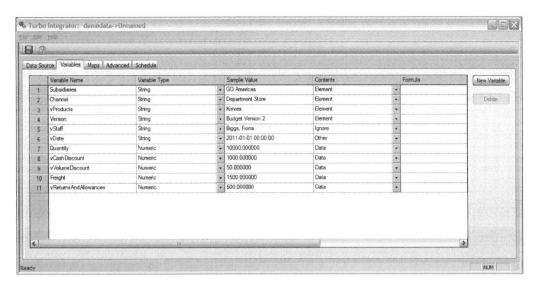

13. In the same **Turbo Integrator** window, under the **Variables** tab, click on the **New Variable** button. Rename the new variable as **vMonth**. Click on **Formula** and in the formula box type:

```
vMonth=NUMBERTOSTRING(MONTH(vDate));
```

14. Click on **Data** in the **Destination** section and click on **Evaluate**.

15. Click on **OK** button to close.

16. For the Variable Name **vMonth** select **String** for **Variable Type** and **Element** for
    Contents. Variables that are mapped to **Elements** or **Consolidation** must be set to
    Element Type String.

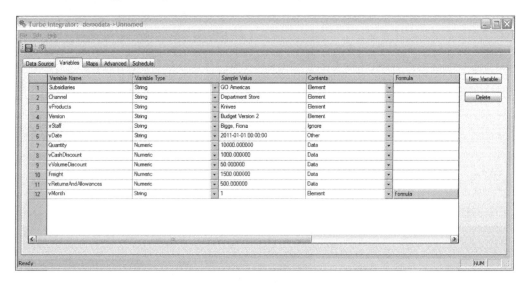

17. Click on the **Maps** tab and then on the **Cube** tab, click on **Update Cube**. Click on the
    drop-down menu beside **Cube Name**, and select **Sales_Plan**. Below **Data Action**,
    click on **Store Values**, as shown in the following screenshot:

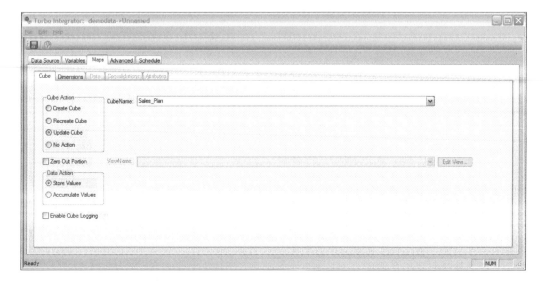

18. Click on the **Dimensions** tab to map the **Element Variable** to the corresponding **Dimension**. As the dimensions have already been created, the **Action** column is set to **As Is**. Refer to the table for valid values assigned to **Dimension** for each **Element Variable** in the preceding screenshot.

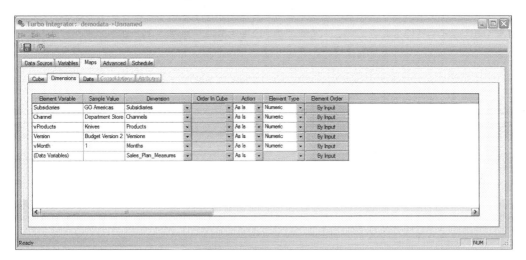

Element Variable	Dimension
Subsidiaries	Subsidiaries
Channel	Channels
vProducts	Products
Version	Versions
vMonth	Months
(Data Variables)	Sales_Plan_Measures

19. Click on the **Data** tab to define mapping for **Sales_Plan_Measures**. For each **Data Variable** click on the arrow under the **Element** column and from the **Subset Editor** select the appropriate elements, as shown in the following screenshot:

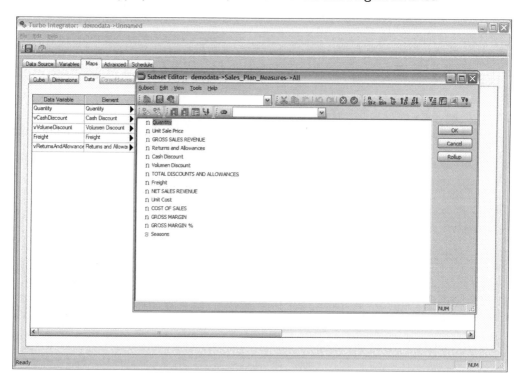

20. Click on the **Advanced** tab, and click on the **Prolog, Metadata, Data**, and **Epilog** tabs. Save the process as **LoadSalesPlanODBC** and then execute the process.

    Click on **OK** and close the **Turbo Integrator**.

21. Go to the **Server Explorer** in TM1 Architect and click on the **Sales_Plan** cube.

22. Click on the **Default** view from the drop-down and click on the **Recalculate** button, as shown in the following screenshot:

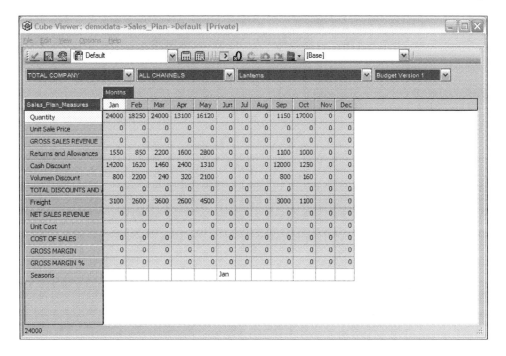

23. If the **Default** view is not already set as shown, arrange the dimensions and save as the default view, as shown in the preceding screenshot.

24. Close the **Cube Viewer**.

Chores

TI processes can be scheduled to run during out of business hours. When scheduling is carried out, TI automatically creates a chore that will be scheduled.

Either a chore or a TI process can be run on demand from the menu, depending on security privileges. There are no built-in functions to allow a user to run a process or a chore from the command line. However, this can be accomplished by using the TM1 API to write your own program. Many such utilities are available on the Internet with complete documentation. A utility called TM1RUNTI.EXE is available with TM1 9.5.2 latest hot fix which enables a user to execute a TI process from the command line.

Chores should be deactivated while being edited so that they don't get executed while being edited. Once editing is done, chores should be reactivated and can be executed at the scheduled date and time.

Clearing data from a cube using a process

In addition to loading data, TI processes can be used to:

- ▸ Clear data
- ▸ Move data from cube to cube
- ▸ Automatic saving

In this recipe, we will see how to clear data from a cube using a Turbo Integrator process.

Getting ready

Ensure that TM1 Admin service is started. The demodata TM1 Server should be running and **Server Explorer** should be open in TM1 Architect.

How to do it...

1. Open the **Server Explorer** window in TM1 Architect.
2. Right-click on **Processes** and select **Create New Process**.
3. On the **Datasource Type** tab click on **IBM Cognos TM1** and select **Cube View** from the drop down.
4. Click on the **Browse...** button, select **demodata:Sales_Plan** and click on the **Create View...** button as shown in the following screenshot:

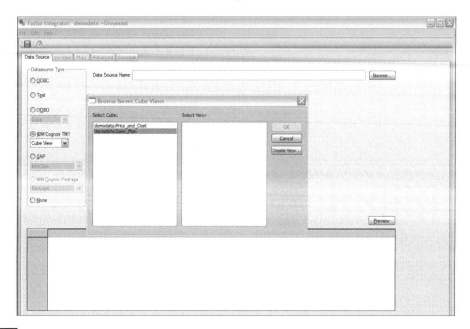

5. The **View Extract** window pops up. Click on **OK** button without making any selections, the default is to select all elements.

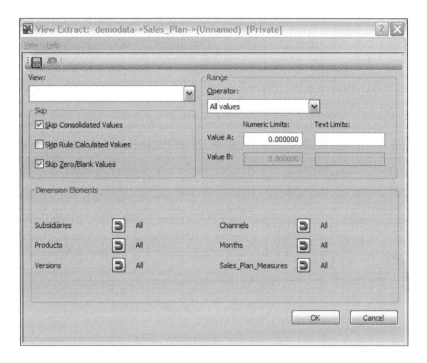

6. In the **TM1 Save View** dialog box, type **zDeleteAll** and click on **OK**.

7. In the **Select View** column, select **zDeleteAll** and click on **OK**.

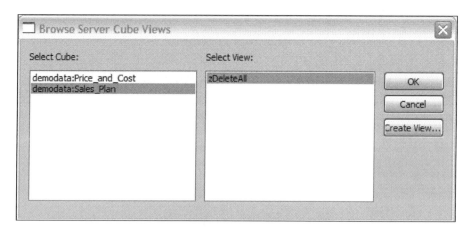

8. Click on **Preview** and you should see the following screen:

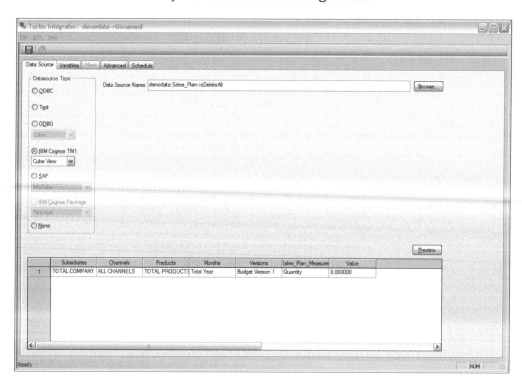

9. Save the process as shown in the following screenshot:

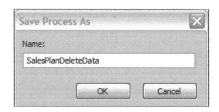

10. Click on the **Variables** tab, then the **Advanced** tab and the **Prolog** tab.

11. A function needs to be added in the generated script which will set all data values to zero in the `Sales_Plan` cube. `VIEWZEROOUT` is such a function, the following is the syntax:

```
ViewZeroOut('CUBE','VIEW_NAME');
```

12. Add the preceding function in the **Prolog** tab at the end of the generated script as shown:

```
ViewZeroOut('Sales_Plan','zDeleteAll');
```

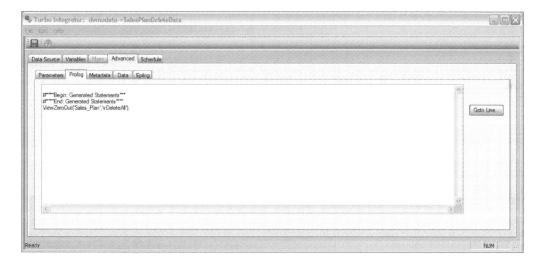

13. Save and execute the process. When the process is completed successfully close the Turbo Integrator window.

14. Open the **Server Explorer** window in TM1 Architect and double-click on the **Sales_ Plan** cube, as shown in the following screenshot.

15. Open the **Default view** from the drop-down in **Cube Viewer** and check if all the cells are correctly set to zero.

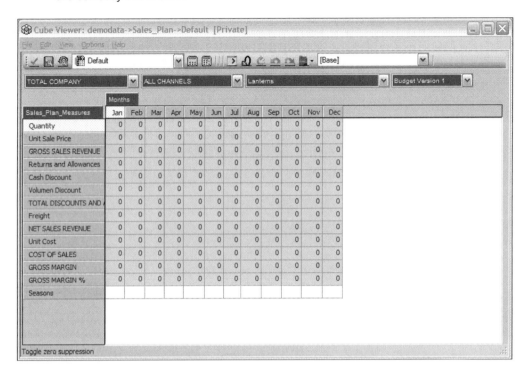

16. Close the **Cube Viewer**.

Accumulating data

In our Load data from ODBC example, **Staff** was an additional column in the Excel spreadsheet, with no corresponding dimension. Normally, TM1 keeps overwriting the present data value for staff with the next incoming data value for staff. Hence, the data cell values in the cube after the load will only have a value for the last staff member loaded. This is because we have fewer dimensions in the cube then the available columns in Excel.

In an ideal scenario, the values for different staff members should accumulate instead of overwriting each other. To achieve this functionality we need to edit the TI process to accumulate data instead of storing data, we will be update the **LoadSalesPlanODBC** process accordingly.

Getting ready

Ensure that the TM1 Admin service is started. The demodata TM1 Server should be running and **Server Explorer** should be open in TM1 Architect.

How to do it...

1. In the **Server Explorer** window, right-click on **LoadSalesPlanODBC** and click on **Edit** to open the **Turbo Integrator** window.

2. Click on the **Maps** tab and check **Accumulate Values** in the **Data Action** section, as shown in the following screenshot:

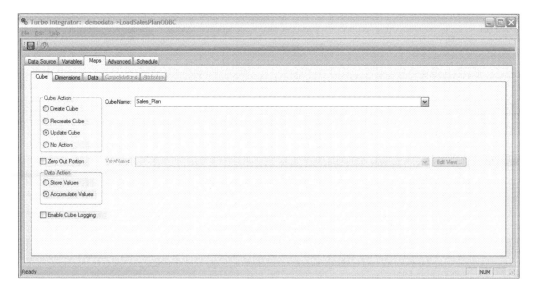

3. In the **Advanced** tab, click on the **Prolog, Metadata, Data**, and **Epilog** tabs to change the underlying scripts.

4. Click on **Save** and **Execute** the process. If completed successfully, close the **Turbo Integrator** window.

5. In the **Server Explorer** window, double-click on the **Sales_Plan** cube.

6. Select **Default view** and click on **Recalculate** to view the loaded data.

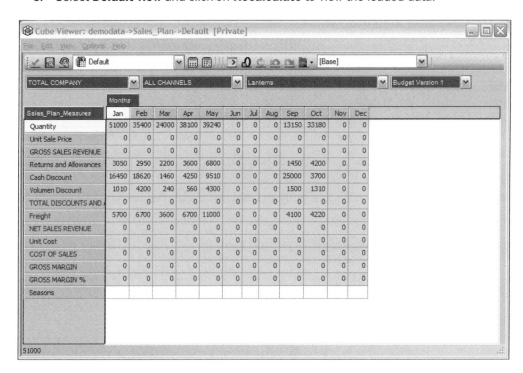

How it works...

Clearly, the data values are much larger then those previously loaded. This is because this time we are accumulating data values for different staff members instead of overwriting them. Therefore, this time we are able to see aggregated values instead of the value for the latest uploaded staff member.

Saving data

All the objects in TM1 reside in the memory until they are saved to the server. When the data server is shut down, the user is prompted to save the changes made. Ideally, there should be a process which runs automatically after a fixed interval and saves all the changes made. We will be creating such a process in this recipe.

Getting ready

Ensure that TM1 Admin service is started. The demodata TM1 Server should be running and **Server Explorer** should be open in TM1 Architect.

How to do it...

1. In the **Server Explorer** window right-click on **Processes** and select **Create New Process**.

 The process will save all the data, not just specifically to a cube or a cube view.

2. In the **Turbo Integrator** window click on the **Advanced** tab.
3. Click on the **Epilog** tab and type in **SAVEDATAALL;** as shown in the following screenshot:

4. Click on the **Schedule** tab.

5. Check **Schedule the Process as a Chore Named:** and type **SaveAllData** in the textbox. For the **Chore Frequency** set the process to run every 2 hours, as shown in the following screenshot:

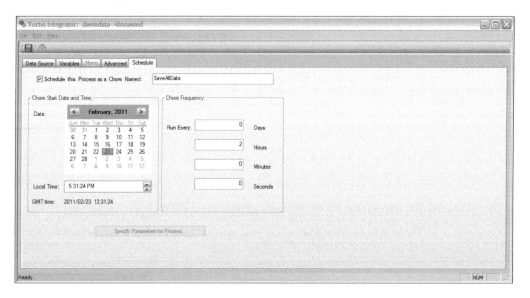

6. Click on **Save** to save the process as **SaveAllData**. Close the **Turbo Integrator** window.

7. The **SaveAllData** processes and chores are visible in the **Server Explorer** window as shown in the following screenshot:

8. The new saved process or chore can be executed by right-clicking on the available menu.

5
Adding Business Rules

In this chapter, we will cover:

- ▶ Creating simple rules
- ▶ Using a rule to override aggregation
- ▶ Creating a rule to share data between cubes
- ▶ Creating a pick list using a rule
- ▶ Reviewing a rules worksheet
- ▶ Doing custom calculations in dimensional hierarchies

Introduction

In previous chapters we have looked at dimensions, cubes, and ways to populate business data for further analysis.

The next and obvious step is to apply business logic on the objects by implementing business rules and storing these in cubes.

Applying business rules ensures:

- ▶ That the same version of calculations are being used by all users
- ▶ Applying custom calculations
- ▶ Reformatting business data
- ▶ Overriding hierarchical calculations
- ▶ Sharing data between cubes

Most of the time, rules are used to store or modify data in target cells of a cube. Therefore, the first step involved in rules creation and implementation is to identify an appropriate cell to store values returned by the rule. A cube is then identified, on which the rule is applied. Rules are applicable to both leaf level elements as well as consolidated elements. These can also be applied to string elements. Rules are applied to the cells in the order written; hence, more specific rules should be written before generic rules. Once a rule is applied to a cell, TM1 stops looking for other rules that apply to that cell.

Rules are stored in text files with the extension `*.rux`.

TM1 provides two types of Editor: the Advanced Rules Editor and a simple version. In order to change the Editor, the `TM1p.ini` file needs to be modified as follows:

AdvancedRulesEditor=F/T for Simple Editor/Advanced Editor

`TM1p.ini` is located at `C:\Documents and Settings\Administrator\Application Data\Applix\TM1` for the Windows, single computer setup being discussed.

Certain folders in the preceding path may be hidden and may need to be made visible before the file can be located. Also, Perspectives needs to be closed down (**Server Explorer**) if the user wants to change certain settings. For example, which nodes are visible, use Advanced Rules Editor or not, and so on.

In the subsequent recipes we will be using the Advanced Rules Editor, therefore the file mentioned above needs to be modified. We will be using the same DemoData setup we have been using for previous recipes and we will be creating an additional cube called **Rules** to demonstrate the concepts, in addition to the existing cubes **Price_and_Cost** and **Sales_Plan**.

Creating simple rules

In this recipe we will be creating a cube and writing rules for it.

Getting ready

Ensure that the TM1 Admin Server service is started and the demodata TM1 Server is up and running. Log on to the demodata Server in TM1 Architect.

How to do it...

1. In a **Server Explorer** window, right-click on **Cubes** and click on **Create New Cube**.
2. In the **Creating Cube** dialog, type **Rules** for the **Cube Name**.

3. Under **Available Dimensions** double-click on **Months** and **Price_and_Cost_Measures** to add them to **Dimension in new Cube**.

4. Click on the **Create Cube** button.

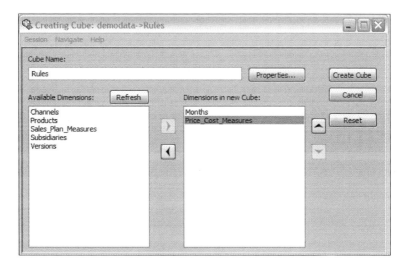

5. In the **Server Explorer** window, under **Cubes**, double-click on the **Rules** cube to open it in the **Cube Viewer**.

6. Click on **Recalculate** to display the data in the cube.

7. In the **Cube Viewer**, expand **Months** to display the data as shown in the following screenshot:

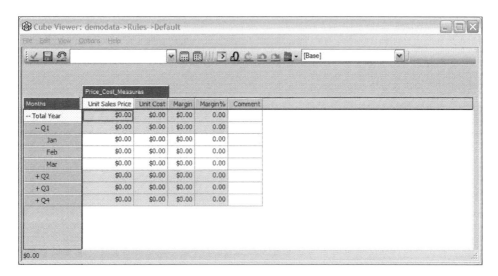

8. In the **Server Explorer** window right-click on the **Rules** cube and click on **Create Rule** to open the **Advanced Rules Editor**.

9. The following screenshot shows the Advanced Rules Editor provided with TM1 to write rules. It has all the required existing functionalities as a text editor such as indent line, undo, redo, delete, cut, copy, paste, and so on.

10. Click on the brackets ⬚ and then on **Price_and_Cost_Measures**, as shown in the following screenshot:

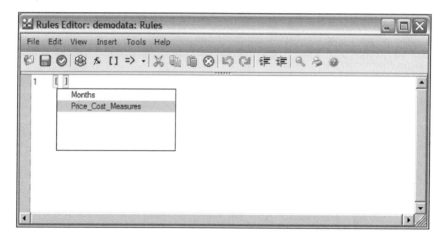

11. It will open the **Subset Editor**, from here you can select one of the measure elements intended to be the target cell. Choose **Unit Sales Price** and then click on **OK** to display the text as shown in the following screenshot:

12. At the end of line 1 type =1; as shown in the following screenshot:

13. In the **Rules Editor** all statements must end with a semicolon.

14. All numbers are displayed in red and all strings in blue. All strings must be enclosed in single quotes.

15. Click on the check syntax icon 🔘 to highlight any syntax errors.

16. Try checking for syntax errors by deleting the semicolon in the first line and clicking on the check syntax icon.

17. The preceding step will throw an error message as shown in the following screenshot:

18. Replace the semicolon to rectify the error and again click on the check syntax icon to ensure there are no errors in the script now.

19. Click on the **Save** button 🔳.

20. In the **Cube Viewer** window for the **Rules** cube click on the **Recalculate** button to show the updated data.

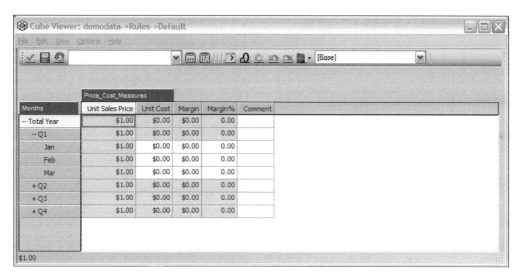

21. All cells corresponding to **Unit Sales Price** are set at $1.00, overriding any consolidations applied.

22. Click on the **Rule Editor**.

23. Delete **=** sign and click on the **Insert Qualifier or Operator** button on the toolbar as shown. Click on **=N**.

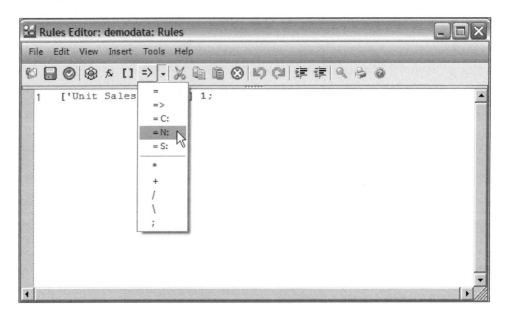

24. Line number 1 should now look like:

```
1    ['Unit Sales Price' ]   = N: 1;
```

25. Click on check syntax icon and click on **Save**.

26. The preceding modification ensures that the rule applies only to leaf level elements and consolidations work as required.

27. Click on **Cube Viewer** and **Recalculate** to show the modified data. Please note that only leaf level elements have been changed to **$1** for the **Unit Sales Price**. These leaf level elements are aggregated as before to form consolidated level elements.

28. Notice the color of the calculated cells, which includes consolidated cells, is grey indicating that no values can be entered manually for them. Rules-driven cells will not accept any data entry.

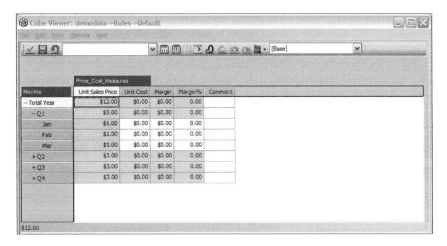

29. Click on the **Rules Editor**.

30. On the first line click after the semicolon and type **C:20;**

31. The resulting first line looks like:

```
1   ['Unit Sales Price' ]   = N: 1; C:20;
```

32. This will ensure leaf level elements are set to 1 and consolidated level elements for **Unit Sales Price** are set to 20. Again this will override the default consolidation which is evident when the **Cube Viewer** window is opened and data is recalculated, as shown in the following screenshot:

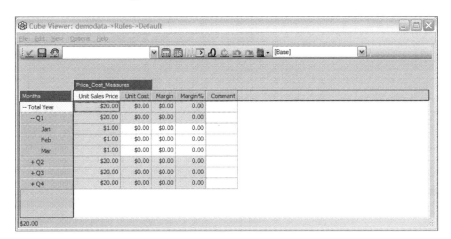

33. Click on the **Rules Editor** window and on the second line type the following statement:

```
1    ['Unit Sales Price' ]    = N: 1; C:20;
2    ['Q1','Unit Sales Price'] = 7;
```

34. The above rule is a more specific rule compared to what is specified in line 1.

35. The rule sets all the cells identified by Q1 and the **Unit Sales Price** to 7.

36. Click on the check syntax icon and then on **Save**.

37. Open the **Cube Viewer** window and **Recalculate**.

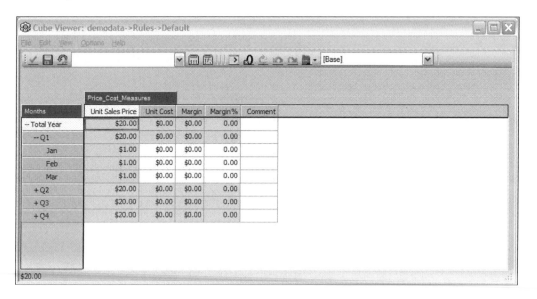

38. Please note that data does not change as we have specified a more generic statement before a specific one in the Rules Editor. Due to the order (Q1, Unit Sales Price), cells have already been changed in rule 1; hence, rule 2 does not have an effect on that.

39. To change cells (Q1, Unit Sales Price) to 7, apply the rule before the current rule 1 and change the order as shown in the next screenshot:

```
1    ['Q1','Unit Sales Price'] = 7;
2    ['Unit Sales Price' ]    = N: 1; C:20;
```

40. Check for the syntax and click on **Save**.

41. Open the **Cube Viewer** window and click on **Recalculate**.

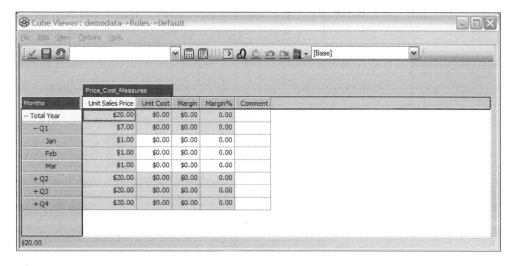

42. In an earlier case, TM1 had already applied a rule to cells (Q1, Unit Sales Price), hence TM1 ignores any other calculation applied on the same cell afterwards. Therefore, more specific rules must be applied before general ones.

43. Save the view as **Default View**.

44. Close the **Rule Editor** and **Cube Viewer**.

45. Go to the **Server Explorer** window.

46. Expand the **Rules** cube and double-click on the **Rules** icon 🗒 to open the **Rules Editor**.

47. On line 3 click the brackets 📋 icon, double-click on **Price_and_Cost_Measures,** and select **Comments** from the **Subset Editor**.

48. Outside the bracket click on the **Insert Qualifier or Operator** icon ⇒ and click on = S.

49. Type 'Winter' after =S: as shown in the next screenshot:

```
1    ['Q1','Unit Sales Price'] = 7;
2    ['Unit Sales Price' ]    = N: 1; C:20;
3    ['Comment']    = S: 'Winter';
```

50. Click on the check syntax icon, save, and open the **Rules** cube in **Cube Viewer**.
Recalculate to see the latest data.

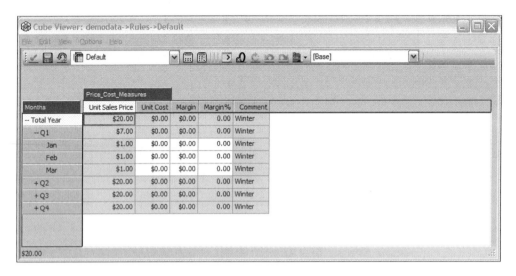

51. Go to the **Rules Editor** to add logic to populate **Winter/Summer** depending on certain
conditions of the **Unit Sales Price**.

52. In the **Rules Editor** on line 3, delete **'Winter'** and add the following logic:

```
1   ['Q1','Unit Sales Price'] = 7;
2   ['Unit Sales Price' ]  = N: 1; C:20;
3   ['Comment']  = S: IF (['Unit Sales Price']>5,'Summer','Winter');
```

53. The preceding rule is expected to return **Summer** if the condition is true, else **Winter**.
The general syntax would be:

```
IF(Condition,Result_on_true,Result_on_false)
```

54. Check the syntax, save the rule. Open the **Cube Viewer** and click on **Recalculate** to
view the latest data.

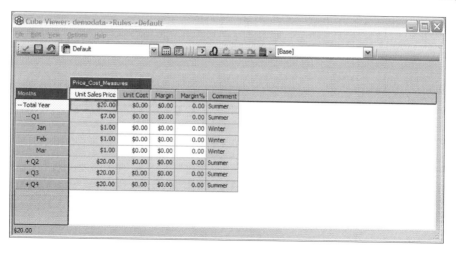

55. The next step would be to exclude **Q1** from the rule by using the **STET** command.

56. To exclude an area from a rule we use the **STET** command immediately before the rule.

57. The syntax for **STET** is STET.

58. In the **Rules Editor** make the changes as shown in the following screenshot:

```
1   ['Q1','Unit Sales Price'] = 7;
2   ['Unit Sales Price' ]  = N: 1; C:20;
3   ['Q1'] = STET;
4   ['Comment']  = S: IF (['Unit Sales Price']>5,'Summer','Winter');
```

59. Check the syntax, save, and open the **Cube Viewer**.

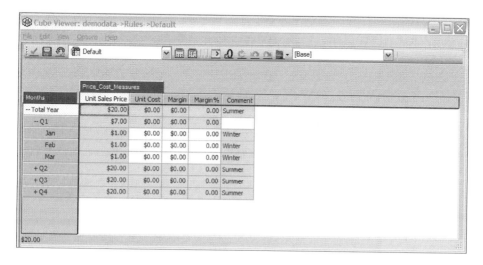

60. Since no rule was applied to the **Q1** cell, it is shown in white.

61. Close **Rule Editor** and **Cube Viewer** without saving any changes to the cube view.

How it works...

In this recipe we have created a cube and added rules to it using the Advanced Rules Editor. These rules come into play when a user browses the cube and data is populated accordingly.

We have just written business logic to copy static values to **Unit Sales Price** and a conditional statement to populate **Comment** in the cube.

Using a rule to override aggregation

Rules can be used to override default aggregation rules applied to leaf level elements, when they are rolled up to consolidated elements along a dimension.

In this recipe, we will elaborate on the concept of using the existing demodata setup, where we want to add elements to compute the average price at the leaf level. At the consolidation level we want to create an average calculation using a leaf level calculation.

Getting ready

Ensure that the TM1 Admin Server service is started and that the demodata TM1 Server is up and running. Log on to the demodata Server in TM1 Architect.

How to do it...

1. Open the **Server Explorer** window, right-click and choose **Edit Dimension Structure** to open in **Dimension Editor**.

2. Right-click on **Margin%** and click on **Insert Element** to open **Dimension Element Insert**.

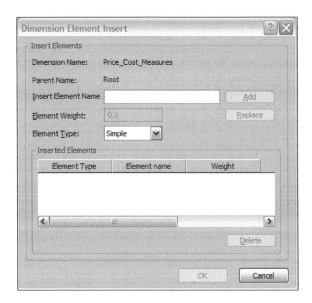

3. Add two new simple elements after **Margin%** as shown.

    ❑   **UnitPrice_Hold**

    ❑   **UnitPrice_Count**

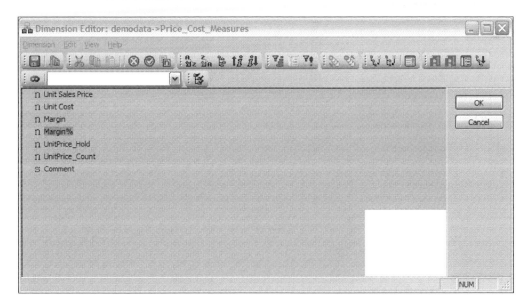

4. Save and close the Dimension Editor.

5. Open the default view of the **Price_and_Cost** cube.

6. Swap **Months** and **Price_Cost_Measures** (displaying **Unit Sales Price**).

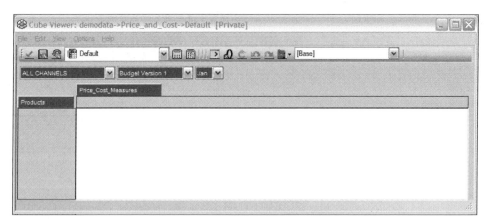

7. Click on **Price_Cost_Measures** to open in **Subset Editor**.

8. In **Subset Editor** click on the **All** icon 🖼, *Ctrl + Click* **Unit Sale Price**, **UnitPrice_ Count**, **UnitPrice_Hold**, right-click and select **Keep** from the menu options.

9. Click on **OK**.

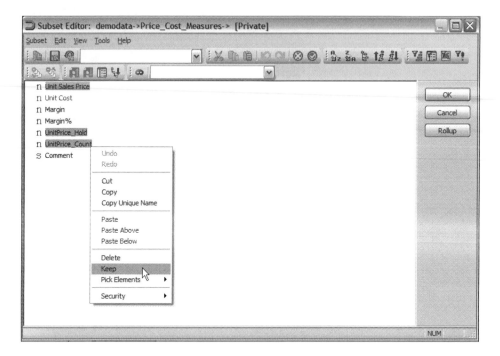

10. In **Cube Viewer** click on the **Recalculate** button to populate the data. If there is no data in the cube execute the `LoadPriceAndCostCSV` process created in *Chapter 4* and then follow the preceding steps.

11. Expand **CAMPING EQUIPMENT** and the data should appear as shown in the following screenshot:

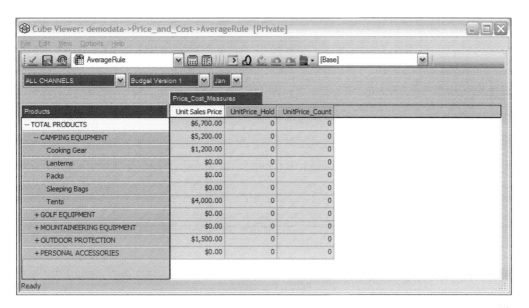

12. Save the view as **AverageRule** by clicking on **Save As** from the **File Menu**.

13. Close the **Cube Viewer** window.

14. In the **Server Explorer** window right-click on the **Price_and_Cost** cube and click on **Create Rule** to open the **Advanced Rule Editor**.

15. On line 1 type, **#Hold Unit Sales price to calculate Average Price**.

> **#** indicates that the rest of the line is a comment and is useful for documentation purposes.

16. Press *Enter* to add another line. Click on the brackets [], and then double-click **Price_Cost_Measures** to open the **Subset Editor**. Select **UnitPrice_Hold** and click on **OK** to return to the **Rules Editor**.

17. Click on the right of , click the **Insert Qualifier or Operator** icon ⇒ ·, and then select ⁼ Nⁱ.

18. Click on the brackets 🔲 and then double-click **Price_Cost_Measures** to open the **Subset Editor**. Select **Unit Sales Price** and click on **OK** to return to the **Rules Editor**.

19. Type a semicolon to end the line, as shown in the following screenshot:

```
1    #Hold Unit Sales Price to calculate Average Price
2    ['UnitPrice_Hold' ]  = N: ['Unit Sales Price' ]  ;
```

20. Click on the check syntax icon and correct any errors.

21. Open the **AverageRule** view for the **Price_and_Cost** cube and click on **Recalculate** 🔲 to display the data as shown in the following screenshot:

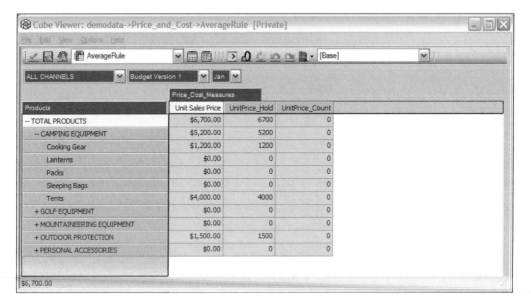

22. The **UnitPrice_Hold** column contains the same values as the **Unit Sales Price** column. The next thing we want to calculate is the number of items that are being counted in the **Unit Sales Price**.

23. In the **Rule Editor** on line number 3, click on **Brackets** and double-click **Price_Cost_Measures**.

24. Click on **UnitPrice_Count** and then click on **OK**.

25. After **Brackets** type **=N:** and click on the insert function icon 🔲.

26. The **Insert a Function** dialog opens up, as shown in the following screenshot:

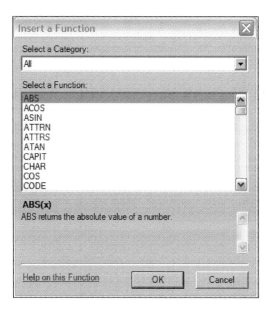

27. For **Select a Category**, click on **Logical** and for **Select a Function**, click on **IF** as shown. Click on **OK** to continue.

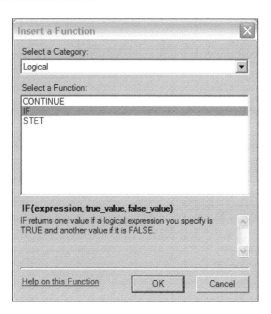

28. The preceding step will open a **Function Arguments** dialog box to enter parameters for the IF function. Enter the values as shown in the following screenshot:

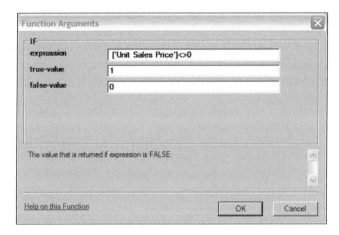

29. Click on **OK**, type a semicolon at the end of the line, check the syntax and click on **Save**.

30. The preceding step will create an IF condition which will populate **UnitPrice_Count** with the number of non-zero **Unit Sales Price** values.

```
1   #Hold Unit Sales Price to calculate Average Price
2   ['UnitPrice_Hold' ]  = N: ['Unit Sales Price' ]  ;
3   ['UnitPrice_Count' ] =N: IF( ['Unit Sales Price']<>0, 1, 0);
```

31. Recalculate the **AverageRule** view and note the values in the **UnitPrice_Count** column.

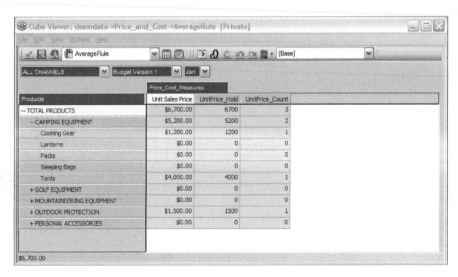

32. Hence, for leaf level elements, **Unit Sales Price** is really the price of a single unit. For consolidated elements, it's actually the sum of the leaf level **Unit Sales Price,** which is wrong. We are actually interested in calculating the average **Unit Sales Price** for consolidated elements.

In the following steps we will be calculating the average unit price by applying a rule.

1. In the **Rules Editor** on line 4 click on **Brackets**, double-click on **Price_Cost_Measures** and select **Unit Sales Price**.

2. Click outside the brackets and type **=C**.

3. Click on **Brackets** and double-click on **Price_Cost_Measures**.

4. Click to the **UnitPrice_Hold** and **OK** to return to the **Rules Editor**.

5. Click on right of the last square bracket and type \.

6. In TM1, \ indicates division, where Divide By Zero is replaced by 0. / can be used for normal division, where Divide By Zero returns **NA**.

7. Now click on **Brackets**, double-click **Price_Cost_Measures** and select **UnitPrice_Count**.

8. Click **OK** and type a semicolon at the end to arrive at the rules as shown.

```
1   #Hold Unit Sales Price to calculate Average Price
2   ['UnitPrice_Hold' ]  = N: ['Unit Sales Price' ]  ;
3   ['UnitPrice_Count' ] =N: IF( ['Unit Sales Price']<>0, 1, 0);
4   ['Unit Sales Price' ] =C: ['UnitPrice_Hold' ] \ ['UnitPrice_Count' ] ;
```

9. Check the syntax, save the rule, and recalculate the **AverageRule** view.

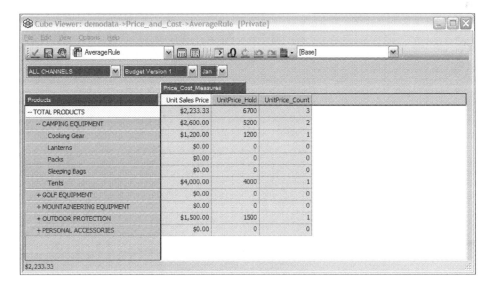

10. Please note the **Average Unit Sales Price** populated in the **Unit Sales Price** column. Close the **Advanced Rules Editor**, save the **AverageRule** view and close.

How it works...

In this recipe, we have overridden the default aggregation rule to do an average of leaf level elements instead of the sum. We have written rules for this and have used an **IF** statement to apply the business logic.

There's more...

A function in a rule can be used to:

- ▶ Reformat data
- ▶ Combine data
- ▶ Do logical operations
- ▶ Share data

A cell in the current cube may be referenced by the element name in brackets. To reference cells in the current cube or across cubes, the DB function can be used in the following form:

```
DB ('Cube_Name','Dimension1','Dimension2'.....'Dimension N')
```

An element name or cube name can be specified in single quotes. The current element of a dimension can be referenced by using an exclamation mark (!) preceding the dimension name.

Note that the order of specifying dimensions has to be the same as what is in the **Server Explorer** tree.

For example, the following code refers to a cell which corresponds to the **Price_and_Cost** cube, the current element of the **Channel** dimension, the **TOTAL PRODUCTS** element, the current element of the **Months** dimension, the current element of the **Versions** dimension, and the element **Unit Sales Price**.

```
DB('Price_and_Cost',!Channels,'TOTAL PRODUCTS',!Months,!Versions,'Unit
Sales Price')
```

Creating a rule to share data between cubes

In the recipe we will see how data can be shared across cubes.

Getting ready

Ensure that the TM1 Admin Server service is started and demodata TM1 Server is up and running. Log on to the demodata Server in TM1 Architect.

How to do it...

1. In the **Server Explorer** window open the default view of the **Sales_Plan** cube.

2. Pick a leaf level element for each dimension, for example:

    - GO AMERICAS REGION
    - Department Store
    - Cooking Gear
    - Budget Version 1

3. Click on **Recalculate** to view the data, as shown in the following screenshot:

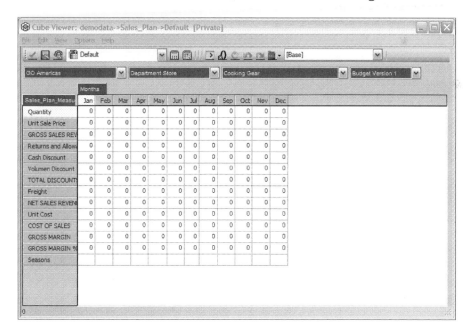

4. In the **Server Explorer** window right-click on **Sales_Plan** cube and click on **Create Rule** to open the **Advanced Rules Editor**.

5. On the first line in **Rules Editor** click on **Brackets** and double-click on **Sales_Plan_Measures** to open the **Subset Editor**. Select **Unit Sales Price** and click on **OK** to return to the **Rules Editor**.

6. Click to the right of the last square bracket and then click on **Insert Qualifier or Operator** icon. Click on **=N:**

7. Click on the **Insert Function** icon and select **DB** from the scrollable list of functions.

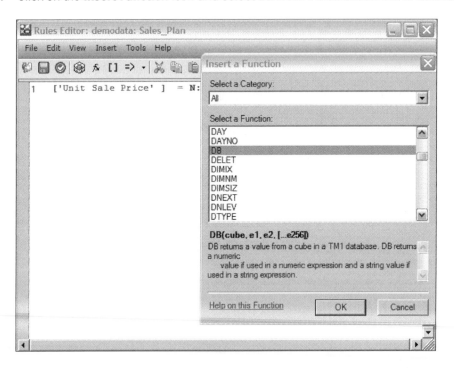

8. Click on **OK** and in the **Insert Cube Reference** dialog pick **Price_and_Cost** in the cube list.

9. The cube reference can also be inserted by clicking the ⊕ icon on the toolbar.

10. All dimensions of the cube are shown in the **Insert Cube Reference** dialog.

11. The references to be used in the DB function are displayed in the **References** column. A specific element can be selected by clicking on the subset icon ▭.

12. In the **Price_Cost_Measures** row click on the subset icon.

13. In the Subset Editor select **Unit Sales Price** and click on **OK** to return, as shown in the following screenshot:

14. Click on **OK** and type a semicolon at the end.

15. On the Subset Editor next line type the following:

```
C:['GROSS SALES REVENUE']\['Quantity'];
```

16. The result will appear as follows:

```
1   ['Unit Sale Price' ]  = N: DB('Price_and_Cost', !Channels,
2           !Products, !Months, !Versions, 'Unit Sales Price');
3   C: ['GROSS SALES REVENUE'] \ ['Quantity'];
```

17. The first rule will pull **Unit Sales Price** from the **Price_and_Cost** cube at the **N:** level, while the consolidated levels will compute the **Unit Sales Price** based on the **Gross Sales Revenue** divided by the **Quantity**, and will not be aggregated at the consolidated levels.

18. Check the syntax and save the rule.

19. Open **Cube Viewer** and click on **Recalculate**.

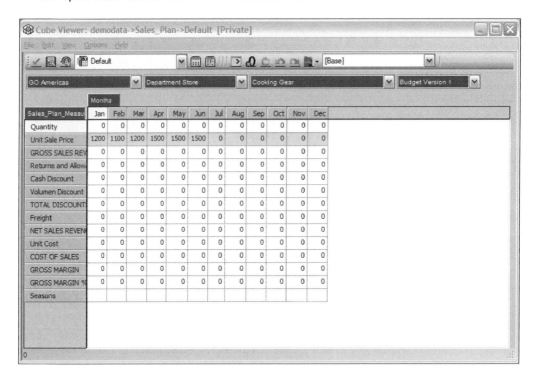

20. Note that now the values for **Unit Sales Price** are populated in the cube.

21. Save the view as **Price** and close **Rules Editor** and **Cube Viewer**.

 In the preceding screenshot, values for **Unit Sales Price** are grey and cannot be changed manually using **Cube Viewer**.

How it works...

In this recipe, we have demonstrated how we can share data across cubes using the **DB** function and writing rules using this function. Hence, the same data does not need to be duplicated and this ensures there is only one version of the same data across cubes, preventing inconsistencies.

Creating a pick list using a rule

A pick list can be populated using rules on a control cube. A control cube is an internal TM1 object used to store metadata about the model such as security, attributes, the pick list, and so on

Control cubes and dimensions are hidden by default. They are preceded by a right curly bracket (}).

A pick list control cube is composed of the same dimension as the regular cube it is associated with, along with an additional dimension named } Pick list.

The } Pick list dimension contains a single string element, named Value.

Getting ready

Ensure that the TM1 Admin Server service is started and demodata TM1 Server is up and running. Log on to the demodata Server in TM1 Architect.

How to do it...

1. In the **Server Explorer** window open the **Price_and_Cost** cube and open the **Price Comment** view created previously.
2. Click to expand **Outdoor protection**.
3. Select **Comment** for **Price_Cost_Measures** and expand **Camping Equipment**.

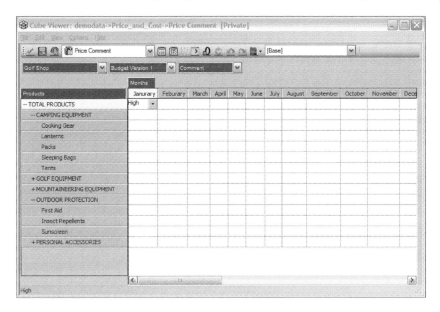

4. In the **Server Explorer** window click on **View** from the toolbar and click on **Display Control Objects**.

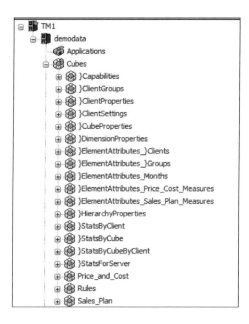

5. Control objects can be identified by curly brackets.

6. Right-click on the **Price_and_Cost** cube and click on **Create Pick List Cube**. A cube is created, as shown in the following screenshot:

7. Double-click on the **}PickList_Price_and_Cost** cube to open in **Cube Viewer**.

8. Arrange the cube as shown in the following screenshot:

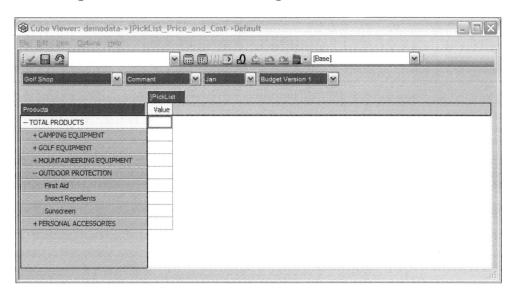

9. Click the value for **Insect Repellents** and type the following:

```
Static: :Jun:Jul:Aug:Sep
```

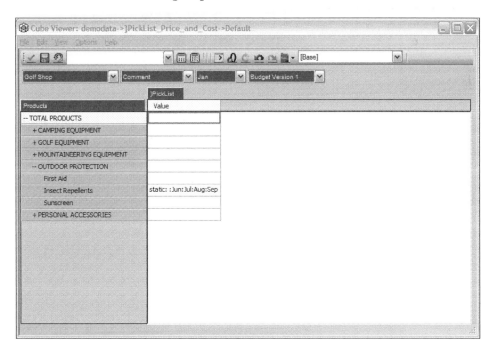

10. Please note that the syntax to specify a pick list by typing in cube cells will remain the same as before:

   ❑ Static: Value1:Value2......ValueN

   ❑ Subset: Dimension_Name:Subset_Name

   ❑ Dimension: Dimension_Name

11. Click on **Recalculate**.

12. Click on the **Price Comment** view of the **Price_and_Cost** cube and then again on **Recalculate**.

13. Click on **OUTDOOR PROTECTION** to expand.

14. Click the cell for **Jan** to display the **Pick List** as shown in the following screenshot:

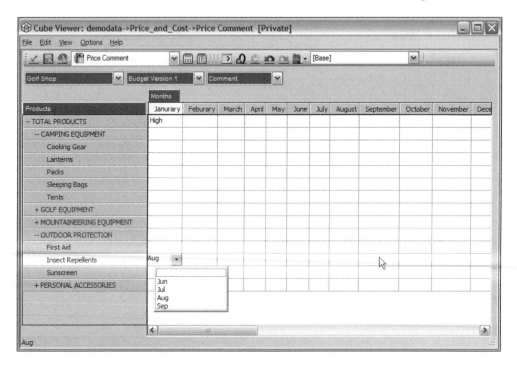

15. Click on **Aug** from the pick list as shown.

16. Click on other cells and the pick list attribute is still in effect. However, using a rule to populate a pick list will override the attribute.

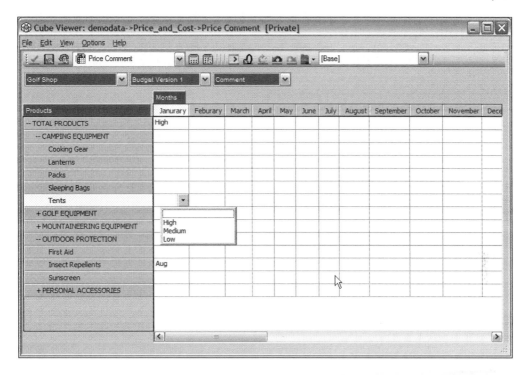

17. Right-click on the }**PickList_Price_and_Cost** cube and then click on **Create Rule** to open the **Advanced Rules Editor**.

18. On line 1, click on the brackets and then double-click on **Products**.

19. *Ctrl + Click* the following elements and click on **OK**.

   - CAMPING EQUIPMENT
   - GOLF EQUIPMENT
   - MOUNTAINEERING EQUIPMENT
   - OUTDOOR PROTECTION
   - PERSONAL ACCESSORIES

20. Click on **Insert Qualifier or Operator** and then click **=S**.

21. Type the following after **=S**.

```
('subset:Months:Months');
```

22. Spaces and line feeds can be entered in Rules Editor to improve readability, as shown in the following screenshot:

```
1   [{'CAMPING EQUIPMENT','GOLF EQUIPMENT','MOUNTAINEERING EQUIPMENT'
2   ,'OUTDOOR PROTECTION','PERSONAL ACCESSORIES'} ]
3   = S: ('subset:Months:Months');
```

23. For the **Price_and_Cost** cube, in the **Price Comment** view click on **Recalculate**.

24. Click on any of the cells for **CAMPING EQUIPMENT/GOLF EQUIPMENT/ MOUNTAINEERING EQUIPMENT/OUTDOOR PROTECTION/PERSONAL ACCESSORIES**, as shown and a pick list showing 12 months become visible as a comment pick list.

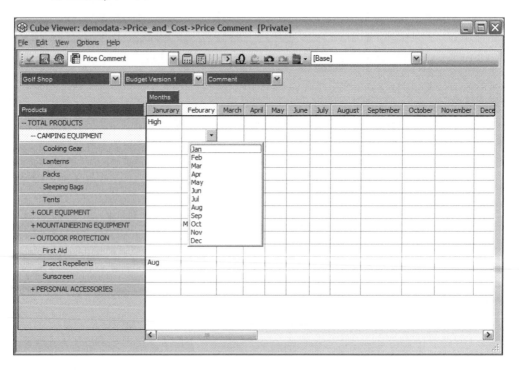

25. Close the view and save the changes.

26. Close the **}PickList_Price_and_Cost** cube and do not save any changes.

27. In the **Server Explorer** window turn off **Display Control Objects** from the **View** menu.

28. Close **TM1 Architect** and any other open windows.

How it works...

In this recipe, we have added a pick list to ensure that a cube always has valid data for the cells for the defined pick list. This reduces the risk of typo errors while a user is manually entering data in cubes.

There's more...

All rules can be found in the folder: . . . TM1\Custom\TM1Data\DemoData\Data as .RUX files. There is one RUX file per cube. It contains all the rules up through the module for which it is named.

RUX files are compiled versions of rules and are the only format that Rules Editor can read/ write to.

In the same folder all TI processes are also stored as .PRO files.

Reviewing a Rules worksheet

Rule worksheets are used to create and format rules in Microsoft Excel in addition to Advanced Rules Editor available with TM1.

Using worksheets helps into:

- ▶ Keep versions of rules together
- ▶ Make rules easier to read with Microsoft Excel formatting options
- ▶ Enhance rules with Microsoft Excel functions

Both Rules worksheets and Rules Editor should not be used for the same cube as that may cause data to be lost. Rules should either be written in a worksheet or in Rules Editor.

While saving rules, the TM1 menu should be used to save the file as * .xru, which will automatically generate a .rux file.

Saving rules as a .xru file directly from the Excel menu will not generate a .rux file, which is the only format Rules Editor understands. Opening a .xru file directly in Rules Editor will not show the latest changes and business logic may get lost.

Using Rules worksheets to create and format rules in Microsoft Excel is an old way of doing things. It is not frequently used anymore. It is discussed as a recipe as it might be useful to certain customers who might already be using it.

Getting ready

Ensure that the TM1 Admin Server service is started and demodata TM1 Server is up and running. Log on to the demodata Server in TM1 Architect.

How to do it...

1. With the **TM1 Admin** and **DemoData** Server started, click on **Start | All Programs | IBM Cognos | TM1** and click on **Perspectives for MS Excel,** as shown in the following screenshot:

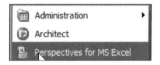

2. Click on **Enable Macros** if prompted.

3. In Microsoft Excel, from the **TM1** menu click on **Connect**.

4. Enter the user credentials as shown in the following screenshot:

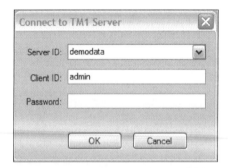

5. From the **TM1** menu click on the **Rule New** icon and click on **demodata:Rules** as shown in the following screenshot:

6. `Rules.xru` opens up with a wide column A. Only statements placed in Column A are compiled. Other columns can be used for documentation purposes.

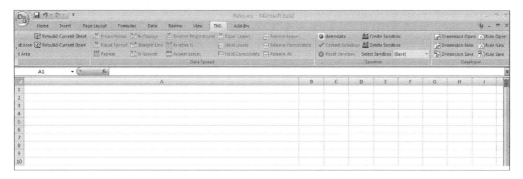

7. Rules created in **Rules Editor** do not appear. Rules worksheet reads and writes to `.xru` files. Therefore, either Rules Editor or Rules worksheet should be used to create rules for a cube. Both the editors should not be used for the same cube.

8. All the rules should be written in column A in the same format as written in **Advanced Rules Editor**.

9. The Rule Save icon `Rule Save` from the TM1 menu should be used to save the Rules worksheets and will save a `.xru` file and generate a compiled `.rux` version, which TM1 understands.

10. Close the **Rules worksheet** without saving it.

11. Close **MS Excel**.

How it works...

In this recipe, we have discussed Rules worksheets which can also be used to maintain Rules in addition to Rules Editor. Either of the two should be used for writing Rules. Use of Rules worksheets has become nonexistent these days. Users prefer using Rules Editor.

Doing custom calculations in dimensional hierarchies

In this recipe, we will define a custom calculation which will calculate the GROSS MARGIN based on NET SALES REVENUE and COST OF SALES.

Getting ready

Ensure that the TM1 Admin Server service is started and demodata TM1 Server is up and running. Log on to the demodata Server in TM1 Architect.

How to do it...

1. Open **DemoData** project and ensure that TM1 Admin service is up and running.

2. Open TM1 Architect and then a **Server Explorer** window.

3. Right-click **Sales_Plan_Measures** under **Dimensions** and click on **Edit Dimension Structure**.

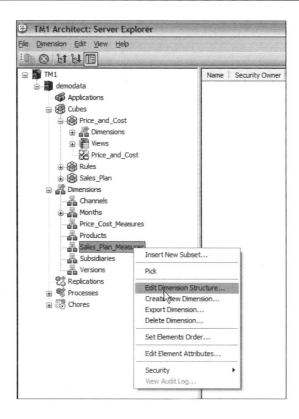

4. In the **Dimension Editor**, click **NET SALES REVENUE** and then from the **Edit menu** click on **Cut**.

5. Click on **OK**.

6. Click **GROSS MARGIN** and then from the **Edit** menu click on **Paste as Child**.

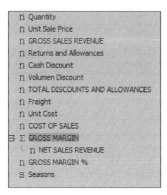

7. Repeat the preceding steps to paste **COST OF SALES** as a child of **GROSS MARGIN**.

8. Right-click **COST OF SALES** and click on **Element Properties**. In the **Element Weight** box type **-1** and click on **OK**. By default, consolidations are summations, but, by specifying the weight as -1, subtraction takes place.

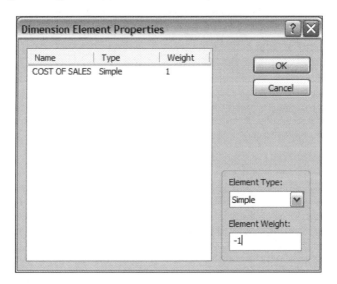

9. Click on **OK**.

10. **GROSS MARGIN** will be calculated/consolidated as **NET SALES REVENUE + (-1) * COST OF SALES** or **NET** SALES **REVENUE – COST OF SALES**.

11. Modify the CSV and load the data for **NET SALES REVENUE** and **COST OF SALES**, so that data is populated for the two elements. Verify if the correct data is calculated for **GROSS MARGIN**.

12. The same could also have been achieved by writing rules on the cube, but consolidations are always much faster than processing rules, hence applying custom calculations by using consolidations is a much more efficient way than writing rules for it.

13. Click on **Save** and close the **Dimension Editor**.

How it works...

In this recipe, we created a custom calculation which calculated the **GROSS MARGIN** based on **NET SALES REVENUE** and **COST OF SALES**. In a similar fashion, a user can add custom calculations in the dimension hierarchy, which is useful in implementing business logic as a whole.

6

Automating Data Load Processes using Scripts

In this chapter, we will cover:

- ▶ Loading data from multiple columns into a single column
- ▶ Creating a dimension and a subset in Turbo Integrator
- ▶ Creating a dimension with uneven/unbalanced hierarchy
- ▶ Exporting data to ASCII Text using Turbo Integrator
- ▶ Moving data between versions
- ▶ Moving data using scripts and parameters
- ▶ Creating and Scheduling a Chore

Introduction

In this chapter, we will use advanced features of Turbo Integrator and use logic in TI scripts to load custom data into a cube. Adding a subset to a dimension will also be demonstrated using a TI module. We will also focus on moving data between versions and exporting data to ASCII. Lastly, we will construct chores to schedule a process, or a chain of processes.

As already explained earlier, Turbo Integrator is an ETL (Extraction, Transformation, and Load) tool in TM1. It can be used to create dimensions, cubes and to populate cubes from various data sources.

TI processes can also be used to write data to ODBC data sources and export data to ASCII files.

Various TI functions and TM1 rules functions can be used with TI Modules to achieve conditional processing of data and metadata.

Every TI process is made up of four additional procedures, which are executed before and after the actual data source is processed by TI processes. By default, these four additional procedures are generated and contain code that is automatically generated by TM1. However, additional functions can be added to achieve required customization while executing TI processes.

These four procedures are executed in succession and can be viewed and edited in the **Advanced Tab** of TM1TI module. Parameters and functions can be added to these procedures which make TI processes flexible according to different required data load scenarios. However, any customizations must be added outside the reserved area.

These four procedures are:

Procedure name	Description
Prolog	Contain series of actions to be executed before the data source is processed.
Metadata	Contains a series of actions that update or create cubes, dimensions, and other metadata structures.
Epilog	The procedure executes after the data source is processed.
Parameters	A set of parameters can be used to generalize a process so that it can be used in different situations.

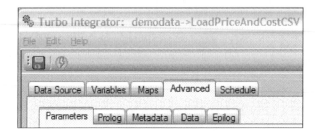

A few things which can be achieved by TM1 module and customizing scripts are:

- ▸ Schedule processes to run periodically
- ▸ Create subsets manually
- ▸ Extract data from a view and move into another
- ▸ Archive a cube

Loading data from multiple columns into a single column

In this recipe, we will be populating data from multiple columns into a single column using a TI process.

Getting ready

Ensure that TM1 admin service is started. Start demodata TM1 server and open **Server Explorer**.

How to do it...

1. Right-click on **Dimensions** and click on **Create New Dimension** to open **Dimension Editor**.

2. From the **Edit** menu click on **Insert Element**.

3. Add following dimension elements by clicking on **Add** after each one.

   □ Gross Sales Revenue

   □ Commission

   □ Commission%

   □ Commission_hold

   □ Commission_count

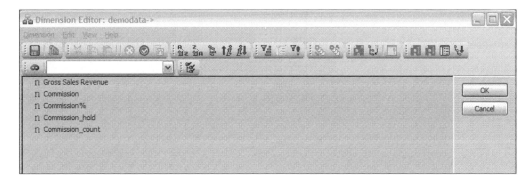

4. Click on **OK** and save dimension as **Commission_Measures**.

5. Close the window.

6. Return to **Server Explorer** window and *right-click* on **Cubes**.

7. Click on **Create New Cube** and name the new cube as **Commissions**.

8. In the **Available Dimensions** list double-click on the dimensions, shown in the following screenshot, in order and move them to the new cube:

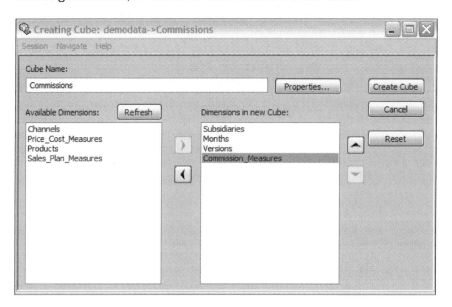

9. Click on **Create Cube** and return to **Server Explorer**.

10. Right-click on **Commissions** cube and click on **Create Rule**.

11. On line 1, type **SKIPCHECK**.

> **SKIPCHECK** and **FEEDERS** are extensively used in IBM Cognos TM1 to optimize rules performance. These are to be written, while rules are written. We will discuss these concepts in later chapters.

12. In the next step we will be pulling data from **Sales_Plan** cube to **Commissions** cube.

13. Click on **Brackets** and double click on **Commission_Measures** to choose the measure dimension.

14. Click on **Gross Sales Revenue** to choose the element and click on **OK**.

15. Click on **=**, and click on **Insert Cube Reference** 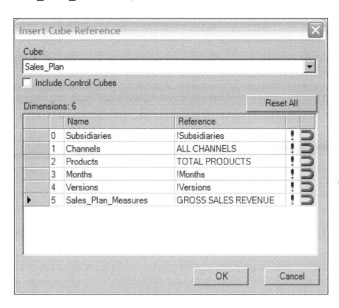 and then in cube list click on **Sales_Plan**. This will insert a reference to the **Sales_Plan** cube.

16. Click on the subset icon next to **Channels**, click on **ALL CHANNELS** to choose the element from the **Subset Editor** and then click on **OK**.

17. Repeat previous step with following:

   ❑ **Products**, click on **TOTAL PRODUCTS**

   ❑ **Sales_Plan_Measures**, click on **GROSS SALES REVENUE**

18. Click on **OK** and return to **Rules Editor**.

```
1   SKIPCHECK;
2   ['Gross Sales Revenue' ] = DB('Sales_Plan', !Subsidiaries,
3    'ALL CHANNELS', 'TOTAL PRODUCTS', !Months, !Versions, 'GROSS SALES REVENUE')
```

19. On Line number 3 click on semicolon; at the end.

20. On next line click brackets and then double-click on **Commission_Measures**.

21. Click on **Commission_hold** and click on **OK**.

22. Click on **Insert Qualifier or Operator** icon and click on **=N:**

23. Click on brackets, double-click on **Commission_Measures** and click on **Commission%**.

24. Click on **OK** and type semicolon "**;**" at the end.

```
1    SKIPCHECK;
2    ['Gross Sales Revenue' ] = DB('Sales_Plan', !Subsidiaries,
3     'ALL CHANNELS', 'TOTAL PRODUCTS', !Months, !Versions, 'GROSS SALES REVENUE');
4    ['Commission_hold' ] =N: ['Commission%' ] ;
```

25. On next two lines, type the following to calculate **Average Commission Percent** at **Consolidated Level** as shown.

```
5    ['Commission_count'] =N:IF(['Commission%']<>0,1,0);
6    ['Commission%'] =C:(['Commission_hold']\['Commission_count']);
```

26. Line number 5 indicates that if **Commission%** is not zero then **Commission_count** = 1 else 0.

27. Next line actually calculates average using *forward-slash* "\" which as explained earlier, will assign zero to **Commission%** if **Commission_count** is zero.

28. On next line type as shown.

```
7    ['Commission'] = N:(['Gross Sales Revenue']*['Commission%'])/100;
```

29. On the next lines type the following. We will discuss **SKIPCHECK** and **FEEDERS** which are used to optimize rules performance in chapter *Optimizing Rules Performance* later.

```
8    FEEDERS;
9    ['Commission%'] => ['Commission'],['Commission_hold'],['Commission_count'];
```

30. Whole code fragment will look as shown in the following screenshot:

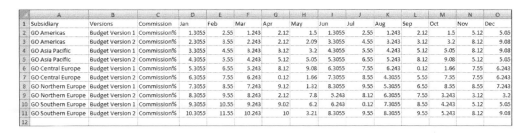

```
1    SKIPCHECK;
2    ['Gross Sales Revenue' ] = DB('Sales_Plan', !Subsidiaries,
3     'ALL CHANNELS', 'TOTAL PRODUCTS', !Months, !Versions, 'GROSS SALES REVENUE');
4    ['Commission_hold' ] =N: ['Commission%' ] ;
5    ['Commission_count'] =N:IF(['Commission%']<>0,1,0);
6    ['Commission%'] =C:(['Commission_hold']\['Commission_count']);
7    ['Commission'] = N:(['Gross Sales Revenue']*['Commission%'])/100;
8    FEEDERS;
9    ['Commission%'] => ['Commission'],['Commission_hold'],['Commission_count'];
10
```

31. Check syntax, save and close the **Rules Editor**.

32. Create `Commissions.csv` as shown and put that in the following path `C:\Program Files\cognos\TM1\Custom\TM1Data\TI_Data`.

	A	B	C	D	E	F	G	H	I	J	K	L	M	N	O
1	Subsidiary	Versions	Commission	Jan	Feb	Mar	Apr	May	Jun	Jul	Aug	Sep	Oct	Nov	Dec
2	GO Americas	Budget Version 1	Commission%	1.3055	2.55	1.243	2.12	1.5	1.3055	2.55	1.243	2.12	1.5	5.12	5.05
3	GO Americas	Budget Version 2	Commission%	2.3055	3.55	2.243	2.12	2.09	3.3055	4.55	3.243	3.12	3.2	8.12	9.08
4	GO Asia Pacific	Budget Version 1	Commission%	3.3055	4.55	3.243	3.12	3.2	4.3055	5.55	4.243	5.12	5.05	8.12	9.08
5	GO Asia Pacific	Budget Version 2	Commission%	4.3055	5.55	4.243	5.12	5.05	5.3055	6.55	5.243	8.12	9.08	5.12	5.05
6	GO Central Europe	Budget Version 1	Commission%	5.3055	6.55	5.243	8.12	9.08	6.3055	7.55	6.243	0.12	1.66	7.55	6.243
7	GO Central Europe	Budget Version 2	Commission%	6.3055	7.55	6.243	0.12	1.66	7.3055	8.55	4.3055	5.55	7.55	7.55	6.243
8	GO Northern Europe	Budget Version 1	Commission%	7.3055	8.55	7.243	9.12	1.32	8.3055	9.55	5.3055	6.55	8.55	8.55	7.243
9	GO Northern Europe	Budget Version 2	Commission%	8.3055	9.55	8.243	2.12	7.8	5.243	8.12	6.3055	7.55	3.243	3.12	3.2
10	GO Southern Europe	Budget Version 1	Commission%	9.3055	10.55	9.243	9.02	6.2	6.243	0.12	7.3055	8.55	4.243	5.12	5.05
11	GO Southern Europe	Budget Version 2	Commission%	10.3055	11.55	10.243	10	3.21	8.3055	9.55	8.3055	9.55	5.243	8.12	9.08
12															

33. In the **Server Explorer** window right-click on **Processes** and click on **Create New Process**.

34. That will open **Turbo Integrator** window. Specify the `Commissions.csv` created above as shown.

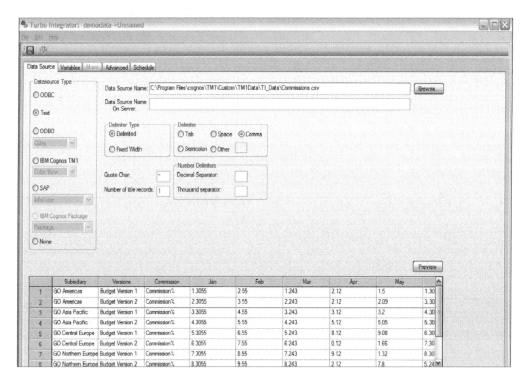

35. Please note **Number of title records** is set to 1. Click on **Preview** to view the sample records.

36. Click on the **Variables** tab and set the options as shown in the following screenshot:

	Variable Name	Variable Type	Sample Value	Contents	Formula
1	Subsidiary	String	GO Americas	Element	
2	Versions	String	Budget Version 1	Element	
3	Commission	String	Commission%	Element	

37. In above snapshots for **Subsidiary**, **Versions** and **Commission**, in the **Contents** column **Element** has been selected.

38. From **Jan** till Dec, in **Variable Type** column, **Numeric** is selected and for **Contents** column **Data** has been selected.

4	Jan	Numeric	▾	1.3055	Data	▾
5	Feb	Numeric	▾	2.55	Data	▾
6	Mar	Numeric	▾	1.243	Data	▾
7	Apr	Numeric	▾	2.12	Data	▾
8	May	Numeric	▾	1.5	Data	▾
9	Jun	Numeric	▾	1.3055	Data	▾
10	Jul	Numeric	▾	2.55	Data	▾
11	Aug	Numeric	▾	1.243	Data	▾
12	Sep	Numeric	▾	2.12	Data	▾
13	Oct	Numeric	▾	1.5	Data	▾
14	Nov	Numeric	▾	5.12	Data	▾
15	Dec	Numeric	▾	5.05	Data	▾

39. Click on **Maps** tab, for **Cube Action** click on **Update Cube** and select **Commissions** cube as **Cube Name**.

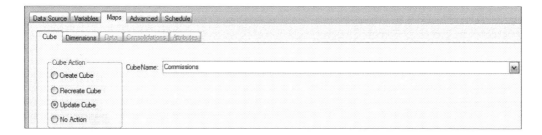

40. In **Dimensions** tab, besides each **Element Variable** click on appropriate **Dimension** as shown in the following screenshot:

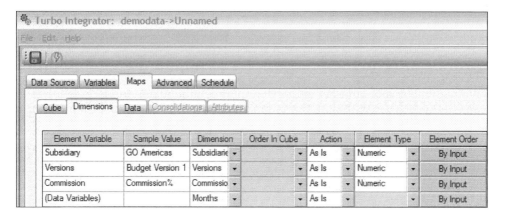

41. Click on **Data** tab. In the **Element** column select from **Subset Editor**, **Jan** till **Dec** matching values in **Data Variable**.

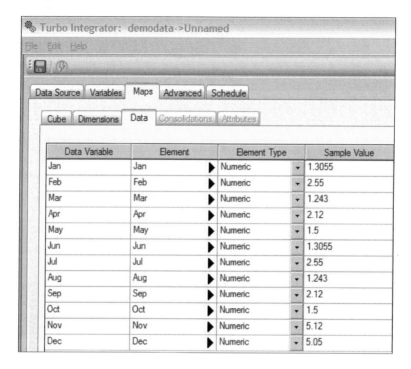

42. Click on **Advanced** tab and click through **Prolog**, **Metadata**, **Data**, and **Epilog** tabs to generate the scripts.

43. Save the process as **LoadCommissionPctCSV** and then click on **Run**.

44. Click on **OK** to close the **Turbo Integrator** and return to **Server Explorer**.

45. Open **Commissions** cube and click on **Recalculate**.

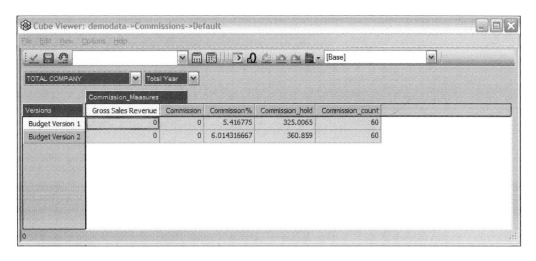

46. Close the **Cube Viewer** without saving the view.

47. In **Server Explorer**, right-click on **Commission_Measures**, and then click on **Edit Element Attributes**.

48. In the **Attributes Editor** select **Gross Sales Revenue** and **Commission** and click on **Format**.

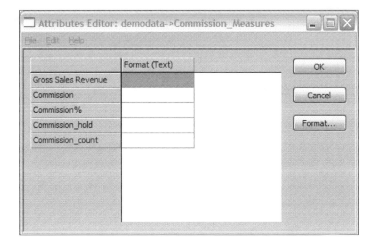

49. Click on **Currency** and click on **OK** twice to close. Return to **Server Explorer**.

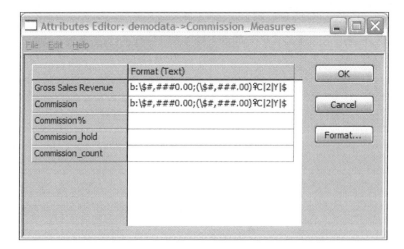

50. Double-click on **Commissions** cube and click on **Recalculate**.
51. Close the **Cube Viewer** without saving.

How it works...

In this recipe we have populated **Gross Sales Revenue** in **Commissions** cube from corresponding column in **Sales_Plan** cube using TI processes.

Creating a dimension and a subset in Turbo Integrator

Other than loading data, Turbo Integrator along with functions, can be used to create and update a dimension in terms of its hierarchy, elements, attributes, and sort order.

These can also be used to create, update, and destroy subsets for a dimension.

Getting started

Ensure that TM1 Admin Server service is started and demodata TM1 server is running.

How to do it...

1. Open the **Server Explorer** window.

2. Right-click on **Processes** and click on **Create New Process**.

3. In **Turbo Integrator** window choose `C:\Program Files\cognos\TM1\Custom\TM1Data\TI_Data\Products.csv` as shown in the following screenshot:

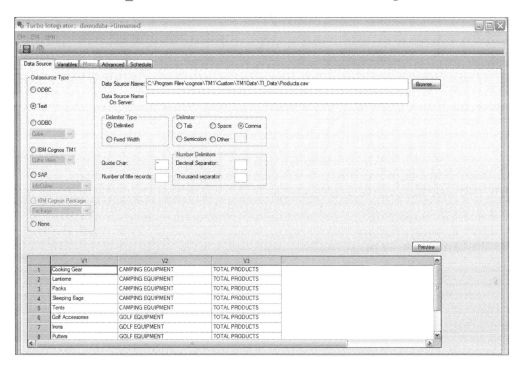

4. Please note **Number of Title Records** is set to blank. Click on **Preview** to view sample records.

5. Click on **Variables** tab and update as shown.

6. **Contents** column for the three variables has been set to **Other**. Also **Variable Name** has been set as shown in the preceding screenshot.

7. **Other** variables are available to TI processes, but will not require mapping to be specified in **Maps** tab.

8. Click on **Advanced** tab, click on **Metadata** and then after the generated statements add the following:

```
IF
(SubsetExists('Products',vProductType)=0);
SubsetCreate('Products',vProductType);
ENDIF;
```

9. The preceding statements check if the given subset (specified by vProductType) already exists in the given Dimension (Products). If not, then it will create the specified subset (vProductType) for the specified Dimension (Products).

10. You can check the online help for various functions and syntax.

11. On next line after ENDIF; type the following. TM1 is case insensitive hence case of the entered statements will not make any difference.

```
SubsetElementInsert('Products',vProductType,vProducts,0);
```

12. The preceding statement inserts elements (specified by variable vProducts), in corresponding subset (specified by variable vProductType) for the given dimension (Products). 0 indicates first position in the index.

13. Resulting statements are as shown in the following screenshot:

14. Save the process as **CreateProductType_subsets**, run the process and then close the **Turbo Integrator**.

15. Go to **Server Explorer** and open **Products**.

16. Click on the **Select Subset** box to view the Subsets created as part of the above generated TI Scripts.

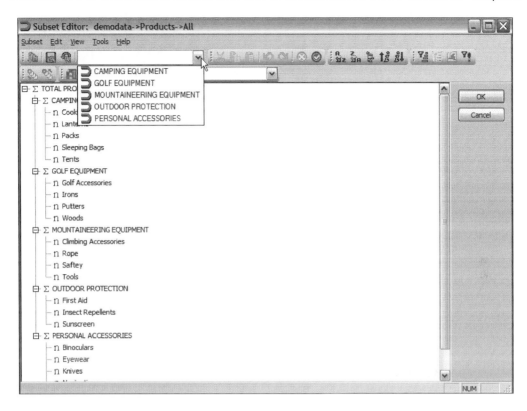

17. Close the subset editor.

18. In the preceding steps we have created subsets for each product type as part of the TI Script. Please note that syntax and semantics of various functions available as part of TI and Rules may differ. Online help should be referred to details of each of these functions and syntax. Help documents are also available from the **Help** menu of the TM1 toolbar.

How it works...

In this recipe we have seen how with the help of TI functions, dimensions and subsets can be created and maintained. We have also checked, if the TM1 object to be created, already exists or not and skip the creation step, if the object already exists.

Creating a dimension with uneven/unbalanced hierarchy

TI functions can be used to transform data before it is loaded into the model. Some examples of such requirements would be change in the data type, loading only relevant part of source data, supporting uneven/unbalanced hierarchy, and so on. We will be using the term uneven hierarchy as a synonym for unbalance hierarchy from now on.

Uneven hierarchy would be a case where parent-child relations in a dimension may differ from case to case. Let's consider a case of a dimension that organizes data into Region | Subsidiaries. In some cases there is only a single subsidiary for a region and hence parent has no child objects. Such a dimension is a classical example of an uneven hierarchy. In this recipe we will see how such hierarchies can be handled in TI processes.

Getting ready

Ensure that TM1 Admin service is started and demodata TM1 server is running.

How to do it...

1. Create a CSV by name of `UnevenSubsidiaries.csv` as shown in the following screenshot:

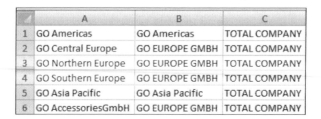

	A	B	C
1	GO Americas	GO Americas	TOTAL COMPANY
2	GO Central Europe	GO EUROPE GMBH	TOTAL COMPANY
3	GO Northern Europe	GO EUROPE GMBH	TOTAL COMPANY
4	GO Southern Europe	GO EUROPE GMBH	TOTAL COMPANY
5	GO Asia Pacific	GO Asia Pacific	TOTAL COMPANY
6	GO AccessoriesGmbH	GO EUROPE GMBH	TOTAL COMPANY

2. Place the CSV at `C:\Program Files\cognos\TM1\Custom\TM1Data\TI_Data`.

3. Open **Server Explorer** window and right-click on **Processes** and then **Create New Process**.

4. In **Turbo Integrator** window select **Text** for **Datasource Type**, provide CSV path and click on **Preview** to view sample data as shown in the following screenshot:

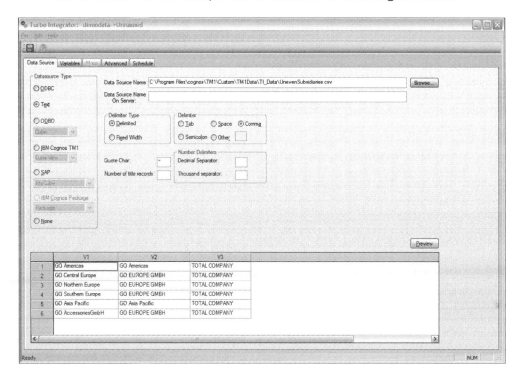

In the preceding screenshot V1 and V2 for many subsidiaries is the same. TM1 requires that elements (leaf level or string level) be unique otherwise TM1 creates dimensions with parents having no child objects.

Two ways to resolve this duplication are altering the CSV manually and creating a Turbo Integrator process to create an uneven hierarchy.

In the following steps we will create a TI process which will not address the duplicates, and then later we will correct the process.

5. Click on **Variables** tab and set the following:

    ❑ Rename **V1** as **vSubsidiary**

    ❑ Rename **V2** as **vRegion**

    ❑ Rename **V3** as **vTotalCompany**

Set the Contents as shown.

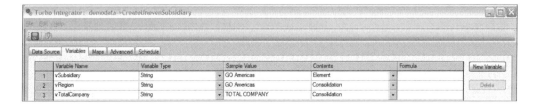

6. Under **Maps,** in the **Dimensions** tab, type **UnevenSubsidiary** in the **Dimension** column, as **Dimension** name. Set **Element Order** to **By Hierarchy** by clicking on **By Input** button and then on **Automatic** and **Hierarchy** option. Click on **OK** to close.

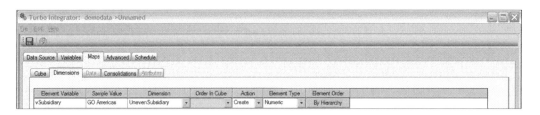

7. Click on **Consolidations** tab and besides **vRegion** under **Child Variable** click on **vSubsidiary** and then besides **vTotalCompany** click on **vRegion**. Click both **By Input** buttons under **Component Order**, and set **Automatic Sort By** to **Name** as shown in the following screenshot:

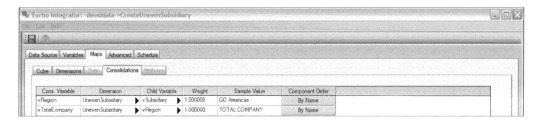

8. On **Advanced** tab click through **Prolog, Metadata, Data** and **Epilog** tabs to generate relevant scripts. Save the process as **CreateUnevenSubsidiaries** and run the process.

9. If an error message appears click on **YES** to view the log file.

10. Double-click on first row and it shows that circular reference indicating that the items at the leaf level are not unique.

11. Close the log file and leave the TI open.

12. In **Server Explorer** double-click on **UnevenSubsidiary**, under **Dimensions |
UnevenSubsidiary**, and then click on **All** icon , and then click on **Hierarchy Sort** .

13. The resulting subset is as shown in the following screenshot:

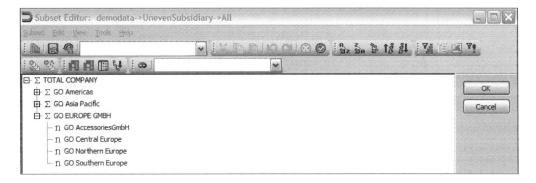

> **GO Americas** and **GO Asia Pacific** should have been created as leaf level elements since they have no children.
>
> Instead these have been created as consolidations with no children and hence data cannot be loaded to these.
>
> Now we will edit the process to handle this duplication.

14. Save the subset as **Subset1** and close the **Subset Editor**.

15. Open the TI process **CreateUnevenSubsidiary** and on **Maps** tab, click on **Dimensions** tab and change **Action** to **Recreate**. As the dimension has already been created we cannot make any changes to the process untill we make **Action** as **Recreate**.

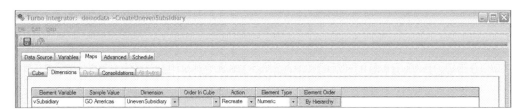

16. On the **Advanced** tab click on **Prolog** tab.

17. Copy everything between **Begin** and **End** and paste it outside the generated script space. Right-click on the generated script space and that allows to copy and paste.

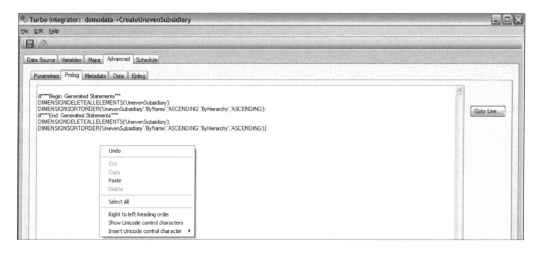

18. Click on **Metadata** tab and repeat the preceding step as shown in the following screenshot:

19. Click on **Variables** tab and then change the **Contents** column for all variables to **Other** as shown.

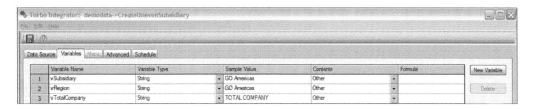

20. Click on **Advanced** and then on **Prolog** tab. Generated script should look as shown in the following screenshot:

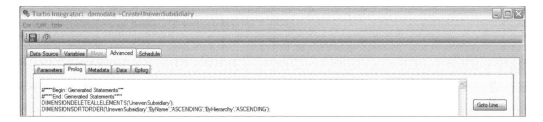

21. Click on **Metadata** tab and generated script should look as shown in the following screenshot:

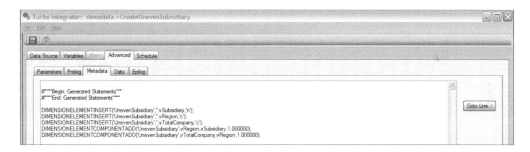

Now we will add IF statement in **Metadata** script to conditionally check if vSubsidiary matches with vRegion or not. If yes, then TI should generate only a two level hierarchy otherwise it will generate a three level hierarchy. Multiple ELSEIF statements can be added in case we want the same logic for greater than a two level hierarchy.

22. After the generated statements in **Metadata** tab type the following.

```
IF(vSubsidiary@<>vRegion);
#Create the three level hierarchy

DIMENSIONELEMENTINSERT('UnevenSubsidiary','',vSubsidiary,'n');
DIMENSIONELEMENTINSERT('UnevenSubsidiary','',vRegion,'c');
```

```
DIMENSIONELEMENTINSERT('UnevenSubsidiary','',vTotalCompany,'c');

#Assigns parent/child relationships and weights to elements in the
hierarchy

DIMENSIONELEMENTCOMPONENTADD('UnevenSubsidiary',
vRegion,vSubsidiary,1.000000);
DIMENSIONELEMENTCOMPONENTADD('UnevenSubsidiary',
vTotalCompany,vRegion,1.000000);

ELSE;
#Ctreate the two level hierarchy

DIMENSIONELEMENTINSERT('UnevenSubsidiary','',vRegion,'N');
DIMENSIONELEMENTINSERT('UnevenSubsidiary','',vTotalCompany,'c');

#Assigns parent/child relationship and weights to elements in the
hierarchy

DIMENSIONELEMENTCOMPONENTADD('UnevenSubsidiary',vTotalCompany,vReg
ion,1.000000);

ENDIF;
```

Refer to comments specified after # for description.

23. The **Metadata** tab looks as shown in the following screenshot:

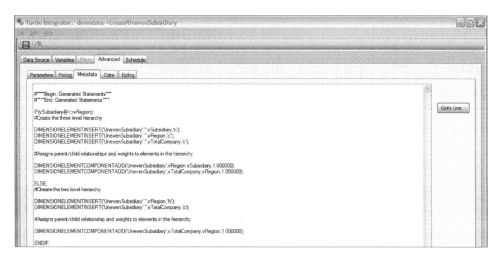

24. Click through the **Advanced** tab, save and run the process. The process runs without errors.

25. Close the **Turbo Integrator** to return to **Server Explorer**.

26. In **Server Explorer** window double-click on the **UnevenSubsidiary** dimension. In **Subset Editor** click on **All** and then do **Hierarchy Sort**.

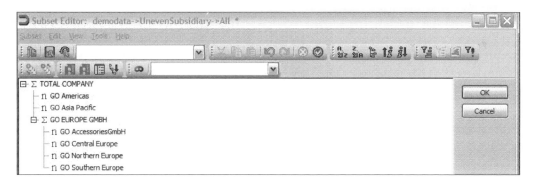

27. Close the **Subset Editor** without saving.

How it works...

In the recipe we have used TI functions to create an uneven hierarchy. We have customized code in **Advanced** tab which gets executed while the TI process is executed and hence forms the **UnevenSubsidiary** dimension.

Exporting data to ASCII text using Turbo Integrator

TM1 can be used as a source of data for external sources by exporting dimensions or cube views to text files. Views can also be created in TI which is properly formatted for exporting. This allows data to be shared among a variety of systems.

Getting ready

Ensure that TM1 Admin service is started and demodata TM1 server is running. Open TM1 Architect from Start Menu.

How to do it...

1. Open the **Server Explorer** window and create a new process with **Datasource Type** set to **TM1 Cube View**.

2. On the same window, for **Data Source Name** select **demodata:Sales_Plan** and click on button **Create View**.

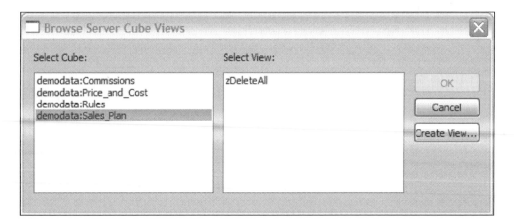

3. **View Extract** window opens. Ensure that **Skip Consolidate Values** and **Skip Zero/ Blank Values** are checked by default.

4. Under **Dimension Elements** on the same window click on subset icon ⊡ besides **Version** and select **Budget Version 1** from the **Subset Editor**. Click on **OK** to return to **View Extract** window.

5. In the **TM1 Save View** box type **vExport view** and keep the view as non private view. TI can only work on public views.

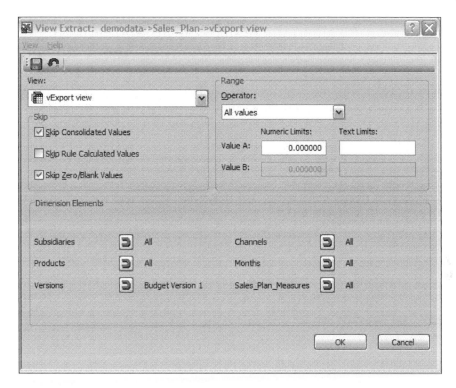

6. Click on **OK** to return to **Browse Server Cube Views** in **Turbo Integrator** and select **vExport view** as shown in the following screenshot. Click on **OK**.

7. Click on **Preview** to view sample records as shown in the following screenshot:

8. Click on the **Variables** tab.

9. For all variables set the **Variable Type** to **String** and **Contents** to **Other** as shown in the following screenshot:

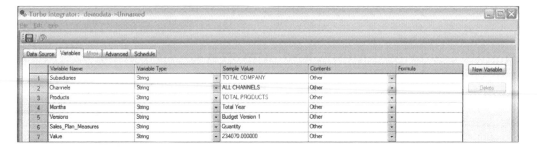

 When exporting data to text or ASCII file all variables must be set to strings, even the data as shown in the preceding screenshot.

10. Click on **Advanced** tab and then click on **Metadata**.

11. Type the following to the **Metadata** tab below the generated statements.

```
#****Begin: Generated Statements***
#****End: Generated Statements****
TextOutput('C:/TextOutput.csv',Subsidiaries,Channels,Products,Mont
hs,Versions,Sales_Plan_Measures,Value);
```

12. The preceding function writes to the text file specified as the first parameter, each of the fields specified after the first parameter. The result appears as shown in the following screenshot:

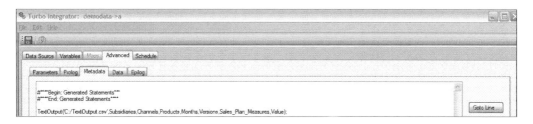

13. Click through all the tabs under **Advanced** tab and save the process as **CreateTextOutput**, and then run the process.

14. Save and close the **Turbo Integrator** window.

15. The preceding process will write the records specified in the `.csv` file mentioned as part of the **TextOutput** function.

16. Open the file and view.

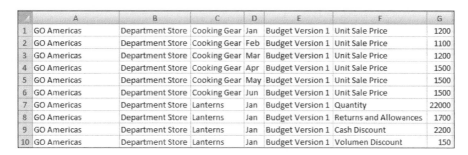

How it works...

In the recipe we have just used **TextOutput** function to write data to a text file. There are other functions available for the same functionality like **AsciiOutput**. Detailed documentation of these is available from Help menu in TM1.

Moving data between versions

This recipe will suggest how unit sales price figures for budget version 1, which need to be approved, in the **Price_and_Cost** cube can be moved to submit version. Hence, we will see how data can be moved from one version to another.

Getting ready

Ensure that TM1 Admin service is started and demodata TM1 server is running. Open TM1 Architect from **Start Menu**.

How to do it...

1. Open **Server Explorer** and right-click on **Versions** dimension.

2. Click on **Edit Dimension Structure**.

3. In **Dimension Editor** click on **Budget Version 2**.

4. From **Edit** menu click on **Insert Element**.

5. Name it **Submit Version**, click on **Add** and then on **OK**.

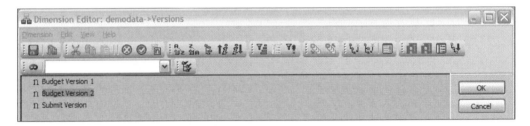

6. Save and close the **Dimension Editor** to return to **Server Explorer**.

7. Create a new process with **Datasource Type** as **TM1 Cube View**.

8. In the **Data Source Name** box click on **Browse** and click on **demodata:Price_and_ Cost** cube.

9. Click on **Create View** on **Browse Server Cube Views** window.

10. On the **View Extract** window besides **Price_Cost_Measures** click on subset icon ⊇, *Cntrl+Click* as shown and click on **OK**.

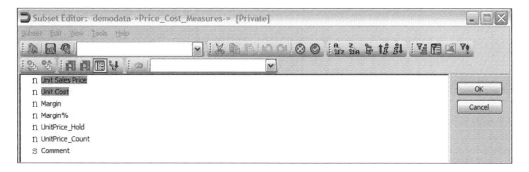

11. Similarly besides **Versions** click on subset icon and select **Budget Version 1**.

12. Click on **OK** and save the view as **Budget Version 1**.

13. For **Select View** click **Budget Version 1** and click on **OK**.

14. Click on **Preview**.

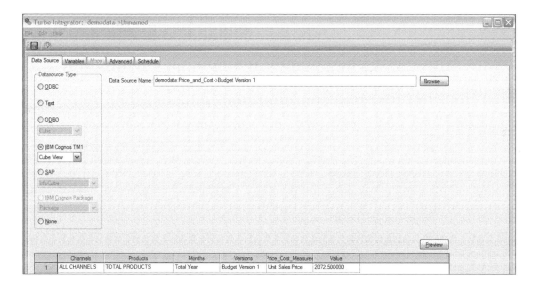

15. Click on the **Variables** tab and then rename the fifth variable **Price_Cost_Measures** as **PCMeasures**.

16. Create a new variable with the variable name as **vVersions**.

17. Click on **Formula** and in the formula box type `vVersions='Submit Version';` and click on **Evaluate**.

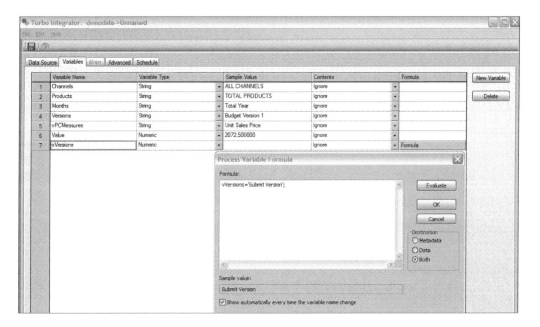

18. Click on **OK**.

19. Under **Variable Type** for **vVersions** click on **String**.

20. Set the **Contents** of the variables as shown:

- **Channels: Element**
- **Products: Element**
- **Months: Element**
- **Versions: Other**
- **vPCMeasures: Element**
- **Value: Data**
- **vVersions: Element**

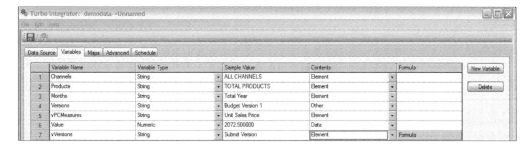

21. Click on **Maps**.

22. Select **Update Cube** and then click on **Price_and_Cost** in the cube name list.

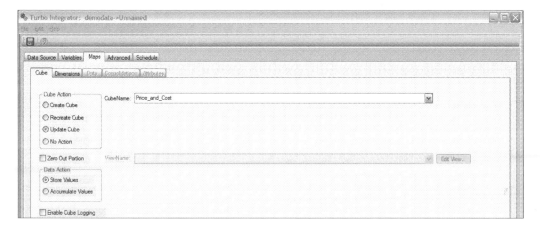

23. Click on the **Dimensions** tab.

24. Set the **Dimension** for each **Element Variable** as shown in the following screenshot:

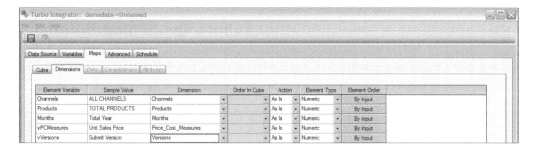

25. Click on **Advanced** tab and click on each tab to refresh the scripts.

26. Save the process as **MoveVersion**.

27. Run the process and close the Turbo Integrator window.

28. In **Server Explorer** open **Price_and_Cost** cube.

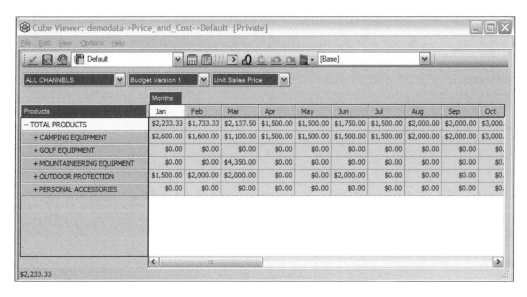

29. Double-click **Budget Version 1** and then click on **All** icon , click on **Submit Version** and click on **OK**.

30. Similarly, double-click on **Price_and_Cost_Measures**, click on **All**, select **Unit Sales Price** and click on **OK** and in **Cube Viewer** click on **Recalculate**.

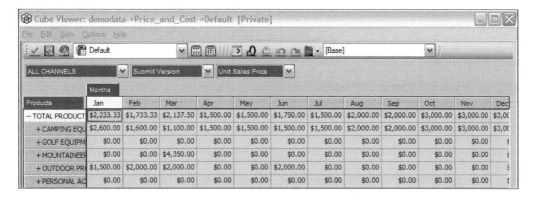

31. Please note data has been copied over to **Submit Version**.
32. Close the **Cube Viewer** without saving any changes.

How it works...

In this recipe we have moved data from one version to another using TI processes. It is useful when users wants to switch data between versions as in above case where data needs to be in submit version to get reviewed and hence, it is moved from draft version 1 to submit version.

Moving data using scripts and parameters

In this recipe we will repeat the outcome from the preceding recipe for **Sales_Plan** cube but using scripts and parameters.

Getting ready

Ensure that TM1 Admin Server service is started and demodata TM1 server is running. Open TM1 Architect from the **Start Menu**.

How to do it

1. Create a new TI process of **Datasource Type: TM1 Cube** view from **Server Explorer** window.
2. Click on **Browse** button and select **Sales_Plan** cube. Click on **Create View** button.

3. In **Extract View** window, besides each of the following dimensions click **Subset Editor** icon as suggested in the preceding recipe, click on **All** icon, click on **Filter by Level**, click on **0** and save the view as **ztrf_MonthVersion** and click on **OK**.

   ❏ Subsidiaries

   ❏ Products

   ❏ Channels

   ❏ Months

   ❏ Versions

4. Leave **Sales_Plan_Measures** as **All**.

5. Select **ztrf_MonthVersion** from **Select View** and click on **OK**.

6. Click on **Preview**.

7. Click on the **Variables** tab.

8. Change the **Contents** column for all the variables to **Other** as shown in the following screenshot:

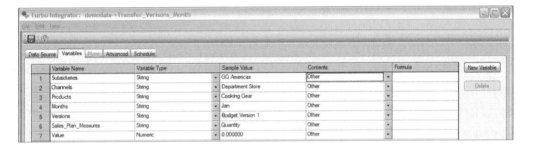

9. Click on **Advanced** and then on **Parameters** tab.

10. Create three parameters as shown in the following screenshot:

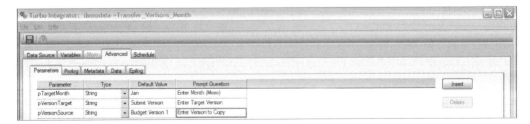

11. The parameter names are:
    - ❑ pTargetMonth
    - ❑ pVersionTarget
    - ❑ pVersionSource

12. **Data Type** for each is set to **String**.

13. For **pTargetMonth Prompt Question** is set to **Enter Month (Mmm)** and **Default Value** is set to **Jan**.

14. Similarly, for **pVersionTarget, Prompt Question** is set to **Enter Target Version** and **Default Value** is **Submit Version**.

15. For **pVersionSource Prompt Question** is set to **Enter Version to Copy** and **Default Value** is **Budget Version 1**.

>
> The **Prompt Question** would be asked of users so that they enter parameter values

16. **Default Value** is exactly same as an element in **Months** and **Versions** dimension.

>
> The **DimensionElementInsert** and **SubsetElementInsert** functions we are using in the code don't do anything if the element already exists. However, in general practice it is advisable to test using a **DIMIX** function which returns zero if the element does not already exist. Syntax of the function is:
>
> **DIMIX(Element)** > 0 implies that the element already exists. A zero value implies that the element does not exist.
>
> Hence, **DIMIX** function coupled with **IF** function can be used to check parameter values input from the user.

17. In **Advanced** tab for **Prolog** sub tab please type the following code:

```
#****End Generated Statements****
Cube = 'Sales_Plan';
Object = '$Transfer'|Cube;
#-----Delete old view if any
VIEWDESTROY(Cube,Object);
#---------Delete old subsets if any
SUBSETDESTROY('Months',Object);
SUBSETDESTROY('Versions',Object);
#Create new subsets
SUBSETCREATE('Months',Object);
SUBSETELEMENTINSERT('Months',Object,pTargetMonth,1);
```

```
SUBSETCREATE('Versions',Object);
SUBSETELEMENTINSERT('Versions',Object,pVersionTarget,1);
#Create view
VIEWCREATE(Cube,Object);
VIEWSUBSETASSIGN(Cube,Object,'Months',Object);
VIEWSUBSETASSIGN(Cube,Object,'Versions',Object);
#Clear view
VIEWZEROOUT(Cube,Object);
#Delete the cleared view
VIEWDESTROY(Cube,Object);
#Delete associated subsets
SUBSETDESTROY('Months',Object);
SUBSETDESTROY('Versions',Object);
#Create new views to use as data source for next step
#Create source subsets
SUBSETCREATE('Months',Object);
SUBSETELEMENTINSERT('Months',Object,pTargetMonth,1);
SUBSETCREATE('Versions',Object);
SUBSETELEMENTINSERT('Versions',Object,pVersionSource,1);
#Create source views
VIEWCREATE(Cube,Object);
VIEWSUBSETASSIGN(Cube,Object,'Months',Object);
VIEWSUBSETASSIGN(Cube,Object,'Versions',Object);
#Reestablish the new view as the data source
DATASOURCECUBEVIEW=Object;
```

18. The window looks as shown in the following screenshot:

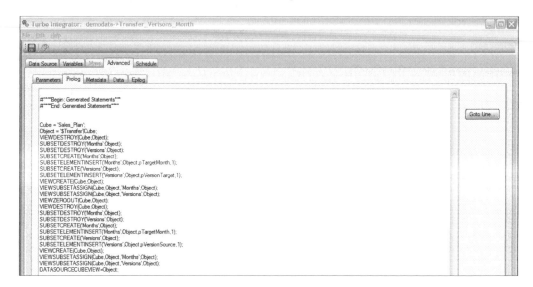

Please refer to online TI functions reference guide from the **Help** menu for various functions, semantics, and syntax.

19. In the script we have written in **Prolog** tab we have:

    ❑ Created a target view to zero out the data (and then destroyed it and its subsets)

    ❑ Created a view for the data transfer based on the source (and then destroyed it and its subsets)

 We typically have added a destroy subset to ensure the subset is based on the input parameter and clean up the system, so there will be no public views left for the users.

20. Nothing is needed on the **Metadata** tab.

21. Similarly, for **Data** tab, code is specified which gets executed for every record in the data source. We should ensure that the TM1 object to be updated in this tab actually exists and is created already.

```
IF(Value_Is_String<>0);
#-------------String
CELLPUTS(SValue,Cube,Subsidiaries,Channels,Products,pTargetMonth,p
VersionTarget,Sales_Plan_Measures);
ELSE;
#-------------Number
#Ignore values where the cell cannot be updated
IF (CELLISUPDATEABLE(Cube,Subsidiaries,Channels,Products,pTargetMo
nth,pVersionTarget,Sales_Plan_Measures)=0);
ITEMSKIP;
ELSE;
CELLPUTN(Value,Cube,Subsidiaries,Channels,Products,pTargetMonth,pV
ersionTarget,Sales_Plan_Measures);
ENDIF;
ENDIF;
```

 # denotes rest of the line is a comment and is for documentation only.

22. Conditional statements in the preceding script will check to see if numeric data or string data is being copied. `Value_Is_String` is TM1 local variable to facilitate the check.

23. Now click on the **Epilog** tab and enter the following code:

```
#Delete old view if any
VIEWDESTROY(Cube,Object);
#Delete old subsets if any
SUBSETDESTROY('Months',Object);
SUBSETDESTROY('Versions',Object);
```

24. The preceding code is added to delete the temporary view and its subsets if any.

25. Save the process as **Transfer_Versions_Month** and run the process.

26. When the process is run it will ask for parameter values as shown in the following screenshot:

27. Please accept the default values and click on **OK**.

28. Close the **Turbo Integrator**.

29. In **Server Explorer** window double-click on **Sales_Plan** cube.

30. Double-click on **Versions** dimension to open in **Subset Editor**.

31. Click on **All** icon, select **Submit Version** and click on **OK**.

32. Return to the **Cube Viewer** and click on **Recalculate**.

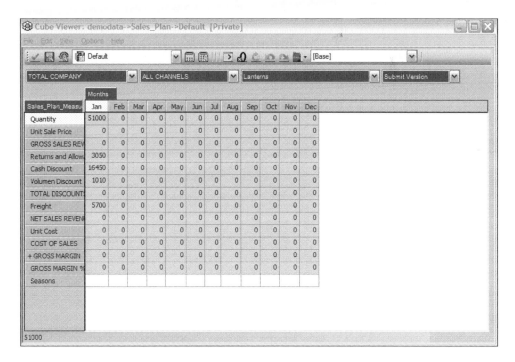

33. Close the **Cube Viewer** without saving.

How it works...

In the recipe we have copied data to submit version for Jan using TI functions.

 It is recommended to go through TI functions semantics and syntax available in TI documentation in **Help** menu and try to achieve the same functionality using different functions.

Creating and scheduling a chore

In this recipe we will create a chore to create and populate the **Product** dimension and then create the **Product Type** subsets.

Getting ready

Ensure that TM1 Admin server is started and demodata TM1 server is running. Open TM1 Architect from the **Start Menu**.

How to do it...

1. In the **Server Explorer** window right-click on **Chores** and **Create New Chore**.

2. Double-click on **CreateProductCSV** and **CreateProductType_subsets** as shown in the following screenshot:

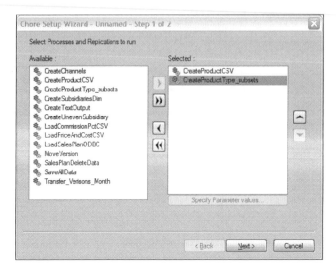

3. Click on **Next** and we will schedule the chore to run after every seven days. **Activate** the chore as shown in the following screenshot:

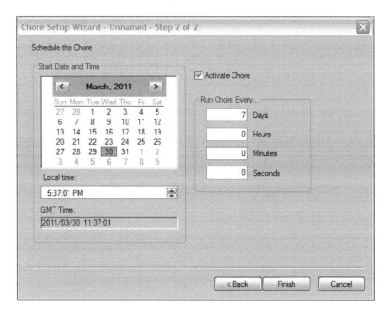

4. Click on **Finish** button and save the chore as **CreateProducts_ProductTypeSubsets**.

5. Here we have created a chore that creates and populates the **Products** dimension and then creates the **Product Type** subsets.

6. Please note that the chore should be deactivated while making changes to the underlying TI process or the chore itself. Nothing in TM1 stops from editing a chore or the underlying TI process without deactivating that, but just to aviod other users unknowingly executing the chore, while the chore or the underlying TI process is being edited, it is recommended to deactivate it and then edit the associated components.

How it works...

In this recipe we have added a chore to execute the TI process as per the schedule set. This is a common business requirement to schedule cube and dimension updates during business hours at fixed time intervals.

7
Customizing Drill Paths

In this chapter, we will cover:

- ▸ Creating a drill-through path to a view in another cube
- ▸ Creating a drill path to an ODBC source

Introduction

In this chapter will explore methods to perform and implement a drill-through in TM1.

A drill-through is a method used to navigate from a data point to other related information present in any other source (a cube or ODBC). For example, if a cell shows revenue figures for the current financial year then the next information which might be useful is the different product lines that have contributed to the total revenue, and the product-specific details for each of these product lines.

Such information should be available with a click on the master cell which shows the total revenue and a drill-through path should be defined to the navigate to detailed product-specific information.

There can be multiple drill-through paths originating from a master data cell, a list of all available drill-through paths should appear if more then one related paths are defined.

Therefore, in this chapter we will see how to define such drill-through paths from a cell to more detail, or to other relevant information.

A TM1 drill-through process can drill to a cube view, an ODBC data source, or any other data source supported by Turbo Integrator.

Creating a drill-through path to a view in another cube

Creating a drill-through path involves following the steps demonstrated in this recipe.

▶ Identifying the source data from which the drill-through process/es will be available.

▶ Identifying the target data which would be navigated to from the source data identified above.

▶ Identifying the parameters on which the target data will be filtered so that the context is maintained from source to target.

▶ Associating all such drill-through (Source Target/Master Detailed) relationships with the source cell.

Getting ready

Ensure that the TM1 Admin Server service is started and demodata TM1 Server is running. Open TM1 Architect from the start menu.

How to do it...

1. In a **Server Explorer** window, double-click the **Price_and_Cost** cube.

2. In the default view, swap **Price_Cost_Measures** with the **Months** dimension.

3. In the **Channels** dimension select **ALL CHANNELS** and then in the **Versions** dimension select **Budget Version 1**.

4. Double-click the **Months** dimension, click on the **All** icon ▨ in **Subset Editor,** and select **Total Year**. Click on **OK**.

5. Double-click the **Price_and_Cost_Measures** dimension, *Ctrl + Click* the **Unit Sales Price** and **Unit Cost** elements, and click on **OK**.

6. Click the **Recalculate** icon ▨ in **Cube Viewer**.

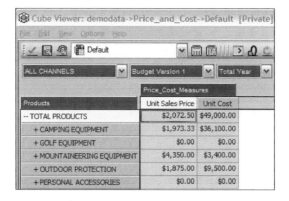

7. Click on **File** and select **Save As** to save the view as **PriceandCostDrillView**. Uncheck the **Private** checkbox to save the view as a non-private view.

8. Click on **OK** to close the view and return to the **Server Explorer** window.

9. In the **Server Explorer** window, right-click the **Sales_Plan** cube, point to **Drill**, and then click on **Create Drill Process**.

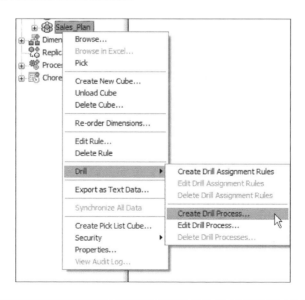

10. Enter the **Parameter Value** for each **Parameter Name** in the first screen of the **Drill Process Setup Wizard**, as shown in the following screenshot:

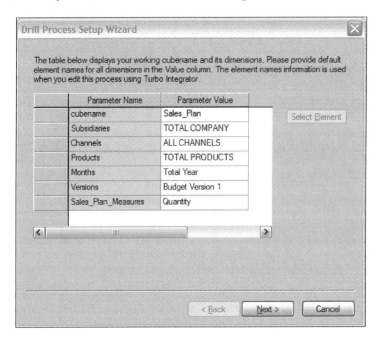

11. In the **Drill Process Setup Wizard** click on **Next** button.

12. On next screen select **Cube View** and then click on **Browse** to select the destination cube view.

13. Under **Select Cube** click the **demodata:Price_and_Cost** cube, then in the **Select View** box select **PriceandCostDrillView** as shown in the following screenshot:

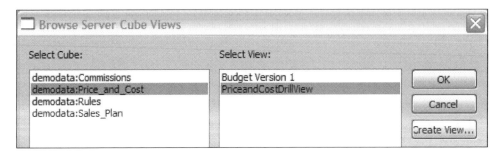

14. Click on **OK** and then the **Finish** button.

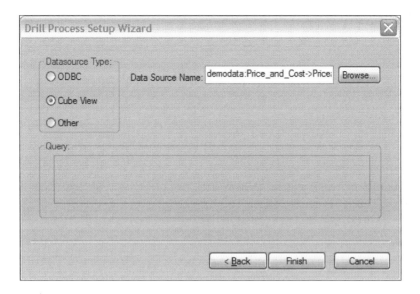

15. When prompted, save the process as **SalesPlantoPriceandCost** and click on **OK** to return to the **Server Explorer** window.

16. In the **Server Explorer** window, right-click on the **Sales_Plan** cube, click on **Drill,** and then click on **Create Drill Assignment Rules** to assign drill-through processes to the source cube.

17. This will open the **Advanced Rules Editor** where we will type assignment rules.

18. Click on the brackets icon and then double-click **Sales_Plan_Measures**.

19. Click on **Unit Sales Price** and then **OK**.

20. Type **=S: 'SalesPlantoPriceandCost';** as shown in the following screenshot:

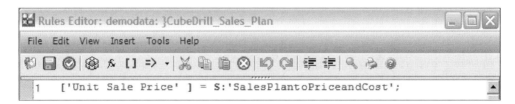

21. This indicates that the drill process specified will run when drilling from any cell in the **Unit Sales Price** dimension.

22. Click on **Save,** Close the **Rules Editor,** and return to **Server Explorer**.

23. In **Server Explorer** double-click the **Sales_Plan** cube.

24. In the **Default View** double-click **Subsidiaries** to open in **Subset Editor**.

25. Expand **GO AMERICAS REGION** and click on **GO Americas,** as shown in the following screenshot:

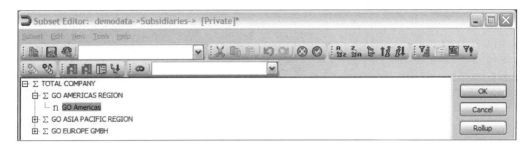

26. Under **Channels** click on **Department Store**.

27. Under **Products** click on **Cooking Gear**.

28. Click on **OK** to ensure the **Cube Viewer** appears as shown in the following screenshot:

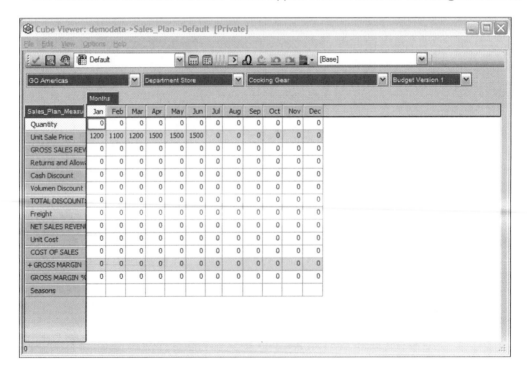

29. Click on **Recalculate** and save the view as non-private **DrillView**.

30. Right-click on **Unit Sales Price** for **Jan** and click on **Drill**.

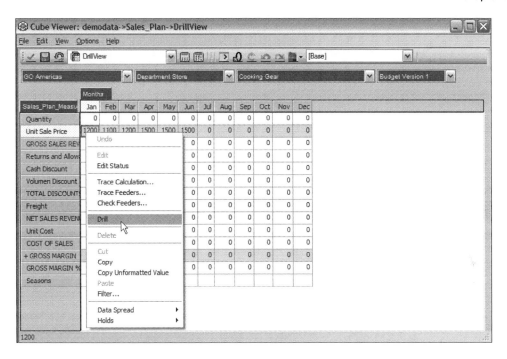

31. It will open a new window showing **PriceandCostDrillView**, saved earlier and specified as the destination view as shown in the following screenshot:

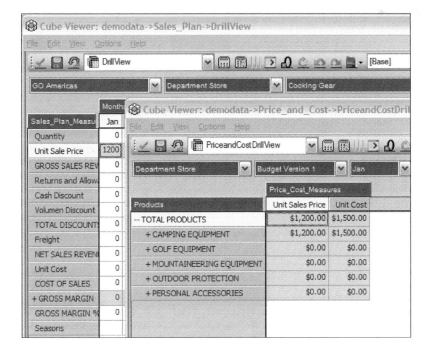

32. Here we can see the data for the **Department Store** and **Jan** combination, which acts as a filter for the **Sales_Plan** cube and data shown is relevant to this combination only. The original **PriceandCostDrillView** has dimensions defaulted to **ALL CHANNELS** and **TOTALYEAR**, and therefore shows complete data without any filter unless drilled from the parent view for a specific combination of dimensions.

33. Close the **PriceandCostDrillView**.

34. In the **Sales_Plan** cube right-click on **Quantity** for **Jan**. Please note that the **Drill** option is disabled here as we have not made the drill process available to elements other then **Unit Sales Price**.

35. Close all windows without making any changes if prompted.

How it works...

In this recipe, we created a drill process from the parent cube to a cube view. We also created a drill assignment rule which will be executed when the user clicks on any cell specified in the rule.

There's more...

In this recipe, we have seen an approach to drill from a cube to a cube view, where the cube acts as a source and the cube view acts as the destination. The following table shows other data source types which can act as the destination:

Destination	Description
ODBC	Drills from the origination cube to an ODBC source. The ODBC source must be accessible from the computer on which the TM1 Server is running.
Cube view	Drills from the origination cube to a different cube view. We can drill to any cube that resides on the same server as the origination cube.
Other	Drills from the origination cube to any data source Turbo Integrator supports.

We have also written a drill assignment rule, this is to link cube cells with related detailed data which can be a cube view, an ODBC source, or any other data source accessible through Turbo Integrator.

We have seen an approach to write a drill assignment rule in this recipe, where the right-hand side of the expression denotes the drill process we have created for the cube in TI, and the left-hand side is the cube name.

Another approach to create a drill assignment rule is to associate each cube area we want to act as source with the detailed data. Again, this can be done in **Advance Rules Editor** by clicking on the **Insert Cube Reference** icon to define an area in the cube; in terms of the source cube, dimension, and element combination, from where a user can drill to the destination data source which can be any of them, as mentioned in the preceding table.

Creating a drill path to an ODBC source

In this recipe, we will be extending drill-through concepts explained in the previous recipe and will create a drill-through path to an ODBC data source.

Getting started

Ensure that the TM1 Admin Server service is started and demodata TM1 Server is running. Open the TM1 Architect tool from the start menu.

How to do it...

1. Right-click on the **Sales_Plan** cube and from the **Drill** menu click on **Create Drill Process**.

2. Click on the **Next** button in the **Drill Process Setup Wizard**.

3. For **Datasource Type** select **ODBC** and click on **Browse**.

4. In the ODBC data source list select **Sales_Plan** and click on **OK**.

5. We have already created the **Sales_Plan** ODBC in a previous chapter which points to `Sales_Plan.xls`, having a range defined by name of **Sales**.

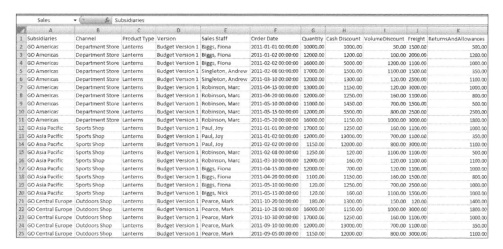

6. Click on **Finish,** save the process as **salesplantosalesplanxls**, and then click on **OK** to return to the **Server Explorer** window.

7. In the **Server Explorer** window right-click on the **Sales_Plan** cube, then from the **Drill** menu click on **Edit Drill Process**.

8. In the **Select** list choose **salesplantosalesplanxls,** as shown in the following screenshot:

9. Click on **OK** to dismiss the error message.

10. In the **Turbo Integrator** window type the following in the **Query Box**:

```
select * from sales
where
Subsidiaries = '?Subsidiaries?'
and Channel = '?Channels?'
and "Product Type" = '?Products?'
and Version = '?Versions?'
```

11. Click on **Preview** and the result is displayed as follows:

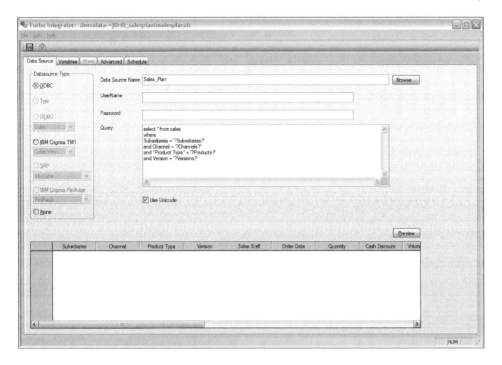

12. The query columns on the left refer to columns in the data source while references on the right refer to the TM1 dimension names in the cube.

13. Click on the **Save** icon .

14. In the dialog box ensure that **Keep all variables** is selected and click on **OK**.

> Turbo Integrator
>
> Modifications to datasource specification caused Turbo
> Integrator to re-read the input and recreate the
> variables. Please specify an action for the existing
> variables.
> ○ Keep derived variables only.
> ◉ Keep all variables.
>
> [OK]   [Cancel]

15. Close the **Turbo Integrator** window to return to the **Server Explorer** window.

16. In the **Server Explorer** window right-click the **Sales_Plan** cube and from the **Drill** menu click on **Edit Drill Assignment Rules**.

17. The preceding step will open the **Advanced Rules Editor** window, as shown in the following screenshot:

18. On row number 3 type:

```
[] = S: IF(ISLEAF=1,'SalesPlanToSalesPlanXLS', '');
```

19. The rule on line 3 states that for all the leaf level elements in the **Sales_Plan** cube the drill path to `Sales_Plan xls` is available. As the first rule is already applied on **Unit Sales Price**, the drill path from **Unit Sales Price** is different from that available from any other measure, such as **Quantity**.

20 Click on **Save** and close the editor to return to **Server Explorer**.

21. In **Server Explorer** double-click **Sales_Plan** to open **Drill View** created as part of the previous recipe.

22. Right-click on the cell corresponding to tuple (**Jan, Quantity**), as shown in the following screenshot, and click on **Drill**.

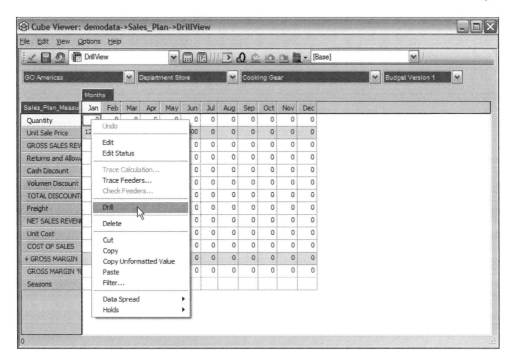

23. It will open default drill view of **Price_and_Cost**, created previously, as shown in the following screenshot. As there is no data for the tuple selected in the source cube, the destination view is empty. This shows that the target view is filtered based on the tuple selected in the source.

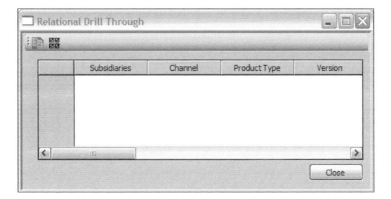

24. If we had right-clicked on **Quantity** for **Q1**, the **Drill** option would not have been available; **Q1** defines a non-leaf level element, and a drill from the non-leaf element is excluded in the rule itself.

25. Close all the cube views without saving anything.

How it works...

In this recipe, we have created a drill-through link from a cube to an ODBC data source. We have changed the TI process definition accordingly and have modified rules to disable the drill option from non-leaf elements.

We have deliberately clicked on the tuple in the source cube for which data does not exist, this is to show how the target view is filtered based on selections in the source cube.

8
Using Rules for Advanced Modelling

In this chapter, we will cover:

- ▶ Creating the Expenses cube
- ▶ Examining a Spread Profile cube, Lookup cube, and virtual cube
- ▶ Moving balances from last month to next month

Introduction

In this chapter, we will be learning about Virtual Cubes, Spread Profile cubes, and Lookup cubes. We will be demonstrating these concepts on the existing demodata TM1 Server. We will start by creating an Expenses cube which we will use in this chapter and onwards. Lastly, we will move balances from last month to next month using rules.

Creating the Expenses cube

In this recipe we will create an Expenses cube, which will be populated in part by data from spreadsheets, rules, and user input. Users will need to spread data in order to project some overhead expenses into different regions.

Getting ready

Ensure that the TM1 Admin Server service is started and demodata TM1 Server is running. Open TM1 Architect from the **Start menu**.

How to do it...

1. Open **Server Explorer** in TM1 Architect.

2. Create `Expenses.csv` as shown and save it in `C:\Program Files\cognos\TM1\Custom\TM1Data\TI_Data`.

A	B	C
Salaries: direct	SALARIES	TOTAL COMPENSATION
Salaries: indirect	SALARIES	TOTAL COMPENSATION
Commission	SALARIES	TOTAL COMPENSATION
Pension Plan%		
PENSION PLAN	BENEFITS	TOTAL COMPENSATION
Social Security%		
SOCIAL SECURITY	BENEFITS	TOTAL COMPENSATION
Health Insurance%		
HEALTH INSURANCE	BENEFITS	TOTAL COMPENSATION
Workers Compensation	BENEFITS	TOTAL COMPENSATION

3. Create a new Turbo Integrator process for **Source**, select **Text**, and for **Data Source Name** provide the above path to `Expenses.csv`. Click on **OK** to close the warning and see the **Preview** as shown in the following screenshot:

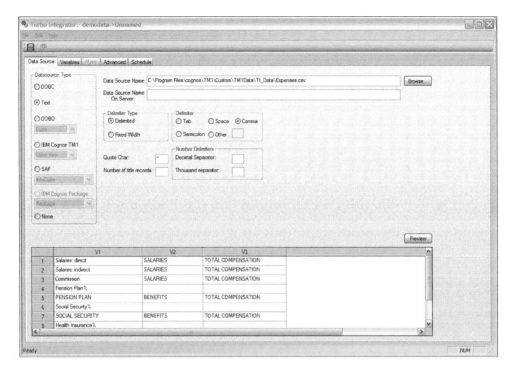

4. Click on the **Variables** tab.

5. Rename **Variable Name** and assign the **Contents** as shown in the following screenshot:

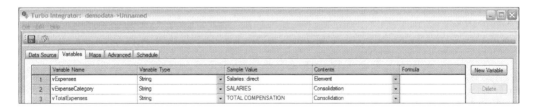

6. Click on **Maps** and then on the **Dimensions** tab to provide the values as shown in the following screenshot:

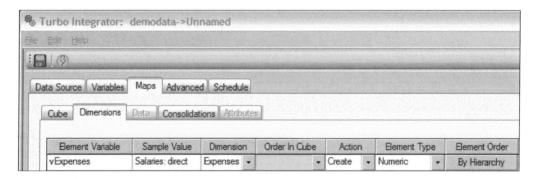

7. For **Element Order** we clicked **By Input**, then in the **Dimension Element Ordering** window we selected **Automatic** and then **Hierarchy** to sort the resulting leaf level elements automatically by hierarchy.

8. We also named the dimension as **Expenses** by typing this in the **Dimension** column.

9. In the preceding steps, we created a leaf level element by the name of **Expenses** which would be populated by the variable **vExpenses**.

10. Now in the **Consolidations** tab for the first row under **Child Variable** select **vExpenses** and for the second row select **vExpenseCategory** under the same **Child Variable** column, as shown in the following screenshot:

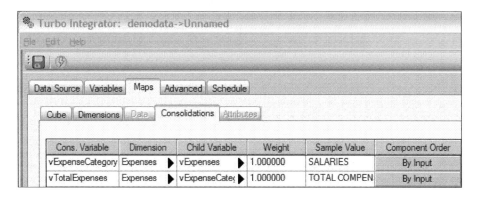

11. Click through the **Advanced** tab and then the **Prolog, Epilog, Metadata,** and **Data** tabs to generate the scripts.

12. Save the process as **CreateExpenseCSV** and execute the process.

13. Click on **Yes** to view the log file and then double-click on the first line.

14. It tells you that the **Consolidated Element** for three of the elements are not found. This is obvious as we have not included consolidated elements for these child level elements in our Expenses.csv.

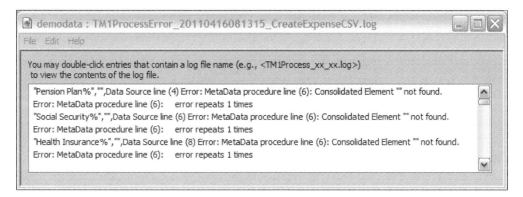

15. This is still fine with us as we will not be using these three elements in our cube. Close **Turbo Integrator** and all the error messages to return to the **Server Explorer** window.

16. Double-click on the **Expenses** dimension to open in the **Subset Editor**.

17. Now we will delete these three elements from the subset, but they will remain as part of the dimension as we are deleting these using **Subset Editor**.

 If we delete the elements using **Dimension Editor** they will be permanently removed.

18. Select the three elements as shown in the following screenshot and click on the **Delete** icon ⊗.

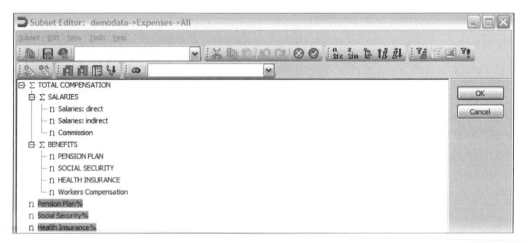

19. Save this as a public default subset, the result should look as shown in the following screenshot:

20. Close the **Subset Editor** to return to the **Server Explorer window**.

21. In the **Server Explorer** window right-click on **Dimensions** and click on **Create New Dimension**.

22. In the **Dimension Editor**, insert two new simple elements named **Amount** and **Percent** as shown in the following screenshot:

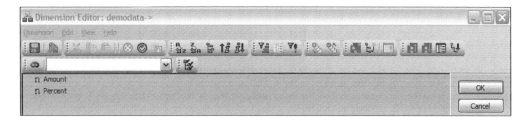

23. Save the dimension as **Expense-Measures** and close the **Dimension Editor** to return to **Sever Explorer**.

24. In the **Server Explorer** window right-click on Cubes and click on **Create New Cube** named **Expenses**.

25. Double-click on the following dimensions:

    ❑ Versions

    ❑ Months

    ❑ Subsidiaries

    ❑ Expenses

    ❑ Expense_Measures

26. The result appears as shown in the following screenshot:

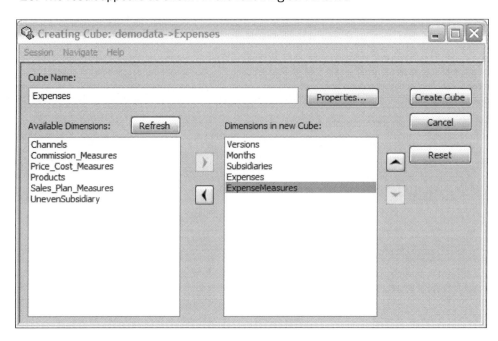

27. Click on **Create Cube** to return to the **Server Explorer** window where a new cube now appears by the name of **Expenses**.

28. Create a CSV called Ben Work Comp.csv to load data into the cube. Save the CSV file to C:\Program Files\cognos\TM1\Custom\TM1Data\TI_Data.

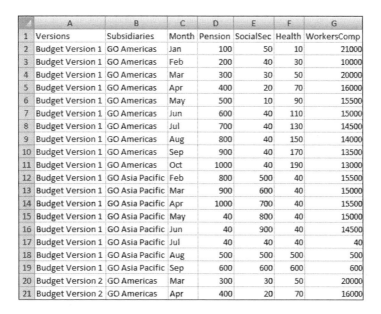

	A	B	C	D	E	F	G
1	Versions	Subsidiaries	Month	Pension	SocialSec	Health	WorkersComp
2	Budget Version 1	GO Americas	Jan	100	50	10	21000
3	Budget Version 1	GO Americas	Feb	200	40	30	10000
4	Budget Version 1	GO Americas	Mar	300	30	50	20000
5	Budget Version 1	GO Americas	Apr	400	20	70	16000
6	Budget Version 1	GO Americas	May	500	10	90	15500
7	Budget Version 1	GO Americas	Jun	600	40	110	15000
8	Budget Version 1	GO Americas	Jul	700	40	130	14500
9	Budget Version 1	GO Americas	Aug	800	40	150	14000
10	Budget Version 1	GO Americas	Sep	900	40	170	13500
11	Budget Version 1	GO Americas	Oct	1000	40	190	13000
12	Budget Version 1	GO Asia Pacific	Feb	800	500	40	15500
13	Budget Version 1	GO Asia Pacific	Mar	900	600	40	15000
14	Budget Version 1	GO Asia Pacific	Apr	1000	700	40	15500
15	Budget Version 1	GO Asia Pacific	May	40	800	40	15000
16	Budget Version 1	GO Asia Pacific	Jun	40	900	40	14500
17	Budget Version 1	GO Asia Pacific	Jul	40	40	40	40
18	Budget Version 1	GO Asia Pacific	Aug	500	500	500	500
19	Budget Version 1	GO Asia Pacific	Sep	600	600	600	600
20	Budget Version 2	GO Americas	Mar	300	30	50	20000
21	Budget Version 2	GO Americas	Apr	400	20	70	16000

29. Create a new Turbo Integrator process to load text data from the above CSV, as shown in the following screenshot. Change **Number of title records** to **1**. Click on **Preview**.

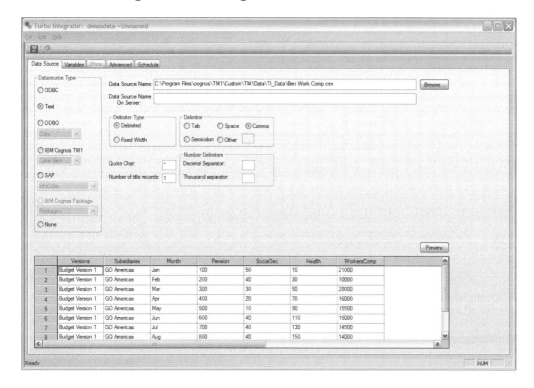

30. Click on the **Variables** tab and create a new variable called **vMeasures** and type the following formula.

```
vMeasures='Percent';
```

31. Click on **Evaluate** and then **OK**.

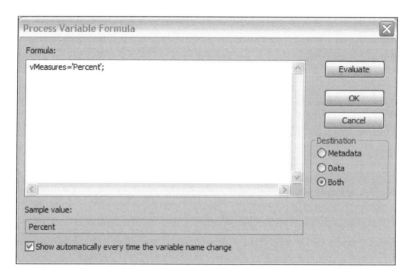

32. Change the **Variable Type** for **vMeasures** to **String**.

33. Rename the **Variable Name** for other variables and set the **Contents** as shown in the following screenshot:

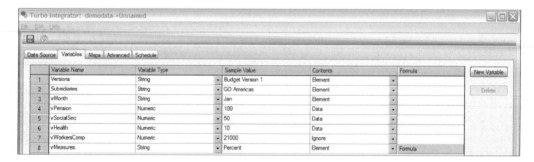

34. Click on **Maps** and select **Update Cube Action**. Select the **Expenses** cube for **Cube Name** as shown in the following screenshot:

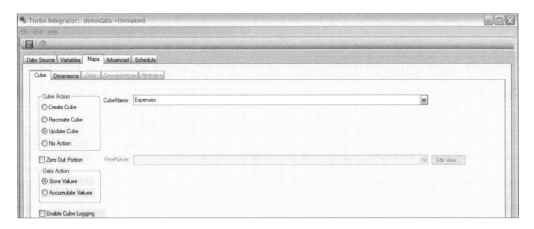

35. Click on the **Dimensions** tab and then map each **Element Variable** to the appropriate **Dimension** column, as shown. Note that the **Action** column is **As Is** as we are not going to add new elements to the dimensions.

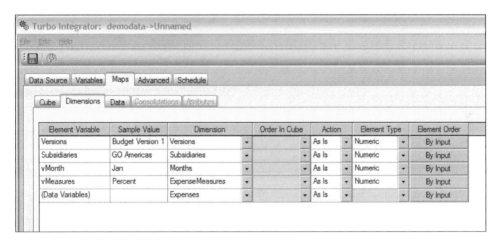

36. Click on the **Data** tab to map the data to the elements.

37. Click all tabs under the **Advanced** tab to generate scripts.

38. Save the process as **LoadBenWorkCompCSVPercent**.

39. Click on **Run** and then click on **OK**.

40. Close **Turbo Integrator** to return to the **Server Explorer** window.

41. In the **Server Explorer** window double-click on the **Expenses** cube and set **Version** to **Budget Version 1**.

42. Click on **Recalculate** to show the loaded data as shown in the following screenshot:

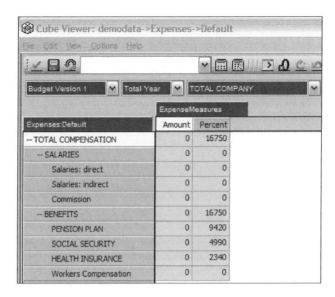

43. Open the **LoadBenWorkCompPercent** process, click on **File** and **Save As** to process **LoadBenWorkCompCSVAmount** to load dollar values.

44. Click on the **Variables** tab and, next to **vMeasures**, click on **Formula**.

45. Change **Percent** to **Amount**.

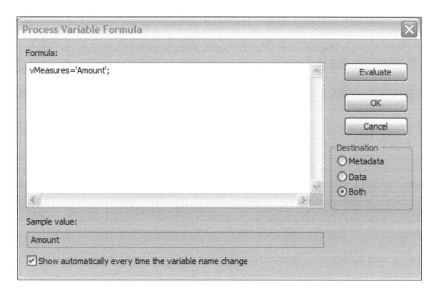

46. Click on **OK**.
47. Next to **vPension**, **vSocialSec**, and **vHealth** change the **Contents** to **Ignore**.
48. Next to **vWorkersComp** change the **Contents** to **Data**.
49. Create a new variable called `vExpense='WorkersCompensation';`
50. Change its variable type to **String** and **Contents** to **Element**.
51. Click on **Maps** and then on the **Dimensions** tab.
52. Map **vExpense** to the **Expenses** dimension.

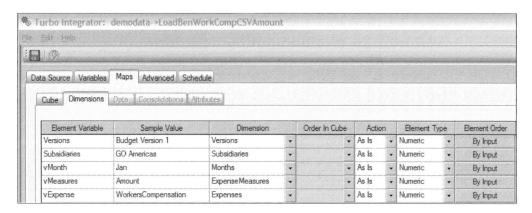

53. Since we have only one data element and it matches with an element in our Measures dimension, we don't have to map it manually.
54. Click on the **Advanced** tab and the tabs under it to generate the scripts.

55. Click on **Save** and **Run**.

56. Close to return to the **Server Explorer** window.

57. Now **Recalculate** the view in the **Expenses** cube to show both the **Amount** and **Percent** values loaded, as shown in the following screenshot:

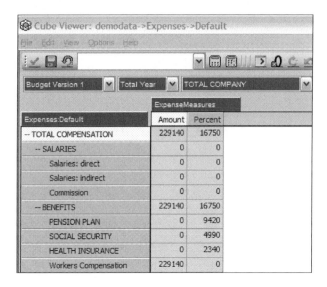

58. Save as the **Default** view and leave the view open.

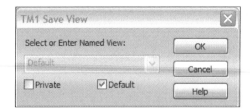

59. In the same **Cube Viewer** window double-click on the **Months** dimension to open in **Subset Editor**, expand **Q1**, click on **Jan**, and then click on **OK**.

60. Double-click on the **Subsidiaries** dimension, in the **Subset Editor** expand **GO AMERICAS REGION**, click on **GO Americas**, and then click **OK**.

61. Click on **Recalculate** and save the view as **GO Americas** view.

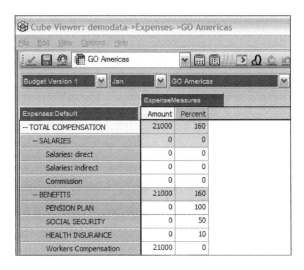

62. Minimize the view window and in the **Server Explorer** window right-click on the **Expenses** cube and click on **Create Rule** to open **Advanced Rules Editor**.

63. On line 1 type `SKIPCHECK;` and then press *Enter*.

64. Click on **Brackets** and then double-click on **Expenses**.

65. Click on **Commission** and then click on **OK**.

66. Inside the square brackets, after **Commission**, type **Amount** and press the *End* key.

67. Type **=:N** and then click on **Insert Cube Reference**.

68. In the **Cube** list click on **Commissions** cube.

69. Click on the **Subset** icon for **Commission_Measures**, click on **Commission** and click on **OK** twice to return to the **Rules Editor**.

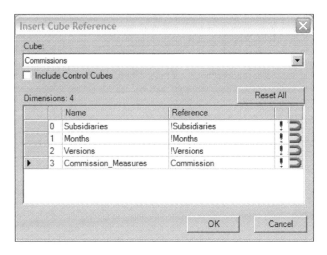

70. In the **Rules Editor** type at the end so that the code looks as shown below:

```
SKIPCHECK;
['Commission','Amount' ] =N:DB('Commissions', !Subsidiaries,
!Months, !Versions, 'Commission');
```

71. Save the rule and click on the **Recalculate GO Americas** view.

72. In the preceding steps we copied commission data from the **Commission** cube to the **Expenses** cube.

73. Now, since we are feeding the **Expense** cube with data in the **Commission** cube, we need to add a **FEEDER** statement under the rules in the **Commission** cube. We will be examining more about SKIPCHECK and FEEDER statements in a later chapter on *Optimizing Rules Performance*.

> **FEEDER** pushes values to another cube and is also a way to tell TM1 that the source cube, where the statement is placed, will act as a source of data for the cubes mentioned on the right-hand side of the statements under the **FEEDERS;** statement. We will see more about these statements in later chapters.

74. Add the following FEEDER to the rules in the **Commission** cube by right-clicking on the **Commission** cube in **Server Explorer** and clicking on **Edit Rules**.

```
['Commission%'] => DB('Expenses',!Versions,!Months,!Subsidiaries,'
Commission','Amount');
```

```
Rules Editor: demodata: Commissions
File  Edit  View  Insert  Tools  Help

1   SKIPCHECK;
2   ['Gross Sales Revenue' ] = DB('Sales_Plan', !Subsidiaries,
3   'ALL CHANNELS', 'TOTAL PRODUCTS', !Months, !Versions, 'GROSS SALES REVENUE');
4   ['Commission_hold' ] =N: ['Commission%' ] ;
5   ['Commission_count'] =N:IF(['Commission%']<>0,1,0);
6   ['Commission%'] =C:(['Commission_hold']\['Commission_count']);
7   ['Commission'] = N:(['Gross Sales Revenue']*['Commission%'])/100;
8   FEEDERS;
9   ['Commission%'] => ['Commission'],['Commission_hold'],['Commission_count'];
10  ['Commission%'] => DB('Expenses',!Versions,!Months,!Subsidiaries,'Commission','Amount');
11
```

75. As the **Commission** cube is the source of data for the **Expense** cube, the FEEDER statement must be placed in the **Commission** cube.

76. Save the rule and close the **Rules Editor** for both cubes.

77. Double-click on the **Expense** cube, click on **Jan** for **Months** and **GO Americas** for **Subsidiaries**, and click on **Recalculate** to view newly loaded commission data in the **Expense** cube, sourced from the **Commission** cube. If no new data is loaded, it implies that the **Commission** cube does not have the commission data for **Jan** or **GO Americas**.

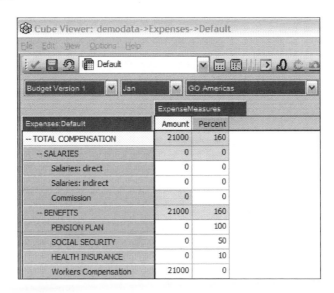

78. Leave the **Cube Viewer** open and return to the **Server Explorer** window.

79. In the **Server Explorer** window right-click on **Expense Measures** and click on **Edit Element Attributes**.

80. For **Amount**, specify currency as the **Format** and click on **OK**.

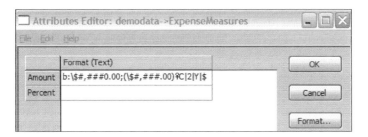

81. In the **Server Explorer** window open the **Rules Editor** for the **Expenses** cube and on line number 3 click on **Brackets**, then double-click on **Expenses**.

82. Click on **PENSION PLAN** and **OK**.

83. Inside the square brackets after **PENSION PLAN**, type **Amount** and then press the *End* key.

84. Now type the following:

```
=N:['SALARIES,'Amount'] * ['PENSION PLAN','Percent'];
```

85. Repeat the preceding step for **SOCIAL SECURITY** and **HEALTH INSURANCE**, so that the code appears as shown in the following screenshot:

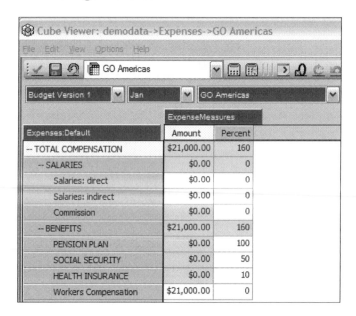

86. Save the rules and **Recalculate** the **GO Americas** cube view to update the data, as shown in the following screenshot:

Expenses:Default	Amount	Percent
-- TOTAL COMPENSATION	$21,000.00	160
-- SALARIES	$0.00	0
Salaries: direct	$0.00	0
Salaries: indirect	$0.00	0
Commission	$0.00	0
-- BENEFITS	$21,000.00	160
PENSION PLAN	$0.00	100
SOCIAL SECURITY	$0.00	50
HEALTH INSURANCE	$0.00	10
Workers Compensation	$21,000.00	0

87. On line number 7, create the following **FEEDERS;** in the **Expenses** cube:

```
FEEDERS;
['SALARIES','Amount'] => ['PENSION PLAN','Amount'], ['SOCIAL
SECURITY','Amount'], ['HEALTH INSURANCE','Amount'];
```

88. Rules on the **Expenses** cube should now look as shown in the following screenshot:

```
Rules Editor: demodata: Expenses
File   Edit   View   Insert   Tools   Help

1   SKIPCHECK;
2   ['Commission','Amount' ] =N:DB('Commissions', !Subsidiaries, !Months, !Versions, 'Commission');
3   ['PENSION PLAN','Amount' ] =N:['SALARIES','Amount'] * ['PENSION PLAN','Percent'];
4   ['SOCIAL SECURITY','Amount' ] =N:['SALARIES','Amount'] * ['SOCIAL SECURITY','Percent'];
5   ['HEALTH INSURANCE','Amount' ] =N:['SALARIES','Amount'] * ['HEALTH INSURANCE','Percent'];
6
7   FEEDERS;
8   ['SALARIES','Amount'] => ['PENSION PLAN','Amount'], ['SOCIAL SECURITY','Amount'], ['HEALTH INSURANCE','Amount'];
9
```

89. Save the rules and **Recalculate** the **GO Americas** cube view.

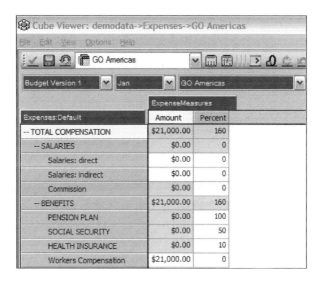

90. Zeros in the view indicates a deficiency in the data present in one of the associated CSVs. Users need to ensure there is good data in CSVs before starting with the recipes.

91. Close the view and save as **GO Americas** if prompted.

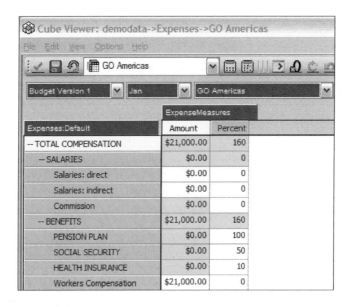

How it works...

In this recipe, we have created a cube that contains expenses. Salary and benefit data has come from data in text files and through calculations, while data for other expenses will come from user input through spreading, as shown in the following recipes.

There's more...

Virtual cubes are special cubes that do not actually store data, but are primarily used to combine data from other cubes to show summary data or for other reporting requirements.

Virtual cubes are totally driven by rules which are used to pull just the required data from, say, a very large cube for specific reporting requirements.

We will examine and use a Virtual cube in the following recipe.

Examining a Spread Profile cube, Lookup cube, and Virtual cube

Lookup cubes are special category cubes used to lookup data in one column and return corresponding data in another column using a rule. They are similar to using a lookup table for populating foreign keys in a fact table. Again, we will look at these in more detail in upcoming sections.

[It is advisable to prefix lookup cubes with special names so that similar purpose cubes appear together in the **Server Explorer** window.]

Spreading data to leaf level elements on the basis of aggregated elements is a concept made possible in TM1 using Spread Profile cubes.Relative spreading refers to distributing data among cells and writing them back to the cubes based on other cubes' data patterns.

Data is inserted into leaf level cells of the target based on the source cube, provided a common dimension exists between the source cube and the target cube.

Source cubes can be referred to as a Spread Profile cubes which act as a lookup cube for relative spread patterns. Based on these patterns, data is written back to leaf level elements in the target cube. The only constraint is the existence of a common dimension between the Spread Profile Source cube and the Target cube.

Getting ready

Ensure that the TM1 Admin Server service is started and demodata TM1 Server is running. Open TM1 Architect from the start menu.

How to do it...

1. We will first manually add a new consolidated element to the **Expenses** dimension and add its children elements, which will be used in this recipe.

2. In the **Server Explorer** window right-click on the **Expenses** dimension and click on **Edit Dimension Structure** to open the **Dimensions Editor**.

3. Insert a consolidated element called **TOTAL EXPENSES**.

4. Under **TOTAL EXPENSES** add child elements as shown in the following screenshot:

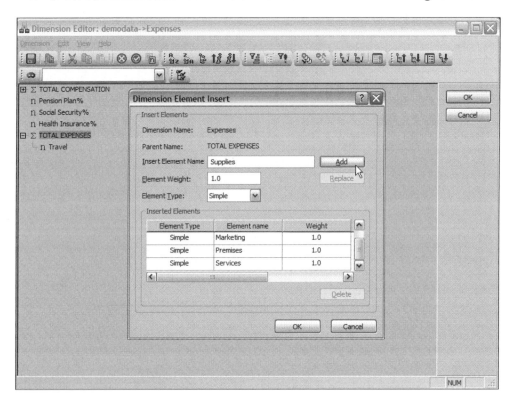

5. The resulting dimension structure should look as shown in the following screenshot:

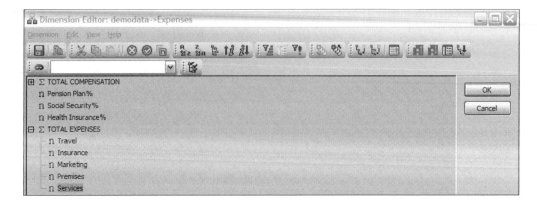

6. Click on **OK** to return to the **Server Explorer** window. Save changes to the dimension when prompted.

7. In the **Server Explorer** window double-click on the default subset for the **Expenses** dimension, as shown in the following screenshot:

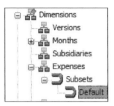

8. In the **Subset Editor** click on the **All** icon 📄.

9. Delete **Pension Plan%**, **Social Security%,** and **Health Insurance%** by clicking on the **Delete** icon ⊗ so that they are deleted from the subset, but remain in the dimension.

10. The resulting subset looks as shown in the following screenshot:

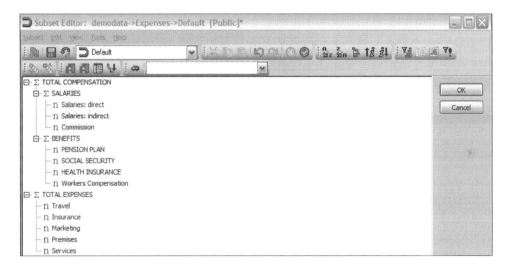

11. Click on **OK** to save the changes and return to **Server Explorer**.

12. In the **Server Explorer** window right-click on **Dimensions** and click on **Create New Dimension**.

13. Insert the following leaf elements:

- Flat
- Quarterly
- 4 4 5
- Business

14. Save the dimension as **SpreadMethod** and then close the Dimensions Editor. The dimension acts as a Lookup dimension.

15. In the **Server Explorer** window right-click on **Cubes** and then click on **Create new Cube**.

16. In the Cube Name box type **Spread_Profiles**.

17. Move the **Months** and **SpreadMethod** dimensions to the new cube.

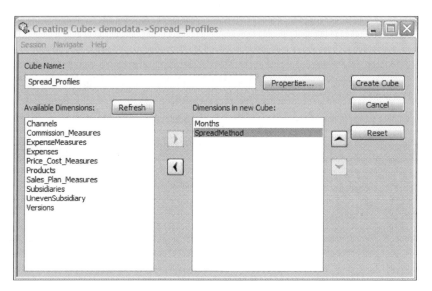

18. Click on **Create Cube** to return to **Server Explorer**.

19. In the **Server Explorer** window double-click on the **Spread_Profiles** cube.

20. Swap the **Months** and **SpreadMethod** dimension so that the former is in the row area.

21. Double-click on the **Months** dimension and select all the **level 0** elements. Click on **Recalculate** to display.

22. Right-click on the cell corresponding to (**Flat, Jan**), and from the **Data Spread** menu click on **Repeat**...

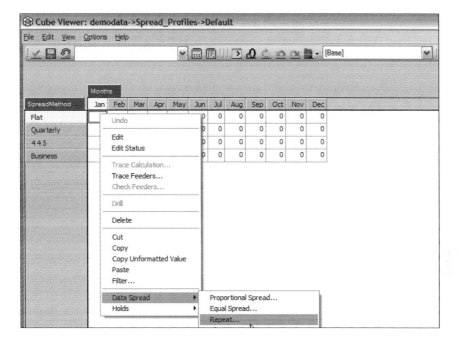

23. In the **Value** box type 1 and then click on **Right**, as shown in the following screenshot:

24. Click on **Apply**.

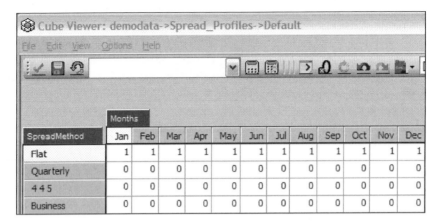

25. You can see that the same cell value 1 is spread across all the cells in that row.

26. Now enter the rest of the values manually.

27. The cube now contains weights which can be used to proportionally spread data along the **Months** dimension, in any other cube containing the **Months** dimension.

28. Click on **Recalculate** and save as default public view.

29. Close the **Cube Viewer** and return to **Server Explorer**.

30. In the **Server Explorer** window open the **GO Americas** view for the **Expenses** cube.

31. Swap **Expense Measures** and **Months**.

32. Click on **Recalculate** and then collapse all sections.

33. Double-click on **Months** and then in the **Subset Editor** click on **All**.

34. *Ctrl+Click* **Total Year** and the leaf elements from **Months**, as shown in the following screenshot, and click on **OK**.

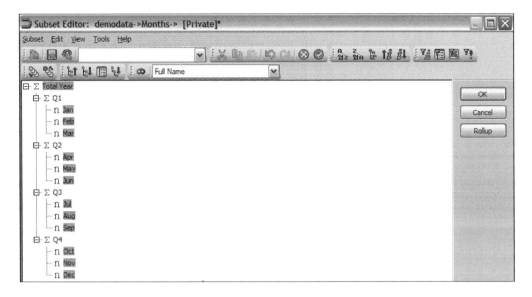

35. In **Cube Viewer** click on **Recalculate** and save as public view by the name **GO Americas Expenses**.

36. Now we will try spreading out **Travel Expenses** for the **Americas** in a **4 4 5** pattern, where they seem to be greater during the last month of the quarter. The budget for the travel expenses is supposed to be 1,000,000 or less for a year.

37. Click on **TOTAL COMPENSATION** to collapse it as shown in the following screenshot:

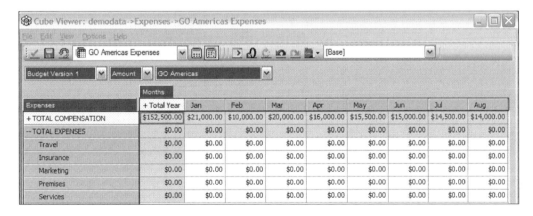

38. Right-click on the cell (Travel, Total Year), and from the **Data Spread** menu click on **Relative Proportional Spread**, as shown in the following screenshot:

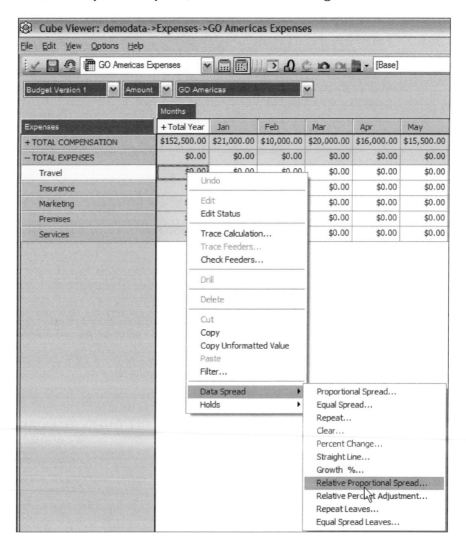

39. In the **Select a Reference Cell** dialog box, for **Cube** select **Spread_Profiles**, under **Dimensions** click on **SpreadMethod**, and select **4 4 5** as shown in the following screenshot:

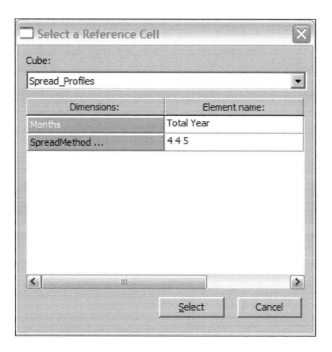

40. Click on **Select** and then for **Value** type **1000000**, click on **Apply** to return to the **Cube Viewer** window.

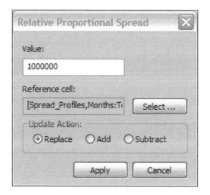

41. As shown in the following screenshot, $1,000,000 is spread into **Months** in the same proportion as the values in the **Spread_Profiles** cube for **Travel Expenses**. Here, we are able to manually write-back data for **Travel Expenses** with the help of spreading logic in the proportion of **4 4 5** when the total budget for **Travel** is fixed.

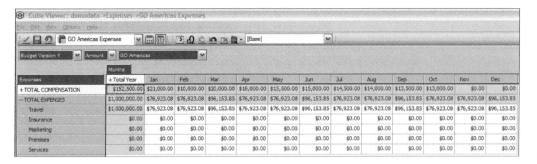

42. Close the **Cube Viewer** by saving **GO Americas Expenses** when prompted and return to the **Server Explorer** window.

43. In the **Server Explorer** window right-click on the **SpreadMethod** dimension and click on **Edit Dimension Structure**.

44. Click on **Business** and add a new element called **Subsidiary**.

45. Save and close the dimension to return to **Server Explorer**.

46. In the **Server Explorer** window right-click on **Cubes** and click on **Create New Cube**.

47. Include **Subsidiaries** and **SpreadMethod** in the cube.

48. Name the cube as **Spread_Profile_Subsidiary**.

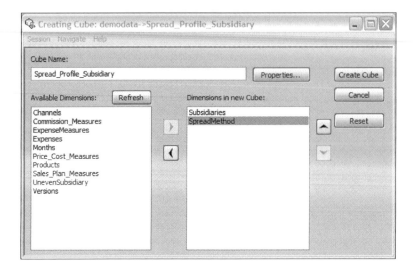

49. Double-click on the **Spread_Profile_Subsidiary** cube to open it in the **Cube Viewer**.

50. Double-click the **Subsidiaries** dimension, click **All**, and then click the **Filter by Level** icon.

51. Click **0** and **OK** to select only leaf level elements, as shown in the following screenshot:

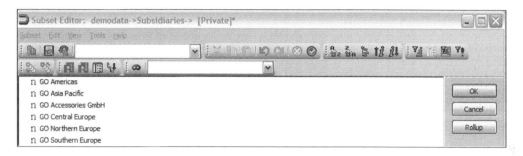

52. Click on **OK** to return to the **Cube Viewer** window.

53. Similarly, double-click on the **SpreadMethod** dimension and then click on the **All** icon.

54. Click on **Subsidiary** and then on **OK**.

55. Click on **Recalculate** and save the view as public default view.

56. Enter values for each subsidiary as shown, recalculate, and close, saving any changes when prompted.

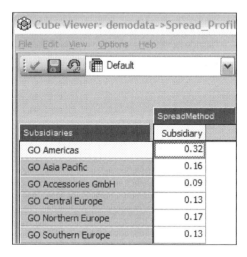

57. We can use this view to spread data by subsidiary. However, it's common to have a requirement where each subsidiary has different monthly proportions; it's imperative to have a method to combine the 4 4 5 proportion with the subsidiary. We will demonstrate this by using a third Spread Profile cube which will combine the two criterions.

58. In the **Server Explorer** window right-click on **Cubes** and click on **Create New Cube** by the name of **Spread_Profile_SubsByMonth**.

59. Include three dimensions for the cube, as shown in the following screenshot:

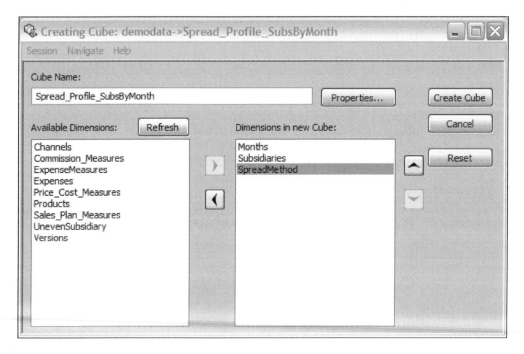

60. Create a public default view on the cube by swapping **Months** with **SpreadMethod**.

61. For **SpreadMethod** click on **Subsidiary**.

62. **Recalculate** to expose view, as shown in the following screenshot:

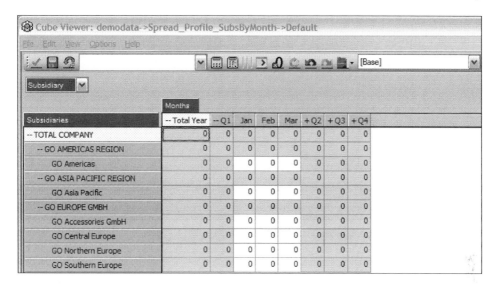

63. Save the view as public default view and keep the view open.

64. In the **Server Explorer** window create the following rule for **Spread_Profile_SubsByMonth**:

```
['Subsidiary'] = DB('Spread_Profile_Subsidiary',!Subsidiaries,'Sub
sidiary') *
    DB('Spread_Profiles',!Months,'4 4 5');
```

65. Save the rule and close the **Rules Editor**.

66. Click on **Recalculate** for the **Spread_Profile_SubsByMonth** cube to show the copied data from the two cubes referenced in the rule, as shown in the following screenshot:

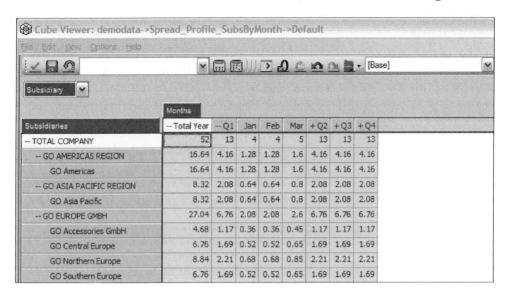

Subsidiaries	-- Total Year	-- Q1	Jan	Feb	Mar	+ Q2	+ Q3	+ Q4
-- TOTAL COMPANY	52	13	4	4	5	13	13	13
-- GO AMERICAS REGION	16.64	4.16	1.28	1.28	1.6	4.16	4.16	4.16
GO Americas	16.64	4.16	1.28	1.28	1.6	4.16	4.16	4.16
-- GO ASIA PACIFIC REGION	8.32	2.08	0.64	0.64	0.8	2.08	2.08	2.08
GO Asia Pacific	8.32	2.08	0.64	0.64	0.8	2.08	2.08	2.08
-- GO EUROPE GMBH	27.04	6.76	2.08	2.08	2.6	6.76	6.76	6.76
GO Accessories GmbH	4.68	1.17	0.36	0.36	0.45	1.17	1.17	1.17
GO Central Europe	6.76	1.69	0.52	0.52	0.65	1.69	1.69	1.69
GO Northern Europe	8.84	2.21	0.68	0.68	0.85	2.21	2.21	2.21
GO Southern Europe	6.76	1.69	0.52	0.52	0.65	1.69	1.69	1.69

67. Roll up both **TOTAL COMPANY** and **Total Year** values in the viewer and they come up to 52 both ways, which means that the 4 4 5 proportion was allocated properly by the subsidiary.

68. Open the **GO Americas Expenses** view of the **Expenses** cube.

69. Change the **Subsidiaries** dimension to display **GO AMERICAS REGION** and then click on **Recalculate**.

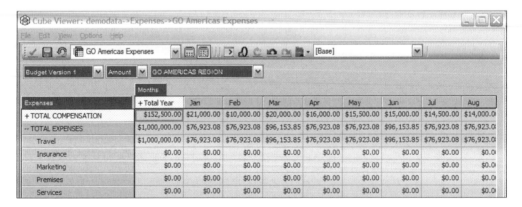

Expenses	+ Total Year	Jan	Feb	Mar	Apr	May	Jun	Jul	Aug
+ TOTAL COMPENSATION	$152,500.00	$21,000.00	$10,000.00	$20,000.00	$16,000.00	$15,500.00	$15,000.00	$14,500.00	$14,000.0
-- TOTAL EXPENSES	$1,000,000.00	$76,923.08	$76,923.08	$96,153.85	$76,923.08	$76,923.08	$96,153.85	$76,923.08	$76,923.0
Travel	$1,000,000.00	$76,923.08	$76,923.08	$96,153.85	$76,923.08	$76,923.08	$96,153.85	$76,923.08	$76,923.0
Insurance	$0.00	$0.00	$0.00	$0.00	$0.00	$0.00	$0.00	$0.00	$0.0
Marketing	$0.00	$0.00	$0.00	$0.00	$0.00	$0.00	$0.00	$0.00	$0.0
Premises	$0.00	$0.00	$0.00	$0.00	$0.00	$0.00	$0.00	$0.00	$0.0
Services	$0.00	$0.00	$0.00	$0.00	$0.00	$0.00	$0.00	$0.00	$0.0

70. Right-click on **Total Year** and **Premises**, click on **Data Spread**, and then **Relative Proportional Spread**.

71. In the **Cube** list select **Spread_Profile_SubsByMonth**. Under **Dimensions**, click on **SpreadMethod**, select **Subsidiary**, and then click **OK**, as shown in the following screenshot:

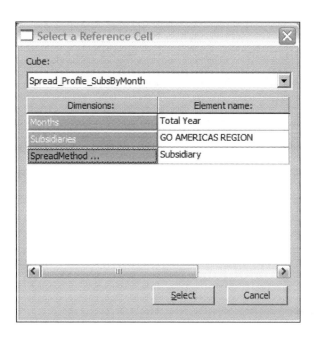

72. Click on **Select** and in the **Value** box type **2000000**, as shown in the following screenshot, and click on **Apply**.

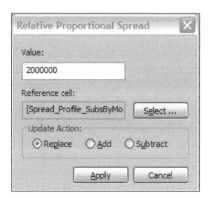

73. The result appears as shown in the following screenshot:

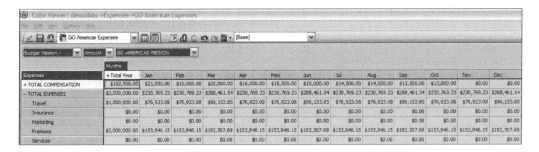

74. The result has been allocated along two dimensions, both **Months** and **Subsidiaries**.

75. Close **Cube Viewer** without saving any changes.

How it works...

In this recipe, we have created three Spread Profile cubes that can be used to spread data to other cubes. These are Lookup cubes. We have also created one Virtual cube (**Spread_Profiles_SubsByMonth**) that allocates data from one cube (**Spread_Profiles**) by the **Subsidiaries** dimension in another cube (**Spread_Profiles_Subsidiary**).

There's more...

Most of the spreading methods available under the **Data Spread** menu on **Cube Viewer** can also be applied through a special syntax and can be entered directly in cells in **Cube Viewer**.

Data spreading syntax cannot be used for Relative Proportional Spread, Relative Percent Adjustment, Repeat Leaves, and Equal Spread Leaves methods. The user interface should be used to apply any of these methods. Similar is the case when a user wants to spread across a selected range of cells; spreading syntax cannot be used in this case either.

Each data spreading syntax expression consists of the following components:

- ▶ Method Code
- ▶ Data Action (optional)
- ▶ Direction Indicators
- ▶ Method Parameter

An example would be **S+<>100**. In this statement S is the method code, + is the data action, <> are direction indicators, and 100 is the method parameter.

Component	Description	Example
Method Code	One or two character code for a data spreading method.	S is the method code for the Equal Spread spreading method.
Data Action	Indicates whether spread values should replace, be added to, or be subtracted from the existing cell values.	Replace – If we do not specify an action, TM1 replaces the existing cell values with the spread values.
		Add – Plus sign (+) adds spread values to the existing cell values.
		Subtract – Tilde (~) subtracts spread values from the existing cell values.
Direction Indicators	Indicates the direction to spread data relative to the point of insertion. The cell from which we initiate data spreading is always included in the spreading. We can use any combination of direction indicators in an expression.	Pipe (	) – Spreads values below the point of insertion.
		Caret (^) – Spreads values above the point of insertion.
		Right arrow (>) – Spreads values to the right of the point of insertion.
		Left arrow (<) – Spreads values to the left of the point of insertion.
Method Parameter	Supplies all parameters required to execute a given spreading method.	

The TM1 user guide should be referenced for a detailed listing of various spreading methods, along with their codes and parameters. For example, the Proportional Spread method has code P, the value to spread needs to be specified while using the syntax for data spread. Typical syntax in this case would be P<>100 which proportionally spreads the value of 100 to all leaf level cells on the row of insertion, and replaces the existing cell values. The user just needs to enter the code (P<>100) for a cell in Cube Viewer and press enter.

Moving balances from last month to next month

Similar to the functionality of lookup cubes, as discussed in the preceding recipe, element attributes can also be used to lookup information. This has been made possible by providing **ATTRN/ATTRS** functions, which can be used to pull data from the attributes of a dimension. While the **ATTRS** function returns a string attribute of a specified element of a dimension, **ATTRN** returns a numerical attribute.

The syntax of both versions are:

```
ATTRS(Dimension, Element, Attribute)
ATTRN(Dimension,Element,Attribute)
```

These are frequently used to lookup an element based on the value of an attribute. In this recipe, we will extend the concept while we try to move balances from last month to next month.

Getting ready

Ensure that the TM1 Admin Server service is started and demodata TM1 Server is running. Open TM1 Architect from the **Start menu**.

How to do it...

1. In the **Server Explorer** window create a new dimension with the structure as shown in the following screenshot:

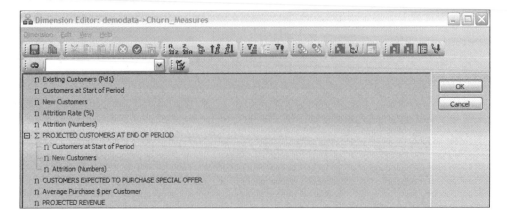

2. **Attrition (Numbers)**, which is a child of **PROJECTED CUSTOMERS AT END OF PERIOD**, has the element weight changed to minus **1**. For all of the other child elements of **PROJECTED CUSTOMERS AT END OF PERIOD**, the element weight is **1**.

3. Save the dimension as **Churn_Measures**.

4. Click on **OK** to close the **Dimension Editor** and return to **Server Explorer**.

5. In **Server Explorer** create a new cube called **Customer_Churn** with the following dimensions:

    ❑   Months

    ❑   Churn_Measures

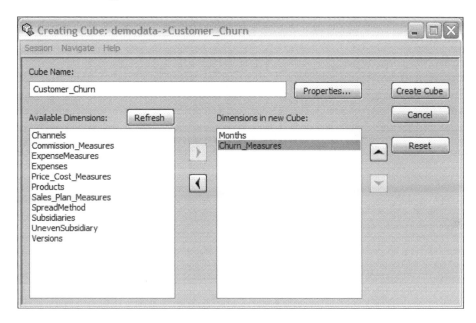

6. Double-click on the **Customer_Churn** cube to open in **Cube Viewer**.

7. Swap **Churn_Measures** and **Months**.

8. Click on **Churn_Measures** to open in **Subset Editor**. Click on **All** and then **OK**.

9. Click on **Months** and then **All**. Select all leaf level elements in **Subset Editor** and click on **OK**.

10. Click on **Recalculate** to show in **Cube Viewer**.

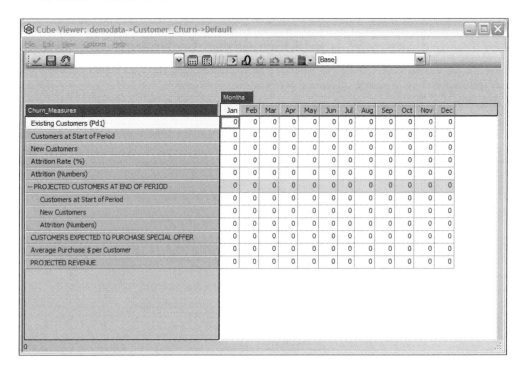

11. Leave the view open and return to the **Server Explorer** window.

12. Create `ChurnData.csv` to load data to the cube, as shown, and save in `C:\ Program Files\cognos\TM1\Custom\TM1Data\TI_Data`.

	A	B	C
1	Existing Customers (Pd1)	Jan	12000
2	New Customers	Jan	15000
3	Attrition Rate (%)	Jan	0.04
4	AveragePurchase $ per Customer	Jan	50
5	New Customers	Feb	7000
6	Attrition Rate (%)	Feb	0.04
7	AveragePurchase $ per Customer	Feb	50
8	New Customers	Mar	8000
9	Attrition Rate (%)	Mar	0.05
10	AveragePurchase $ per Customer	Mar	100
11	New Customers	Apr	8000
12	Attrition Rate (%)	Apr	0.02
13	AveragePurchase $ per Customer	Apr	300
14	New Customers	May	9000
15	Attrition Rate (%)	May	0.05
16	AveragePurchase $ per Customer	May	300
17	New Customers	Jun	9000
18	Attrition Rate (%)	Jun	0.05
19	AveragePurchase $ per Customer	Jun	100
20	New Customers	Jul	9000
21	Attrition Rate (%)	Jul	0.05
22	AveragePurchase $ per Customer	Jul	200

13. Create a TI process in **Server Explorer** to read the CSV, as shown in the following screenshot:

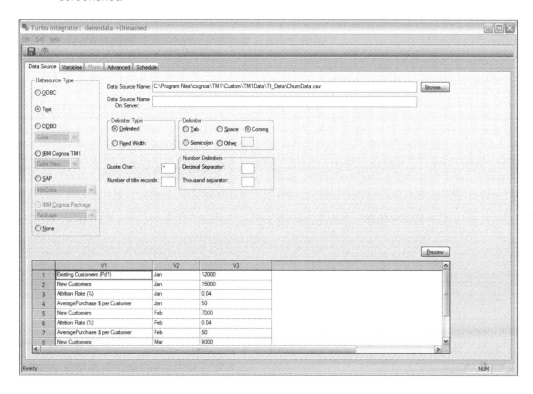

14. Move to the **Variables** tab on the TI process and map the following:

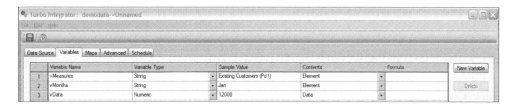

15. In the **Maps** tab click on **Update Cube** and for **Cube Name** select **Customer_Churn**.

TM1 worksheet functions are available (valid only in worksheets) to send numeric and string values to a TM1 cube and can be used instead of TI processes here. DBS and DBSS are two such functions to send numeric and string data, respectively. The TM1 Developers Guide needs to be referred to for detailed listing of TM1 worksheet functions and their documentation.

16. In the **Dimensions** tab assign the dimensions, as shown in the following screenshot:

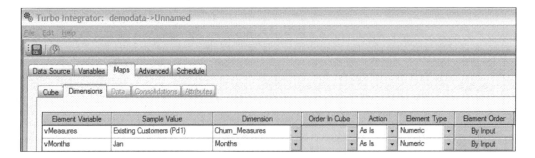

17. Click on the **Advanced** tab and the tabs within to generate the scripts.

18. Save the process as **LoadChurnDataCSV** and **Run** the process.

19. Close **Turbo Integrator** and **Recalculate** the view, as shown in the following screenshot:

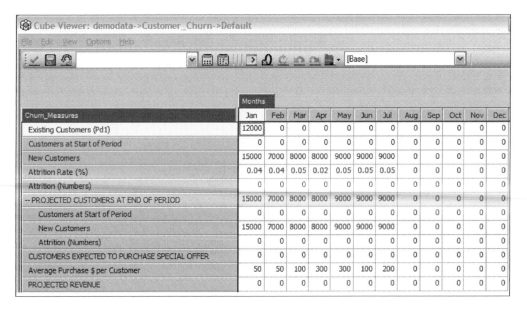

20. Leave the view open and return to the **Server Explorer** window.

21. Create a new rule in the **Customer_Churn** cube.

22. Enter the following rule to move **Existing Customers (Pd1)** to **Customers at Start of Period**:

```
['Customers at Start of Period','Jan' ]  = N:['Existing Customers
(Pd1)','Jan' ] ;
```

23. Enter the following rule to multiply **Customers at Start of Period** by **Attrition Rate (%)** and store the value **in Attrition (Numbers)**.

```
['Attrition (Numbers)' ] = N:['Customers at Start of Period' ] *
['Attrition Rate (%)' ] ;
```

24. Enter the following rule to calculate the number of **CUSTOMERS EXPECTED TO PURCHASE SPECIAL OFFER**, which is 90% of the **Customers at Start of Period**.

```
['CUSTOMERS EXPECTED TO PURCHASE SPECIAL OFFER' ] = N:(['Customers
at Start of Period' ] *.9);
```

25. Enter the following rule to calculate **PROJECTED REVENUE**.

```
['PROJECTED REVENUE' ] = N:['CUSTOMERS EXPECTED TO PURCHASE
SPECIAL OFFER' ] * ['Average Purchase $ per Customer' ] ;
```

Rules Editor: demodata: Customer_Churn

File Edit View Insert Tools Help

```
1  ['Customers at Start of Period','Jan' ]  = N:['Existing Customers (Pd1)','Jan' ] ;
2  ['Attrition (Numbers)' ] = N:['Customers at Start of Period' ] * ['Attrition Rate (%)' ] ;
3  ['CUSTOMERS EXPECTED TO PURCHASE SPECIAL OFFER' ] = N:(['Customers at Start of Period' ] *.9);
4  ['PROJECTED REVENUE' ] = N:['CUSTOMERS EXPECTED TO PURCHASE SPECIAL OFFER' ] * ['Average Purchase $ per Customer' ] ;
5
```

26. Save and **Recalculate** the view.

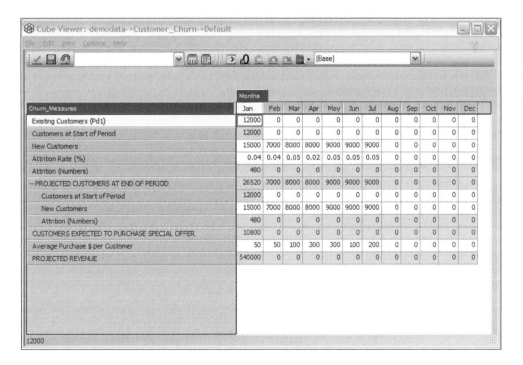

Churn_Measures	Months Jan	Feb	Mar	Apr	May	Jun	Jul	Aug	Sep	Oct	Nov	Dec
Existing Customers (Pd1)	12000	0	0	0	0	0	0	0	0	0	0	0
Customers at Start of Period	12000	0	0	0	0	0	0	0	0	0	0	0
New Customers	15000	7000	8000	8000	9000	9000	9000	0	0	0	0	0
Attrition Rate (%)	0.04	0.04	0.05	0.02	0.05	0.05	0.05	0	0	0	0	0
Attrition (Numbers)	480	0	0	0	0	0	0	0	0	0	0	0
--PROJECTED CUSTOMERS AT END OF PERIOD	26520	7000	8000	8000	9000	9000	9000	0	0	0	0	0
Customers at Start of Period	12000	0	0	0	0	0	0	0	0	0	0	0
New Customers	15000	7000	8000	8000	9000	9000	9000	0	0	0	0	0
Attrition (Numbers)	480	0	0	0	0	0	0	0	0	0	0	0
CUSTOMERS EXPECTED TO PURCHASE SPECIAL OFFER	10800	0	0	0	0	0	0	0	0	0	0	0
Average Purchase $ per Customer	50	50	100	300	300	100	200	0	0	0	0	0
PROJECTED REVENUE	540000	0	0	0	0	0	0	0	0	0	0	0

12000

27. Now we need to pull over the **PROJECTED CUSTOMERS AT END OF PERIOD** in **Jan** to the **Customers at Start of Period** for **Feb**.

28. In the **Rules Editor** for **Customer_Churn** cube on next line type the following:

    ```
    ['Customers at Start of Period' ] = N:
    ```

29. Click on **Insert Cube Reference** and for **Cube** select **Customer_Churn**.

30. Click on the **Subset Editor** icon for **Churn_Measures** and select **PROJECTED CUSTOMERS AT END OF PERIOD**, as shown in the following screenshot:

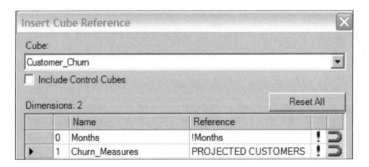

31. Click on **OK** to return to the **Rules Editor** and add a semicolon to the end:

    ```
    ['Customers at Start of Period' ] = N: DB('Customer_Churn',
    !Months, 'PROJECTED CUSTOMERS AT END OF PERIOD');
    ```

32. `!Months` will retrieve the current month name for the given data point. Instead, we want to retrieve the previous month to pull that data into the starting balance of this current month. We will use the `ATTRS` function in the place of `!Months` to retrieve the previous attribute for any given month.

33. In the preceding snippet of code replace `!Months` with:

    ```
    ATTRS('Months',!Months,'Previous')
    ```

34. The preceding function will return the **Previous** attribute for the current element (`!Months`), in the current cube (`Customer_Churn`), in the **Months** dimension.

35. The code now looks like this:

```
['Customers at Start of Period' ] = N: DB('Customer_Churn', ATT
RS('Months',!Months,'Previous'), 'PROJECTED CUSTOMERS AT END OF
PERIOD');
```

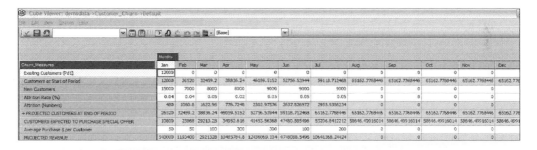

36. Save the rule and **Recalculate** the view.

37. In the preceding screenshot **PROJECTED CUSTOMERS AT END OF PERIOD** for **Jan** has been transferred to **Customers at Start of Period** for **Feb**, and so on.

38. In the **Rules Editor** for the **Customer_Churn** cube, add **SKIPCHECK** at the start of the rule statements and **FEEDERS** at the end of rules statements.

39. After **FEEDERS** type the following:

```
['Existing Customers (Pd1)','Jan' ] => ['Customers at Start of
Period' ,'Jan'] ;
['Attrition Rate (%)' ] => ['Attrition (Numbers)' ] ;
['Customers at Start of Period' ] => ['CUSTOMERS EXPECTED TO
PURCHASE SPECIAL OFFER' ] ;
['Average Purchase $ per Customer' ] => ['PROJECTED REVENUE' ] ;
['PROJECTED CUSTOMERS AT END OF PERIOD' ] => DB('Customer_Churn',
ATTRS('Months',!Months,'NEXT'), 'Customers at Start of Period');
```

40. In order to feed the **Customers at Start of Period**, we need to place a marker in the **PROJECTED CUSTOMERS AT END OF PERIOD** to push to the **Next** month.

41. The code snippet looks as shown in the following screenshot:

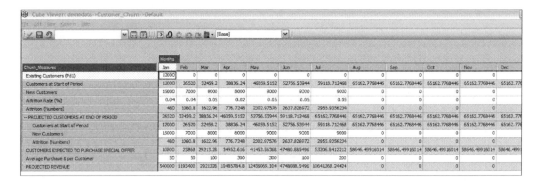

42. Save and **Recalculate** the view.

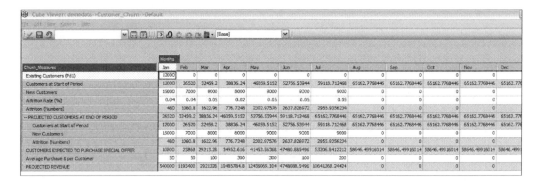

43. Now we want to adjust the rules so the opening and closing balances do not aggregate across time.

44. In the **Customer_Churn** view click on **Months** to open in **Subset Editor**.

45. Click on **All**, then on **Total Year**, and then click on **OK**.

46. Click on **Recalculate** and then expend **Total Year** and **Q1**.

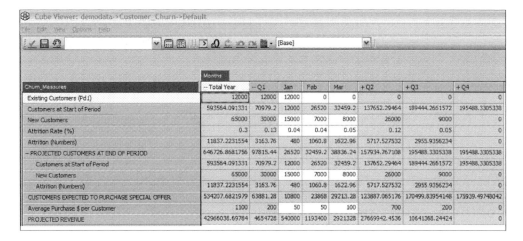

47. Open the rules for the **Cutomer_Churn** cube.

48. Replace the rule for **Customers at Start of Period** at line number 2 with the following:

```
['Customers at Start of Period',{'Jan','Q1','Total Year'} ]  =
N:['Existing Customers (Pd1)','Jan' ] ;
```

49. Remove :N from line number 7 for **Customers at Start of Period**. This will override the aggregation by allowing the **Customers at Start of Period** to be computed at the consolidated level as well as at the base level.

50. Add the following rules before the **FEEDERS** to set the year and quarters to the last month closing balance:

```
['PROJECTED CUSTOMERS AT END OF PERIOD','Q1' ] = C:['Mar' ] ;
['PROJECTED CUSTOMERS AT END OF PERIOD','Q2' ] = C:['Jun' ] ;
['PROJECTED CUSTOMERS AT END OF PERIOD','Q3' ] = C:['Sep' ] ;
['PROJECTED CUSTOMERS AT END OF PERIOD','Q4' ] = C:['Dec' ] ;
```

51. Remove the last **FEEDER** statement as we have removed :N from **Customers at Start of Period** on line number 7. Now this rule is being calculated for consolidated levels as well as the N level.

52. The code snippet now looks as shown in the following screenshot:

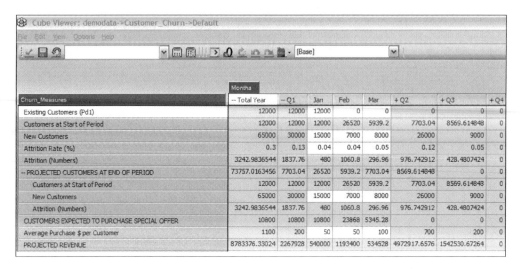

```
   SKIPCHECK;
   ['Customers at Start of Period',{'Jan','Q1','Total Year'}] = N:['Existing Customers (Pd1)','Jan'];
   ['Attrition (Numbers)'] = N:['Customers at Start of Period'] * ['Attrition Rate (%)'];
   ['CUSTOMERS EXPECTED TO PURCHASE SPECIAL OFFER'] = N:{['Customers at Start of Period'] *.9};
   ['PROJECTED REVENUE'] = N:['CUSTOMERS EXPECTED TO PURCHASE SPECIAL OFFER'] * ['Average Purchase $ per Customer'];

   ['Customers at Start of Period'] = DB('Customer_Churn', ATTRS('Months',(Months,'Previous'), 'PROJECTED CUSTOMERS AT END OF PERIOD');

   ['PROJECTED CUSTOMERS AT END OF PERIOD','Q1'] = C:['Mar'];
   ['PROJECTED CUSTOMERS AT END OF PERIOD','Q2'] = C:['Jun'];
   ['PROJECTED CUSTOMERS AT END OF PERIOD','Q3'] = C:['Sep'];
   ['PROJECTED CUSTOMERS AT END OF PERIOD','Q4'] = C:['Dec'];

   FEEDERS;

   ['Existing Customers (Pd1)','Jan'] => ['Customers at Start of Period','Jan'];
   ['Attrition Rate (%)'] => ['Attrition (Numbers)'];
   ['Customers at Start of Period'] => ['CUSTOMERS EXPECTED TO PURCHASE SPECIAL OFFER'];
   ['Average Purchase $ per Customer'] => ['PROJECTED REVENUE'];
```

53. Save and close the **Rules Editor** and views and return to the **Server Explorer**.

54. In **Server Explorer**, right-click on the **Customer_Churn** cube and click on **Unload Cube** to unload the selected cube from the server's memory.

55. Open the default view of **Customer_Churn**, click on **Months**, then **All**, then on **OK**, and swap **Months** with **Churn_Measures**. Similarly, for **Churn_Measures**, click to open in **Subset Editor** and click on **All**. Click on **OK** and then **Recalculate**.

Churn_Measures	-- Total Year	-- Q1	Jan	Feb	Mar	+ Q2	+ Q3	+ Q4
Existing Customers (Pd1)	12000	12000	12000	0	0	0	0	0
Customers at Start of Period	12000	12000	12000	26520	5939.2	7703.04	8569.614848	0
New Customers	65000	30000	15000	7000	8000	26000	9000	0
Attrition Rate (%)	0.3	0.13	0.04	0.04	0.05	0.12	0.05	0
Attrition (Numbers)	3242.9836544	1837.76	480	1060.8	296.96	976.742912	428.4807424	0
-- PROJECTED CUSTOMERS AT END OF PERIOD	73757.0163456	7703.04	26520	5939.2	7703.04	8569.614848	0	0
Customers at Start of Period	12000	12000	12000	26520	5939.2	7703.04	8569.614848	0
New Customers	65000	30000	15000	7000	8000	26000	9000	0
Attrition (Numbers)	3242.9836544	1837.76	480	1060.8	296.96	976.742912	428.4807424	0
CUSTOMERS EXPECTED TO PURCHASE SPECIAL OFFER	10800	10800	10800	23868	5345.28	0	0	0
Average Purchase $ per Customer	1100	200	50	50	100	700	200	0
PROJECTED REVENUE	8783376.33024	2267928	540000	1193400	534528	4972917.6576	1542530.67264	0

56. Close all the open windows, saving the view as public default view.

How it works...

In this recipe, we have used attributes in rules and used them along with TI functions to move balances across periods.

By now we have implemented a completed churn model, using only a handful of rules and two attributes.

We have also discussed Virtual cubes, Lookup cubes, and Spread Profile cubes, and have used these to move, enter, and edit data.

9
Converting Currencies

In this chapter, we will cover:

- ► Creating currency dimension and attributes
- ► Creating a currency cube
- ► Populating currency attributes using control cubes
- ► Creating rules to apply exchange rates and calculate equivalent amount in target currency

Introduction

In the previous chapters, we have been discussing various aspects of TM1 modelling and rules to best analyze business data. Apart from obvious business requirements, an analyst may have to deal with multiple currencies and may have different reporting requirements. For example, our fictitious company has multiple subsidiaries that span across multiple regions and continents. Each of these may have a different currency. It is desirable to have central organizational reporting done in a common reporting currency. This calls for ways to tackle the existence of multiple local currencies, but using a single reporting currency. Again, currency rates may change with time making it more difficult to report in a single currency in a consistent manner.

Hence, in this chapter, we will demonstrate a combination of techniques in TM1, which allows us to deal with non-uniform currency issues. These techniques are primarily based on the following:

- ▶ Lookup cubes
- ▶ Attributes
- ▶ Rules
- ▶ Rules tracer
- ▶ Control cubes
- ▶ Dimension worksheets

Some of these, we have already seen in previous chapters and some we will learn afresh.

Creating currency dimension and attributes

In this recipe, we will create a currency and currency type dimension for our model. We will also add a currency attribute to existing **Subsidiaries** and **ExpenseMeasures** dimension.

Getting ready

Ensure that TM1 Admin Server is started and demodata TM1 server is running. Open TM1 Architect from **Start Menu**.

How to do it...

1. Open **Server Explorer** window for demodata TM1 server.
2. In the Server Explorer window, expand **Dimensions**, right-click on **Subsidiaries** and then click on **Edit Element Attributes**.

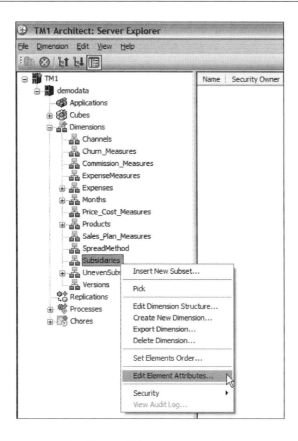

3. From the **Edit** menu in **Attributes Editor**, click on **Add New Attribute**.

4. In the **Name** box, type **Currency** and click on **OK**.

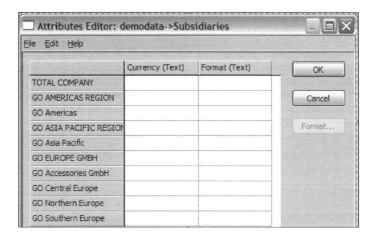

5. Similarly, add **Currency** attribute to the **ExpenseMeasures** dimension.

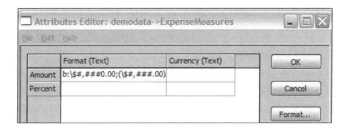

6. Return to the **Server Explorer** window, right-click on the **ExpenseMeasures** dimension and click on **Edit Dimension Structure** to open the dimension in **Dimension Editor**.

7. Click on the **Percent** element and then select **Insert Element** from the **Edit** menu.

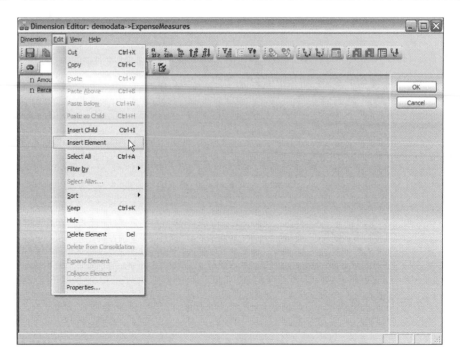

8. Add the following elements:

   ❏ Reporting USD

   ❏ Reporting EUR

   ❏ Reporting JPY

9. Click on **OK** to show the resulting dimension.

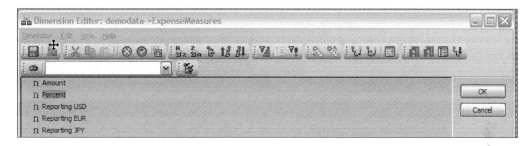

10. Save and close the dimension to return to the **Server Explorer** window.

11. In the **Server Explorer** window, right-click on **Dimensions** and click on **Create New Dimension**.

12. In the **Dimension Editor** from the **Edit** menu, click on **Insert Element** and add the following currency symbols:

    ❏ BRL

    ❏ GBP

    ❏ CAD

    ❏ EUR

    ❏ JPY

    ❏ SEK

    ❏ USD

13. Save the dimension and name it **Currency**.

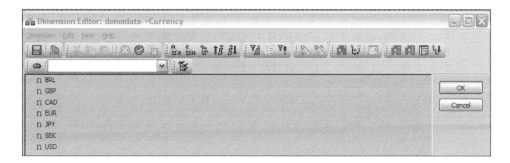

14. Close the **Dimension Editor** to return to the **Server Explorer**.

15. Similarly, create a new dimension with the name **CurrencyType** and consisting of the following elements:

  ❑ Reporting

  ❑ Yearly Rate

  ❑ Spot Rate

  ❑ Monthly Rate

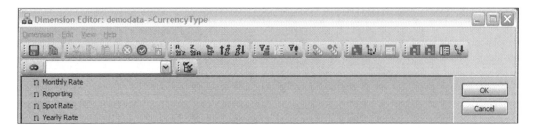

16. Now again, create a new dimension called **CurrencyConvertTo** with the following elements. The elements we are going to include in this dimension are the same as the elements we have inserted in the **Currency** dimension, but as we cannot use the same dimension more than once in the same cube, we are creating a copy. We can also create the dimension by performing a **Save As** on **Currency** dimension.

  ❑ BRL

  ❑ GBP

  ❑ CAD

  ❑ EUR

  ❑ JPY

  ❑ SEK

  ❑ USD

17. Close the **Dimension Editor** and return to the **Server Explorer** window.

How it works...

In the preceding recipe, we have added a **Currency** attributes to **ExpenseMeasures** and **Subsidiaries** dimension. This will associate the **Currency** as a property of each element of the dimension.

We have also added currency-specific elements to the **ExpenseMeasures** dimension (Reporting USD/JPY). Hence, the **Reporting JPY** element will have reporting figures in Japanese yen, and should have **JPY** as the **Currency** attribute. Users can add similar elements to **ExpenseMeasures** dimension, specific to the desired currency, and **Currency** attribute for each should be set accordingly, for which we will write rules in later sections.

We have also added a **Currency** and **CurrencyConvertTo** dimension, which has all the desired currencies as elements. **Currency** dimension has all desired base currencies while **CurrencyConvertTo** will have target currencies. Hence, if a user intends to convert **USD** to **JPY**, then the **Currency** dimension will point to **USD** while **CurrencyConvertTo** points to **JPY**.

We will also need a rule to set **Currency** attribute for **Subsidiaries** dimension correctly. Hence, **GO AMERICAS REGION** and its children should have **USD** as **Currency** attribute. We will discuss this rule afterwards.

The design requirement is to have the **Amount** element in the **ExpenseMeasure** dimension in local currency, which depends on the **Subsidiary** it is associated with. Hence, for example, if a cell corresponds to **GO Americas** (rule will set **Currency** attribute for **GO Americas** as **USD**) and **Amount**, then the base currency would be **USD** (Amount is interpreted as in **USD**). Such a cell will have a corresponding value for the **Amount JPY** element (having **Currency** attribute set to **JPY** using a rule) as well and should be calculated after conversion from base currency (**USD** in this case) to target currency (**JPY** in this case), again by a rule (**CurrencyConvertTo** point to **JPY** in this case).

We will discuss these rules in the following sections.

Creating a currency cube

Now in this recipe, we will create a currency cube to hold currency exchange rates data, which is assumed to be updated on a monthly basis. We are assuming that the business wants to apply updated rates on a monthly basis for simplicity. In real-life scenarios, it may vary and dimensions, cubes, and model may change accordingly, but the basic process remains same. If business wants to apply new rates on a daily basis, then the currency cube should include a time dimension having granularity, untill day level. In our case, we are using **MONTHS** dimension for time aspect and hence, assuming that the business is interested in keeping track of the updated exchange rate on a monthly basis.

Getting ready

Ensure that TM1 Admin Server is started and demodata TM1 data server is running. Open TM1 Architect from the **Start Menu**.

How to do it...

1. In the **Server Explorer** window, create a new cube with the name **zRate** and consisting of the following dimensions:

    ❑ Months

    ❑ CurrencyType

    ❑ Currency

    ❑ CurrencyConvertTo

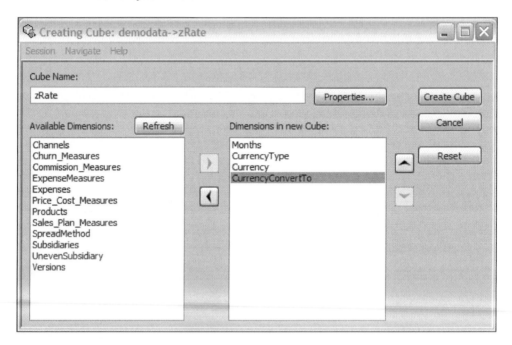

2. Create cube to return to the **Server Explorer**.
3. Double-click on the **zRate** cube to open it in the **Cube Viewer**.
4. Double-click on the **Months** dimension and click on **All** in **Subset Editor**.
5. In the drop-down for **Currency Type**, click on **Reporting**.
6. In the drop-down for the **Months** dimension in **Cube Viewer**, select **Jan** and click on **Recalculate**.

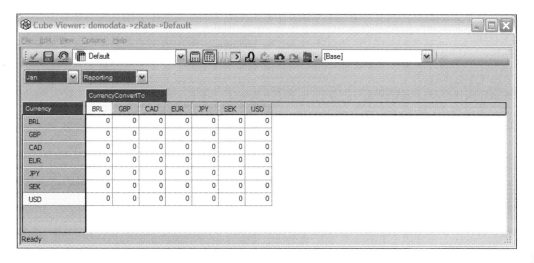

7. Save the view as default view.

8. Minimize the **Cube Viewer** window and create an excel file to load currency rates in the cube.

9. Name the excel file `CurrencyRates.xls` with the data as shown in the following screenshot:

B2				f_x	1		
	A	B	C	D	E	F	G	H
1		BRL	GBP	CAD	EUR	JPY	SEK	USD
2	BRL	1	0.0757	0.5097	0.4377	0.1453	0.2569	0.5713
3	GBP	0.324	1	0.4908	0.7925	0.4725	0.8352	0.5108
4	CAD	0.66	0.0366	1	0.6142	0.9624	0.1701	0.0405
5	EUR	0.4088	0.2617	0.6193	1	0.5962	0.1057	0.6445
6	JPY	0.5682	1.593	3.858	67.71	1	0.6746	8.098
7	SEK	0.8763	0.9617	5.8713	9.454	0.6523	1	6.111
8	USD	0.6343	0.9574	0.9608	0.5514	0.9249	0.1635	1

10. Copy all the rates by selecting cells **B2:H8**, as shown in the following screenshot:

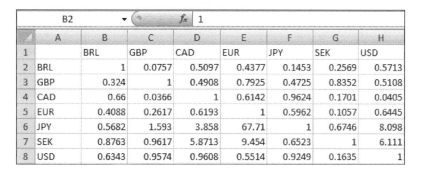

11. Select all the cells in the **Cube Viewer** and paste.

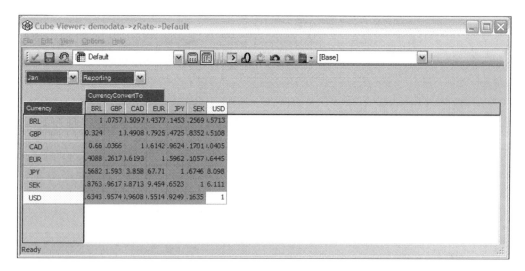

12. Click on the **Automatic Recalculate** icon and copy the cells for each **Month** in the same fashion so that each **Month** will have the same exchange rates. We need to copy the exchange rates for each month at a time since cube viewer is two dimensional and we need **Currency** and **CurrencyConvertTo** along the two dimensions. A small rule can also be written in the fashion we described earlier to ensure that diagonal elements are always equal to one. Similarly, cells below diagonal axis will be 1/x where x are cell values above diagonal axis. For the sake of simplicity, we are updating data manually from the excel sheet.

13. Close the **Cube Viewer** to return to **Server Explorer**.

How it works...

In this recipe, we have added a **zRate** cube to hold exchange rates for various base and target currency combinations, which can be updated on a monthly basis.

We can add a variety of rules here. So, instead of manually populating the whole of today using excel, rules can be written to load currency exchange data, which would be less tedious.

For the sake of simplicity, we have shown data entered manually.

Populating currency attributes using control cubes

In this recipe, we will be creating rules to populate the **Currency** attributes for the **ExpenseMeasures** and **Subsidiaries** dimensions.

Getting started

Ensure that TM1 Admin Server service is started and demodata TM1 server is running. Open TM1 Architect from the **Start Menu**.

How to do it...

1. In the **Server Explorer** from the **View** menu, click on **Display Control Objects**. This will expose control cubes in the **Server Explorer** window, which are used to store information about the application, that is, metadata including attributes. We are mainly interested in the control cube by the name of **}ElementAttributes_ Subsidiaries** 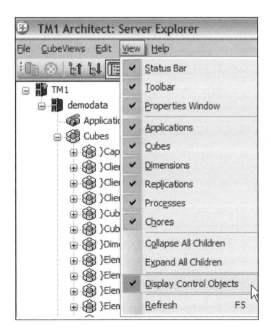 that is used to store element attributes for **Subsidiaries** dimension. We are going to write a rule on the cube to make maintenance of the currency attribute automatic. We will add a rule to apply parent currency rate to its children.

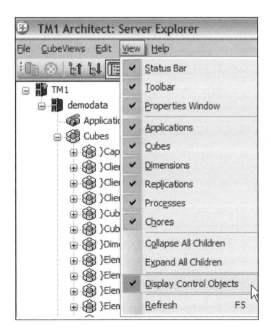

2. Right-click on **}ElementAttributes_Subsidiaries** and click on **Create Rule** to open in advanced **Rules Editor**.

3. The rule uses the following functions:

Function	Syntax	Notes
ELPAR	ELPAR(dimension,element,index)	Returns the parent of an element in the specified dimension. Index refers to the index of the dimension hierarchy which will usually be 1 unless there is more then one hierarchy in the dimension.
IF	IF(expression,true_value,false_value)	Returns a true value if logical expression specified is true otherwise it returns a false value.

4. In the **Rules Editor**, enter the following rule:

```
['Currency'] =S:IF(ELPAR('Subsidiaries',!Subsidiaries,1)@='GO
AMERICAS REGION','USD',continue);
```

5. The rule states that for the currency, refer to the Element's parent. If parent is **GO AMERICAS REGION**, then the currency will be **USD**, otherwise `continue`.

6. The `continue` statement allows many rules over the same area and we will use **STET** at the end to allow cells not covered by this function to be entered manually.

7. Save the rule and return to the **Server Explorer** window.

8. Double-click on the **}ElementAttributes_Subsidiaries** cube and **Recalculate**.

9. Now add the following rules to the cube:

```
['Currency' ] =S:IF(ELPAR('Subsidiaries',!Subsidiaries,1)@='GO
 ASIA PACIFIC REGION','JPY',continue);
['Currency' ] =S:IF(ELPAR('Subsidiaries',!Subsidiaries,1)@='GO
 EUROPE GMBH','EUR',continue);
```

10. Save the rules and recalculate the view, as shown in the following screenshot. As stated previously, the rule will assign currency attribute to each subsidiary, however, in many real-life scenarios currency for each subsidiary is loaded from the source file itself through a TI process.

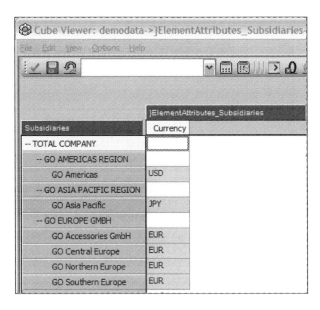

11. Close the **Rules Editor** and the view without saving the view.

12. In **Server Explorer** window, right-click on the control cube called **}ElementAttributes_ ExpenseMeasures** and calculate the view. We have applied formatting to **Amount** already with a dollar sign, but that does not mean that it's in **USD**. **Amount** is intended to be in local currency and the **$** sign just signifies any currency symbol for that matter.

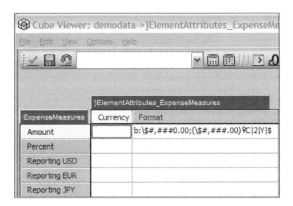

13. In **Server Explorer** window, right-click on **}ElementAttributes_ExpenseMeasures** and click on **Create Rule** to open the advanced **Rules Editor**. Now we will be assigning **Currency** attributes to **ExpenseMeasures**. We can just as well hard code these, but we will use rules to make this more flexible, which might be useful in real-life scenarios.

14. In the rule, we will be using **SUBST** function, which returns a substring of the given string. Its syntax is as follows:

```
SUBST(string,beginning_position,length)
```

15. Enter the following rule:

```
['Currency' ]   = S: IF(SUBST(!ExpenseMeasures,1,9)@='Reporting',
   SUBST(!ExpenseMeasures,11,3),  STET);
```

16. Save the rule and **Recalculate** the view as shown in the following screenshot:

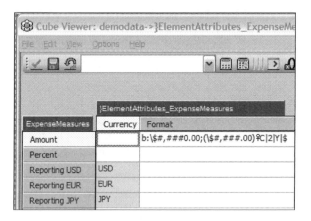

17. The rule refers to the element name to determine the value for the reporting currency. If we add a new reporting currency, according to the naming convention, applied to the previous element, then the rule will update the currency attribute automatically. In case of hard coding, we need to change the currency manually. For example, if a user adds a new measure element by name of **Reporting GBP**, then the rule will automatically save its **Currency** attribute to **GBP**. No need to manually go and update the attribute, just follow the naming convention while adding a new measure element.

18. Close all the control cube rules and views.

How it works...

In this recipe, we have two basic use cases. First is to populate the Currency attribute for each element in Subsidiaries dimension. We have written our first rule for on **}ElementAttributes_ Subsidiaries** for this.

Secondly, we want to provide flexibility to users so that they can add currency-specific measure elements such as **Reporting USD**, **Reporting JPY** (which are already added) and so on. **Currency** attributes for such elements should be populated by default based on the last three characters of the elements. For example, if a user adds Reporting GBP, then the rule should populate **Currency** attribute for the element with GBP. We have discussed such a rule in the second part of the recipe.

Creating rules to apply exchange rates and calculate an equivalent amount in target currency

In this section, we will write rules to apply conversion based on the zRate. We will use Currency attribute and previously created dimension.

Getting started

Ensure that TM1 Admin Server service is started and demodata TM1 server is running. Open TM1 Architect from the **Start Menu**.

How to do it...

1. In the **Server Explorer** window from the **View** menu, click on **Display Control Objects** to turn off display of the control cubes.

2. In the **Server Explorer** window, double-click on the **Expenses** cube and create a new view called **ReportingCurrencies**.

3. In the **Cube Viewer**, double-click on **ExpenseMeasures** and in **Subset Editor**, click on **All** and then on **OK**.

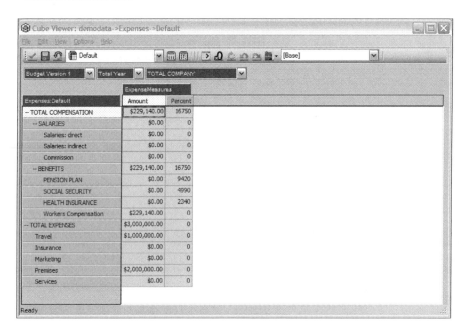

4. In the **Cube Viewer** window, click on **Recalculate** to update the view.

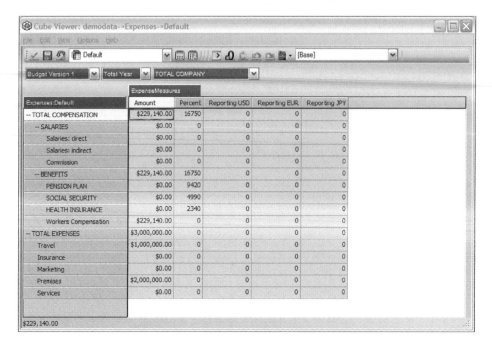

5. Add to the rules for **Expenses** cube by right-clicking on it and then selecting **Create Rule** in the **Server Explorer** window.

6. Now we will be multiplying the dollars by the exchange rate that will be pulled from **zRate** cube by using **FROM** currency specified as the attribute in **Subsidiaries** dimension and **TO** currency specified as the attribute in **ExpenseMeasures** dimension.

7. Enter the following code snippet just before the **FEEDERS** statement:

```
['Reporting USD'] = N:['Amount']*DB('zRate',!Months,
   'Reporting',ATTRS('Subsidiaries',!Subsidiaries,'Currency'),
   ATTRS('ExpenseMeasures',!ExpenseMeasures,'Currency'));
```

8. In preceding rule, we have inserted a cube reference to the **zRate** cube that can also be inserted in the code fragment by clicking on **Insert Cube Reference** in the **Rules Editor**. Hence, in preceding rule, we have calculated the **Amount** in **USD** and assigned it to **Reporting USD** (it has **USD** as **Currency** attribute as determined by the rule on **}ElementAttributes_ExpenseMeasures**). Base currency will be derived from the **Currency** attribute in the **Subsidiary** dimension. This attribute again is determined by a rule we have written on **}ElementAttributes_Subsidiaries**.

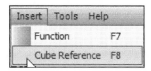

9. In the resulting dialog for **Cube**, specify **zRate** and for subset icon in **Reference**, **Reporting** needs to be selected from the **Subset Editor**.

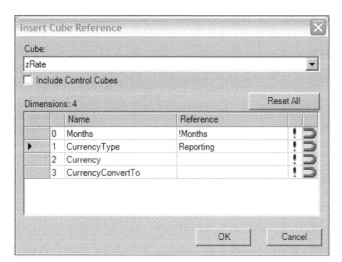

10. **ATTRS** function is used to get the **Currency** attribute of the **Subsidiaries** dimension for the current subsidiary.

11. The code will look like the following screenshot with the newly added highlighted part:

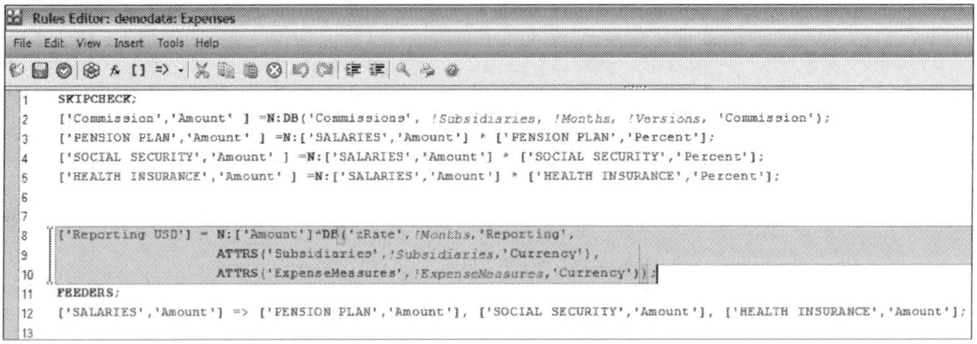

```
Rules Editor: demodata: Expenses
File  Edit  View  Insert  Tools  Help

1   SKIPCHECK;
2   ['Commission','Amount' ] =N:DB('Commissions', !Subsidiaries, !Months, !Versions, 'Commission');
3   ['PENSION PLAN','Amount' ] =N:['SALARIES','Amount'] * ['PENSION PLAN','Percent'];
4   ['SOCIAL SECURITY','Amount' ] =N:['SALARIES','Amount'] * ['SOCIAL SECURITY','Percent'];
5   ['HEALTH INSURANCE','Amount' ] =N:['SALARIES','Amount'] * ['HEALTH INSURANCE','Percent'];
6
7
8   ['Reporting USD'] = N:['Amount']*DB('zRate', !Months,'Reporting',
9                   ATTRS('Subsidiaries',!Subsidiaries,'Currency'),
10                  ATTRS('ExpenseMeasures', !ExpenseMeasures,'Currency'));
11  FEEDERS;
12  ['SALARIES','Amount'] => ['PENSION PLAN','Amount'], ['SOCIAL SECURITY','Amount'], ['HEALTH INSURANCE','Amount'];
13
```

12. Now add a feeder as shown in the following line of code:

```
['Amount'] => ['Reporting USD'];
```

13. The code will look like the following screenshot:

```
Rules Editor: demodata: Expenses
File  Edit  View  Insert  Tools  Help

1   SKIPCHECK;
2   ['Commission','Amount' ] =N:DB('Commissions', !Subsidiaries, !Months, !Versions, 'Commission');
3   ['PENSION PLAN','Amount' ] =N:['SALARIES','Amount'] * ['PENSION PLAN','Percent'];
4   ['SOCIAL SECURITY','Amount' ] =N:['SALARIES','Amount'] * ['SOCIAL SECURITY','Percent'];
5   ['HEALTH INSURANCE','Amount' ] =N:['SALARIES','Amount'] * ['HEALTH INSURANCE','Percent'];
6
7
8   ['Reporting USD'] = N:['Amount']*DB('zRate', !Months,'Reporting',
9                   ATTRS('Subsidiaries',!Subsidiaries,'Currency'),
10                  ATTRS('ExpenseMeasures', !ExpenseMeasures,'Currency'));
11
12  FEEDERS;
13  ['Amount'] => ['Reporting USD'];
14  ['SALARIES','Amount'] => ['PENSION PLAN','Amount'], ['SOCIAL SECURITY','Amount'], ['HEALTH INSURANCE','Amount'];
15
```

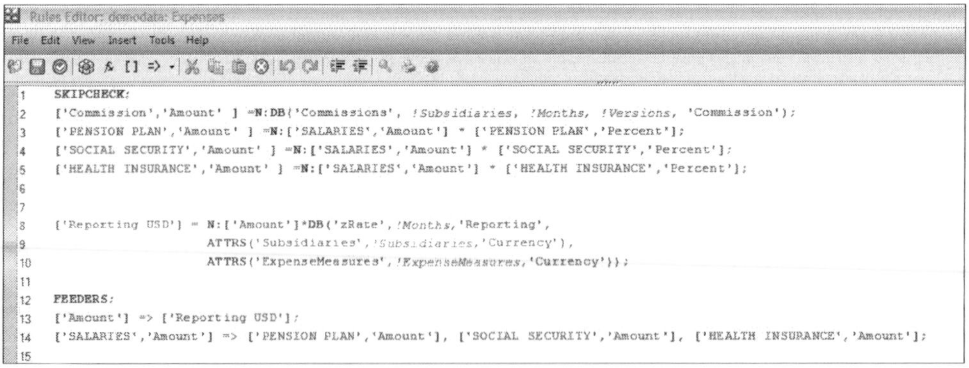

14. Copy the rule at line number 8 and modify for EUR and JPY as shown in the preceding screenshot. Instead of copy and paste, the assignment to the elements can also be done using single line of code using the following syntax:
    `[{'Reporting USD', 'Reporting JPY', 'Reporting EUR'}] =N:...` We are using copy paste for the sake of simplicity, so it's easier for readers to understand.

    ```
    ['Reporting JPY'] = N:['Amount']*DB('zRate',!Months,'Reporting',
      ATTRS('Subsidiaries',!Subsidiaries,'Currency'),
      ATTRS('ExpenseMeasures',!ExpenseMeasures,'Currency'));
    ['Reporting EUR'] = N:['Amount']*DB('zRate',!Months,'Reporting',
      ATTRS('Subsidiaries',!Subsidiaries,'Currency'),
      ATTRS('ExpenseMeasures',!ExpenseMeasures,'Currency'));
    ```

15. Copy the rule as shown in the following screenshot:

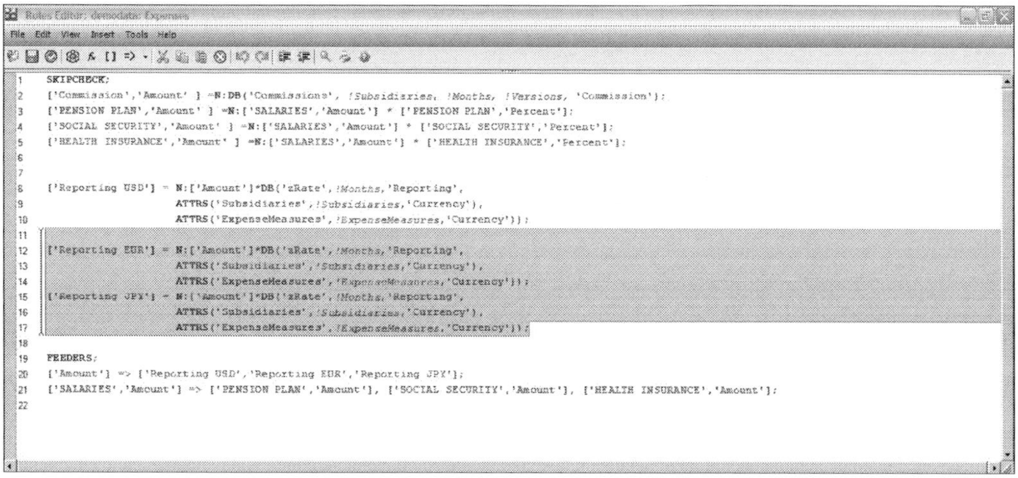

16. Modify the corresponding **FEEDER** statement as shown in the following line of code:

```
['Amount'] => ['Reporting USD','Reporting EUR','Reporting JPY'];
```

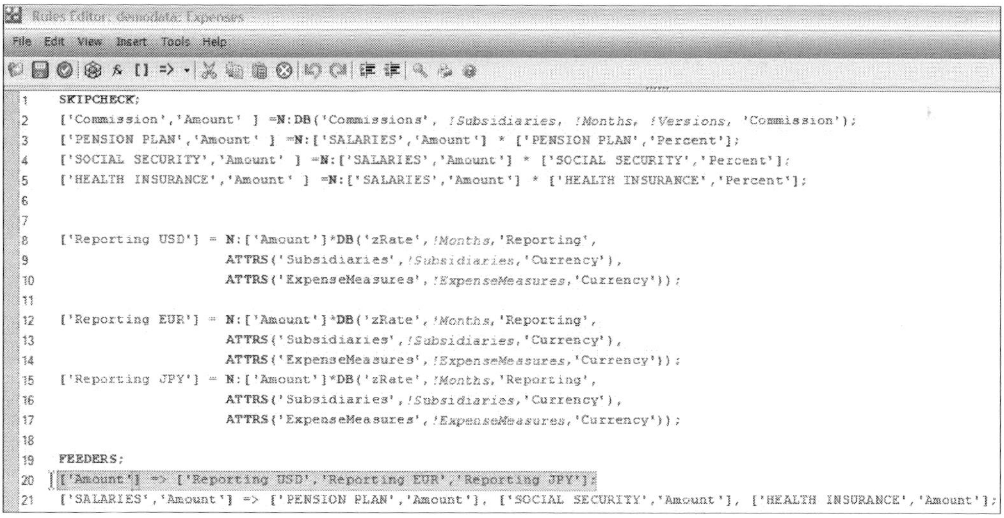

17. Save the rule and **Recalculate** the view.

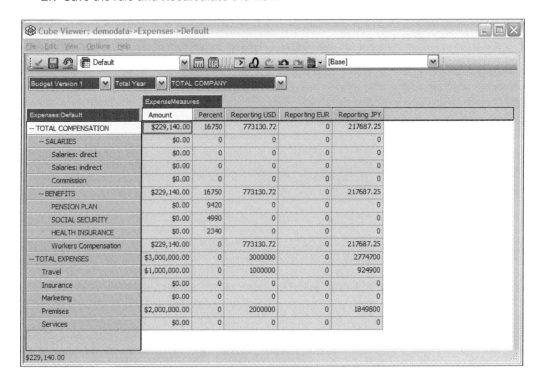

18. Close all open views and the **Rules Editor**.

How it works...

In this recipe, we have written rules to do currency conversion from base currency to the target currency. The rules populate currency-specific measures (Reporting USD, Reporting JPY, and Reporting EUR), for each subsidiary. The base currency is determined using the **ATTRS** function on **Subsidiaries** dimension. Target currency again is determined using the **ATTRS** function on **ExpenseMeasures** dimension. Hence, if a user has added an element to **ExpenseMeasures** with the name **Reporting GBP**, its **Currency** attribute is set to **GBP**. When the rule is applied on a cell, for example, at the intersection of Reporting GBP and a **Subsidiary** element **GO Central Europe**, **ATTRS** function on Subsidiaries will return EUR, which will be base currency. The function when applied to **ExpenseMeasures** will return **GBP**, which will be target currency. Hence, **zRate** cube cell will have **Currency** as **EUR**, **CurrencyConvertTo** as **GBP**, and current month will be returned and multiplied by base **Amount** and the result stored in **Reporting GBP**.

10
Modelling for Different Fiscal Requirements

In this chapter, we will cover:

- ▶ Adding a year dimension
- ▶ Creating a continuous time model

Introduction

In any BI/DW implementation, time dimension always plays a crucial role to the extent that having a clean and precise implementation of time dimension has become indispensable.

In TM1, time aspect can be included to facilitate time-based analysis of data. Hence, in this chapter, we will focus on creating and maintaining time dimension. The approach is similar to what we have for other dimensions.

Before starting with time dimension, it is very important to decide on the level of time granularity the business would need to analyze the data, and the existing granularity at the source that feeds data into the TM1 cubes.

This chapter will discuss two main implementations of time dimension in TM1. They are as follows:

- ▶ Discrete time dimension
- ▶ Continuous time dimension

Discrete time dimensions refer to the simplest form of implementations, which does not consider weekends or holidays. These are typically used for backward looking financial cubes. These are easier to maintain and intuitive to users.

However, these are not advisable where rolling forecasts need to be done.

Adding a year dimension

In this recipe, we are going to create a new version of **Franchise_Revenue** cube that contains **Year** dimension as well as **Months**. The year should contain three years starting with 2008, and next, we will load data for 2008.

Getting ready

Ensure that TM1 Admin Server service is started and demodata TM1 server is running. Open TM1 Architect from the **Start Menu**.

How to do it...

1. In the **Server Explorer**, create a new dimension with base level elements as follows:
    - **2008**
    - **2009**
    - **2010**

2. Save the dimension as **Years** and close the **Dimension Viewer** to return to **Server Explorer**.

3. Create a new cube called **Franchise_Revenue2** with following dimensions included:
    - Subsidiaries
    - Years
    - Months
    - Versions

4. The cube now appears in **Server Explorer** window as shown in the following screenshot:

5. Create `Franchiserev.CSV` to load data into **Franchise_Revenue2** cube as shown. Data in the MS Excel is for 2008 and **Month** column in the sheet has format **d-mmm**. Hence, the first row has data for `11th day of Jan 2008`.

	A	B	C	D
1	Subsidiaries	Month	Budget1	Budget2
2	GO Americas	11-Jan	1200	1250
3	GO Americas	11-Feb	1300	1350
4	GO Americas	11-Mar	1500	1450
5	GO Americas	11-Apr	1200	1000
6	GO Americas	11-May	1230	3212
7	GO Americas	11-Jun	1218	3453
8	GO Americas	11-Jul	1222	1220
9	GO Americas	11-Aug	1000	1000
10	GO Americas	11-Sep	2050	2500
11	GO Americas	11-Oct	54000	123434
12	GO Americas	11-Nov	1200	12344
13	GO Americas	11-Dec	12345	2132434
14	GO Asia Pacific	11-Jan	1250	1200
15	GO Asia Pacific	11-Feb	1350	1300
16	GO Asia Pacific	11-Mar	1450	1500
17	GO Asia Pacific	11-Apr	1000	1200
18	GO Asia Pacific	11-May	3212	1230
19	GO Asia Pacific	11-Jun	3453	1218
20	GO Asia Pacific	11-Jul	1220	1222

6. Place the `.csv` at `C:\Program Files\cognos\TM1\Custom\TM1Data\TI_Data`.

7. From the **Server Explorer** window, create a new TI process with the preceding file specified as **Data Source Name** and **Number of title records** specified to **1**. Click on **Preview** to show the sample data present in the file.

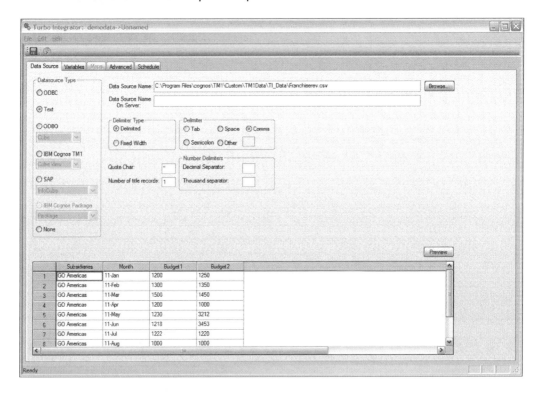

8. Click on the **Variables** tab. Name and map variables as shown in the following screenshot:

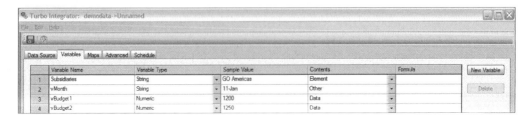

9. On the same tab, create a new variable called **vDate** with the following formula:

```
vDate=SUBST(vMonth,4,3);
```

10. The preceding ling of code will extract substring starting from the 4th position till three characters and load months into the variable **vDate**.

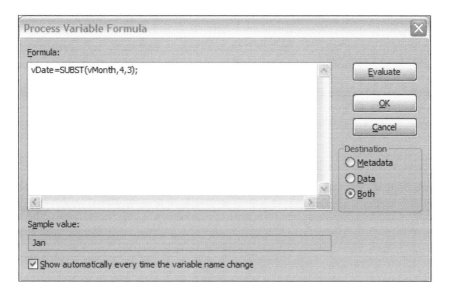

11. For **vDat**e in **Variables** tab, under **Variable Type**, **String** needs to be specified and under **Contents**, click on **Element**, as shown in the following screenshot:

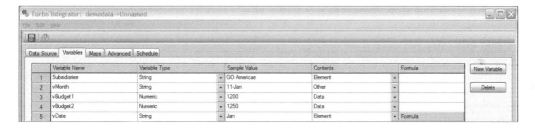

12. On the same **Variables** tab, create another variable called **vYear** with **Variable Type** as **String** and **Contents** as **Element**. Type the following formula:

```
vYear = '2008';
```

We are using the TI process to load data for **2008** only, hence we have hardcoded **vYear** to **2008**. As stated earlier, the **Months** column in MS Excel sheet has format as **d-mmm**, which has day and month part. Year part is assumed to be 2008 as the sheet is meant to have data for that year only. If we had other year's worth of data in the same spread sheet, then we should have used the **SUBST** function to extract year in the same way we had done for **vDate**.

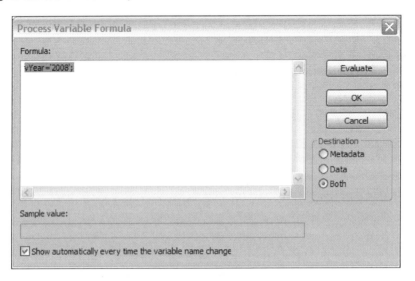

13. Completed, the **Variables** tab now looks like the following screenshot.

14. Now click on the **Maps** tab. Click on **Update Cube** and for **Cube Name** specify **Franchise_Revenue2**.

15. Click on the **Dimensions** tab and map variables with the dimensions they load, as shown in the following screenshot:

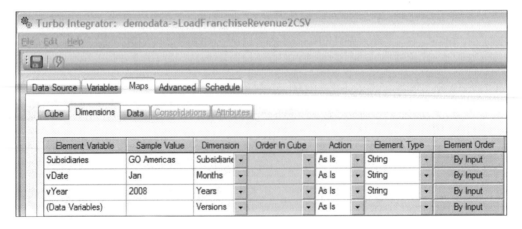

16. Click on the **Data** tab to specify mappings to measure elements, as shown in the following screenshot:

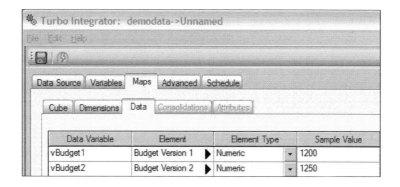

17. Click on the **Advanced** tab and all tabs underneath to generate common scripts.

18. Save the process as **LoadFranchiseRevenue2CSV** and run the process. Ignore the message by clicking on **OK**.

19. Close the **Turbo Integrator** and open the **Franchise_Revenue2 cube**.

20. On the **Default** view, swap **Months** and **Subsidiaries**, and then **Months** and **Versions**.

21. Double-click on **Months** to open in the **Subset Editor**. Click on **All**, *Ctrl+click* on **Q1** and **Q2**, as shown on the following screenshot, and click on **OK**.

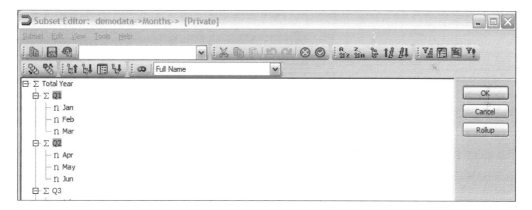

22. Drag **Years** to the column area (to the left of **Months**) to stack the **Dimensions**.

23. In the **Versions** list, select **Budget Version1**.

24. Click on **Recalculate** to refresh the view with data, as shown in the following screenshot:

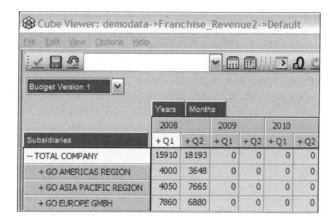

25. Save the view as default public view and close the view to return to **Server Explorer**.

26. The resulting cube proves useful in order to compare same months or quarters over time. If the user needs greater granularity or more time-specific information such as comparing weekends to weekdays, and so on, a continuous time dimension may serve the purpose as discussed in the next recipe.

 Years and **Months**, in the preceding screenshot, are different dimensions altogether. Hence, if we are looking at months or quarters, then we must have year on the columns, to provide the context; otherwise numbers will be wrongly added together, that is, Jan will show the total of Jan 2008 + Jan 2009 + Jan 2010.

How it works...

In this recipe, we have assumed that we are interested in monthly level of granularity while we analyze data. Hence, we have created a time dimension **Months** with years at the top level, preceded by quarters and months. We have also loaded data for 2008 in the cube and have seen how time-based cube views can be created, hence providing time aspects to the business data while doing analysis.

Creating a continuous time model

A continuous time dimension is implemented by creating a time cube that enables a user to compare the current and previous period for current as well as prior years.

This provides more flexibility in reporting by supporting forecast applications that span year boundaries.

Hence, continuous time dimensions provide more flexibility, but are hard to maintain.

In this recipe, we will implement the continuous time dimension model and demonstrate the flow using a cube called **Franchise_Revenue**.

Getting ready

Ensure that TM1 Admin Server service is started and demodata TM1 server is running. Open TM1 Architect from the **Start Menu**.

How to do it...

1. Open the **Server Explorer** window and create a new cube, name it **Franchise_ Revenue** with following dimensions:

    ❑ Subsidiaries

    ❑ Months

    ❑ Versions

2. Please note that the cube will be loaded from the previously created **Franchiserev.CSV**.

3. In the **Server Explorer** window, under **Processes** open **LoadFranchiseRevenue2CSV** and save it as **LoadFranchiseRevenueCSV**.

4. In the existing process, under the **Variables** tab, delete the **vYear** variable so that **Variables** tab now looks like the following screenshot:

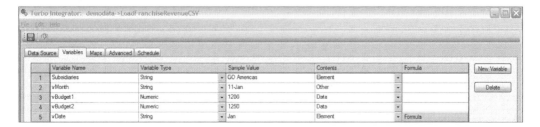

5. Under the **Maps** tab, change the **Cube Name** to **Franchise_revenue** cube.

6. The **Dimensions** tab should be updated as follows:

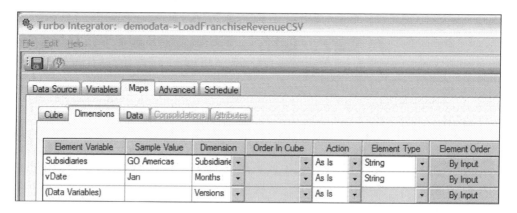

7. Take note of the **Data** tab as shown in the following screenshot:

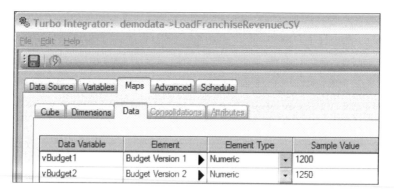

8. Save the process and run it to populate the cube.

9. Close the TI process and return to the **Server Explorer** window. Double-click on the **Franchise_Revenue** cube to open the default view as shown in the following screenshot.

10. Change the default view to show data in the layout as follows:

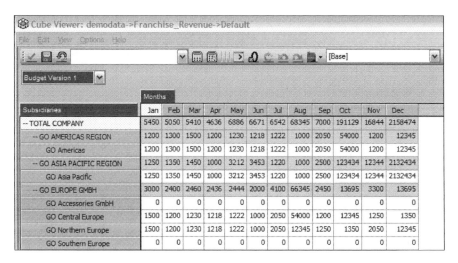

11. Save the view as default public view.

12. Now we will be creating a continuous time dimension using Turbo Integrator.

13. In the **Server Explorer**, right-click on **Processes** and click on **Create New Process** to create a turbo integrator process for the same.

14. Now we will create SLTime.csv file consisting of three years worth of data to create the dimension.

15. Take a note of the structure of the .csv, as shown in the following screenshot:

	A	B	C	D	E	F
1	Mo	Quarter	Yr	MoYear	Mo01	MonthLongName
2	M1	Q1	Y1	8-Jan	M01	January
3	M2	Q1	Y1	8-Feb	M02	February
4	M3	Q1	Y1	8-Mar	M03	March
5	M4	Q2	Y1	8-Apr	M04	April
6	M5	Q2	Y1	8-May	M05	May
7	M6	Q2	Y1	8-Jun	M06	June
8	M7	Q3	Y1	8-Jul	M07	July
9	M8	Q3	Y1	8-Aug	M08	August
10	M9	Q3	Y1	8-Sep	M09	September
11	M10	Q4	Y1	8-Oct	M10	October
12	M11	Q4	Y1	8-Nov	M11	November
13	M12	Q4	Y1	8-Dec	M12	December
14	M13	Q5	Y2	9-Jan	M01	January
15	M14	Q5	Y2	9-Feb	M02	February
16	M15	Q5	Y2	9-Mar	M03	March
17	M16	Q6	Y2	9-Apr	M04	April
18	M17	Q6	Y2	9-May	M05	May
19	M18	Q6	Y2	9-Jun	M06	June
20	M19	Q7	Y2	9-Jul	M07	July
21	M20	Q7	Y2	9-Aug	M08	August
22	M21	Q7	Y2	9-Sep	M09	September
23	M22	Q8	Y2	9-Oct	M10	October
24	M23	Q8	Y2	9-Nov	M11	November
25	M24	Q8	Y2	9-Dec	M12	December
26	M25	Q9	Y3	10-Jan	M01	January

16. Note that preceding CSV has 36 rows of data and the first row as title record. Hence, the `.csv` has three years worth data at monthly granularity. While the first three columns will be mapped to elements (simple and consolidate), the last three are just attributes.

 These CSV files can be downloaded from the PACKT website.

17. Place the CSV at `C:\Program Files\cognos\TM1\Custom\TM1Data\TI_Data.`

18. The given data will facilitate the user to view the **Franchise_Revenue** cube with a continuous time period that spans three years beginning with Jan 1, 2008.

19. Another version of the **Franchise_Revenue** cube is to be created that should enable a user to compare data for current and previous period, both this year and the last year.

20. Now we will continue with creating the dimension using `SLTime.csv` and the **Turbo Integrator** process.

21. In the already opened Turbo Integrator window, specify **Data Source Name** as **SLTime.csv** with **Number of title records** specified as **1**.

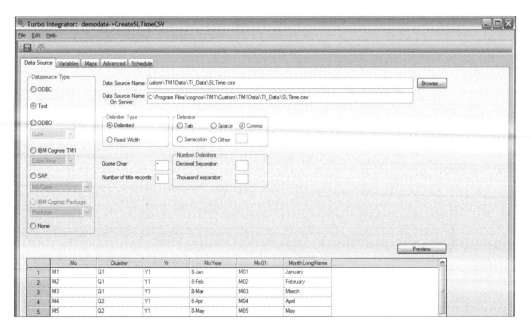

22. Click on the **Variables** tab. Specify the entries as shown in the following screenshot:

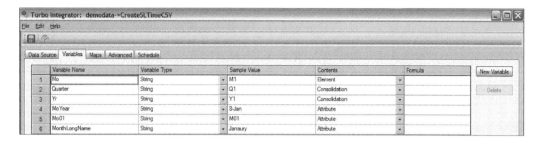

23. Click on the **Maps** tab and then on the **Dimensions** tab in order to map the variables with the dimensions.

24. In the **Dimension** column for **Mo**, type **SL_Time** and then click on **By Input**.

25. Click on **Automatic**, click on **Hierarchy** and then click on **OK**.

26. The resulting **Dimensions** tab looks like the following screenshot:

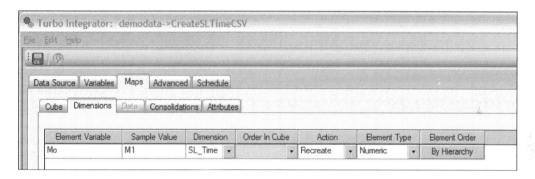

27. Please note that the **Element Type** is specified as **Numeric**.

28. Now, click on the **Consolidations** tab and specify mapping for consolidated elements, as shown in the following screenshot.

29. Click on the **Child Variable** cell for **Quarter**, select **Mo** and then click on **OK**.

30. Now for **Child Variable** cell for **Yr**, select **Quarter** and then click on **OK**.

31. The results appear as follows:

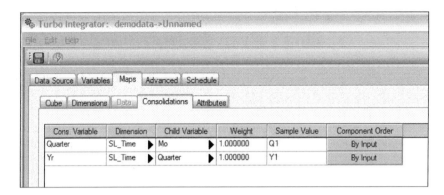

32. Click on the **Attributes** tab to specify mapping for attributes.

33. Set the **Element Variable** to **Mo** for all the three attributes.

34. Now for the **Attribute** column, type the following:

  ❑   MoYear: MonthYear

  ❑   Mo01: M00

  ❑   MonthLongName: Full Name

35. Under the **Attribute Type** column, type the following:

  ❑   MoYear: Alias

  ❑   Mo01: Text

  ❑   MonthLongName: Text

36. Resulting pane looks like the following screenshot:

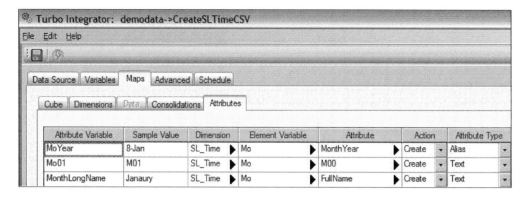

37. Click on the **Advanced** tab and then all the tabs below it will generate automated scripts.

38. Save the process as `CreateSLTimeCSV` and then run it.

39. Close the **Turbo Integrator** process to return to **Server Explorer** window.

40. Double-click on the **SL_Time** dimension and the result appears as follows:

41. On the **Subset Editor**, click on the use aliases icon 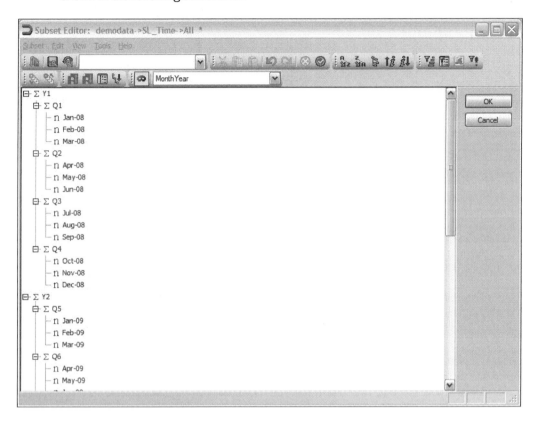 and view the changes as shown in the following screenshot:

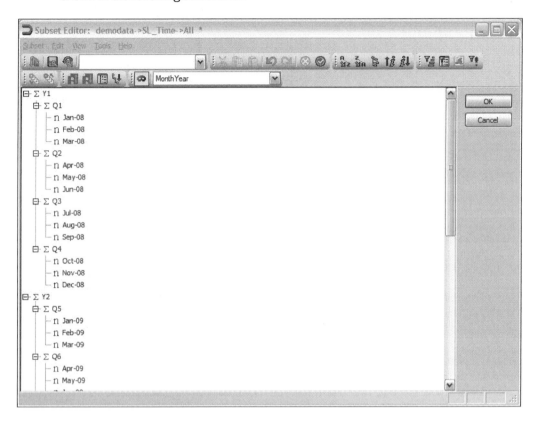

42. Now close the **Subset Editor**.

43. In following steps, we will create a time navigation dimension consisting of the following elements:

      ❑   Prior_Period

      ❑   Next_Period

      ❑   Same_Period_LY

      ❑   Prior_Period_LY

      ❑   Same_Period_NY

      ❑   Next_Period_NY

44. In the **Server Explorer** window, create a new dimension with the name **Time_ Navigation** and insert the preceding string elements.

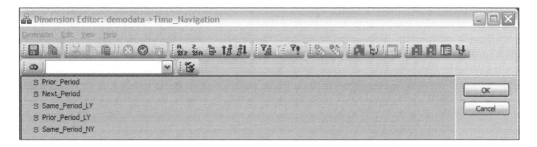

45. Now we will be creating and populating a time navigation cube.

46. In the **Server Explorer** window, create a new cube with the name **zTime_Navigation** consisting of the following dimensions:

    ❑ SL_Time

    ❑ Time_Navigation

47. In the **Server Explorer** window, double-click on the **zTime_Navigation** cube to open the default view.

48. Click on the **SL_Time** dimension, and in the **Subset Editor** click on the **All** icon in order to select all the elements into the view.

49. Click on **Recalculate** and save the view as public default view.

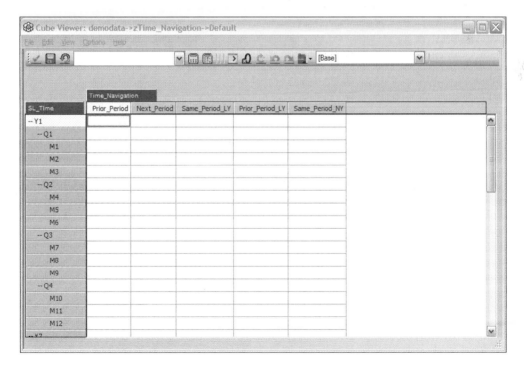

50. Populate the cube through the view manually by entering data in cells, as shown in the following screenshot:

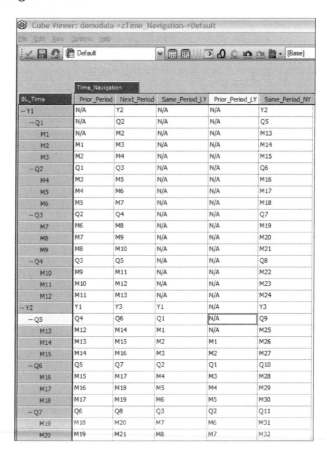

SL_Time	Prior_Period	Next_Period	Same_Period_LY	Prior_Period_LY	Same_Period_NY
-- Y1	N/A	Y2	N/A	N/A	Y2
-- Q1	N/A	Q2	N/A	N/A	Q5
M1	N/A	M2	N/A	N/A	M13
M2	M1	M3	N/A	N/A	M14
M3	M2	M4	N/A	N/A	M15
-- Q2	Q1	Q3	N/A	N/A	Q6
M4	M3	M5	N/A	N/A	M16
M5	M4	M6	N/A	N/A	M17
M6	M5	M7	N/A	N/A	M18
-- Q3	Q2	Q4	N/A	N/A	Q7
M7	M6	M8	N/A	N/A	M19
M8	M7	M9	N/A	N/A	M20
M9	M8	M10	N/A	N/A	M21
-- Q4	Q3	Q5	N/A	N/A	Q8
M10	M9	M11	N/A	N/A	M22
M11	M10	M12	N/A	N/A	M23
M12	M11	M13	N/A	N/A	M24
-- Y2	Y1	Y3	Y1	N/A	Y3
-- Q5	Q4	Q6	Q1	N/A	Q9
M13	M12	M14	M1	N/A	M25
M14	M13	M15	M2	M1	M26
M15	M14	M16	M3	M2	M27
-- Q6	Q5	Q7	Q2	Q1	Q10
M16	M15	M17	M4	M3	M28
M17	M16	M18	M5	M4	M29
M18	M17	M19	M6	M5	M30
-- Q7	Q6	Q8	Q3	Q2	Q11
M19	M18	M20	M7	M6	M31
M20	M19	M21	M8	M7	M32

51. Save the view as public default view.

52. Close the view and return to the **Server Explorer** window.

53. In the **Server Explorer** window, create a new dimension with the name **Franchise_ Revenue_Measures** dimension consisting of the following elements:

- Current Period
- Prior Period Ending
- Next Period Ending
- Same Period Ending LY
- Prior Period Ending LY

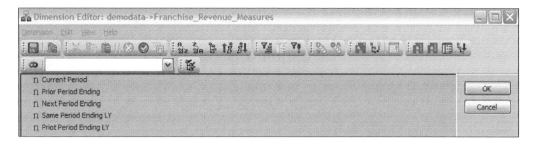

54. Save the dimension and close the **Dimension Editor** to return to the **Server Explorer** window.

55. In the **Server Explorer** window, create a new cube with the name **Franchise_Revenue3** and consisting of the following dimensions:

 ❑ Subsidiaries

 ❑ SL_Time

 ❑ Versions

 ❑ Franchise_Revenue_Measures

56. Double-click on the cube in **Server Explorer** to open the default view.

57. Arrange the cube as shown in the following screenshot:

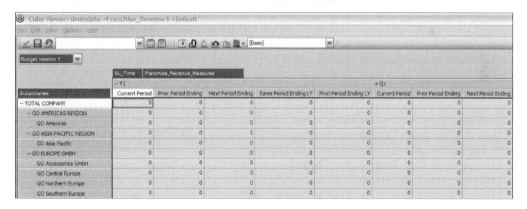

58. Click on **SL_Time** to open the **Subset Editor**. *Ctrl+Click* on **Q1**, **M1**, **M2**, and **M3**, and then from the **View** menu, click on **Expand Above**. Click on **OK** in order to return to the **Cube Viewer**.

59. Save the view as default public view and return to the **Server Explorer** window.

60. Open the process **LoadFranchiseRevenue.csv**, from the **Processes** menu in **Server Explorer**.

61. In the **Variables** tab, add a new variable, with the name **vMeasures**. Apply the following formula for the variable:

```
vMeasures='Current Period';
```

62. Please note that the **Variable Type** of the new variable will be **String** and **Contents** will be set to **Element**, as shown in the following screenshot:

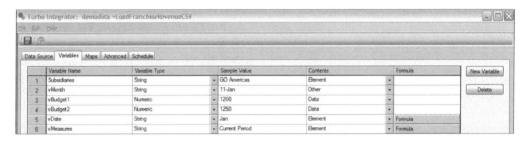

63. In the same **Variables** tab, click on **Formula** for **vDate** where we want to concatenate **–YY** to the existing **vMonth**, as shown in the preceding screenshot. Hence, MMM part of vMonth (Jan par from 11-Jan, that is, 11th Day of Jan) will be concatenated to -08 (2008) to arrive at the **vDate** in the required format (Jan-08), which is MMM-YY. The Year part has been hardcoded for 2008 as we have loaded data from the `.csv` that has 2008 data only.

```
vDate=SUBST(vMonth,4,3)|'-08';
```

64. Click on the **Maps** tab, and change the **Cube Name** to **Franchise_Revenue3**, by choosing that from the cube list. Keep the **Cube Action** set to **Update Cube**.

65. Click on the **Dimensions** tab and map dimensions as shown in the following screenshot:

66. Click on the **Data** tab and map **Data Variables** to **Budget Version 1** and **Budget Version 2**, as shown in the following screenshot:

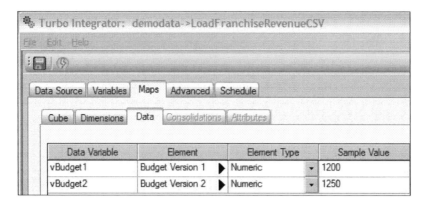

67. Click all the tabs under **Advanced** tab to generate the scripts. Save the process as **LoadFranchiseRevenue3CSV** and run the process.

68. Close to return to the **Server Explorer**.

69. **Recalculate** the default view of **Franchise_Revenue3** to verify that **Current Period** now has data populated, as shown in the following screenshot:

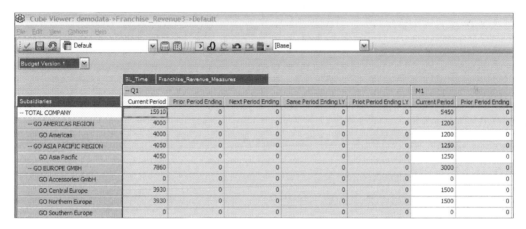

70. Now we will create rules to calculate time measures for the **Franchise_Revenue3** cube.

71. Return to the **Server Explorer** window and open advanced **Rules Editor** for the **Franchise_Revenue3** cube.

72. Enter the following code snippet:

```
SKIPCHECK;
['Prior Period Ending' ]   = N: DB('Franchise_Revenue3',
  !Subsidiaries
, DB('zTime_Navigation', !SL_Time, 'Prior_Period')
, !Versions, 'Current Period');
```

Rules Editor: demodata: Franchise_Revenue3

File   Edit   View   Insert   Tools   Help

```
1   SKIPCHECK;
2   ['Prior Period Ending' ]   = N: DB('Franchise_Revenue3', !Subsidiaries
3   , DB('zTime_Navigation', !SL_Time, 'Prior_Period')
4   , !Versions, 'Current Period');
5
```

73. In the preceding rule, for every **Prior Period Ending** cell in the **Franchise_Revenue3** cube, a corresponding **Prior Period** is looked up from the **zTime_Navigation** cube and a **Current Period** value for that looked up tuple is copied over to the cell.

74. For example, for **M2-2008**, it will look up the **zTime_Navigation** cube and will return **M1-2008** as **Prior Period**. The **Current Period** value for the returned **M1-2008** tuple is then copied to **Prior Period Ending** value of the **M2-2008**, which is the required behavior.

75. Add following **FEEDER** at the end.

```
FEEDERS;
['Current Period' ] =>  DB('Franchise_Revenue3', !Subsidiaries
, DB('zTime_Navigation', !SL_Time, 'Next_Period')
, !Versions, 'Prior Period Ending');
```

Rules Editor: demodata: Franchise_Revenue3

File   Edit   View   Insert   Tools   Help

```
1   SKIPCHECK;
2   ['Prior Period Ending' ]   = N: DB('Franchise_Revenue3', !Subsidiaries
3                               , DB('zTime_Navigation', !SL_Time, 'Prior_Period')
4                               , !Versions, 'Current Period');
5
6   FEEDERS;
7   ['Current Period' ] =>  DB('Franchise_Revenue3', !Subsidiaries
8                           , DB('zTime_Navigation', !SL_Time, 'Next_Period')
9                           , !Versions, 'Prior Period Ending');
```

76. Save the rule and close the editor to return to the **Server Explorer**.

77. **Recalculate** the view on **Franchise_Revenue3** and verify if the data is being populated for **Prior Period Ending** as well.

Cube Viewer: demodata->Franchise_Revenue3->Default

Subsidiaries	SL_Time ~Q1 Current Period	Prior Period Ending	Next Period Ending	Same Period Ending LY	Priot Period Ending LY	M1 Current Period	Prior Period Ending
-- TOTAL COMPANY	15910	10500	0	0	0	5450	0
-- GO AMERICAS REGION	4000	2500	0	0	0	1200	0
GO Americas	4000	2500	0	0	0	1200	0
-- GO ASIA PACIFIC REGION	4050	2600	0	0	0	1250	0
GO Asia Pacific	4050	2600	0	0	0	1250	0
-- GO EUROPE GMBH	7860	5400	0	0	0	3000	0
GO Accessories GmbH	0	0	0	0	0	0	0
GO Central Europe	3930	2700	0	0	0	1500	0
GO Northern Europe	3930	2700	0	0	0	1500	0
GO Southern Europe	0	0	0	0	0	0	0

78. Close the **Cube Viewer**.

How to do it...

In this recipe, we have implemented continuous time dimension model and have the view to retrieve the **Prior Period** as specified in the **zTime_Navigation** cube.

There's more...

We can extend the recipe to make it easier for users comparisons between this year's and last year's data. For that we need to add calculations for same (or current) period of last year's balance. We have already created a time navigation cube for these calculations. To do this we need to perform the following:

1. Add calculations for **Same Period LY** and **Prior Period Ending LY**

2. Add **FEEDERS**

We need to add rules to **Franchise_Revenue3** cube in advanced **Rules Editor** as shown in the following code snippet:

```
SKIPCHECK;
['Prior Period Ending' ]  = N: DB('Franchise_Revenue3', !Subsidiaries
  , DB('zTime_Navigation', !SL_Time, 'Prior_Period')
  , !Versions, 'Current Period');
['Same Period Ending LY' ] = N: DB('Franchise_Revenue3',
!Subsidiaries,
```

```
      DB('zTime_Navigation', !SL_Time, 'Same_Period_LY'),
      !Versions, 'Current Period');


   ['Priot Period Ending LY' ]  = N: DB('Franchise_Revenue3',
   !Subsidiaries,
      DB('zTime_Navigation', !SL_Time, 'Prior_Period_LY'),
      !Versions, 'Current Period');


   FEEDERS;
   ['Current Period' ] =>  DB('Franchise_Revenue3', !Subsidiaries
      , DB('zTime_Navigation', !SL_Time, 'Next_Period')
      , !Versions, 'Prior Period Ending'),
      DB('Franchise_Revenue3', !Subsidiaries,
      DB('zTime_Navigation', !SL_Time, 'Same_Period_LY'),
      !Versions, 'Same Period Ending LY' ),
      DB('Franchise_Revenue3', !Subsidiaries,
      DB('zTime_Navigation', !SL_Time, 'Next_Period_NY'),
      !Versions, 'Prior Period Ending LY' );
```

```
Rules Editor: demodata: Franchise_Revenue3
File  Edit  View  Insert  Tools  Help

1   SKIPCHECK;
2   ['Prior Period Ending' ]  = N: DB('Franchise_Revenue3', !Subsidiaries
3                             , DB('zTime_Navigation', !SL_Time, 'Prior_Period')
4                             , !Versions, 'Current Period');
5
6   ['Same Period Ending LY' ] = N: DB('Franchise_Revenue3', !Subsidiaries,
7                             DB('zTime_Navigation', !SL_Time, 'Same_Period_LY'),
8                             !Versions, 'Current Period');
9
10  ['Priot Period Ending LY' ]  = N: DB('Franchise_Revenue3', !Subsidiaries,
11                            DB('zTime_Navigation', !SL_Time, 'Prior_Period_LY'),
12                            !Versions, 'Current Period');
13
14  FEEDERS;
15  ['Current Period' ] =>  DB('Franchise_Revenue3', !Subsidiaries
16                        , DB('zTime_Navigation', !SL_Time, 'Next_Period')
17                        , !Versions, 'Prior Period Ending'),
18                        DB('Franchise_Revenue3', !Subsidiaries,
19                        DB('zTime_Navigation', !SL_Time, 'Same_Period_LY'),
20                        !Versions, 'Same Period Ending LY' ),
21                        DB('Franchise_Revenue3', !Subsidiaries,
22                        DB('zTime_Navigation', !SL_Time, 'Next_Period_NY'),
23                        !Versions, 'Prior Period Ending LY' );
```

The preceding screenshot shows a revised piece of code as viewed through **Rules Editor** on the **Franchise_Revenue3** cube. This should populate **Same Period Ending LY** and **Prior Period Ending LY** as well, which enables a user to compare between the current year's and last year's data. It can be verified by checking LY values for year 2009.

11
Optimizing Rules Performance

In this chapter, we will cover:

- ▸ Adding SKIPCHECKS and FEEDERS
- ▸ Troubleshooting rules and feeders

Introduction

So far, we have seen how rules play a critical role while implementing even the simplest of business-specific solutions in TM1. An additional consideration may be the performance of these rules, when it comes to billions and billions of cells in any decent sized cube.

Business definitely does not want to wait hours and hours while cubes are being created due to mammoth volumes of data. Number crunching and analysis has to be fast and precise.

With this on the cards, the TM1 engine has been designed to optimize performance in various ways. Some require the user to do configurations and some just happen in the background, without the user even knowing about it.

In this chapter, we will look at such concepts to be able to use TM1 in the most efficient way. We will look at:

- ▸ Consolidations and sparsity
- ▸ Using SKIPCHECKS and FEEDERS to enhance rules performance

Consider a typical business scenario, where we have three regular dimensions, a Time dimension and two elements in the Measure dimension. So, we have 100 elements each for Products, Region, and Customer, and we are interested in two years worth of data with daily granularity. Daily granularity over two years will have at least (365*2 = 730) points. So our cube ends up having (730*100*100*100*2) cells, which is still a conservative estimate of the volume of data we have in a real, decent sized organization. When one customer buys one product in a region on a specific day, the corresponding cell out of the 1460 million possible intersections will have a value. Hence, most of the intersection will be null or empty. Now, if the preceding data has, say, 1% of the values as non-zeros and nulls then it is much faster and efficient to do consolidation on just that 1%, rather then wasting resources on the other 99% of zeros and nulls.

In any practical business scenario, it's common to have more than 80% of the values as zeros and nulls, and we don't want the consolidation engine to waste time over those while rolling up. Moreover, rolling over these nulls and zeros will result in more of such values, which will unnecessarily result in a cube size explosion, which we don't want to happen.

To avoid such situations, the TM1 consolidation engine automatically skips zero and null values while doing consolidations and hence saves lots of resources.

When we write a rule that is being executed, it also has an effect on the above said consolidation process. As soon as a rule is added to the cube, TM1 checks every cell to see if the rule applies to it. If yes, then it is evaluated to a non-zero value. TM1 will then consolidate only non-zero values. Cells which are now populated by rules are seen as having no values by the consolidation engine.

The above rule checking happens as soon as a rule file is associated with a cube, even if it contains no rules. This can significantly increase the time it takes to aggregate data while doing consolidations. We can turn off this checking by using the SKIPCHECK statement in the rules file.

Now, in the proceeding section, we will extend the same idea of using SKIPCHECKS to optimize rules performance.

SKIPCHECKS are added at the top of the rules file to skip the automatic checking of all cells. Doing this will enable the values at the base levels to be calculated correctly, but figures at the consolidated levels will be zero if the base level figures have been derived by the rules. This is because the consolidation engine considers everything calculated by rules to be zero and hence it skips it while doing aggregation. Adding SKIPCHECK will remove automatic checking on the cell if that evaluates to non-zero values and hence zeros at the consolidated levels (if the corresponding base level cells have been derived by a rule).

In general, as a direct consequence of doing consolidations only on non-zero and non-null values, storage space is conserved, as the cube only stores non-zero and non-null values. Time is another resource which is saved due to such sparsity-driven behavior of the TM1 consolidation engine.

Hence, to summarize:

- ▶ The TM1 consolidation engine considers only non-zero and non-null values while doing aggregation. This saves time and storage space used by the cubes.

- ▶ When a rule is applied to a cube, a rule file is generated, which is checked by the TM1 engine even if it doesn't contain a single rule.

- ▶ Every cell is evaluated by the TM1 engine and checked to see if a rule is applicable to that cell. If yes, does it evaluate to a non-zero value? Consolidations are then performed on non-zero and not-null values.

- ▶ Adding SKIPCHECKS at the top of the RULE file will skip this checking by the TM1 engine, and will save time and storage. As a consequence, all consolidated level cells which are derived using rules will have zeroes, as cells populated by rules are seen as having no value by the consolidation engine.

- ▶ Values at the base level are still calculated correctly.

As a direct consequence of skipping cells, we end up having the wrong zero values in consolidated cells even if the base cells have correctly populated non-zero values calculated by rules. We consider the following scenario to highlight the problem. We will assume that the total year consolidates Q1 and Q2 separately, and not Q1 + Q2 and Q3 + Q4. Q1 + Q2 are not consolidated but are calculated using the rules.

	Total Year	Q1	Q2	Q1+Q2	Q3+Q4
Total Products	30	10	20	0	0
Product 1	10	10	0	10	20
Product 2	20	0	20	20	0
Product 3	0	0	0	0	10
Product 4	0	0	0	0	40

Here, in the preceding scenario, we have the last two columns that have calculations and hence the total products column ignores the values in them.

To correct this problem we write FEEDERS to tell TM1 which calculated cells will receive non-zero values via rules. This will cause TM1 not to skip the calculated cells, derived through rules, only if they contain non-zero and not-null values. These non-zero and not-null values are then consolidated. Hence, this improves the speed while preserving accuracy at the same time.

FEEDERS are typically written at the end of the rules file to specify which cells will contain values used in the rules and which N level cells are to be calculated by TM1.

Feeders are typically written for every set of values populated by a rule. When written in the rule file at the bottom of the rules, it tells TM1 which elements on the right-hand side of the rules will determine if there would be a non-zero, not-null values on the left-hand side of the rule. For example, in the following rule:

['Revenue'] =N:['Quantity'] * ['Unit Price'];

Quantity determines if there is going to be a non-zero and not-null value in Revenue, and hence for this rule the following FEEDER statement will be written after FEEDERS; statement at the bottom of the rules file:

['Quantity'] => ['Revenue'];

This clearly tells TM1 that Revenue is fed by Quantity; hence, place an internal marker in the Revenue cell if there is a value for the Quantity, which is seen by the consolidation engine while processing values for the Revenue rule.

Feeders are activated when a cube is first loaded into the memory, and thereafter whenever a zero value is changed to a non-zero value in the cube. On the contrary, a rule is activated whenever a value is requested by the user.

When we feed a cell, a small marker is stored in that cell which takes up a small amount of memory. This will cause TM1 to evaluate any rule which is applicable to that cell and consider it while consolidating, even if that cell eventually returns a zero value. Hence, we should be careful when writing a FEEDER statement, as not needed feeders will be an extra overhead on processing times, as well as on storage. This overhead is more when a cube is first loaded in to the memory, as at this point in time the processor has to evaluate all the feeders. Thereafter, this burden is less as TM1 needs to evaluate feeders only when a value changes from zero to non-zero, and only to those feeders that are related to the value that was changed.

Hence, overfeeding will cause performance bottlenecks as it effectively returns us to the state that was before a SKIPCHECK was added.

As a rule, feeders should be applied only to simple cells that are calculated using a rule. For instance:

- We write a feeder for: [X] =N: [Y]*[Z];
- We don't write a feeder for: [X] =C: [Y]*[Z];

We do not feed rules that apply to consolidated cells unless using Suppress Zeros.

When using multiplication and division, we feed using the least data, as shown:

[Revenue] = N:[Quantity] * [Price];

[Quantity] => [Revenue];

In addition, subtraction, or logic, feed using each section:

[HalfYear] = N:[Q1]+[Q2];

[Q1]=>[HalfYear]; [Q2]=>[HalfYear];

It's typically a better idea to overfeed than to underfeed, underfeeding calculated cells that may actually have non-zero values will result in the wrong consolidation as there would be certain cells considered as zeros, even if the calculation could have resulted in a non-zero value.

We may also need to feed both consolidations and base level cells when users turn on Suppress Zeros for a view. Suppress Zeros hides all values displaying only zeros in an entire row or column. If both the base level and consolidated level calculation is not fed, Suppress Zeros may hide the columns or rows containing calculations.

We have seen earlier that rules can also pull data from other cubes. In such cases, feeders put a marker in the source cells and push it to the calculated cell in the target cube.

While the rule resides in the target cube, feeders generally reside in the source cube. From the modeler point of view, if the source cells are in another cube, then the FEEDER statement needs to be there too.

We typically use a `FEEDSTRINGS;` statement to feed rules applied to string cells when:

- ▸ The rule pulls the string into another cube
- ▸ The rule is populating a pick list
- ▸ The target is using Suppress Zeros

To enable the feeding of string cells, we need to insert a FEEDSTRINGS declaration by having a `FEEDSTRINGS;` statement as the first line of the rule. FEEDER statements are then placed under the FEEDERS declaration after the rule statements.

Once a FEEDSTRINGS declaration is in place, only then can we set up feeders for string cells in the cube view and rely on the string to be available to other rules, even if the view is zero suppressed.

Adding SKIPCHECKS and FEEDERS

The objective of this recipe is to improve the performance of calculations in the **Price_and_Cost** cube using SKIPCHECKS and FEEDERS.

Getting ready

Ensure that the TM1 Admin Server service is started and demodata TM1 Server is running. Open TM1 Architect from the **Start menu**.

How to do it...

1. Start the DemoData Server and open the **Server Explorer**.

2. In the **Server Explorer**, open the default view for the **Price_and_Cost** cube and expand **CAMPING EQUIPMENT**.

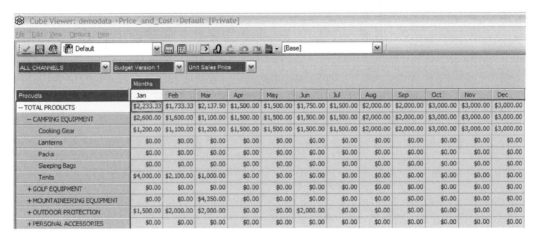

3. Open the **Rules Editor** for the **Price_and_Cost** cube.

4. Insert a new line at the top and type SKIPCHECK;.

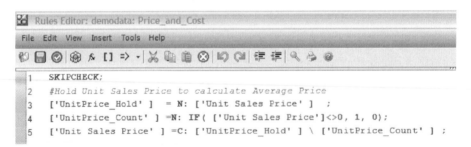

5. Save the rule and **Recalculate** the default view for the **Price_and_Cost** cube.

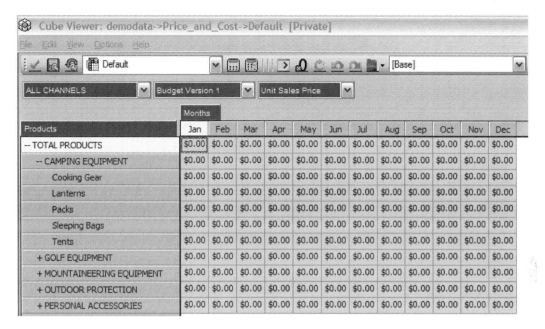

6. The consolidations no longer calculate the average because TM1 does not see the calculated values in **N:** level elements **UnitPrice_Hold** and **UnitPrice_Count**. They contain calculations that are stored only in the memory, but TM1 doesn't know they contain values to compute and are seen as 0 when aggregating consolidated values.

7. We need to feed the **N:** level calculations so that values for those cells can be used in other calculations.

8. In the piece of code shown in the next screenshot, we will feed **N:** level calculations for **UnitPrice_Hold** and **UnitPrice_Count** using **Unit Sales Price** so that they are used to calculate **Unit Sales Price** at the consolidated levels.

9. Now add the **FEEDERS** as shown at the bottom of the rules:

```
FEEDERS;
['Unit Sales Price' ] => ['UnitPrice_Hold' ],['UnitPrice_Count' ];
```

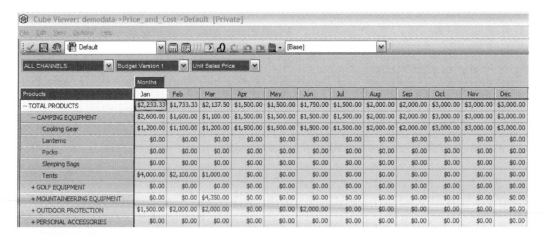

10. Save the rules and **Recalculate** the view. This wil be updated as shown in the following screenshot:

Products	Jan	Feb	Mar	Apr	May	Jun	Jul	Aug	Sep	Oct	Nov	Dec
-- TOTAL PRODUCTS	$2,233.33	$1,733.33	$2,137.50	$1,500.00	$1,500.00	$1,750.00	$1,500.00	$2,000.00	$2,000.00	$3,000.00	$3,000.00	$3,000.00
-- CAMPING EQUIPMENT	$2,600.00	$1,600.00	$1,100.00	$1,500.00	$1,500.00	$1,500.00	$1,500.00	$2,000.00	$2,000.00	$3,000.00	$3,000.00	$3,000.00
Cooking Gear	$1,200.00	$1,100.00	$1,200.00	$1,500.00	$1,500.00	$1,500.00	$1,500.00	$2,000.00	$2,000.00	$3,000.00	$3,000.00	$3,000.00
Lanterns	$0.00	$0.00	$0.00	$0.00	$0.00	$0.00	$0.00	$0.00	$0.00	$0.00	$0.00	$0.00
Packs	$0.00	$0.00	$0.00	$0.00	$0.00	$0.00	$0.00	$0.00	$0.00	$0.00	$0.00	$0.00
Sleeping Bags	$0.00	$0.00	$0.00	$0.00	$0.00	$0.00	$0.00	$0.00	$0.00	$0.00	$0.00	$0.00
Tents	$4,000.00	$2,100.00	$1,000.00	$0.00	$0.00	$0.00	$0.00	$0.00	$0.00	$0.00	$0.00	$0.00
+ GOLF EQUIPMENT	$0.00	$0.00	$0.00	$0.00	$0.00	$0.00	$0.00	$0.00	$0.00	$0.00	$0.00	$0.00
+ MOUNTAINEERING EQUIPMENT	$0.00	$0.00	$4,350.00	$0.00	$0.00	$0.00	$0.00	$0.00	$0.00	$0.00	$0.00	$0.00
+ OUTDOOR PROTECTION	$1,500.00	$2,000.00	$2,000.00	$0.00	$0.00	$2,000.00	$0.00	$0.00	$0.00	$0.00	$0.00	$0.00
+ PERSONAL ACCESSORIES	$0.00	$0.00	$0.00	$0.00	$0.00	$0.00	$0.00	$0.00	$0.00	$0.00	$0.00	$0.00

11. Close the **Rules Editor** and **Cube Viewer**.

How it works...

In this recipe, we have improved performance by adding SKIPCHECKS to the rules. We have also ensured that consolidated level elements are calculated correctly by adding FEEDERS.

There's more...

When we feed a consolidated element, all children are fed; whereas when we start feeding from a consolidated cell, we feed from every child implicitly.

It is also worth exploring the idea of Persistent Feeders, which improves the reload time of cubes with complex feeders. There is a configuration parameter, **PersistentFeeders**, which can be set to true (T) to store the calculated feeders to a `.feeders` file. Any installation with server load times of over five minutes can probably improve their performance using this parameter.

When this parameter is set to T and the server encounters a persistent feeder file, it loads the saved feeders which reduces the time normally taken to recalculate those feeders. Feeders are saved when data is saved or rules are edited. We do not have to explicitly save the feeders. Hence, for installations with many complex feeder calculations, persisting feeders and then reloading them at server startup will improve performance.

Troubleshooting rules and feeders

The Rules tracer is a feature provided with TM1 to troubleshoot rules and feeders. They are typically used to:

- ▶ Trace calculations
- ▶ Trace feeders
- ▶ Check feeders

The Rules tracer has two panes:

- ▶ The top pane shows the current cell definition and calculations
- ▶ The bottom pane shows the components of calculations and feeders

The user can right-click on any of the cell and choose Trace Calculation to trace it to the base level or lead level elements.

Trace feeders is another utility which is enabled only at base or leaf level cells and checks the way the selected cell feeds other cells.

If a cube contains a rule with SKIPCHECK and FEEDERS statements, the Rule tracer can be used to check if all of the components of the consolidation have been fed or not.

If the Tracer pane is empty, it means the consolidation is fed; otherwise a **not fed** message is displayed for all leaf level cells that ought to be fed.

Getting ready

Ensure that the TM1 Admin Server service is started and demodata TM1 Server is running. Open TM1 Architect from the **Start menu**.

How to do it...

1. Open the **Server Explorer** window for the already started DemoData Server.

2. Open the **AverageRule** view on the **Price_and_Cost** cube, as shown in the following screenshot:

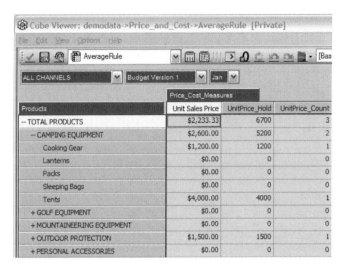

3. Right-click on **CAMPING EQUIPMENT** for the **Unit Sales Price** column cell and then click on **Trace Calculation**.

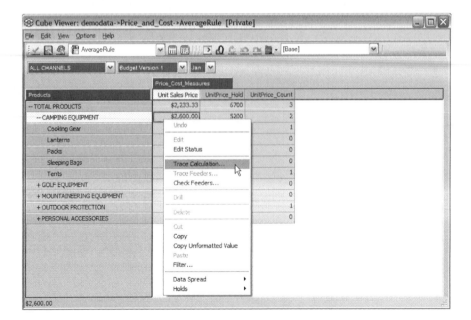

4. The top pane shows the calculation (consolidation) and the bottom pane shows the values that make up the calculation above.

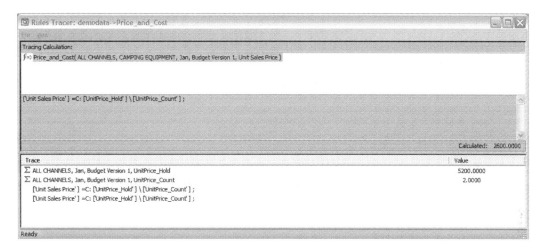

5. We can double-click on a value in the bottom pane to trace it.

6. In the preceding window, double-click on the first line in the bottom pane and under the **Tracing Calculation** pane it displays the path we are tracing.

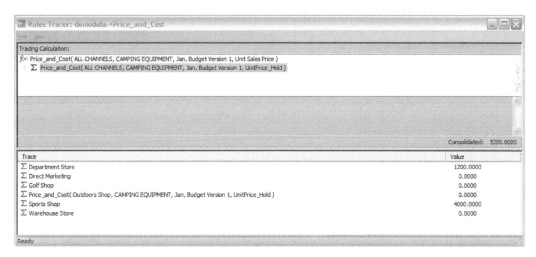

7. We can double-click on an expression in the **Tracing Calculation** pane to return to the previously traced expression.

8. The bottom most element is displayed with a gray bullet to indicate that there is nothing left to trace and we are already at the base level element.

9. Click on **File** and then on **Exit** to close the window.

10. Now we will try the **Check Feeders** utility by right-clicking on the **CAMPING EQUIPMENT/Unit Sales Price** cell in the **Cube Viewer** as shown in the following screenshot:

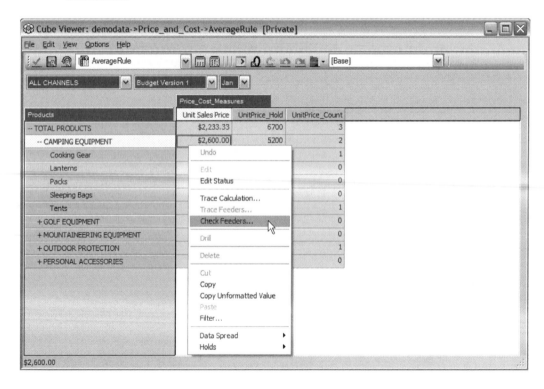

11. In the resulting window, nothing is displayed in **Rules Tracer** except for the calculation that tells us that consolidation has been fed properly and is the desired result.

12. Had the FEEDER statements not been used correctly in this rule, we would have seen the elements making up this consolidation and not being fed properly.

> We can only check the FEEDERS for a cell once per TM1 session. The action of checking the FEEDERS actually feeds the components of the consolidation. Any subsequent checking of the FEEDERS does not yield accurate results. If we want to check the FEEDERS for a cell more than once, we must recycle (shut down and restart) the TM1 Server before every check.

13. The **Trace Feeder** option can be used to show the exact cells that are being fed, these are displayed in the bottom pane, fed by the feeder in the top pane.

14. The **Trace Feeder** option is available only at the base level elements, for consolidated elements it is disabled.

How it works...

In the recipe we have:

- Used the Rules tracer to review the calculations
- Verified the leaf level elements feeding other calculations using **Trace Feeder**
- Verified that calculations are being fed by the correct base cells by using **Check Feeders**

12
Working with Managed Planning Applications

In this chapter, we will cover:

- ▶ Installing and configuring IBM Cognos TM1 Contributor components
- ▶ Installing Apache Tomcat 6.0.18 for IBM Cognos TM1 Contributor
- ▶ Installing IBM Cognos TM1 Contributor
- ▶ Deploying IBM Cognos TM1 Contributor on Tomcat Server
- ▶ Configuring IBM Cognos TM1 Contributor with Microsoft IIS
- ▶ Running IBM Cognos TM1 Contributor for the first time
- ▶ Installing IBM CognosTM1 Contributor Administration tool
- ▶ Contributing data to managed planning application
- ▶ Introducing IBM Cognos TM1 Contributor Workflow screen
- ▶ Navigating the TM1 Contributor workspace
- ▶ Opening a node and modifying a view
- ▶ Entering, editing, and distributing data
- ▶ Reviewing data
- ▶ Creating and deploying managed planning applications to the Web
- ▶ Setting security and access rights
- ▶ Assigning security to managed planning applications

Introduction

Through previous chapters we have been going through various TM1 objects which form the crux of the TM1 planning application. These include dimensions, cubes, rules, TI processes, views, and chores. As we have been learning, these objects are created using TM1 Architect and reside on TM1 server.

A managed planning application contains an additional application layer which facilitates users to access TM1 core components, to analyze, and contribute the data.

The application layer includes following additional components which needs TM1 Contributor to be installed and configured properly. Take a note of typical managed planning application architecture.

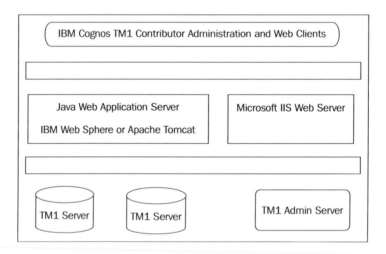

In the preceding diagram additional tier 1 component is TM1 Contributor, which has web clients and administration tool installed and configured. These will be covered in detail later as the chapter proceeds.

Second tier is a Web Server (Web Sphere or Tomcat) and Microsoft IIS, which are necessary for Contributor to be installed and configured.

Third tier, as we have learned previously, has one or more TM1 Servers, which hold data and TM1 objects, for planning application (demodata in our case) and a TM1 Admin Server. TM1 Admin Server is a process that keeps track of all TM1 Servers running on the network.

TM1 Contributor communicates with the TM1 Admin Server to determine which TM1 Servers are available on the network as every running TM1 Server has to register itself with the TM1 Admin Server.

In our case each of these components resides on a single computer and hence a single computer installation.

TM1 contributor combines the power of IBM Cognos TM1 with the capabilities of IBM Cognos Enterprise Planning tool.

Contributor is a web-based planning platform that enables hundreds of users from multiple locations to contribute planning data, to a central repository, which in turn acts as a single source of accurate planning data.

Once contributor application is built, users can access a web grid to enter data using an intranet or a secure Internet connection.

When users log on to the contributor web application, they see a graphical overview of all the areas they are responsible for and the status of the data. The user who is logged on can only enter data that they are authorized to.

Contributor also enables to the building of complex calculations in the model itself so that users only need to enter data known to them. Users can enter relevant data through a web grid interface or through Excel interface.

TM1 Contributor includes:

- ▶ TM1 Contributor web client
- ▶ TM1 Contributor Administration

TM1 Contributor web client is used to browse and contribute data within the TM1 planning application.

TM1 Contributor Administration is a configuration, design and management tool used by administrators to build planning applications and set security on applications.

Installing and configuring IBM Cognos TM1 Contributor components

In this recipe, we will be installing and configuring IBM Cognos TM1 Contributor Version 9.5.1/9.5.2 and will configure it to work with existing demodata TM1 server.

Getting ready

Here we will be assuming a single computer installation of contributor and its components. Take a note of the installation steps in sequence. Please note that installation steps of 9.5.2 are same as 9.5.1. There are slight differences in the UI which we will see later, but for now we can take the following installation on 9.5.1/2 whichever is available to you.

How to do it...

1. Install Microsoft .NET 3.5 SP1 Framework.
2. Install Microsoft Internet Information Services (IIS) (ASP) 32 bit /64 bit.
3   Install Java SE runtime environment (JRE) version 6 for Windows.
4. Install one of the following Java-based web servers:

    ❑   IBM Web Sphere Application Server Community Edition (CE) V2.1.1.2

    ❑   Apache Tomcat 6.0.X

5. Install TM1 Contributor using TM1 Installation Wizard.
6. Determine security authentication mode to use.
7. Deploy TM1 Contributor on a Java-based web server.
8. Start up and configure TM1 Contributor.
9. Install the TM1 Contributor Administration Tool.
10. Configure additional TM1 servers, if necessary.

> When running TM1 Contributor, platform versions should be consistent. For instance, if 64 bit version of JRE is being used, then same version of Apache Tomcat should be used (64 bit). Same would be the case with 32 bit versions.

Here we will be using Apache Tomcat as Web Server. However, IBM Web Sphere Application Server Community Edition (CE) V2.1.1.2 can be used.

Although the initial steps are straightforward, installing Java-based web servers needs more focus and hence will be discussed in the next recipe.

Installing Apache Tomcat 6.0.18 for IBM Cognos TM1 Contributor

In this recipe we will be installing Apache Tomcat 6.0.18. As discussed previously, it is necessary to install a Web Server to get the TM1 Contributor components working.

How to do it...

1. Download and install Apache Tomcat from `http://tomcat.apache.org/` website.

2. On the download page for Tomcat 6.0, go to **Binary Distributions** section, and then in the **Core** sub-section select **Windows Service Installer** in .exe format as shown in the following screenshot:

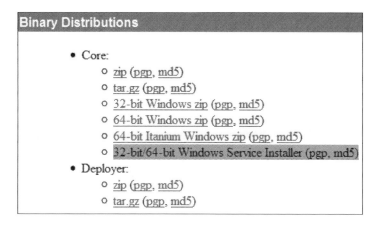

3. Make sure that Apache Tomcat Encoding is set to UTF-8.

4. Make sure that the web server we are installing is not using the same TCP port number as any other application on the same computer.

We are following single computer installation on Windows XP for all the recipes in the book.

5. Above steps will add an entry for Apache Tomcat 6.0 in the start menu after successful installation.

6. Refer to documentation available on `http://tomcat.apache.org/download-60.cgi` for further details.

There's more...

We can also use IBM Web Sphere Application Server Community Edition (CE) V2.1.1.2 as a web server with TM1 Contributor. In this book, we are using Apache Tomcat 6.0.X and hence discussed installation of the same above. Refer to the documentation at `http://publib.boulder.ibm.com/infocenter/ctm1/v9r5m0/index.jsp?topic=%2Fcom.ibm.swg.im.cognos.tm1_rdm.9.5.2.doc%2Ftm1_rdm_id48installing.html` for installation steps of Web Sphere Application Server Community Edition (CE) V2.1.1.2.

Installing IBM Cognos TM1 Contributor

This recipe describes the installation steps needed for TM1 Contributor. TM1 Contributor and all its components can be installed using TM1 Installation Wizard. TM1 Contributor and its components can be installed using the same wizard by selecting the last option (**TM1 Contributor**) on **Choose a Product to Install** screen, which includes and installs everything (TM1 Server and Clients, TM1 Web, and TM1 Contributor along with its components), as shown in this recipe.

How to do it...

1. Run the setup for TM1 installation and answer the introductory prompts.
2. If we are doing fresh TM1 installation, select **TM1 Contributor**. In the following figure, option two **(TM1)** is selected which will install only TM1 Server and its Clients. In the context of this recipe, we must select option four **(TM1 Contributor)** which will install TM1 Contributor and its components in addition to TM1 Server and Clients.

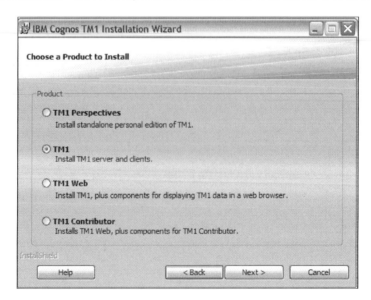

3. Click on **Next** after selecting last option.

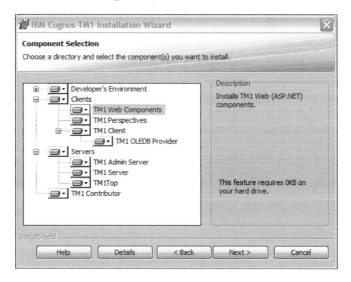

4. If we are installing contributor on existing TM1 installation, then modify the existing setup and select **TM1 Contributor** and other components as shown in the preceding screenshot.

5. The remaining steps are same as explained in *Chapter 1*. We are just interested in installing an additional component TM1 Contributor on top of existing installation, in our case. Hence, we will modify the existing setup as shown in the following screenshot:

Deploying IBM Cognos TM1 Contributor on Tomcat Server

Now after installation of TM1 Contributor, we will be deploying TM1 Contributor application on the web server. In this recipe, we will be deploying the TM1 Contributor application we have just installed on Apache Tomcat Server.

How to do it...

1. We have successfully installed the web server and TM1 Contributor, now we need to manually deploy the Contributor application on the web server.

2. To deploy TM1 Contributor on Java-based web server, we will use the TM1 Contributor web application archive file called `pmpsvc.war` which is located in the following directory: `C:\Program Files\Cognos\TM1\Cadmin`

   In our case, we will be deploying the WAR file on Apache Tomcat Server as it is our web server. Please follow below steps to deploy the contributor application on the Tomcat server.

3. Stop the Apache Tomcat Web server.

   ❑ In Windows, click on **Start | Programs | Apache Tomcat 6.0 | Configure Tomcat**.

   ❑ The **Apache Tomcat Properties** dialog box opens.

   ❑ On the **General** tab, click on **Stop**.

4. Using a text editor, open the Apache Tomcat `tomcat-users.xml` file to make sure the encoding is set to **utf-8**.

   ❑ This file is typically located here:

   `C:\Program Files\Apache Software Foundation\Tomcat 6.0\conf`

   ❑ Locate and edit the following line as follows:

   `<?xml version='1.0' encoding='utf-8'?>`

5. Start the Apache Tomcat web server.

   ❑ In Windows, click on **Start | Programs | Apache Tomcat 6.0 | Configure Tomcat**.

   ❑ On the **General** tab, click on **Start**.

6. Open the **Tomcat Manager**.

   ❑ In Windows, click **Start | Programs | Apache Tomcat 6.0 | Tomcat Manager**.

   ❑ If prompted, enter a valid user name and password that exists in the `tomcat-users.xml` file. This file is typically located at:

   ```
   C:\Program Files\Apache Software Foundation\Tomcat 6.0\
   conf
   ```

   ❑ **Note:** If you edit the `tomcat-users.xml` file, you must stop and restart the Tomcat web server to apply the changes.

   ❑ After a successful login, the **Tomcat Web Application Manager** page opens.

7. In **Tomcat Manager**, scroll down to the **Deploy** section and locate the **WAR file to deploy** sub-section.

8. Click on **Browse**, locate and select the **TM1 Contributor Web** application archive file, `pmpsvc.war`. The typical location of this file is `C:\Program Files\Cognos\TM1\Cadmin`

9. Click on **Open** after selecting the `pmpsvc.war` file.

10. In **Tomcat Manager**, click on **Deploy**.

11. Tomcat extracts, installs, and starts the TM1 Contributor Web application. This process may take a few minutes to complete.

12. When completed, TM1 Contributor is listed as `/pmpsvc` in the **Applications** section of **Tomcat Manager**.

13. When the deployment is complete we can log on to the TM1 Contributor, details of which are given in later sections.

There's more...

Refer to the documentation at the following link to deploy TM1 Contributor application on IBM Web Sphere Application Server Community Edition: `http://publib.boulder.ibm.com/infocenter/ctm1/v9r5m0/index.jsp?topic=%2Fcom.ibm.swg.im.cognos.tm1_rdm.9.5.2.doc%2Ftm1_rdm_id48installing.html`

In this recipe we have explained steps with Apache Tomcat Server as we are using that for our setup.

Now in the next recipe we will configure TM1 Contributor with another necessary component, which is Microsoft IIS server.

Configuring IBM Cognos TM1 Contributor with Microsoft IIS

TM1 Contributor uses Microsoft Internet Information Services (IIS) to run the TM1 Contributor Client. We use the TM1 Contributor Client to view and edit planning application data in grid format. In this recipe, we will learn how to configure the TM1 Contributor, with Microsoft IIS, to run TM1 Contributor Client.

How to do it...

1. When we install TM1 Contributor, the required files for the TM1 Contributor Client are copied to the TM1 Web installation location. Typically, this location is: `C:\Inetpub\wwwroot\TM1Web`. The application file for TM1 Contributor Client is `contributor.aspx` which is present in the preceding location.

2. We must configure the **TM1 Web Client URL** parameter while configuring TM1 Contributor, to point to the `contributor.aspx` file, in this location. For example: `http://WebServer/TM1Web/contributor.aspx`. Please take a note of the exact steps as discussed below.

3. Use the **TM1 Contributor Configuration** page to set the **TM1 Web Client URL** parameter:

   □ If you are running TM1 Contributor for the first time, use the **Configuration** page that opens when you start the program.

   □ For more details, refer to the following section which discusses *Running IBM Cognos TM1 Contributor for the first time*.

   □ If you are already using TM1 Contributor, you can re-open the Configuration page by clicking on the **Administer IBM Cognos TM1 Contributor** button 🔳 on the toolbar of the **TM1 Contributor Portal** page.

4. In the **TM1 Web Client URL** field, enter the URL location of the `contributor.aspx` file.

Running IBM Cognos TM1 Contributor for the first time

In this recipe, we will be determining start-up link for TM1 Contributor depending on which web server it is running on and how it is configured. We will then try running the TM1 contributor for the first time and then logging on to the TM1 contributor.

How to do it...

1. The typical link for TM1 Contributor running on IBM Web Sphere Application Server is `https://WebServer:PortNumber/pmpsvc`, for instance `https://localhost:8443/pmpsvc`.

2. Similarly, for Apache Tomcat the link would be `http://WebServer:PortNumber/pmpsvc`, for instance `http://localhost:8085/pmpsvc`.

3. The **WebServer** parameter in the link can be one of the following:

   ❑ The keyword **localhost**, if you are currently logged on to the web server that is running TM1 Contributor.

   ❑ The machine name or domain name of the web server hosting the TM1 Contributor Web application.

   ❑ The IP address of the web server hosting the TM1 Contributor Web application.

4. The **PortNumber** depends on the actual port number you configured with IBM Web Sphere or Apache Tomcat.

   ❑ IBM Web Sphere: Click on the **Web Server** link in the **Web Sphere Administrative Console** to view and edit port settings.

   ❑ Apache Tomcat: Open the Apache Tomcat `server.xml` file at the following location to view and edit the port settings: `C:\Program Files\Apache Software Foundation\Tomcat 6.0\conf\server.xml`.

5. Now we will be running TM1 Contributor for the first time. In our case we are using Apache Tomcat and hence the URL to start the Contributor application is `http://localhost:8080/pmpsvc`

6. As advised earlier port number is taken from `server.xml` file, which is placed in the following location: `C:\Program Files\Apache Software Foundation\Tomcat 6.0\conf`

```
- <Service name="Catalina">
    <!-- The connectors can use a shared executor, you can define one or more named thread pools -->
  - <!--
        <Executor name="tomcatThreadPool" namePrefix="catalina-exec-"
            maxThreads="150" minSpareThreads="4"/>

    -->
  - <!--
        A "Connector" represents an endpoint by which requests are received
            and responses are returned. Documentation at :
            Java HTTP Connector: /docs/config/http.html (blocking & non-blocking)
            Java AJP  Connector: /docs/config/ajp.html
            APR (HTTP/AJP) Connector: /docs/apr.html
            Define a non-SSL HTTP/1.1 Connector on port 8080

    -->
    <Connector port="8080" protocol="HTTP/1.1" connectionTimeout="20000" redirectPort="8443" />
    <!-- A "Connector" using the shared thread pool -->
  - <!--
        <Connector executor="tomcatThreadPool"
                port="8080" protocol="HTTP/1.1"
                connectionTimeout="20000"
```

7. A TM1 server must be specified, before we run TM1 Contributor. The very first time TM1 Contributor is started, the program prompts for the following configuration information:

   ❑ TM1 Admin Host

   ❑ Server Name

   ❑ TM1 Web Client URL

8. When we start TM1 Contributor for the first time, the configuration page opens and required configuration information needs to be entered as suggested.

Field	Description
TM1 Admin Host	Specify the computer name or IP address of the Admin Host on which the TM1 Admin Server is running.
	Note: The **TM1 Admin Host** and **Server Name** fields appear blank if we have not started the TM1 Admin Server and at least one TM1 server.
Server Name	Sets the name of the TM1 server to use with TM1 Contributor.
	For example: planning sample
	Click on the **Refresh** button to refresh the list of available servers.
TM1 Web Client URL	Specify the URL location of the `contributor.aspx` file.
	TM1 Contributor uses this file, along with Microsoft Internet Information Services (IIS), to display data in grid and chart format.
	This URL points to the TM1 Web server. For example:
	`http://WebServer/TM1Web/contributor.aspx`
IBM Cognos 8 Gateway URI	These parameters are only displayed if we are using TM1 Contributor with IBM Cognos 8 security.
IBM Cognos 8 Dispatcher URI	

9. Click on **OK** to proceed.

10. Once correctly entered, the configuration information is saved and the contributor is run for the second time, this time the user will not be prompted to enter the information again.

11. After entering information log on to the contributor using the username and password.

12. In our case we will be using demodata as TM1 server and hence username and password in our case would be Admin for user and we leave password blank.

13. If we need to edit these settings in the future, click on the **Administer IBM Cognos TM1 Contributor** button  on the toolbar of the **TM1 Contributor Portal** page.

14. TM1 Servers can be added using the same screen by clicking on **Add** below **Server Name:** pane. All the TM1 Servers added here have to use same security authentication and include same administrator username and password. After adding multiple TM1 servers they are available when we use the **TM1 Contributor Administration** tool to design the planning applications.

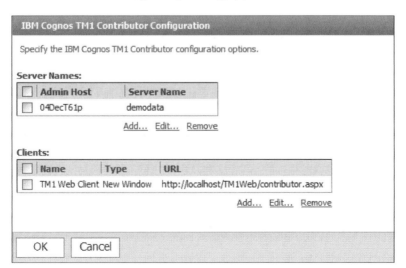

15. Every time we log on to the contributor we are prompted for the username and password. For this recipe and for all the future recipes we will be using demodata setup as the TM1 Server and hence as explained earlier username for the application would be Admin and for password we leave the text box blank and click on **Login** button.

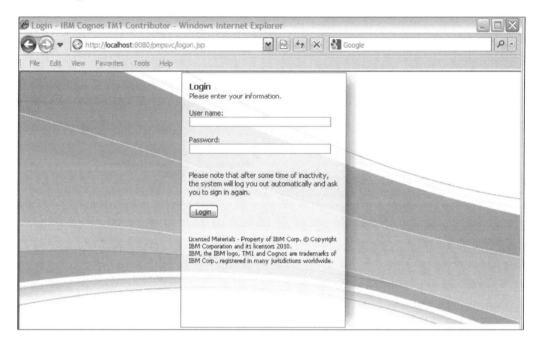

16. After logging on and starting to use TM1 Contributor, the application may require the installation of the IBM Cognos Rich Client Framework. This framework provides the foundation and support files for the TM1 Contributor Administration tool. We will be discussing this in the next section on installing the TM1 Contributor Administration tool.

Installing IBM CognosTM1 Contributor Administration tool

The TM1 Contributor Administration tool requires the IBM Cognos Rich Client Framework. The installation for this framework is provided with the .msi installation package files that are included in the TM1 Contributor Web application. TM1 Contributor users who have administrator rights can automatically install the TM1 Contributor Administration tool and required framework on their computer, the first time they click on the **Design an Application** button 📋 on the **TM1 Contributor Portal** page.

TM1 Contributor users with administrator rights can automatically download and install the TM1 Contributor Administration tool on their own computer using the following steps, depending on which web browser they are using.

We will install the tool with Internet Explorer in the recipe. Installation with other browsers can be referred to, in online TM1 9.5.2 documentation available at: `http://publib.boulder.ibm.com/infocenter/ctm1/v9r5m0/index.jsp?topic=%2Fcom.ibm.swg.im.cognos.tm1_rdm.9.5.2.doc%2Ftm1_rdm_id48installing.html`.

How to do it...

1. Start and log on to IBM **Cognos TM1 Contributor** using Microsoft Internet Explorer.

   ❑ The TM1 Contributor Portal page opens.

2. Click on the **Design an Application button** 🖼.

   ❑ The **Provisioning - IBM Cognos TM1 Contributor** page appears, and you are prompted to install the IBM Cognos Rich Client Framework.

3. Click on **Install Now**.

   ❑ A **File Download** dialog box appears for the `CognosRCP.msi` file.

4. Click on **Run** to install the `CognosRCP.msi` file.

5. If a security dialog box appears, click on **Run** to verify and continue the installation.

6. After the installation has finished, close and then restart your web browser.

7. Log on back to TM1 Contributor.

8. Click on the **Design an Application** button 🖼.

   ❑ A **Progress** dialog box appears and automatically downloads and installs the required components for the TM1 Contributor Administration tool.

   ❑ When this process has finished, the TM1 Contributor Administration window opens.

9. The IBM Cognos Rich Client Framework and the IBM Cognos TM1 Contributor Administration tool are now installed.

There's more...

TM1 contributor can also be configured to use IBM Cognos 8 security. Exact steps can be found in the user guide for IBM Cognos TM1 9.5.1/9.5.2.

Lastly, we also have discussed how additional TM1 servers can be added in the existing setup in the previous section.

In the upcoming recipes we will use the TM1 Contributor setup we have prepared to explore the tool's capabilities and how the whole planning application works.

Contributing data to managed planning application

In the previous sections we have already installed and configured TM1 Contributor which is a web portal that lets end users contribute data to planning applications.

In this section we will use TM1 Contributor, installed and configured above to contribute to a plan in an existing managed planning application.

The people who build the applications are referred to as TM1 Contributor Administrators. TM1 Contributor Administrators use the contributor portal to:

- ▶ Create and maintain applications
- ▶ Manage rights to secure applications
- ▶ Import and export applications
- ▶ Activate and deactivate applications

When an existing application (**Test** in this case) is opened for the first time, a workflow screen appears which contains a tree and a table as shown in the following screenshot:

The following screenshot shows the **Test** application, detailing who are data contributors, who are data reviewers, and status of tasks assigned to each:

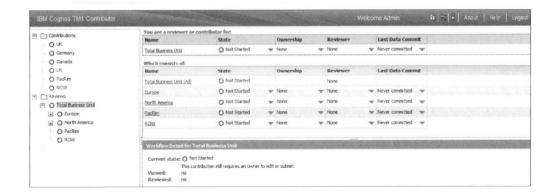

- ▶ Tree Hierarchy displays the areas where the logged in user is responsible for contributing and reviewing data.

- ▶ Corresponding table refers to details about each area such as workflow state, current owner, current reviewer, and when the data was last committed.

We have logged in as Admin user; hence, we are able to see complete application and all areas. A specific user depending on security settings will be responsible for a certain area as a contributor, as a reviewer or both. Hence, he is expected to complete a certain task and this is a workflow which can be in different states depending on if he has started his task (contributing, reviewing, or both), is in the middle of the task, not started at all, or completed the task.

In the preceding screenshot, an item is referred to as node, hence UK, Germany, PacRim are different nodes. Depending on security privileges a user can be a contributor, a reviewer, or both and hence, will see either or both the trees accordingly.

Clicking on a node on the left-hand side tree will show corresponding details on right-hand side table.

Clicking a node in the right-hand side table will open the data, for the node, in web client. The web client presents the data in a grid like interface which primarily enables the user to enter and edit the data. Details regarding that will be covered in later sections.

The approval hierarchy under review tree directly maps to one of the subset from the model that application designer has specified, depending on the approval hierarchy in the organization.

In the preceding example, we have used a subset which has nodes for different business units (Europe, UK, Germany, North America, and so on). This must correspond to the approval hierarchy of the organization.

In any planning process, contributing and reviewing data are two activities which are performed on nodes. Depending on how far the user has gone in terms of the tasks (review data, edit data, or both) assigned to him/her, workflow state of the corresponding node may change accordingly.

Consider a scenario when a user has just logged in and the screen shows him/her various nodes for which he/she needs to contribute data. Here the initial state of nodes is **Not Started** as no data has been saved untill now. After user enters data he/she can choose to either save it for later additional work or **Submit** the node for review.

Once the contributor submits their contribution the reviewer examines it and can then either **Submit** it for next level, **Reject** it or edit if reviewer has edit rights.

Contributions displayed on the left-hand side pane directly map to one or more cube views from the model.

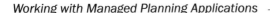

The mapping between views and contributions, subsets and reviews are defined by the Administrator. He/She also defines security policies in terms of which user and group plays role of contributor and reviewer and for which nodes.

The TM1 Contributor Administrator is responsible for creating and maintaining TM1 contributor applications.

Administrator role includes:

Task	Explanation
Defining views	Selecting public views from the model, include in the application and set their properties
Defining an approval hierarchy	Choose the dimension subset from the model which reflects the approval hierarchy of the organization to define workflow for the application
Deploying an application	Making the application available to the users on the IBM Cognos TM1 Contributor portal
Defining security	Defining security to determine which users play role of contributors and reviewers and for which areas

Contributors are responsible for entering data into the application through the Web. They can enter/edit data for only those nodes for which they have security privileges defined by the Administrator. Once done with entering data, contributors can save data to the server so that it is available to other users and then eventually submit data.

Once data is submitted it cannot be edited unless the reviewer rejects it.

Reviewers approve the contributions that are submitted by the contributors. Once data has been submitted, the reviewer can reject, edit, or submit the data. Editing is allowed to the reviewer only if administrator allows that by defining security policies.

There can be multiple reviewers and nodes needed to be approved and submitted by lower level reviewers before it is forwarded to upper level reviewers, depending on the approval hierarchy.

A node depending on what contributors/reviewers have been doing or not doing, can assume different workflow states as explained in the following table:

	Not Started (V 9.5.1)/Available (V 9.5.2)	The node has not been opened and data has not been changed or saved
	Work in Progress	The user has taken ownership but not submitted
	Locked	The data was submitted and waiting to get reviewed. It is read only and the state is returned to Work in Progress only if node is rejected.
	Incomplete	Applies to review nodes and signifies that at least one child node of this parent node is Not Started and at least one other child node is Work in Progress, Locked, or Ready.

*TM1 Version 9.5.1/ Version 9.5.2

	Ready	All child nodes of this parent node are locked. This parent node is ready to be submitted to the next level in the hierarchy.

*TM1 Version 9.5.1/ Version 9.5.2

Next recipe will demonstrate different sections on workflow screen.

Introducing IBM Cognos TM1 Contributor workflow screen

This recipe describes the different sections on the workflow screen. We will create a small sample application based on existing TM1 Server demodata which we have been following up so far in the book.

Getting ready

Ensure that TM1 Admin Server service is started and demodata TM1 server is running. Launch TM1 Architect from the start menu. Ensure that Apache Tomcat Server is started by clicking on **Configure Apache Tomcat** from **Start Menu > Apache Tomcat 6.0**.

How to do it...

1. Open the **Franchise_Revenue** cube and create a new subset under **Subsidiaries** dimension by doing **Save As** of the existing **Subsidiaries** dimension.

2. Name the new subset as **Subsidiary Approver** as shown in the following screenshot:

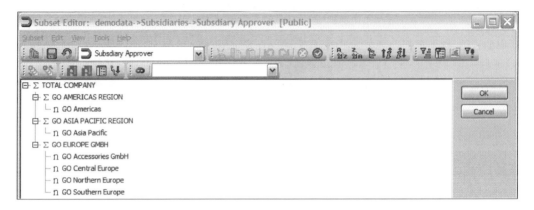

3. Create a new view on the cube **Franchise_Revenue** by name of **Revenue Entry** as shown in the following screenshot:

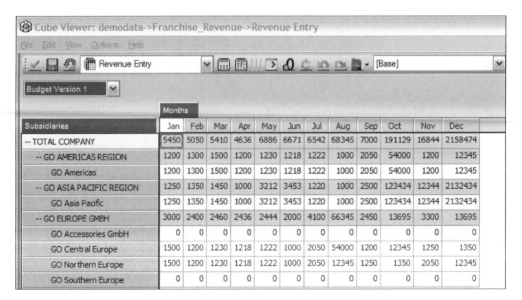

4. Open the TM1 Contributor using the link obtained from the previous recipe *Running IBM Cognos TM1 Contributor for the first time for instance* in our case it is: `http://localhost:8080/pmpsvc`.

5. Enter login credentials as Admin with blank password, the same as what we have been using for demodata application in TM1 Architect.

 Please note that Admin is the administrator user and all TM1 servers hosted on contributor should share same credentials for applications to work.

6. That should open the **IBM Cognos TM1 Contributor** portal as shown in the following screenshot. Here is the place where an Administrator can create and manage planning applications. New TM1 Servers and web clients can be added from the same interface.

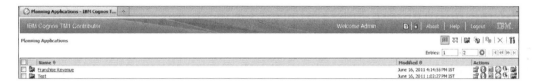

7. Click on [icon] icon to open **IBM Cognos TM1 Contributor Configuration** page. Here is the place where existing TM1 Server connections can be viewed and new TM1 Server connections can be added.

8. In the preceding screenshot we can see that currently two TM1 servers have been added which are **demodata** and **planning sample**. First one is **demodata**, which is created by us in previous chapters and we have been building on. Second one is **planning sample**, which is shipped with TM1 installation package by default. This needs to be started as Windows service first.

9. There is a separate pane **Clients:** to add one or more web clients. A web client is a grid like interface through which planning data can be added/edited.

10. We have one web client already specified there by default.

11. Now return to the home page and click on the **Design an Application** icon 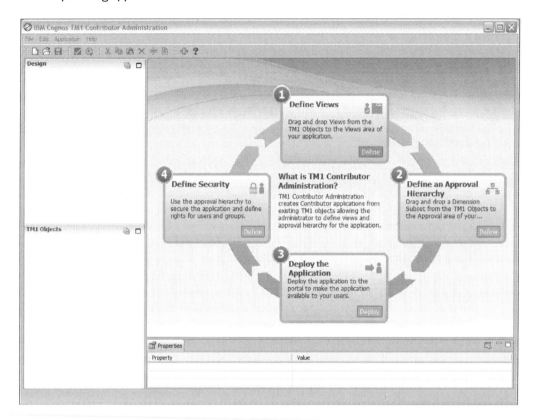 which should open **IBM Cognos TM1 Contributor Administration,** an interface to author a planning application.

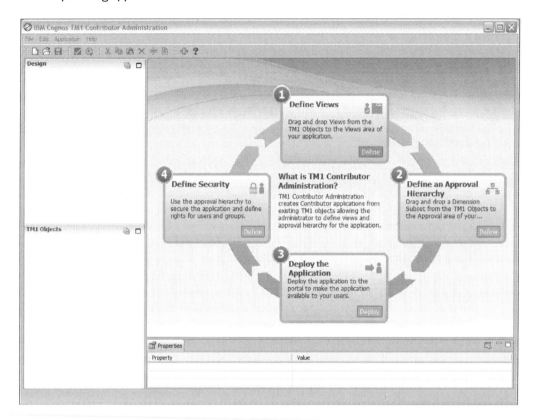

12. To create a new application, from the **File** menu click on **New**.

13. Create a new application by name of **DemoContr1**.

14. The new application would be based on our Demodata TM1 Server.

15. Alternatively, **planning sample** TM1 Server could also have been used by selecting from the drop down as shown in the following screenshot. That way our application would have been based on **planning sample** TM1 Server (Cubes, Dimensions, and other TM1 Objects available on that server). For now we will go with demodata TM1 server.

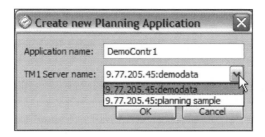

16. That will open the TM1 Objects defined in **demodata** TM1 Server and the authoring pane as shown in the following screenshot:

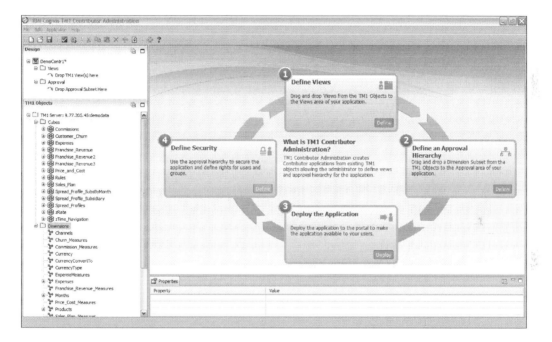

17. As shown in the preceding screenshot top-most left pane has two folders defined by default. First one is **Views** where multiple cube views can be dropped to define nodes where data needs to be entered. Second folder **Approval** represents approval hierarchy, where reviewers need to be defined by dropping a single subset. The subset should define the approval hierarchy of the organization.

18. Drag **Revenue Entry** cube view to **Views** folder in **Design** pane as shown in the following screenshot.

Drag-and-drop **Subsidiary Approver** subset to **Approval folder** as shown in the following screenshot:

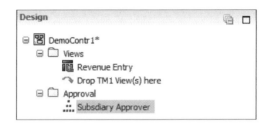

19. Here in the example we have made **Subsidiary** hierarchy as approval hierarchy while data is entered for **Franchise Revenue** by users. Users can be created and assigned to user groups. Data entry nodes hence created are assigned to users for contributing and reviewing.

20. Save the application and validate by clicking on the ✅ icon from the toolbar.

21. Deploy the application by clicking on 🔄 icon.

22. After successful validation and deployment you can exit.

23. Return to the **IBM Cognos TM1 Contributor** page to see the new application **DemoContr1**. Here we need to activate the application by clicking on the 🖼 icon which is in extreme right section of **DemoContr1**.

24. After activating the application, click on 🔵 icon, from the same section, to open the application.

25. This will open the newly created application in the **IBM Cognos TM1 Contributor**. This tree table type layout is now familiar to us, as we have seen earlier.

26. The screen appears differently in TM version 9.5.1 and version 9.5.2. Content remains same but layout is different as shown in the preceding tree table layout screen which is in 9.5.1 and below screen which is in 9.5.2. Apart from this screen, other UIs do not have many changes. Rest of the recipes will be based on version 9.5.2 until and unless specified.

27. Tree table layout in 9.5.2 looks as shown in the following screenshot:

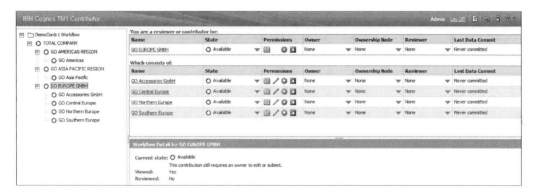

28. Based on the security and role assignments defined in the application, the contribution hierarchy will show who will be able to contribute to the planning process and where. In our case the users need to contribute data to the plan based on the Subsidiary they belong to, hence users belonging to the **GO Americas** can contribute planning data for **GO AMERICAS REGION**. Similarly, users assigned to **GO Accessories GmBH**, **GO Central Europe** can contribute data for **GO EUROPE GMBH**, and so on.

29. In our example we have not set any security privileges so far and we are logged in as **Admin** user as visible on top right-hand side corner of the window.

30. As we have not started contributing data to any of the nodes the workflow states are shown as **Not Started**. Corresponding terminology used in 9.5.2 is **Available** but icon remains the same as before ⊙.

31. In the **Contributions** tree click on **GO Central Europe**. The bottom of the table now displays details for **GO Central Europe** as shown (in TM Version 9.5.1) in the following screenshot:

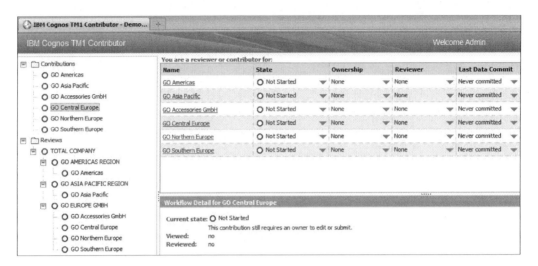

32. Same thing stated same as above in TM Version 9.5.2.

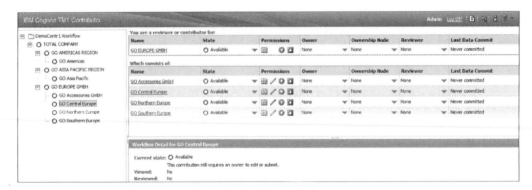

33. The **Current state** is **Not Started/Available**. A particular user assigned to **GO Central Europe** needs to take ownership of the plan and commence the planning process. After that, ownership column will show the correct data. The reviewers for **GO Central Europe** can then accept or reject the planning data. He/She can also edit data if permitted. So far we have not created any users and are just playing around using **Admin** user.

34. Don't close the application and keep the windows open.

How it works...

In this recipe we have created a planning application and introduced TM1 Workflow Screen. We will see how to apply security in later sections.

Navigating the TM1 Contributor workspace

In this recipe we will navigate and explore various options in different UIs of TM1 Contributor.

Getting ready

Ensure that TM1 Admin Server service is started. Start Apache Tomcat server and ensure that demodata TM1 Server is running. We will use IBM Cognos TM1 Contributor screens, still active from the preceding recipe.

How to do it...

1. Right click on **GO Central Europe** and select **Open TM1 Web Client**.

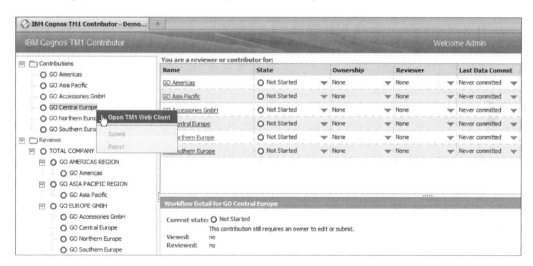

2. This will open a grid like interface which is IBM Cognos TM1 Contributor Web Client used to enter/edit the data.

3. The Contributor Web Client window opens up with the data pertaining to **Central Europe** in a grid like interface.

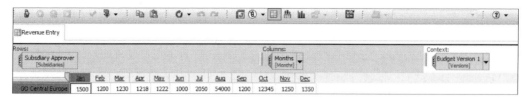

4. We had right-clicked on **GO Central Europe** and hence same data being displayed in web client. Take a note of the grid interface which facilitates data entry and update.

5. On version 9.5.2 the same menu appears as shown in the following screenshot:

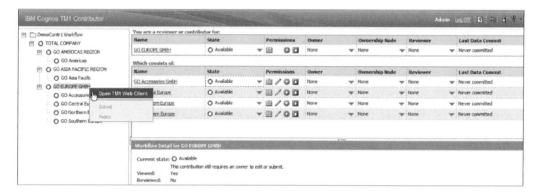

Click on **Open TM1 Web Client** from the menu to display the following screen:

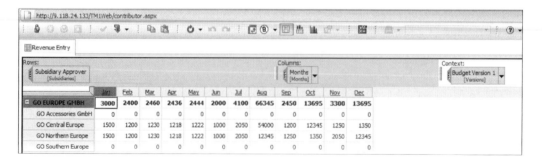

6. Now we will have a closer look at the TM1 Contributor web client interface itself. We will follow TM1 version 9.5.2 consistently. We will go to the workflow screen, right-click on **GO Europe GMBH** and open that in web client. The TM1 Contributor web client should now display combined data for all the four child subsidiaries.

7. Take a note of the grid symbol at the left-most top corner which displays the name of the application. Grid format is more or less similar to cube viewer in TM1 Architect with rows, column, and data context drop downs. Central grid facilitates data entry and update. Within a TM1 Contributor grid we can:

   ❑ Combine multiple views/tabs within a common window

   ❑ Move and nest dimensions

   ❑ Sort data

   ❑ Suppress zeros

   ❑ Apply filters

   ❑ Create and edit subsets

8. We can also add charts and have the option to view grid, view chart, or view both grid and chart together. Users who are familiar with Cognos analysis and query studio know the functionality is quite common to use in these. Most of the things in contributor web client are intuitive and flexible to the extent that the user can:

   ❑ Stack and reorganize views

   ❑ Reset the grid

   ❑ Drag-and-drop views to create desired grid layouts as in cube viewer in TM1 Architect

   ❑ Move and reorder tabs

   ❑ Change type, color, and legend of the charts

   ❑ Change other properties of the charts such as 3D appearance, X/Y axis, appearance, and so on

9. The preceding pointers are just a few things out of loads of options provided in the contributor portal. Different options can be tried out by clicking on various icons available in the toolbar.

10. Exporting data to Excel and PDF is also available on a click of ▣▾ an icon in the toolbar.

11. We will now demonstrate some of the functionality using existing **DemoContr1** application which we have created on demodata. As said earlier we will use the latest TM1 version available which is 9.5.2.

Opening a node and modifying a view

In this recipe we will do some basic tasks on DemoContr1 application. This will further strengthen the use cases which can be achieved using TM1 Contributor.

Getting ready

Make sure that TM1 Admin Server service and Apache Tomcat Server is started. Ensure that demodata TM1 Server is running.

How to do it...

1. Open the workflow screen from **IBM Cognos Contributor** page by clicking on the **DemoContr1** link directly or on [icon] on extreme right of **DemoContr1**.

2. The screen is opened by executing URL `http://localhost:8080/pmpsvc/applications.jsp` and logging in as Admin with blank password.

3. This should open workflow screen with tree table layout.

4. Right-click on **GO EUROPE GMBH** and click on **Open TM1 Web Client** to start Contributor Web Client in the new window.

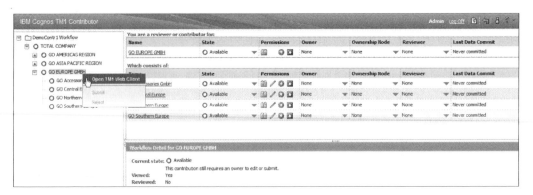

5. This will open **GO EUROPE GMBH** in the TM1 Contributor Web Client grid in a separate window as shown in the following screenshot:

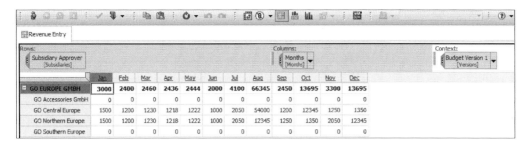

6. Please note the ⊞Revenue Entry icon on the top which displays current view name. In case there is more than one view in the application, views can be switched by clicking on the grid icon.

7. In the dimension bar click on **Months** dimension and drop under rows.

8. Similarly, drag-and-drop **Subsidiary Approver** dimension to columns area.

9. Click on recalculate icon 🖾 to update the view.

10. In dimension bar under rows, click on **Months** dimension's ▾ icon, and select **Jan**, **Feb**, **Mar using** *Ctrl* **key**. Select and recalculate.

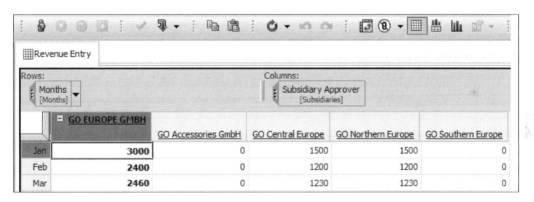

11. Click on swap rows and columns 🖾 icon to swap rows and columns.

12. Click on Suppress Zero values icon and then on Recalculate icon .

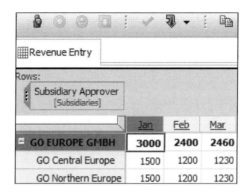

13. Now again we will introduce back all 12 months in the view, hence click on **Months** in the dimension bar, select subset **Months** in the drop down, click **OK** and then on **Recalculate**.

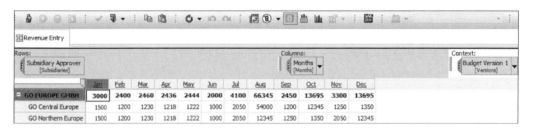

14. Click on **Jan** column to open filter options as shown in the following screenshot:

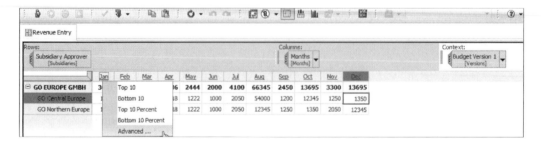

15. Click on **Advanced...** to open advanced filter options which enables the user to set filters and apply.

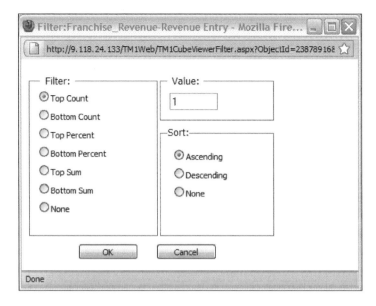

16. Apply filter as shown in the preceding screenshot and click on **Recalculate** to view the updated output.

17. Click on **Jan** once again and click on **Remove Filter** entry.

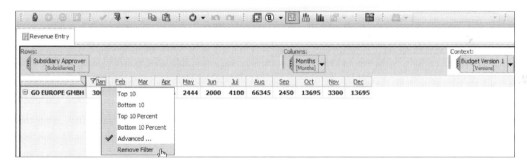

18. **Recalculate** and view the updated output.

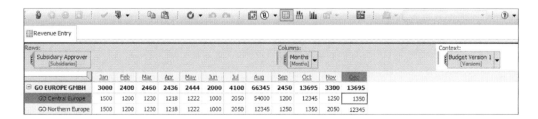

19. On the toolbar click on view chart icon.

20. Click chart properties icon and select **Bar**.

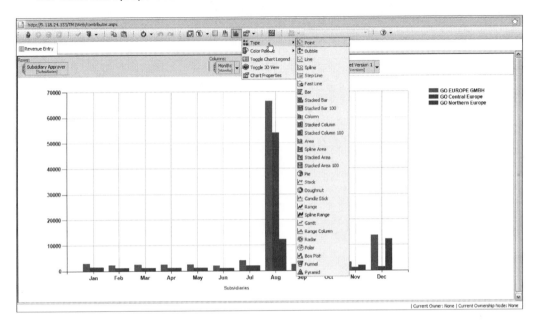

21. Click on **View chart and grid** to view both chart and grid.

22. Click on **View grid** to view only grid.

23. On the toolbar click on **Export** .

24. Export **Slice to Excel** maintains dynamic link to TM1 while export **Snapshot to Excel** does not. **Export to PDF** is also an option.

25. Click on **Snap to Excel**. New window will open to let user choose number of rows and dimension titles to export. It will also tell user number of sheets that will be generated.

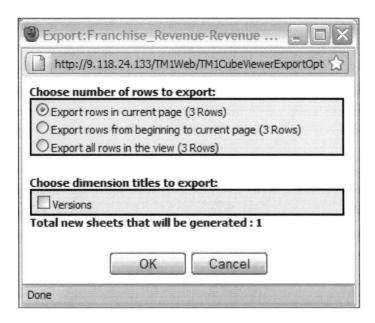

26. Click on **OK** to select default options and view data in Excel. Adjust column widths to accommodate the data. Cells store actual values and not the formulas which link cells with TM1, hence data is static. In export **Slice to Excel** cells are linked with TM1 using a DBRW formula.

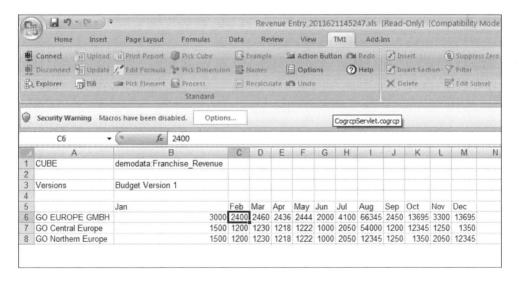

27. Now we will reset this to the original by clicking on **Reset Current view** icon .

28. We will use another view which is default view on **Sales_Plan** cube by including that in our **DemoContr1** application. We will combine the two views in Contributor Web Client.

29. Close the current window of both web client and workflow.

30. Open in TM1 Architect the demodata application, and save as default view on **Sales_ Plan** cube as a public view, **Sales_Plan_V** as shown in the following screenshot:

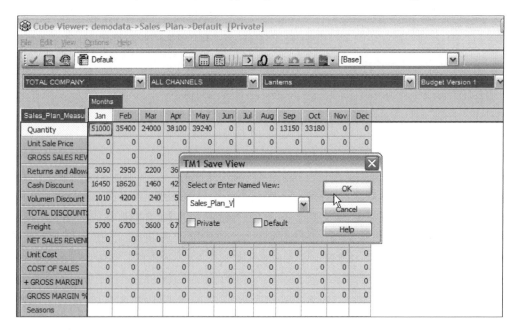

31. Log on to the **IBM Cognos TM1 Contributor** page and click on **Update Application: DemoContr1** icon , from the extreme right of **DemoContr1**. This should open the application in the workflow screen.

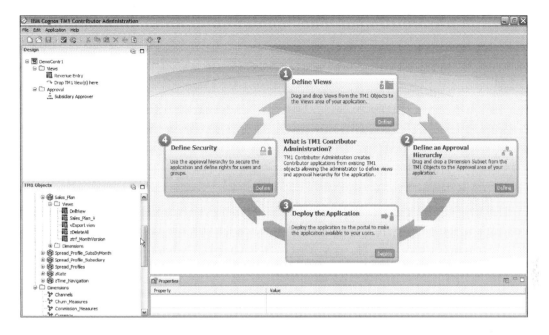

32. Drag the view **Sales_Plan_V** under **Sales_Plan** cube, and drop under existing **Views** folder in **Design** area as shown in the following screenshot:

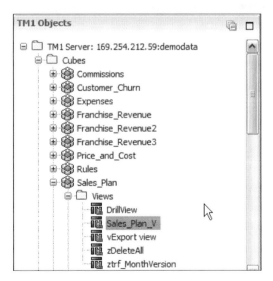

33. Save the application. Validate and deploy ⬚.

34. Close the workflow screen to return to the IBM Cognos TM1 Contributor page, open application and launch Web Client for **TOTAL COMPANY**.

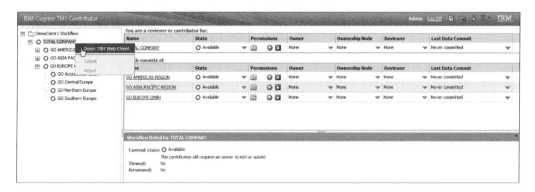

35. Now we can see two views: that is **Revenue Entry** and **Sales_Plan_V** which can be combined in the same window.

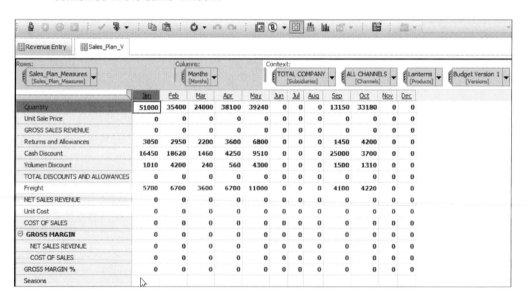

36. Click the **Revenue Entry** tab to make it current view. Now click on **Sale_Plan_V** tab and drag it to the bottom of the grid. The cursor will change to the multiple folders 🗐. Keep dragging the tab until drop area is highlighted and an arrow indicating the placement of the tab.

37. Now the tabs are displayed vertically.

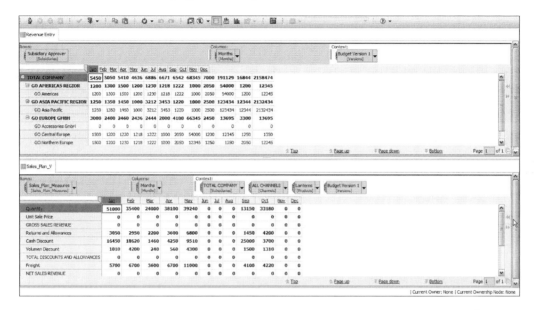

38. This way both views can be monitored and data can be entered/updated so that sync is maintained if required. Assuming the two views have a field in column, changes in one of the views to that field would have been reflected in the other.

39. Now reset both views and tabs by clicking on the 🔄 ▾ icon and selecting reset both views and tabs.

40. Consolidated cells are displayed in bold. These when these are changed, the new values are distributed automatically in a proportional manner to the child cells. For instance under **Revenue Entry** view, change value for (**TOTAL COMPANY, Jan**) to 51000 by double-clicking on the cell and entering new value. Press *Enter* to commit. Corresponding child values are spread as shown in the following screenshot:

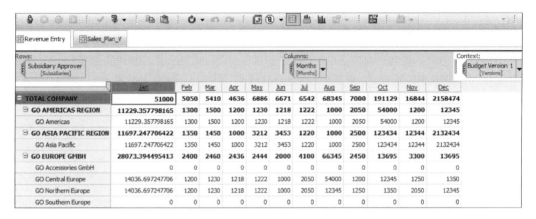

	Jan	Feb	Mar	Apr	May	Jun	Jul	Aug	Sep	Oct	Nov	Dec
TOTAL COMPANY	**51000**	**5050**	**5410**	**4636**	**6886**	**6671**	**6542**	**68345**	**7000**	**191129**	**16844**	**2158474**
⊟ **GO AMERICAS REGION**	**11229.357798165**	**1300**	**1500**	**1200**	**1230**	**1218**	**1222**	**1000**	**2050**	**54000**	**1200**	**12345**
GO Americas	11229.357798165	1300	1500	1200	1230	1218	1222	1000	2050	54000	1200	12345
⊟ **GO ASIA PACIFIC REGION**	**11697.247706422**	**1350**	**1450**	**1000**	**3212**	**3453**	**1220**	**1000**	**2500**	**123434**	**12344**	**2132434**
GO Asia Pacific	11697.247706422	1350	1450	1000	3212	3453	1220	1000	2500	123434	12344	2132434
⊟ **GO EUROPE GMBH**	**28073.394495413**	**2400**	**2460**	**2436**	**2444**	**2000**	**4100**	**66345**	**2450**	**13695**	**3300**	**13695**
GO Accessories GmbH	0	0	0	0	0	0	0	0	0	0	0	0
GO Central Europe	14036.697247706	1200	1230	1218	1222	1000	2050	54000	1200	12345	1250	1350
GO Northern Europe	14036.697247706	1200	1230	1218	1222	1000	2050	12345	1250	1350	2050	12345
GO Southern Europe	0	0	0	0	0	0	0	0	0	0	0	0

41. Here TM1 has used proportional spread method to distribute changed consolidated value to child values. We can also specify custom spread which would be discussed later.

42. In the same **Revenue Entry** view double-click on any child cell, enter/edit a value and press *Enter* to commit. For instance, for **Revenue Entry** view change value for (**GO Central Europe, Feb**) to 1000 and press *Enter*.

43. Cells displayed in white cells can only be edited. Grey cell (Read only) values cannot be changed because of one of the following reasons:

   ❑ User has not taken the ownership of the grid

   ❑ The element is calculated

44. Hence, a user must take ownership of a cube before he can edit values. Ownership cannot be taken for a locked cube.

45. Now close all the portals without saving data if asked.

Entering, editing, and distributing data

Data can be entered in grid like interface once user has logged on to the TM1 Contributor Web Client. Data entry methods are the same as what we have seen for other TM1 components. Hence data can be edited/entered by:

▸ Typing directly in the cells

▸ Using shortcuts

- ▸ Using data spreading
- ▸ Simple copy-paste

Data can be entered/edited in consolidated cells using one of the spreading methods provided by TM1.

 As soon as data is entered in TM1, it is automatically saved in user's own personal view of data which is referred to as sandbox. It does not contain actual data, but only changes which are made to the existing values. The administrator can enable multiple sandboxes per user, but by default there is only one per user.

To save the data to the database user needs to commit the data. As soon as user/contributor submits the plan, the particular node gets locked.

When entering data manually the color of the text changes according to the processing state. Black indicates that text is saved. Blue indicates that user has pressed the *Enter* key after typing the text. Green indicates that user typed text and used *Tab* key, *arrow*, or mouse key to navigate within the grid.

The color of the code helps differentiate between data that is entered in the grid but not committed (blue, green) and data that is saved to the database and hence contributed (black).

The color scheme described above is the default behavior and can be customized by the administrator.

When the user logs on the web client he/she sees data from the database which is base data. When data has been entered/edited by the user it is saved to the sandbox of that user which is his/her own personal area. It is only visible to the user. When user does commit, the sandbox data is saved to the database. User can still continue working after committing, as node is still work in progress.

Hence, while commit just saves the sandbox data back to the database, submit actually locks the node in addition to saving back to database, and hence the user is not able to edit data anymore, unless it is rejected by the reviewer. Data options, commit and submit, apply to entire grid and not just the current tab being viewed. When contributing to the plan user can update the data displayed in the view with the most recent changes saved to the server anytime.

It is important to understand that commit just saves the user's private sandbox data to public database, so that the changes now can be viewed by other users as well. The user who committed data can still continue to work on the data.

When a user submits a plan it commits the whole plan to the database and the user can no longer edit any part of the grid. The data becomes read only and state of the node changes from "in progress" to "locked".

Until the user takes ownership of a particular node he will not be able to commit or submit data. The icons to commit and submit will be disabled for a non-owner.

Ownership of the node can be taken by clicking on the 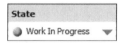 icon as shown in the Contributor Web Client.

When a user takes the ownership of a node, workflow state of the node changes to **Work In Progress** as shown in the following workflow screen:

State
⚪ Work In Progress ▼

A user with appropriate rights can take away ownership of a node from the current owner, while it is being edited.

This is important if the current user is not available or if multiple people are responsible for the same node. Losing ownership to someone else does not result in loss of data even when the grid is refreshed, as everything goes to the sandbox.

Now we will have a look at the practical steps in the recipe.

Getting ready

Ensure that TM1 Admin Server service is started and so is Apache Tomcat Server. Ensure that demodata TM1 Server is running. Log on to the IBM Cognos TM1 Contributor page.

How to do it...

1. Log on to the **DemoContr1** application, right-click on **TOTAL COMPANY** and select **Open in TM1 Web Client**.

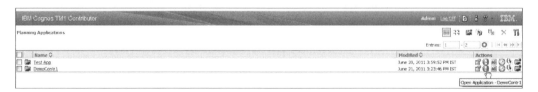

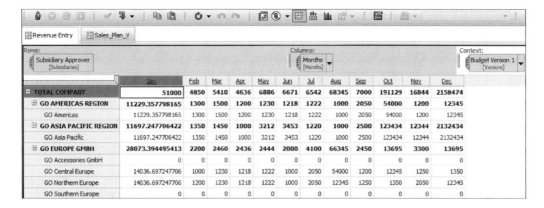

	Jan	Feb	Mar	Apr	May	Jun	Jul	Aug	Sep	Oct	Nov	Dec
TOTAL COMPANY	51000	4850	5410	4636	6886	6671	6542	68345	7000	191129	16844	2158474
GO AMERICAS REGION	11229.357798165	1300	1500	1200	1230	1218	1222	1000	2050	54000	1200	12345
GO Americas	11229.357798165	1300	1500	1200	1230	1218	1222	1000	2050	54000	1200	12345
GO ASIA PACIFIC REGION	11697.247706422	1350	1450	1000	3212	3453	1220	1000	2500	123434	12344	2132434
GO Asia Pacific	11697.247706422	1350	1450	1000	3212	3453	1220	1000	2500	123434	12344	2132434
GO EUROPE GMBH	28073.394495413	2200	2460	2436	2444	2000	4100	66345	2450	13695	3300	13695
GO Accessories GmbH	0	0	0	0	0	0	0	0	0	0	0	0
GO Central Europe	14036.697247706	1000	1230	1218	1222	1000	2050	54000	1200	12345	1250	1350
GO Northern Europe	14036.697247706	1200	1230	1218	1222	1000	2050	12345	1250	1350	2050	12345
GO Southern Europe	0	0	0	0	0	0	0	0	0	0	0	0

2. We have logged on as **Admin**. Click on 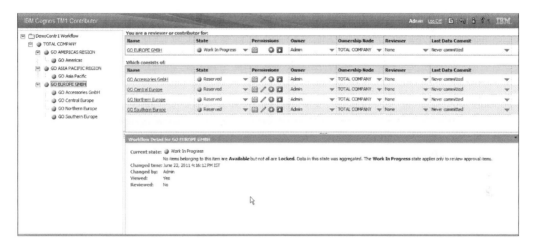 icon on the toolbar to take the ownership of the node, **TOTAL COMPANY**. Take a note of the change in the workflow screen.

3. Also, note the changes in the Contributor Web Portal screen toolbar as shown in the following screenshot:

4. Note that, take ownership icon gets disabled for the current user Admin and icons to commit and submit get enabled.

5. Status bar at the bottom of the window changes to display the current owner and current ownership node.

| Current Owner: Admin | Current Ownership Node: TOTAL COMPANY

6. Now as we have taken ownership of the node from the Admin user, let us modify a child cell data value for example, click on (**GO Southern Europe, Jan**) cell and edit the value to an arbitrary value say 5000. Press *Tab* without pressing *Enter* and the color of the text becomes green. Data is currently in the grid but not saved to the sandbox.

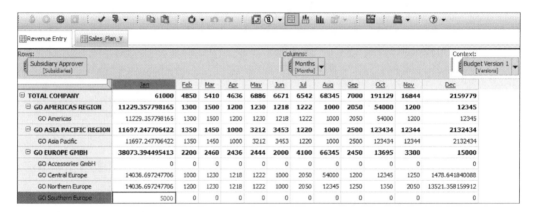

7. Press *Enter* and the text color changes to blue indicating that values are not yet saved back to the database. Change in the color indicates that though values have not been saved back to the database, these are saved to the sandbox. Sandbox data is private to the user and not visible to other users Once it is committed to the database it is made public to other users as well. However, when the data is saved only to Sandbox, it is available to other tabs/views open for the same user, as sandbox is specific to the user. New sandboxes can be added by a user or an existing sandbox can be deleted depending on user rights specified by the administrator. Take a note of the ![icon] icon on the toolbar for that.

8. Now we will try and change data for a consolidated cell using one of the spread methods.

9. In the same grid click on (**GO EUROPE GMBH, Dec**) and then right-click to open the following menu options:

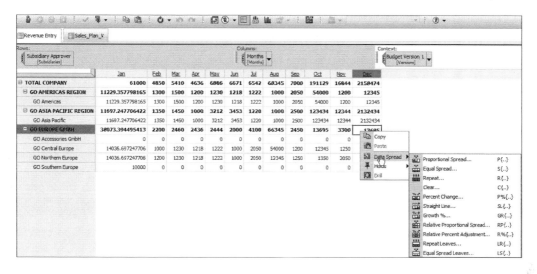

10. **Data Spread** submenu shows a variety of options which are provided by TM1 to spread consolidated value entered to child cells.

11. Here we will click on first option that is **Proportional Spread** to open a submenu using which we can specify intended value for the consolidated cell and how we want to spread the value proportionally.

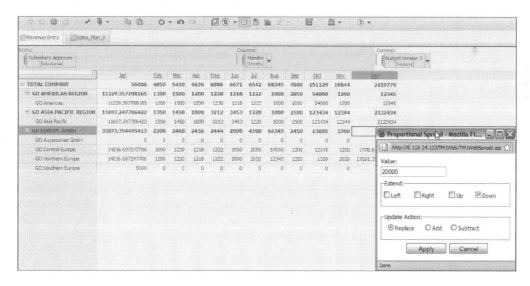

12. Here we want to spread 20000 downwards and we want to replace existing values. Select required options and click on **Apply**.

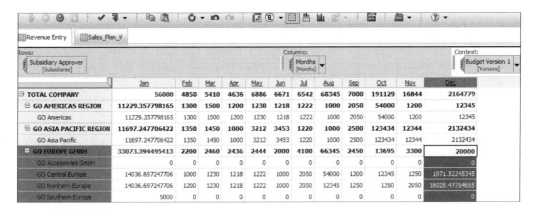

	Jan	Feb	Mar	Apr	May	Jun	Jul	Aug	Sep	Oct	Nov	Dec
TOTAL COMPANY	56000	4850	5410	4636	6886	6671	6542	68345	7000	191129	16844	2164779
GO AMERICAS REGION	11229.357798165	1300	1500	1200	1230	1218	1222	1000	2050	54000	1200	12345
GO Americas	11229.357798165	1300	1500	1200	1230	1218	1222	1000	2050	54000	1200	12345
GO ASIA PACIFIC REGION	11697.247706422	1350	1450	1000	3212	3453	1220	1000	2500	123434	12344	2132434
GO Asia Pacific	11697.247706422	1350	1450	1000	3212	3453	1220	1000	2500	123434	12344	2132434
GO EUROPE GMBH	33073.394495413	2200	2460	2436	2444	2000	4100	66345	2450	13695	3300	20000
GO Accessories GmbH	0	0	0	0	0	0	0	0	0	0	0	0
GO Central Europe	14036.697247706	1000	1230	1218	1222	1000	2050	54000	1200	12345	1250	1971.52245345
GO Northern Europe	14036.697247706	1200	1230	1218	1222	1000	2050	12345	1250	1350	2050	18028.47754655
GO Southern Europe	5000	0	0	0	0	0	0	0	0	0	0	0

13. Take a note of the changed values in blue colored text.

14. Similarly, we can use other options according to the business requirements. Detailed definition of each spread method and its parameters are available in the **Contributor Help** menu which is available from the toolbar as shown in the following screenshot. Note that the spreading is not dynamic (not rules calculated). One-off only.

15. There are various shortcuts available to enter and edit the data quickly without going through and updating each value. These shortcut functions need to be typed in the individual cells and data is automatically updated/entered along the direction specified (left, right, up, down) in the required manner (decreasing, increasing, % increase, % decrease, and so on). Documentation of these shortcut functions is available in same help menu. The user can decide to enter data step-by-step as shown above or these shortcut functions can also be used conveniently.

16. If at any point in time the user is not satisfied with the data entered/edited, he/she can roll back changes or even reset the view.

17. Redo option is also provided on doing an undo.

18. Once satisfied with the values the user needs to click on the commit icon to save data back to the database. Now after commit, data is public and made available to other users as well. After commit, text color for all values changes to black as shown in the following screenshot:

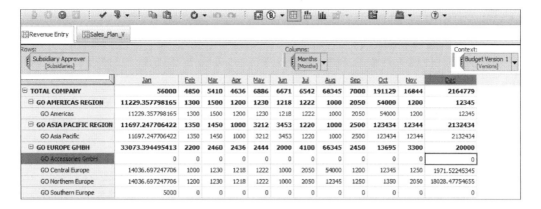

	Jan	Feb	Mar	Apr	May	Jun	Jul	Aug	Sep	Oct	Nov	Dec
⊟ TOTAL COMPANY	56000	4850	5410	4636	6886	6671	6542	68345	7000	191129	16844	2164779
⊟ GO AMERICAS REGION	11229.357798165	1300	1500	1200	1230	1218	1222	1000	2050	54000	1200	12345
GO Americas	11229.357798165	1300	1500	1200	1230	1218	1222	1000	2050	54000	1200	12345
⊟ GO ASIA PACIFIC REGION	11697.247706422	1350	1450	1000	3212	3453	1220	1000	2500	123434	12344	2132434
GO Asia Pacific	11697.247706422	1350	1450	1000	3212	3453	1220	1000	2500	123434	12344	2132434
⊟ GO EUROPE GMBH	33073.394495413	2200	2460	2436	2444	2000	4100	66345	2450	13695	3300	20000
GO Accessories GmbH	0	0	0	0	0	0	0	0	0	0	0	0
GO Central Europe	14036.697247706	1000	1230	1218	1222	1000	2050	54000	1200	12345	1250	1971.52245345
GO Northern Europe	14036.697247706	1200	1230	1218	1222	1000	2050	12345	1250	1350	2050	18028.47754655
GO Southern Europe	5000	0	0	0	0	0	0	0	0	0	0	0

19. Go back to workflow screen to show **Last Data Commit** field. For child nodes workflow state has been changed to **Reserved** which means that data has been committed for these nodes, but not yet submitted. The owner can edit or submit a node in this state. Parent nodes are approval nodes and are in **Work In Progress** state which applies only to the review approval items. This state indicates that no items belonging to this item are **Available**, but not all are **Locked**. Data in this state was aggregated.

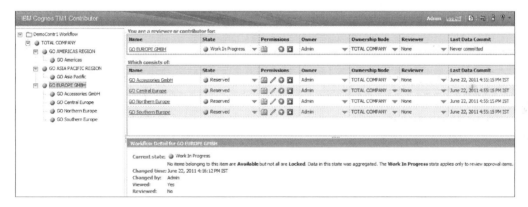

20. Now if we are satisfied with the data we will submit data. The user can submit a node to the next reviewer in the hierarchy when satisfied with the data it contains. After the user has submitted the node, it is locked and no further changes to the data can be made. The reviewer can either accept or reject the changes that user has made to the node.

21. To submit data, user must have rights to submit. If the administrator has enabled multiple sandboxes, the user cannot submit the node from the workflow page. If multiple sandboxes are being used, the user must select the sandbox he wants to submit in TM1 Contributor.

22. Depending on the current node user is working with, and the rights provided to the user for that node, he can submit a single leaf node, multiple leaf nodes, or a consolidated node.

23. We can click on ⊙ icon to submit consolidated node or a single leaf node or on ⊕ icon to submit all leaf nodes under a consolidated node.

24. For this recipe, as we have logged on as Admin and we have submitted rights for all the nodes, we will click on ⊕ icon on the tool bar to submit all leaf nodes under the consolidated node that is **TOTAL COMPANY** in our case, as shown in the following screenshot:

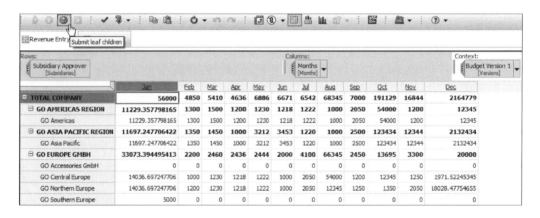

25. After submit, grid becomes read only. The grid has been locked until the reviewer either accepts or rejects the plan.

26. Go back to the workflow screen to view the changes in workflow states. Note that currently we have logged on as Admin, which has submit as well as reviewer rights. Also we have configured an option, which allows the reviewer to edit data in administrative console, which we will see later.

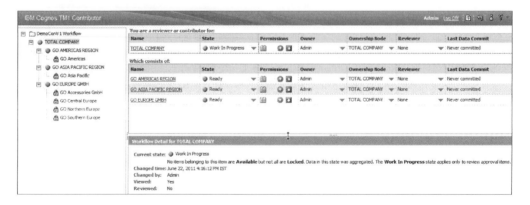

27. Since we have logged on as Admin who is also a reviewer, in workflow screen we are able to see options to submit/accept or reject. For an ordinary user having no approval rights, the grid in the contributor web client would have been read only.

28. In workflow screen, all the child level elements are now in **Locked** state which means the data was submitted and the approval item was locked. Data in this state is read only. If an approval item is rejected, its state returns to **Reserved**.

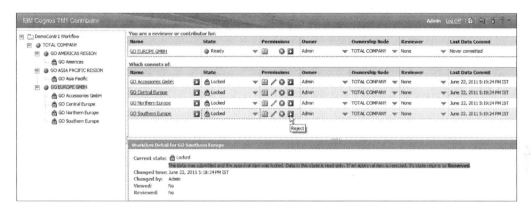

29. Now close the grid and log out from the workflow screen. Save while we shut down the demodata TM1 Server.

There's more...

In the following recipe, we will take a closer look at reviewing data. We will again log on as Admin, review the plan which was submitted, edit the plan if required then either accept it or reject it. In our case we have not created any additional user and not assigned any rights to any user specifically. In our case Admin is playing role of admin, contributor to all nodes and reviewer to all nodes. As we proceed we will see how we can create users and assign them different rights and privileges to contribute or review or both over one or more nodes. The following recipe will deal with the review process in detail.

Reviewing data

Once data has been submitted by contributors, it needs to be reviewed by reviewers. Administrators need to define which users and user groups play the role of contributors, reviewers or both. Whether reviewer will be able to edit data is also defined by administrator, at the time of application design.

We will see how admin assigns various privileges in later sections. Let us look at the following recipe to understand the review process. We will follow same ContrDemo1 application which we have created on top of demodata TM1 server. We have seen how a user has logged on as Admin and submitted the plan he is exposed to. We will now see how the same Admin user can review, edit and accept/reject the plan.

Getting ready

Ensure that TM1 Admin Server service is started and so is Apache Tomcat. Ensure that demodata TM1 Server is running.

How to do it...

1. Open IBM Cognos TM1 Contributor page as Admin, to see the **DemoContr1** application.

2. Open **DemoContr1** application as Admin by clicking on 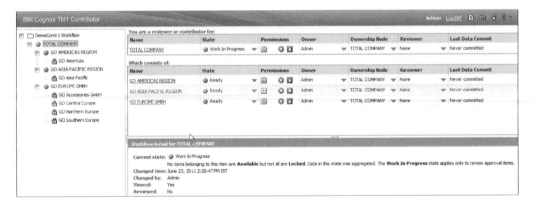 (2107-12-108) icon.

3. Take a note of the workflow screen which now shows updated status of the application, after we had submitted as Admin user. The plan data is ready to get reviewed now. In our case we are using only one user, which is Admin and acting both as contributor and reviewer. We also have edit rights assigned to reviewer which is default setting.

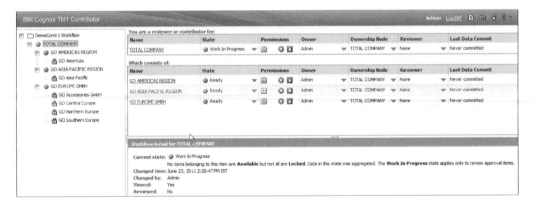

4. Now as shown in the workflow screen data state of the **GO AMERICAS REGION**, **GO ASIA PACIFIC REGION**, and **GO EUROPE GMBH** nodes is in **Ready** state and can be reviewed. Let us click on **GO AMERICAS REGION** and see the information on the right-hand side window.

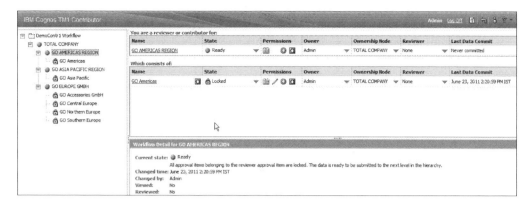

5. Clearly, by looking at right-hand side window we can see that **GO AMERICAS REGION** node is in **Ready** state and logged on user that is Admin has rights to view 📖, Accept/submit 🟢, and Reject 🟥 the plan data.

6. It also says in that the **GO AMERICAS REGION** node consists of **Go Americas** child node which is currently in **Locked** state. Hence, other contributors cannot edit its data. As a reviewer, currently logged on **Admin** user, can edit, view, accept/submit, or reject the plan data.

7. Click on **Go Americas** link to open its data in contributor web client. Since edit rights have been assigned to reviewer as well, we can edit data in the grid otherwise it would have been read only view.

8. Note that we have 🟥 icon besides **Go Americas** link to reject the data directly from the workflow screen. We also have reject icon in contributor web client for child nodes.

9. The web client screen shows data only for the current node which we have clicked that is **Go Americas**. We can view data and if not satisfied we can directly reject it from Contributor Web Client.

10. We can also edit data in the Contributor Web Client.

11. Now close the window and return to workflow screen. Note that reject icon is only for leaf level elements/nodes. However, we can approve from the Contributor Web Client when at the consolidated level. Click on **GO AMERICAS REGION** icon to open it in Web Client.

12. So here we don't have a reject icon which can only be done from leaf level elements (from workflow screen or contributor web portal). We do have a submit icon here which enables user to accept/submit data for the current consolidated node. User can view data and edit and if satisfied submit/accept data to forward that to higher level if applicable, depending on the hierarchy displayed in the workflow screen. Here next level of approval is at **TOTAL COMPANY** level which is currently in **Work In Progress** state, as seen on workflow screen , as lower levels have not been submitted/accepted by reviewers.

13. As soon as reviewer accepts/submits data for lower levels which are displayed below in **Ready** state on workflow screen, the higher level **TOTAL COMPANY** will also change to **Ready** State.

	GO AMERICAS REGION
+	GO ASIA PACIFIC REGION
+	GO EUROPE GMBH

14. Close the contributor web client to return to the workflow screen. Click on **Reject** icon for **GO Southern Europe** to state that reviewer is not satisfied with the data pertaining to the node.

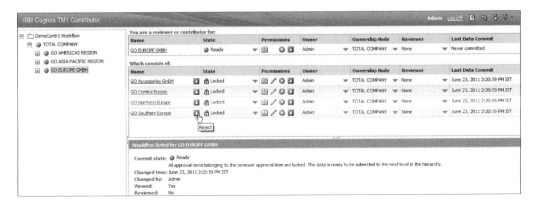

15. Note the changes in the workflow states visible on the workflow screen.

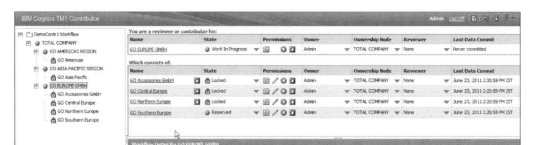

16. **GO Southern Europe** again changed from **Locked** to **Reserved** so that the user who acted as a contributor can now log on and make required changes. State for **GO EUROPE GMBH** also has changed to **Work In Progress** as one of its child nodes is not ready for review and still under update process. States for all other nodes remain as they were before.

17. In the nutshell, all the leaf level elements have to be reviewed by reviewer and can be rejected if plan data for respective node is not satisfactory. Once reviewer is satisfied with all the leaf level elements, he can approve/submit at the approval level which is at consolidated level. Approval at one level will change the state of next higher level from **Work In Progress** to **Ready** (for review) which again needs to be reviewed and so on, until plan goes through complete hierarchy and is submitted/accepted.

18. Until this happens leaf level elements flip flop between **Locked** and **Reserved** state depending on if contributor has submitted data and reviewer has rejected or contributor has not submitted data.

19. Change in state at the lower level will change the state of immediate higher level accordingly.

20. At the end of the recipe try and submit data for **GO ASIA PACIFIC REGION** by opening that in web client and clicking on **Submit** button.

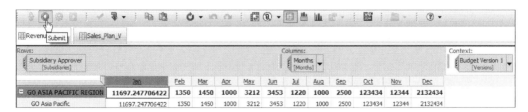

21. This will submit data for the current node that is **GO ASIA PACIFIC REGION**. Note changes in the workflow states for **GO ASIA PACIFIC REGION**, which is now locked and read only as data for this node has been finalized, submitted, reviewed, and accepted.

22. State for **TOTAL COMPANY** is still **Work In Progress** as **GO AMERICAS REGION** has not been reviewed and plan data for one of the child elements of **GO EUROPE GMBH** that is **GO SOUTHERN EUROPE** has been rejected.

23. Once data for these two have been finalized similar to **GO ASIA PACIFIC REGION**, state for **TOTAL COMPANY** will change to **Ready** (for approval) state. Currently it is **Work In Progress** state.

There's more...

In the following recipe we will focus on creating such managed planning applications in IBM Cognos TM1 Contributor and will see user creation and privileges in detail.

Creating and deploying managed planning applications to the Web

In the recipe we will discuss in detail:

▸ Purpose and benefits of a managed planning application

▸ Creating a managed planning application

▸ Applying security to a managed planning application

Throughout previous sections we have been using IBM Cognos TM1 Contributor to create, deploy access, and manage planning applications. This is referred to as IBM Cognos TM1 Contributor Administration.

IBM Cognos TM1 Contributor Administration is used to:

- ▸ Build a managed planning application
- ▸ Maintain a managed planning application
- ▸ Activate and deactivate a managed planning application
- ▸ Assign security rights and privileges
- ▸ Define and validate workflow, contributors, and reviewers
- ▸ Import and export applications

As a general rule we build and maintain applications in IBM Cognos TM1 Administration. We select application content from the IBM Cognos TM1 objects, public views, and public dimension subsets.

Contribution to the applications is done through TM1 contributor interface we have seen earlier which is a zero footprint, browser-based version of TM1 web cube viewer. It supports both Internet Explorer and Firefox.

TM1 servers which will be part of managed planning application must be defined beforehand in the TM1 Contributor Administration tool. Similarly, in the same interface web clients need to be defined. We have seen this earlier also.

Once we are done with defining TM1 servers and web client, managed application needs to be created. TM1 objects included in the TM1 Servers, defined in the above step, are presented as potential content for the managed planning application.

Only public views and subsets, defined in TM1 already can be selected in administration as the content. Multiple public views can be selected and included in the application. This forms content of the application. We can preview the content by double-clicking on the views. The corresponding data is presented in read-only format (gray background) and available for slice and dice. Please note that views are created in TM1 and made public before selecting them in contributor.

Application structure is then defined by selecting a public subset from the available TM1 objects, which forms approval hierarchy for the application. All planning applications have one and only one approval hierarchy which cannot be shared across applications. The hierarchy usually represents an organization chart, a chart of accounts, list of products, or geographical representation of some important aspect of the company such as sales regions. The hierarchy is represented by a public dimension subset and each dimension element represents a node in the planning application. The node is assigned to a user who can be a contributor or a reviewer depending on the security assignments.

Hence, each node represents a contribution entry point where each user depending on the privileges can view, edit, review, or submit the data.

Users take ownership of a node and then can enter data. Each leaf level element must have only one parent that is only one top most node.

Please note that contributor can delete any existing element level security on the approval hierarchy dimension and then apply his/her own element level security in its place.

Next step is to validate, deploy, and secure the application within the context of the IBM Cognos TM1 Contributor Administration.

Hence, four steps required to create a managed planning application are:

- ▸ Selecting TM1 public views which provide data
- ▸ Selecting dimension subset, an approval dimension which provides the structure
- ▸ Deploying the application
- ▸ Assigning security to the application

Getting ready

Ensure that TM1 Admin Server service is started and so is Apache Tomcat Server. Ensure that planning sample TM1 Server is running as a window service as shown. The planning sample TM1 Server is shipped as an example with the TM1 installation package.

If Planning Sample TM1 server is started, log on to the TM1 Architect and open Planning Sample application in TM1 **Server Explorer** window. Note that user ID has been changed to Admin with blank password to make it compatible with existing TM1 servers on contributor (demodata shares same password and all TM1 servers defined on contributor must have same user credentials).

How to do it...

1. In TM1 Architect click on cubes to expand and double-click on **plan_BudgetPlan** to open in the **Cube Viewer** as shown in the following screenshot:

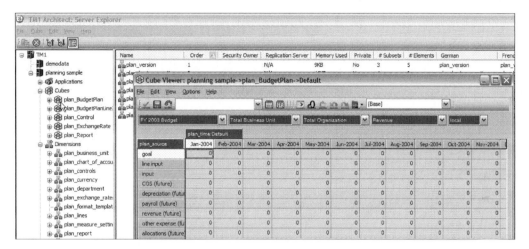

2. In the **Select View** list click on **Budget Input Detailed** and click on **Recalculate**.

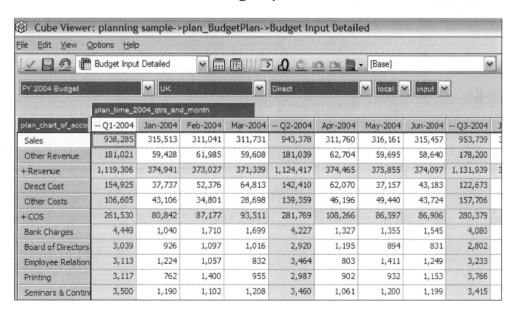

3. This view will be used by contributors for their budgeting and planning applications.

4. Double-click on **UK** to open **Subset Editor**.

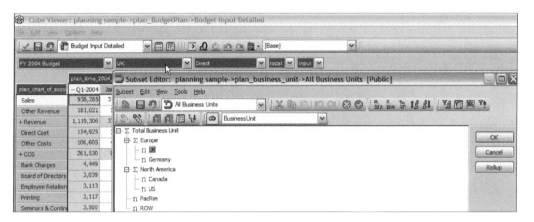

5. The **plan_business_unit** dimension reflects the approval process hierarchy in this application.

6. Click on **OK** to close the **Subset Editor**. Close **Cube Viewer** and **TM1 Architect** without saving any changes.

7. We will now open TM1 Contributor Administration tool.

8. Open the browser and type `http://localhost:8085/pmpsvc` in the address bar to open the log on page for TM1 Contributor Administration. Enter user ID as Admin with blank password.

9. Click on **OK** for the message regarding demodata TM1 server could not be reached, as we have not started the **demodata** TM1 server, but previously defined that in the Admin console. We can choose not to start any TM1 servers we are not using even though it has been defined in the Admin console.

10. On IBM Cognos TM1 Contributor page, click on **Administer IBM Cognos TM1 contributor** (2107-12-131) icon to view which TM1 Servers and web clients are defined.

11. Click on **OK** to return without changing anything.

12. From the **Planning Applications** toolbar on IBM Cognos TM1 Contributor page click on design an application 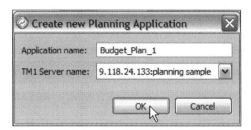 icon.

13. This will open **IBM Cognos TM1 Contributor Administration** tool 9.5.2.

14. Under **File** menu click on **New**.

15. For **Application name** type **Budget_Plan_1**.

16. Note that planning sample TM1 server is specified in the **TM1 Server name** box. Hence, the application will use TM1 objects defined on the **Planning Sample** TM1 Server.

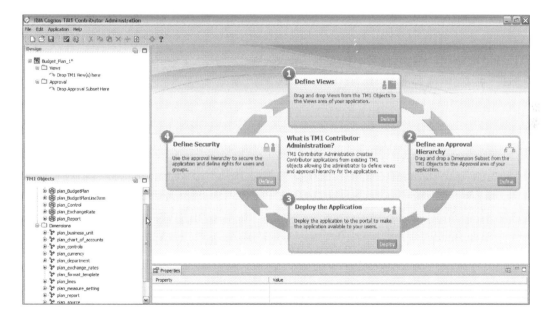

17. So we are able to see TM1 objects available to use on **Planning Sample** TM1 Server.

18. Now we will select multiple TM1 Cube Views and include those in the application.

19. In the lower left hand side window under **TM1 Server | Cubes | plan_BudgetPlan | Views** click on **Budget Input Detailed** view as shown in the following screenshot. This is the cube view in **plan_BudgetPlan** cube we had seen in above steps in **TM1 Architect**.

20. Drag–and-drop the view in **Design** window under **Budget_Plan_1 > Views**.

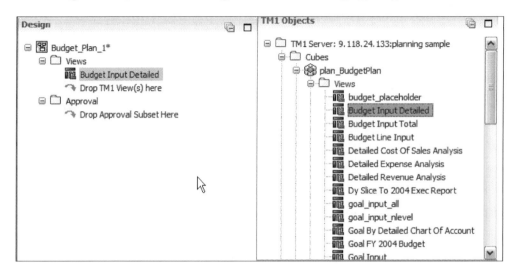

21. Similarly, *Ctrl+Click* to select following views and drag to **Views** area in the **Design** window.

    ❑ **Budget Input Total**

    ❑ **Goal FY 2004 Budget**

    ❑ **Budget Line Input**

    ❑ **Detailed Cost of Sales Analysis**

    ❑ **Detailed Expense Analysis**

▶ **Detailed Revenue Analysis**

    ❑ **Goal by Detailed Chart of Accountant**

    ❑ **Goal Input**

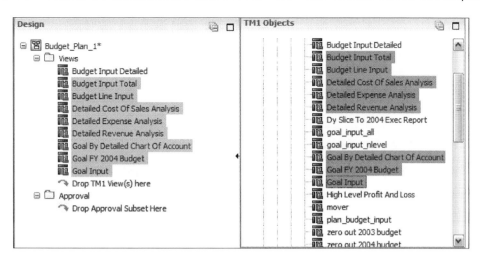

22. Now we will select a public subset containing the approval structure.

23. In the **TM1 Objects** pane expand **Dimensions | plan_business_unit | Subsets** and select **All Business Units** as shown in the following screenshot:

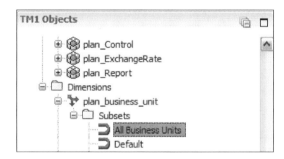

24. Drag **All Business Units** subset to the **Approval** folder in **Design** pane.

25. Click on **Yes** to use the subset as approval dimension.

26. Note that when deployed, current element level security on the approval dimension will be removed and replaced by contributor security which we will define in later sections.

27. From the **File** menu click on **Save As** to save the application by name of **Budget_Plan_1** at C:\Program Files\Cognos\TM1\Custom\TM1Data\PlanSamp.

28. It is saved as .XML file ![Budget_Plan_1.xml].

29. From the **Application** menu click on **Validate** and **Deploy** ☑ ⬢.

30. From **File** menu click on **Exit** to close the IBM Cognos TM1 Contributor Administration.

31. In the IBM Cognos TM1 Contributor window click on refresh 🔃 icon to display the application.

Now next sections will focus on assigning security privileges and will use same application created above, hence keep the IBM Cognos TM1 Contributor open.

Setting security and access rights

Access rights can be explicitly applied to specific nodes in the approval hierarchy of the application, instead of using either IBM Cognos native or IBM Cognos 8 security.

If rights are explicitly applied to the parent node then child node inherits those rights. Child can have a different set of privileges than the parent, but in no case can these rights exceed rights of the respective parents.

At any given point in time only one user has exclusive write access or ownership of a specific node.

Different rights which can be assigned in IBM Cognos TM1 Contributor are:

Access type	Description
View	Read only access to the node. Cannot take ownership of the node.
Edit	Have edit rights and can take ownership of the node.
Submit	Can take ownership of a node. Can edit values and submit the node for review. Can reject submission from child nodes.
Review	Can edit or submit their own nodes. Can review and reject child nodes which have been submitted. If allow reviewer edit is enabled users can take ownership of any child node which has not been submitted edit values and submit the node.

While managing rights for the application there are two important settings which are useful. These are review depth and view depth settings. We will see these along with assigning above rights to users in one of the recipes in later sections. For now we will look at the significance of these two settings in theory.

The review depth option is enabled only when the review or submit right is selected. The review depth determines how many levels beneath the current node will inherit the selected access right. For instance, if user wants only immediate children of the current node to inherit rights, one (1) needs to be selected.

The view depth determines how many levels below the current node are visible to the user group. For instance, if we want members of the user group to be able to view only the current node and its immediate children, one (1) needs to be selected.

The review depth setting can never be greater than the view depth setting.

Before security to nodes is assigned in IBM Cognos TM1 Contributor, users must have access to the model. Typically, users are given access to TM1 Server and assigned to groups. Groups are then given access to different TM1 objects like cubes elements and dimensions.

These users and groups can be defined in Cognos 8 or IBM native security but in our example we will create users and groups manually in TM1 using TM1 security.

Once users are assigned to groups, groups are then given, one of the following privileges to TM1 Objects, in TM1 Architect.

Privilege	Description
READ	See it Not modify it
WRITE	Write to data
LOCK	Permanently locks it unless the user unlocks it
ADMIN	May do anything. Edit, Create, Delete, and so on
NONE	May not do anything
RESERVE	Temporarily lock it until the serve is reset or the admin or the user unlocks it

Let's see all this in detail, in the recipe on *Assigning security to managed planning applications*.

Assigning security to managed planning applications

In this recipe we will assign security to our previously created planning application. This would be based on planning sample TM1 Server, we have seen earlier.

Getting ready

Ensure that TM1 Admin Server and planning sample service are started. Apache Tomcat Server should be up and running. Open TM1 Architect from the start menu and log on to the planning sample.

How to do it...

1. Right-click on **Planning Sample** in **TM1 Architect: Server Explorer** and click on **Security | Clients/Groups**.

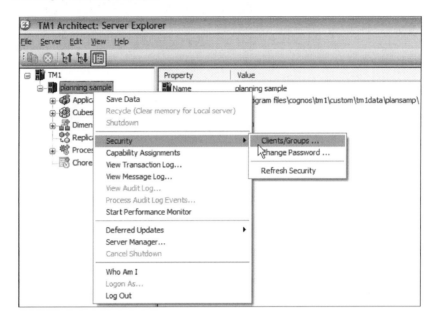

2. In the resulting screen all the users and groups pertaining to **Planning Sample** TM1 Server are shown along with their access rights on TM1 Objects.

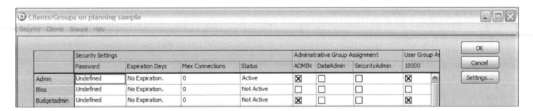

3. Users are shown in rows. **Security Settings** are shown in first four columns and then groups are listed along columns.

4. **ADMIN, DataAdmin, SecurityAdmin** are groups defined by default in TM1 and their privileges may not be altered.

5. The groups that follow along columns are defined by administrator or modeler.

6. Users are assigned to groups by clicking on checkboxes ☒ (2107-12-144) at the intersection of **Users** and **Groups**.

7. **Client** menu can be used to add new users.

8. **Groups** menu is used to add new groups.

9. Take a note of the **BUDGET_PLANNER** and **BUDGET_REVIEWER** groups which need to have access to the cubes in our managed planning application (**Budget_Plan_1** in the preceding recipe).

10. We will use TM1 Contributor to assign the groups, access rights to nodes. Hence element level privileges will be specified using TM1 Contributor.

11. Close the window without saving anything to return to **Server Explorer**.

12. Right-click on **Cubes** and click on **Security Assignments**.

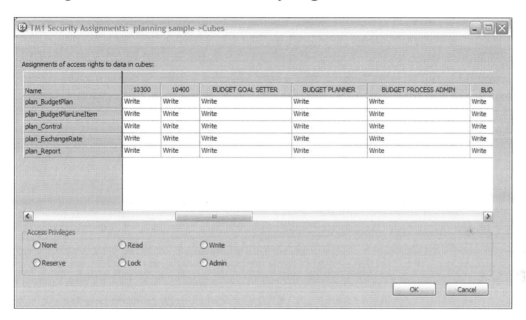

13. In the preceding window, cubes are listed along rows and user groups along columns. Access privileges to a cube can hence be defined for user groups by clicking on the intersecting cell and clicking the privilege.

14. In our application (**Budget_Plan_1**) we are using **plan_BudgetPlan** cube and **BUDGET_REVIEWER. BUDGET_PLANNER** has **WRITE** access to the cube. Close the window without saving any changes.

15. Minimize the **TM1 Architect**.

16. Now we need to activate our newly created managed planning application that is **Budget_Plan_1** in TM1 Contributor.

17. Make sure that Apache Tomcat Server is started and log on to the TM1 Contributor.

18. In IBM Cognos TM1 Contributor click on the **Activate Application** ![icon] for **Budget_ Plan_1**.

19. For **Budget_Plan_1** application click on **Manage Rights for Application** ![icon].

20. This will open interface to assign element/node level security to users and groups as explained.

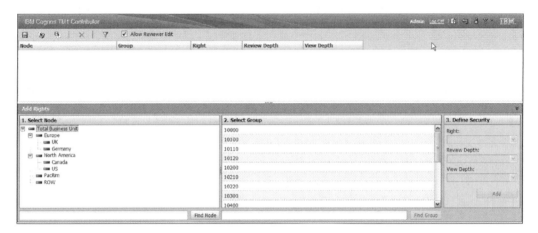

21. From the **Add Rights** section the **Select Node** pane displays approval hierarchy defined as part of the application. We will select **Select Group** that has access to these nodes. Note that these groups have been defined in TM1 and given access to these elements by defining security on **Dimensions** in TM1 Architect.

22. As a rule we are giving access to these TM1 Objects, to users and groups in TM1 Architect first and then assigning element/node level security in Contributor.

23. Now under **Select Node** pane select **North America** which is consolidation of **Canada** and **US**. In the **Select Group** box next to it, in **Find Group** text box type **BUDGET REVIEWER**.

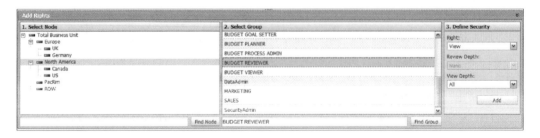

24. Under **Define Security** box select **Review** from the **Right:** drop-down list. Leave the defaults for **Review Depth:** and **View Depth:**. Click on **Add**.

25. Hence we have defined that **BUDGET REVIEWER** group defined in TM1 has **Review** rights for **North America** node and hence its children **US** and **Canada**.

26. The result is shown in upper pane.

27. Now in the **Select Node** pane type **Canada** and then click on **Find Node**.

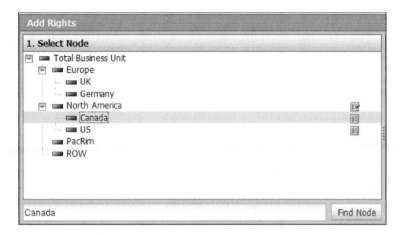

28. In the **Select Group** pane, type **BUDGET PLANNER** and click on **Find Group**.

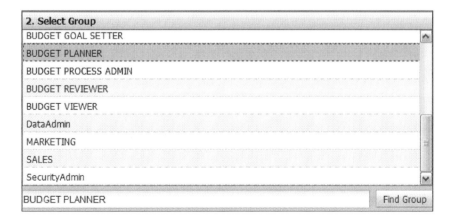

29. Click on **BUDGET PLANNER** and in the **Define Security** pane, click on **Submit** from the **Right:** drop down list.

30. Leave the defaults for **Review Depth** and **View Depth**. Click on **Add** button.

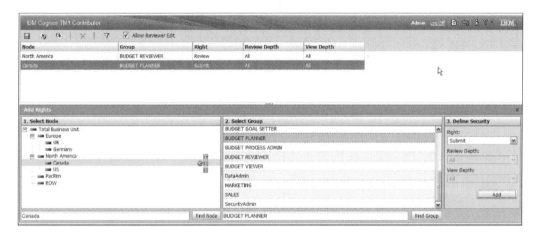

31. Hence, **Canada** node by default inherits **BUDGET REVIEWER** as **Reviewer** from its parent **North America**. In addition to that **BUDGET PLANNER** has submit rights defined explicitly on **Canada** node/element.

32. On the toolbar click on **Save** and then on the return ⬎.

33. Note that as we have not started demodata TM1 Server, contributor will throw a warning stating that the TM1 Server (demodata) cannot be reached. Click on **OK** to dismiss the warning every time it appears.

34. Click on **Log off** from IBM Cognos TM1 Contributor.

35. In TM1 we have a user called **Howell** assigned to **BUDGET PLANNER** group, but not to the **BUDGET REVIEWER** group as shown in the TM1 Architect window, which we have seen earlier also.

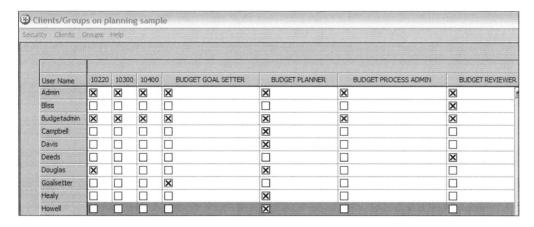

36. Use the same user **Howell** to log on to IBM Cognos TM1 Contributor.

37. Observe that now we have limited functionality as we have logged on as a non Admin user.

38. Click on **Budget_Plan_1** as shown to open IBM Cognos TM1 Contributor Workflow Screen.

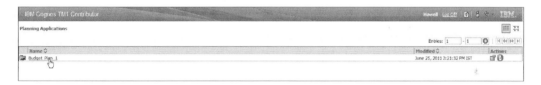

39. Observe that as a **BUDGET PLANNER, Howell** only has **Submit** rights to **Canada**. Click on **Canada** in the left pane under **Budget_Plan_1Workflow**, right-click and select **Open in TM1 Web Client**. Note initial state of the node which is **Available** now with no owner. In TM1 Contributor 9.5.1 status would have been **Not Started** instead of **Available** but semantics are the same.

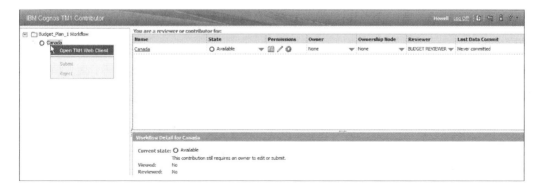

40. Hence in the resulting screen in web client, we can see that views selected are represented by tabs at the top. Also the **plan_business_unit** reflects the **Canada** node. The grid now can be used to contribute data for **Canada** and submit results for approval. Close all the windows without saving anything.

How it works...

This marks end of the section at the end of the section in which we have already seen basic concepts regarding managed planning applications and we should now play around in more detail.

13
Defining Workflow

In this chapter, we will cover:

- ▶ Adding users and groups to the TM1 Security
- ▶ Installing IBM Cognos TM1 Workflow
- ▶ Adding a new process and task using IBM Cognos TM1 workflow
- ▶ Reviewing submitted tasks

Introduction

In the preceding chapter, we looked at different aspects of a managed planning application. We created different TM1 objects and used those in contributor as part of creating our first web-based managed planning application. We used contributor extensively which was previously part of IBM Cognos Enterprise Planning suite and integrated with IBM Cognos TM1 later.

In this chapter, we will talk about one more such component, TM1 Workflow, which was called Planning Manager prior to TM1 version 9.4. This component is pretty old and has been practically replaced by newer components such as IBM Cognos TM1 Contributor. Hence readers can skip this chapter, if TM1 Workflow is not relevant to them.

We will start with installing TM1 Workflow which is a simple click and finish interface. We will configure TM1 Workflow and will have a look at the use cases.

We will also review TM1 security, part of which we have already seen while discussing managed planning applications in the previous chapter.

Before installing and using TM1 Workflow, TM1 needs to be configured in following manner:

- ▸ User, groups, and roles need to be defined.
- ▸ Cubes contain a Version dimension that reflects task and review structure.

Workflow will create elements in the Version dimension that reflect task and review structure of the organization. Dimension must be named as Version.

As seen previously, dimension which reflects task and review structure of the organization may include region, subsidiaries, accounts, or a combination of these dimensions.

In our case subsidiary will be the dimension which reflects task and review structure.

Users will be having responsibility for one or more tasks defined as part of the workflow. This requires TM1 security allowing the user access to any associated elements.

In the following recipe, we will focus on TM1 Security.

Adding users and groups to the TM1 Security

Now after we have learned basic and advanced features of TM1 Objects, we will look at applying basic security to these. We are now familiar with various terms and terminologies as well as basic use cases, and therefore in a much better position to understand how, when, and why to put the additional layer of TM1 Security in place.

In the recipe we will be:

- ▸ Creating users and groups.
- ▸ Assigning access to TM1 Objects at cube, dimension and element level.

TM1 provides interface:

- ▸ To create users, who can access server.
- ▸ Define the number of connections to the server, allowed for each user.

Users are then assigned to one of the user groups. User groups then give access to individual TM1 Objects and give privileges such as:

- ▸ Admin
- ▸ Read
- ▸ Write
- ▸ Lock
- ▸ Reserve
- ▸ None

Security defined in TM1 Contributor will override any other element level security settings defined in TM1 Architect as we are about to see in the next sections.

We will demonstrate the preceding security related concepts in this recipe which is based on the demodata TM1 Server, which we have been following up.

Getting ready

Ensure that TM1 Admin Server service is started. Make sure that demodata TM1 server is running. Open TM1 Architect from the Start Menu, and log on to demodata TM1 server with admin user and blank password.

How to do it...

1. In **Server Explorer** right-click on demodata TM1 server, point to **Security** and then click on **Clients/Groups**.

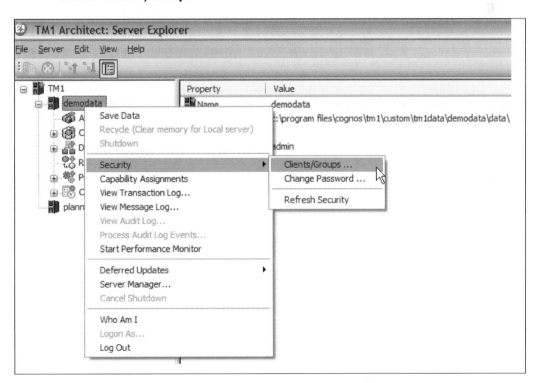

2. By default **Admin** user is created and is assigned to **ADMIN** group.

3. We will now add users and groups from the **Client** menu as shown in the following screenshot:

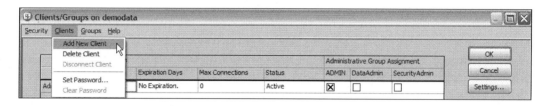

4. Add a user by name of Fiona.

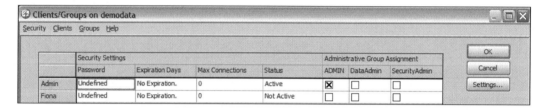

5. Similarly add few more users such as Nick, Joy, Sam, Troy, and Isha.

6. Now let's add a group from the **Groups** menu as shown in the following screenshot:

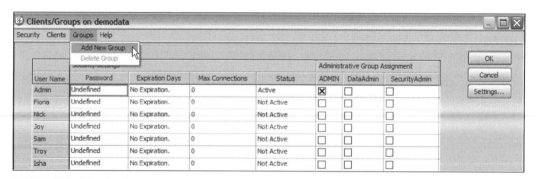

7. Add the group's CFO, Executive, and Manager.

8. These appear as columns at the end of the same window.

9. Now we will assign users to the groups by selecting the intersection cells between users and groups.

10. Next to **Fiona** select check box under **CFO** as shown in the following screenshot:

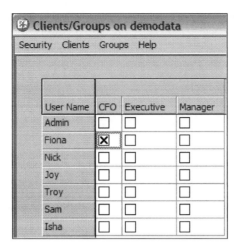

11. Similarly let's define **Nick** and **Joy** as **Executives** and the rest as **Managers**.

12. Click on **OK** to close the window.

13. Now we will define element level security for **Subsidiaries** dimension.

14. In the **Server Explorer** window, under **Dimensions**, right-click on **Subsidiaries**, point to **Security** and then click on **Elements Security Assignments**.

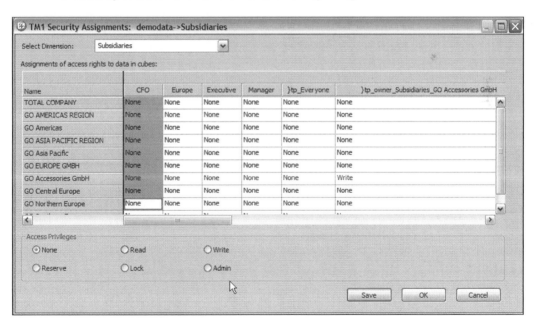

15. As shown in the preceding screenshot we have recently added groups displayed along columns and dimension elements displayed as rows. Each cell displays security type assigned to that intersection which can be changed by clicking a radio button at the bottom.

16. Assign access privileges to elements, for **CFO**, **Executive**, and **Manager** security group as shown. Clearly **CFO** has right to **Write** for each child and parent subsidiary. **Executive** has **Read** privilege for individual subsidiary, but has **Write** access to the whole region. Individual **Manager** has **Write** rights to individual subsidiaries, but only **Read** rights to the consolidated grouping.

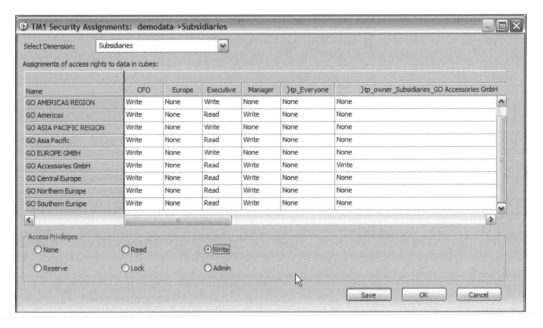

17. Click on **OK** to close.

18. Before data can be edited or entered from MS Excel Perspectives, to the Cubes, make sure that user groups defined by us have necessary rights on relevant cubes and dimensions. Hence cubes should allow users to enter data and dimensions should be readable from UIs.

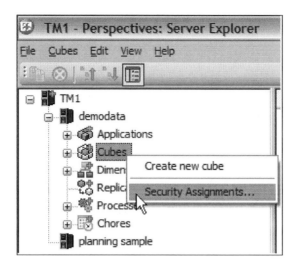

19. If we wanted to enter data for **Expenses** cube only, through **CFO**, **Executive,** and **Manager** groups, we would have given **Write** privileges only on that cube. Rest of cubes would have not been available for **Write** (and **Access Privileges** set to **None**).

20. Similarly in **Server Explorer**, right-click on **Dimensions** and ensure **Read** privileges are given to our groups on relevant dimensions as shown in the following screenshot:

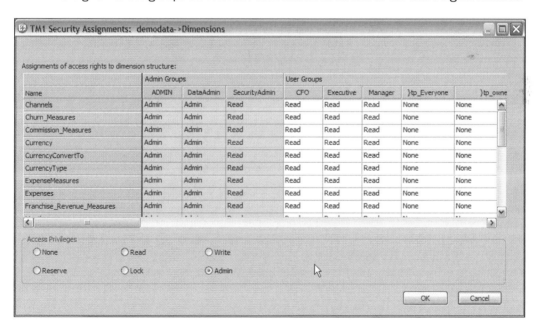

21. Hence whatever exercises we want to carry out, we will give necessary privileges on associated TM1 Objects only.

How it works...

We have created users and groups on demodata TM1 Server and assigned them to specific elements for specific privileges. These users will be now assigned tasks related to their roles in budgeting and forecasting process.

Installing IBM Cognos TM1 Workflow

In this recipe we will be installing IBM Cognos TM1 Workflow 9.5.2 and will get that working. We will use the same TM1 Workflow setup later in the recipes.

Getting ready

Close the TM1 Data Server, saving changes if prompted. From **Control Panel** open **Add/Remove Programs** and remove TM1 Workflow if installed already. Restart machine and then ensure that TM1 Admin Server service is started.

How to do it...

1. Double-click on setup file for IBM Cognos TM1 Workflow 9.5.2 and follow simple instructions.

2. The installation consists of:

    ❑   TM1 Web toolbar on the web server

    ❑   Microsoft Excel Toolbar and the add-in

    ❑   TM1 Control Cubes in the TM1 Server data directory

    Once installation is complete, restart the machine and follow these steps to attach the Workflow with demodata TM1 server.

3. Copy all the files at `C:\Program Files\Cognos\TM1\Custom\TM1Data\TM1 Planning Manager V2\` to copy all the workflow control objects.

4. Paste all the files and folders to `C:\Program Files\Cognos\TM1\Custom\TM1Data\DemoData\Data` which is the data directory for demodata TM1 Server.

5. Now start the demodata TM1 Server in the **Server Explorer**. Log on to the demodata TM1 Server using **admin** user.

6. Now from the **Start Menu** go to **IBM Cognos | TM1** and click on **Perspectives for MS Excel**.

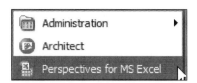

7. It will open **Perspectives for MS Excel**, which is another client, using which users can access TM1 Objects through MS Excel. It gets installed with TM1 Server, but requires existing Microsoft Excel installed on the workstation.

8. Click on **Enable Macros** when starting **Perspectives for MS Excel**. Note that MS Excel toolbar has additional add-ins for **TM1** and **TM1 Workflow**.

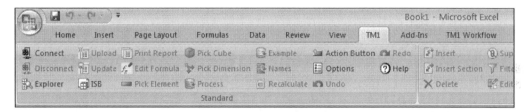

9. Under **TM1 Workflow** tab, click on **Load** ![Load] icon to load the TM1 Workflow Toolbar.

10. It will prompt to connect to a TM1 Server. Select demodata and log in as Admin with blank password.

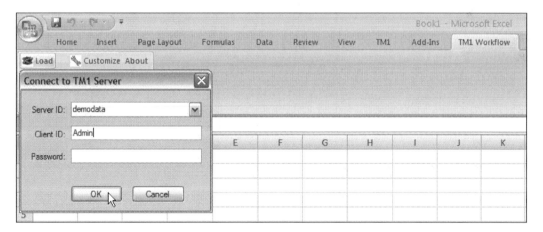

11. We are now connected to TM1 Server **demodata** through TM1 **Perspectives for MS Excel** and **TM1 Workflow** is available to the user Admin.

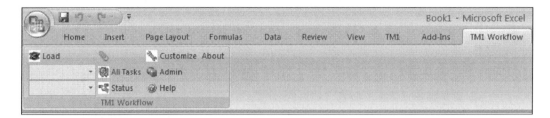

How it works...

The concept is same what we have seen in earlier sections about IBM Cognos TM1 Contributor. In the following recipe, we will see details about IBM Cognos TM1 Workflow in particular. Based on availability of tools either IBM Cognos TM1 Contributor or IBM Cognos TM1 Workflow or both can be used.

Adding a new process and task using IBM Cognos TM1 Workflow

As seen earlier, a workflow process is a series of tasks representing a business process. It consists of primarily a task and review structure which is similar to what we have in IBM Cognos TM1 Contributor. Tasks are assigned to an owner, which gets reviewed by reviewers.

In this recipe we will be using demodata TM1 Server and use TM1 Perspectives for MS Excel as main interface. We will also create another cube called ExpenseDetails and attach its view to a workflow process so that data can be entered, edited, submitted, and reviewed.

Getting ready

Ensure that TM1 Admin Server service is started. Start demodata TM1 Server and log in to the TM1 Architect.

How to do it...

1. In the **Server Explorer** right-click on **Cubes** and create a new cube by name of **ExpenseDetails** as shown in the following screenshot:

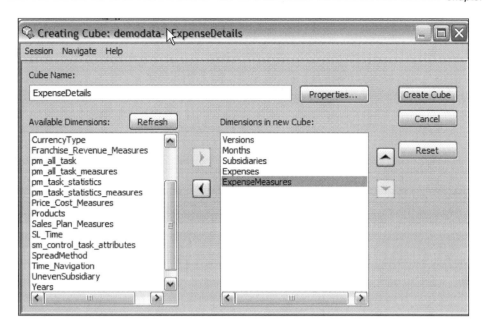

2. Create and save a public view named **ExpenseDetails** as shown in the following screenshot:

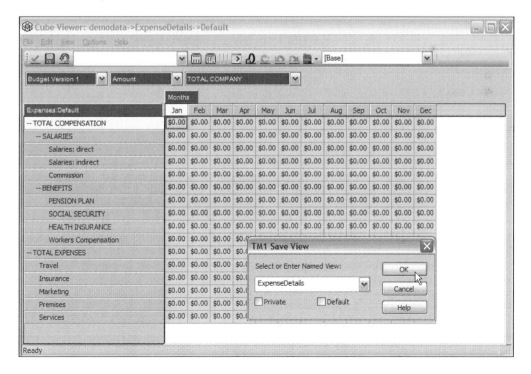

3. Now right-click on **Applications** from **Server Explorer** and click on **Create New Application**.

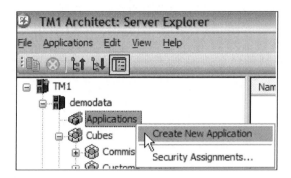

4. Rename the newly created application as **ExpenseDetails** and make it public as shown in the following screenshot:

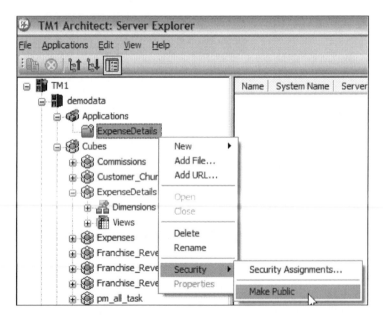

5. Close the **Server Explorer** and keep the demodata server running.

6. **Enable Macros** when prompted. Click on the **TM1** tab and say **Connect**.

7. Log on as **admin** on demodata server.

8. Once connected open the **Server Explorer** ![Explorer].

9. It will pop up a window **TM1 – Perspectives: Server Explorer** showing similar interface as of TM1 Architect as shown in the following screenshot:

10. Under **Cubes** open **ExpenseDetails** cube view as shown in the following screenshot:

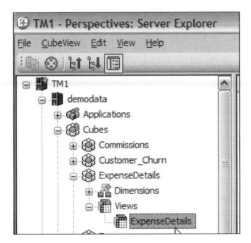

11. On **Cube Viewer** click on **Slice** ![icon] icon.

12. It will open the current **Cube Viewer** in TM1 **Perspectives for MS Excel**.

13. Rename the sheet as **ExpenseDetails** as shown in the following screenshot:

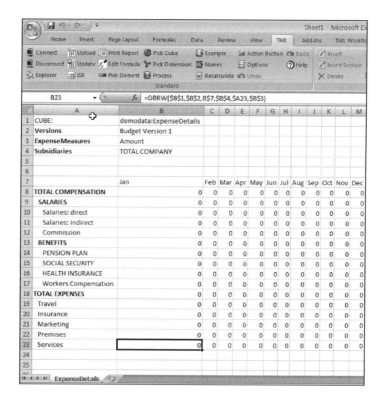

14. Name the range as **ExpenseDetails**.

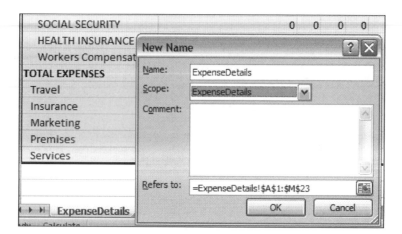

15. Apply whatever formatting is required using MS Excel and TM1 options wherever applicable. Save the excel sheet as `ExpenseDetails.xls` at following locations.

  ❏ `C:\Program Files\cognos\TM1\Custom\TM1Data\PData`

  ❏ `C:\Program Files\cognos\TM1\Custom\TM1Data\DemoData\Data`

16. While the first path is data directory of TM1 Admin Server, second one is data directory for demodata TM1 Server. From MS Excel interface also, excel sheet can be saved on TM1 Server (**TM1 Menu | Save Workbook on TM1 Server**) and then upload **New Application** file to **TM1 Server**).

17. Now from the **TM1** menu click on [Upload] icon to upload the excel sheet to the **ExpenseDetails** application folder.

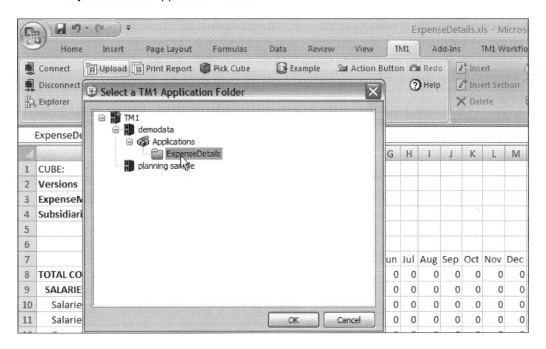

18. Click on **OK** and from the **TM1 – Perspective: Server Explorer**, make the excel sheet as public so that icon changes to ExpenseDetails.xls .

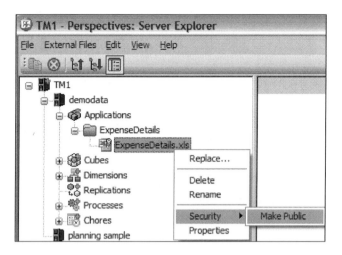

19. Now close the workbook and **TM1 – Perspective: Server Explorer**. From the IBM Cognos **TM1 Perspectives for MS Excel**, go to **TM1 Workflow** tab. Make sure that Admin user is still connected.

20. We will now define the workflow process to enter, submit, and approve the expense figures for 12 months, based on **ExpenseDetails** worksheet. Data will be fed into **ExpenseCube** through **Perspectives for MS Excel** or TM1 Web Interface. We will look at TM1 Web Interface in later sections.

21. In the **Perspectives for MS Excel**, from the **TM1 Workflow** tab click on **Admin** Admin icon.

22. It will pop up a new window, **Process Wizard**, to create a new workflow process.

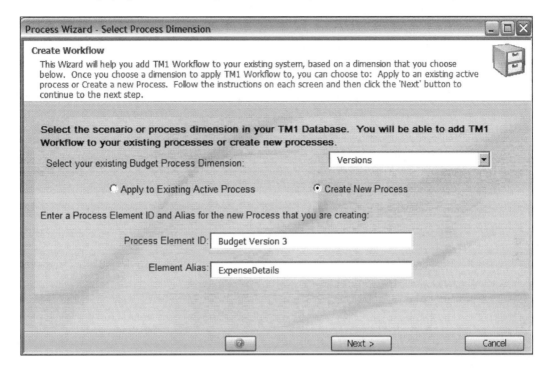

23. On first screen of **Process Wizard** that is **Select Process Dimension**, we have options to either use an existing process or create a new process. We need to make sure that **Versions** dimension is selected for **Select your existing Budget Process Dimension**.

24. Hence we are up to creating a new workflow process. A new element **Budget Version 3** with alias **ExpenseDetails** will be created for **Versions** dimension. Data entered will be available for **Budget Version 3** under **Versions** dimension.

25. Click on **Next** button.

26. Next window would be **Process Wizard – Build Task and Review Hierarchy** which will have **Create Task and Review Template**. It is divided into two panes. Left pane allows user to specify dimensions and subsets which should reflect organizational structure. It is same as the reviewer dimension we discussed in previous chapter on IBM Cognos TM1 Contributor. The only difference being that multiple dimensions and subsets can be used to generate review structure of the workflow.

27. In the **Create Task and Review Template**, in left-hand side pane for **Dimension** click on **Subsidiaries.**

28. This defines review and approval structure of the organization. Click on **TOTAL COMPANY** element in left-hand side pane, drag-and-drop it to the right-hand side pane as shown in the following screenshot:

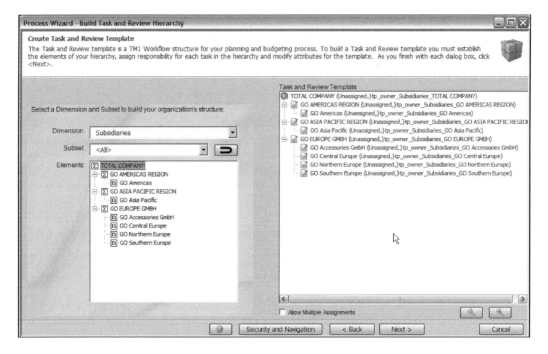

29. Hence we have defined **Task and Review Template** for the process. We can add, or remove subsets from multiple dimensions as opposed to IBM Cognos TM1 Contributor where we can have only one dimension selected for task and review structure. This way TM1 workflow is more flexible, hence elements and subsets can be added, removed, renamed, created, and edited from one or more dimensions as well. Click on **Next**.

30. In the **Process Wizard - Assign Responsibility** window, expand the **CFO** group, select **Fiona** and drag on top of **TOTAL COMPANY**.

31. Now the TM1 user **Fiona** has been assigned responsibility for **TOTAL COMPANY** data.

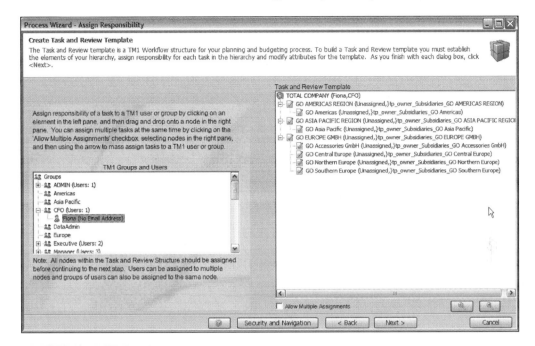

32. Repeat above step to assign users as shown in the following screenshot:

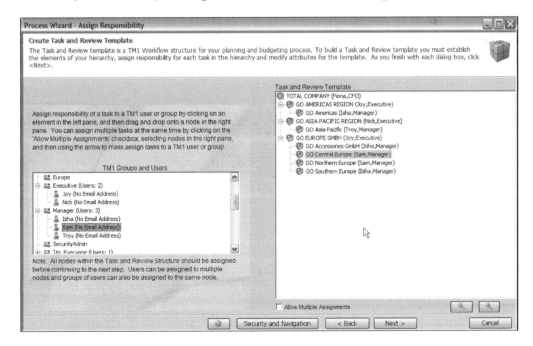

33. Click on **Next**.

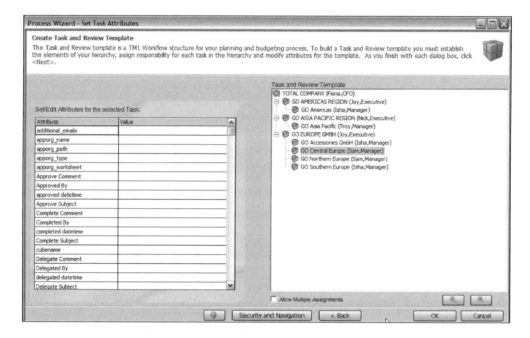

34. In the **Process Wizard - Set Task Attributes** window, select the **GO Americas** task and scroll down to the **Name** attribute.

35. There are a number of attributes for each task which include **Due Date**, **Owner**, **owner group**, and **Post Action TI Process** which can be executed when the task is completed.

36. Scroll down to **Submit Subject** and click on ellipses next to it. On the **Subject** line type as shown in the following screenshot:

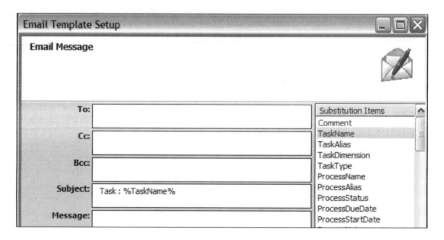

37. Now when the selected task is submitted, an e-mail will be sent to the reviewer stating the given subject in the subject line. **%TaskName%** indicates variable which gets updated depending on the task that gets updated. Click on **OK**.

Submit Comment	
Submit Subject	Task : %TaskName%
Submitted By	
submitted datetime	

38. On the **Process Wizard – Initialize Workflow**, click on **Security and Navigation** button.

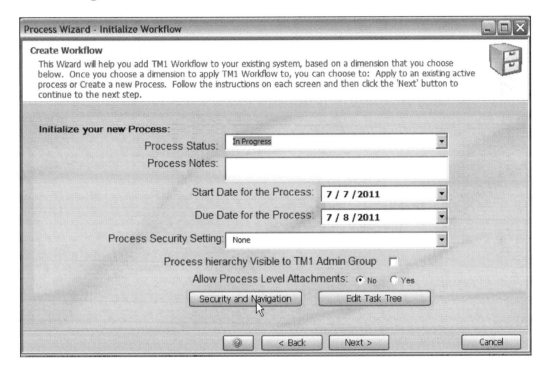

39. It will open **Security and Navigation** wizard as shown in the following screenshot:

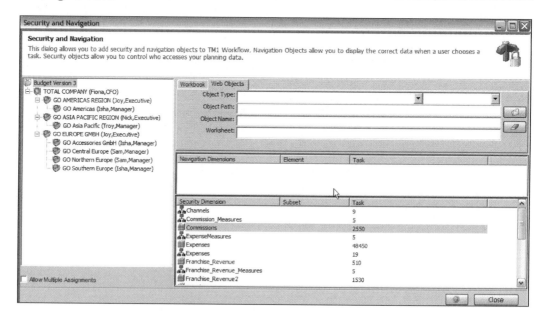

40. In this window we will assign a workbook to be used for all the tasks listed.

41. Select the **Allow Multiple Assignments** box in the lower left corner of the window.

42. Select the checkboxes for **TOTAL COMPANY** and all its children as shown in the following screenshot:

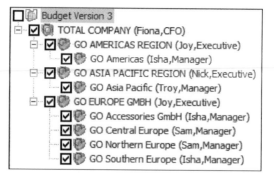

43. Click the **Workbook** tab.

44. Select 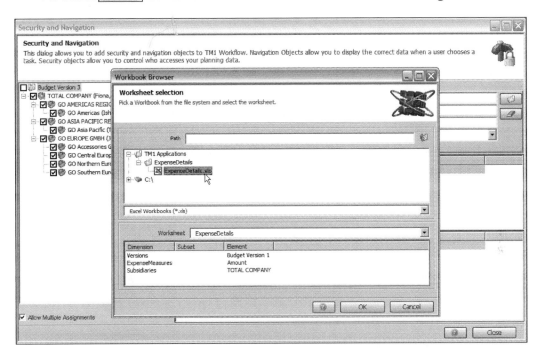 icon to select workbook **Path** as shown in the following screenshot:

45. Click on **Close** button to return to **Process Wizard – Initialize Workflow** window.

46. In the **Process Wizard – Initialize Workflow** window besides **Due Date for the Process** increase the current month by one.

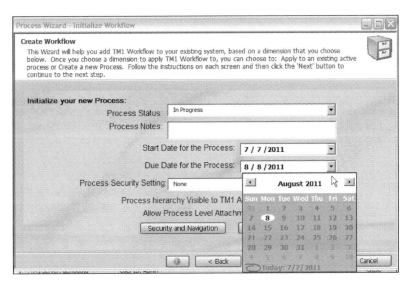

47. Select the **Process hierarchy Visible to TM1 Admin Group** checkbox.

48. Click on **Yes** for **Allow Process Level Attachments**.

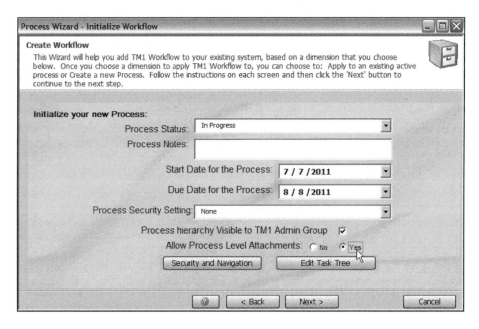

49. Click on **Next** to review the details.

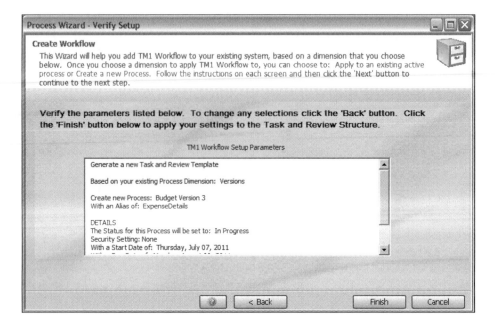

Generate a new **Task** and **Review Template**

Based on your existing **Process Dimension: Versions**

Create new **Process: Budget Version 3**

With an alias of: **ExpenseDetails**

DETAILS

The Status for this Process will be set to: **In Progress**

Security Setting: **None**

With a Start Date of: Thursday, July 07, 2011

With a Due Date of: Monday, August 08, 2011

Notes:

50. Click on **Finish** button without notifying users and click on **Close**.

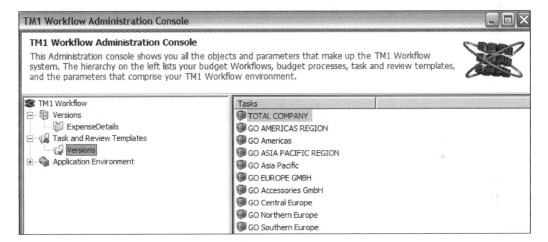

51. From the **Perspectives for MS Excel** interface click on **Admin** from the **TM1 Workflow** tab.

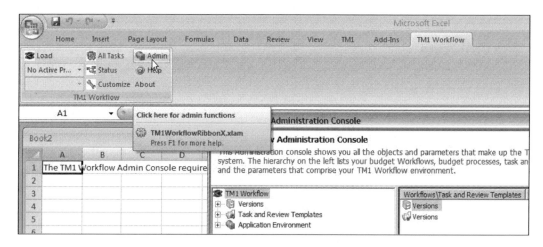

52. Expand **Versions** to view the **ExpenseDetails** process we have just created.

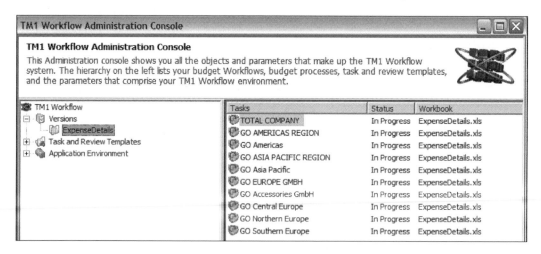

53. Close the **TM1 Workflow Administration Console** and **Perspectives for MS Excel**. Ensure that the demodata server is running.

54. Open TM1 Architect and log in as admin user. Make sure following security assignments are in place.

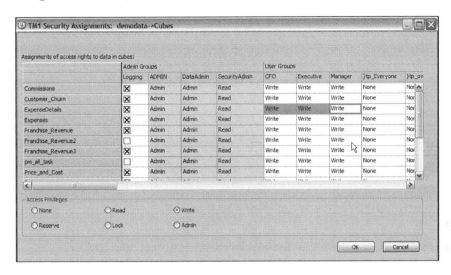

55. Right-click on **Versions** dimension and navigate to **Elements Security Assignments**.

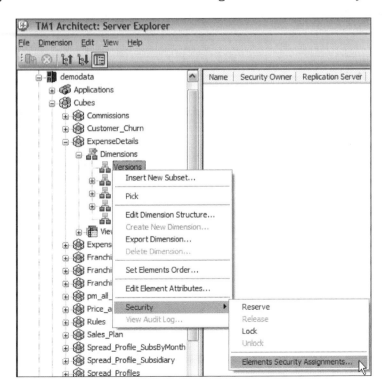

56. A new element **Budget Version 3** has been created as shown in the following screenshot:

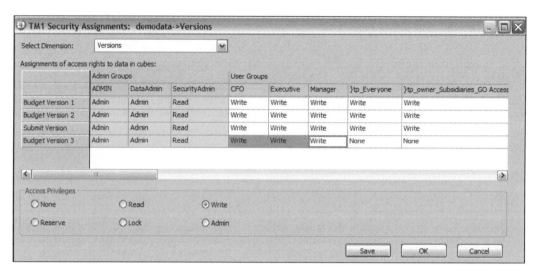

57. Take a note of the security privileges.

58. Now log out as admin user, close the TM1 Architect window and **open TM1 Perspectives for MS Excel** from the **Start** Menu.

59. In the **TM1 Perspectives for MS Excel**, under the **TM1 Workflow** tab click on 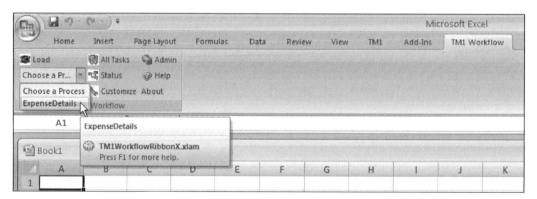 icon.

60. Connect to the TM1 Server demodata with username specified as **Isha** who is responsible to enter data for **GO America**.

61. Click on **Choose a Process** and select the process **ExpenseDetails**.

62. Click on **Choose a Task** and select **GO Americas** which is currently **In Progress**.

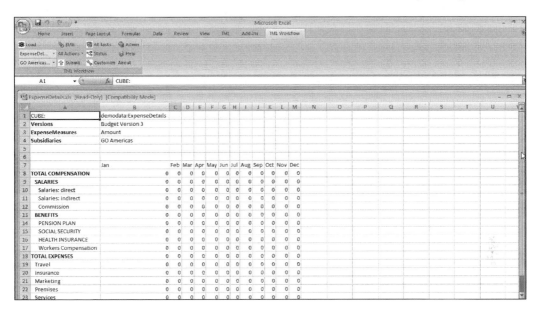

63. The preceding window displays the data entry view we had created in the **ExpenseDetails** cube. Since **Isha** is responsible to enter data for **GO Americas** subsidiary, she has got exactly the interface where she has access to data entry functions similar to what we saw in IBM Cognos TM1 Contributor Web Client.

64. Now we will see how to enter data in these cells and what are the various options provided to **Isha** to enter data for **GO Americas** subsidiary she is responsible for.

65. Right-click on the **Travel** cell for **Jan**, point to **Data Spread** and then click on **Growth%**.

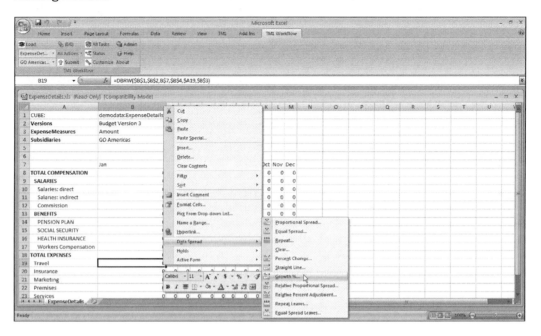

66. Set in such a way that the data spreads towards the right, starting from 50000 and then increasing by 3%, replacing existing values as shown in the following screenshot:

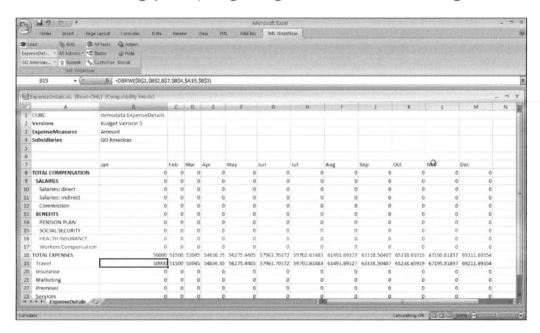

67. Now manually update cells for **Insurance**, **Jan** to 60000 and do equal spread towards right.

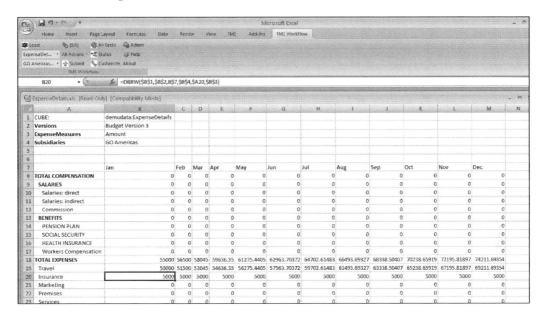

68. Now we will submit the budget whatever has been completed so far to the next level of hierarchy, which is **GO AMERICAS REGION**. **Joy** is responsible for **GO AMERICAS REGION** and all subsidiaries underneath it; hence he will be reviewer of the task submitted by **Isha**.

69. We will now submit the figures by clicking on ⬆ Submit (2107-13-59) icon from Isha's login.

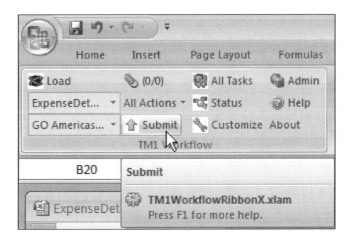

70. It will open an **Action Confirmation** box which lets the task submitted by user update the submit action with comments and other necessary information.

71. We could also have sent mail with the comments, added attachments, and so on. Now click on the All Tasks ⟨ All Tasks ⟩ icon.

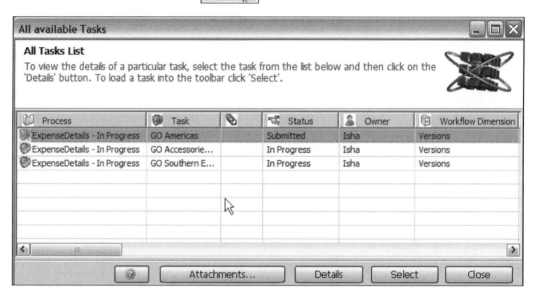

72. In the preceding screenshot note that **Isha** has just submitted task for **GO Americas** region while two other tasks are still pending.

73. Close the spreadsheet and TM1 **Perspectives for MS Excel** without saving any changes.

Reviewing submitted tasks

In this recipe we will see how the task submitted can be reviewed through:

- ▶ TM1 Excel Perspectives
- ▶ TM1 Web

Getting ready

We will use the same sample process we have created in the preceding recipe. Ensure that TM1 Admin Server service is started and demodata TM1 Server is running.

How to do it...

1. Log on to the TM1 **Perspectives for MS Excel** with user name as **Joy**.

2. Go to the **TM1 Workflow** tab and click on **Load** icon.

3. Choose the task **ExpenseDetails** and that will populate review tasks assigned to **Joy**. In the drop down, we see the list of tasks out of which **GO Americas** task is in **Submitted** state. Let's select that and see what data has been submitted.

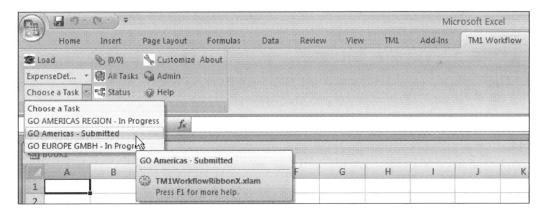

4. So **Joy** is now able to see the **Submitted** data and he can **Approve** that by clicking on ⊘ Approve icon on the toolbar.

5. He can also **Reject** and or **Revoke** the task by clicking on one of the choices as shown in the following screenshot:

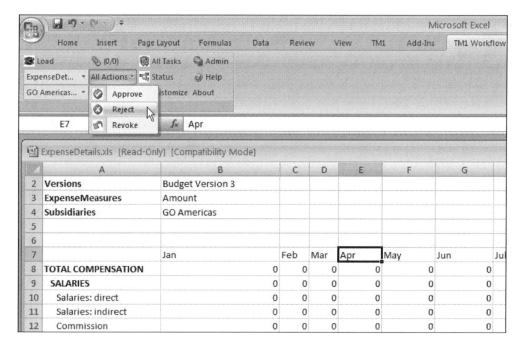

6. Close the TM1 **Perspectives for MS Excel** without saving anything.

7. Now let's review the task using TM1 Web through following link.

   `http://localhost/tm1web/`

8. It will open **IBM Cognos TM1 Web Login** screen as shown in the following screenshot:

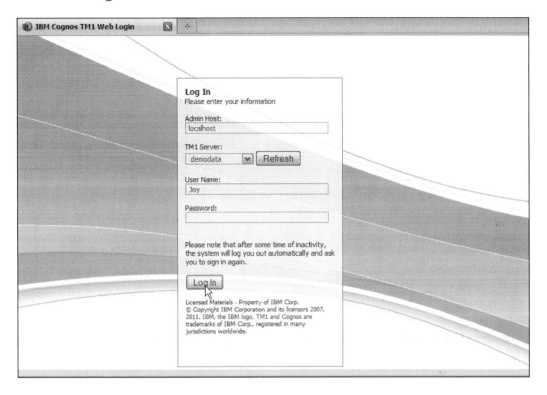

9. Log on to the demodata TM1 Server as **Joy**, shown in above figure.

10. Choose the **ExpenseDetails** process similar to what we did in **TM1Perspectives for MS Excel**. Again it will populate all the tasks assigned to **Joy**.

11. Similar to what we did while we were exploring **TM1Perspectives for MS Excel**, click on **GO Americas task** which is now in **Submitted** state.

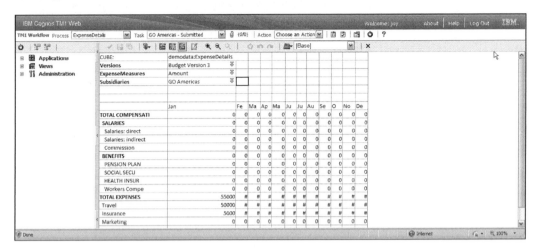

 Due to lesser column width the data in a few cells is not properly visible. Select such cells and click on **Autofit** selected column width icon to adjust width of the cells so that data is visible.

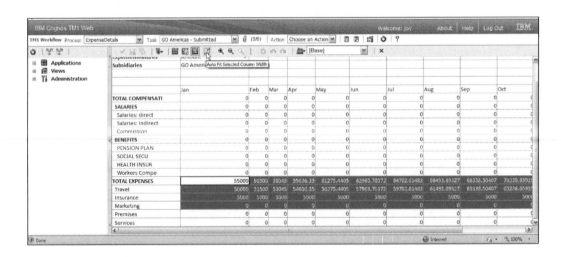

12. Now click on **Action** drop down as shown, to **Approve**, **Reject**, or **Revoke** data entered.

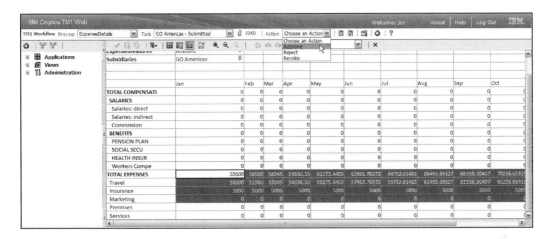

13. Click on **Reject** and enter the following comments as shown in the following screenshot:

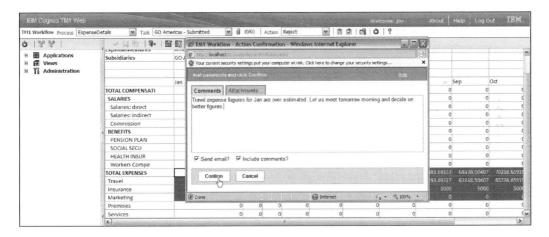

14. Click on **Confirm** button to send comments after the task is rejected so that submitter can make changes and submit again. Submitter cannot edit data before reviewer takes any action (**Approve/Reject/Revoke**).

15. Now log out and log in to **TM1 Perspectives for MS Excel** again with **Isha** as the user name.

16. After loading task note that **GO Americas** task has been **Rejected** as shown in the following screenshot:

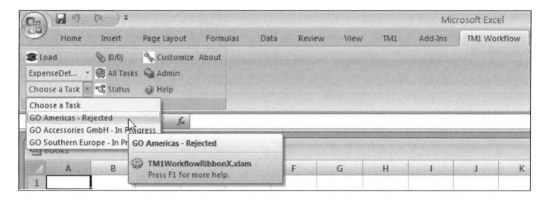

17. Click on **All Tasks** All Tasks (2107-13-74) icon under **Add-Ins** tab as shown in the following screenshot:

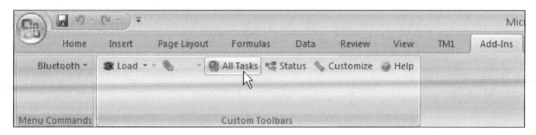

18. Click on **GO Americas** and then click on **Details** button.

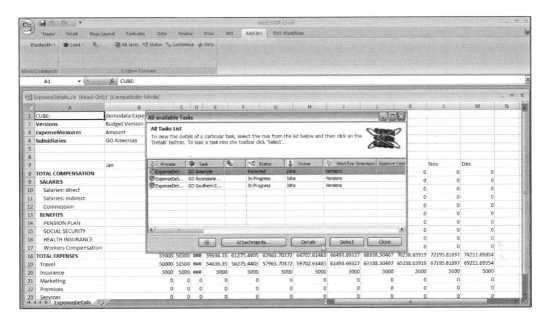

19. It will open another new window and will show details along with **Reject Comment** sent by **Joy**. Close all open windows without saving any changes.

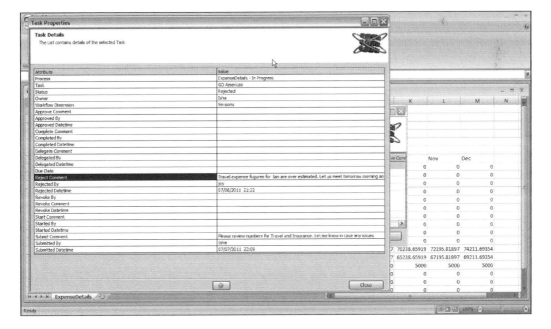

How it works...

We are now done with understanding basic concepts around TM1 Workflow, TM1 Perspectives for MS Excel, and IBM Cognos TM1 Web Client.

There's more...

TM1 contributor was added to TM1 much later and comes from IBM Cognos Enterprise Planning suite which is another Cognos Planning and Budgeting tool similar to TM1.

Prior to the integration, TM1 used to have TM1 Workflow, Perspectives for MS Excel, and TM1 Web Client, solely for user groups management, defining UIs for the application and playing around with the data. TM1 Architect remains the major component which comes from TM1, and is used to model business data in the form of various TM1 Objects.

So now we can have:

▶ IBM Cognos TM1 Architect as modelling tool to create cubes, dimensions, and TI processes.

▶ Either or both IBM Cognos TM1 Contributor Web Client or IBM Cognos TM1 Web client as an interface to enter, edit, review, and submit data through the Web.

▶ IBM Cognos TM1 Perspectives for MS Excel to do above functions through Microsoft Excel interface.

▶ Either or both IBM Cognos TM1 Workflow or IBM Cognos TM1 Contributor Workflow to create and manage the planning application and define workflow based on organizational structure of the organization. Both workflow components have administrative console available to the application designer.

Which components to use actually depends on business use cases and available licenses.

In the next chapter we will deal with integration points between IBM Cognos TM1, IBM Cognos Enterprise Planning, and IBM Cognos BI (starting with version 8 onwards). This may or may not be useful to most of the readers, but just nice to know.

14
Integration with IBM Cognos BI

In this chapter, we will cover:

> ► Integrating IBM Cognos TM1 with IBM Cognos 8 BI

Introduction

Untill now, we have seen different aspects of IBM Cognos TM1. Before proceeding with this chapter, please be aware of the existence of the following tools under the IBM Cognos umbrella:

> ► IBM Cognos 8 BI is a performance management tool with a focus on reporting. We will use the same Cognos BI Version 8 in this chapter. However, the same steps hold good for the latest version of Cognos BI which is version 10.

> ► The IBM Cognos Enterprise Planning tool is a similar planning and budgeting tool as IBM Cognos TM1. It existed as part of the Planning and Budgeting offerings by Cognos. Later, Cognos took over Applix and hence the TM1. (TM1 was originally the Planning and Budgeting tool by Applix before the acquisition.)

We will be discussing the integration of IBM Cognos TM1 with IBM Cognos 8 BI in detail. However, basic knowledge of Cognos 8 BI is assumed throughout the chapter.

We have already learnt and seen each and every way through which we can create and manage complex planning applications. These are as follows:

Component name	Use case	Comments
IBM Cognos TM1 Architect	Creating Dimensions, Cubes, and TI processes. Defining users, groups, and roles. Defining access rights to Cubes, Dimensions, Elements, and even cell level security can be defined here.	
IBM Cognos TM1 Web	Data entry, review, and submit through a web interface.	
IBM Cognos TM1 Perspectives	Data entry, review, and submit through Microsoft Excel interface.	
IBM Cognos TM1 Administration and Workflow	Create workflow, define organizational structure, and hence review hierarchy. Data entry users, groups, and roles and access rights assignments to different business views.	
IBM Cognos TM1 Contributor Administration and Workflow	Create workflow, define organizational structure, and hence review hierarchy. Data entry users, groups, and roles and access rights assignments to different business views. Users and groups can also be defined along with access rights. These will take precedence over security defined using #1.	Previously part of enterprise planning. Now integrated with TM1. Has better UI but functionally similar to #4.
IBM Cognos TM1 Contributor Web	Data entry, review, and submit through a web interface.	Previously part of enterprise planning. Now integrated with TM1. Has better UI but functionally similar to #2.

▶ Note that depending on the business requirements, a user can choose a custom installation, which can be a single computer (as shown in the book) or a distributed installation. Users can also choose between the components, for example, IBM Cognos Contributor components may not be needed at all.

▶ The same infrastructure can be taken further to work with existing IBM Cognos BI components or Planning and Budgeting applications wherever possible.

It is however recommended to separate the BI Server and TM1 Server for performance reasons and the TM1 server's memory requirements.

- ▶ We will discuss BI-TM1 in this chapter, though it is not absolutely necessary and also needs prior understanding of BI concepts, which every reader may not have. TM1-Enterprise Planning integration is made possible in a similar fashion and will not be discussed in this chapter; though please be aware that TM1 Cubes can be used in Enterprise Planning applications as well and integration concepts revolve around the same core, which we will be discussing with regards to TM1-BI integration.

Before diving into the details, please note the following points:

- ▶ TM1 was originally a product by Applix which merged with Cognos and, hence, is now referred to as Cognos TM1 and later IBM Cognos TM1 after IBM acquired Cognos.

- ▶ Enterprise Planning (EP) is a Planning and Budgeting tool by Cognos, similar to TM1 in functionality. After Applix merged with Cognos and Cognos with IBM, we now have two popular Planning and Budgeting tools, EP and TM1.

- ▶ Contributor is the basic component of EP which has an intuitive UI and is now integrated with TM1 as well so that users can have the best of both worlds. They can have fast client-side number crunching by the TM1 engine combined by the user intuitive and jazzy interface of the contributor workflow and contributor web client.

- ▶ Cognos BI is a performance management tool by Cognos which, after acquisition of Cognos by IBM, is referred to as IBM Cognos BI in this book. It is a tool dedicated to reporting, analysis, MOLAP, and event management. It has a modelling tool called Framework Manager and Studios to create, view, and distribute reports and cubes. These four studios are Report Studio, Query Studio, Analysis Studio, and Event Studio.

- ▶ Seamless integration between Cognos BI and Planning Applications (EP and TM1) is made possible in Cognos version 8 onwards.

- ▶ Hence, it has been made possible to have different tools for different business use cases and each of these tools talks to others in a seamless manner, part of which we will explain in this chapter.

Now we will be focusing on the integration of IBM Cognos TM1 with IBM Cognos 8 BI. It is assumed that readers are absolutely familiar with IBM Cognos 8 BI aspects, tools, and procedures. As a recap let's have a look at the Cognos BI components in a brief manner.

IBM Cognos 8 BI is a suite of the following tools;

Component name	Component type	Use case	Access type
Framework Manager	Metadata modelling tool.	Used to import metadata from various data sources, establish relationships between different database objects, and publish the resulting package to connection for use in authoring reports in one of the designer studios.	Desktop-based and to be installed for each metadata model designer.
Cognos Connection	Web-based interface, used to host and access metadata models and reports.	Metadata model (package) is published from Framework Manager to the web-based Cognos connection portal on which users can log on. Depending on user privileges, they can access packages and reports and create more reports in different studios introduced below.	Web based access after single server or distributed installation of Cognos BI server.
Report Studio	Web-based interface used to create reports.	Web-based interface in which packages published through Framework Manager can be opened and metadata can be used to create complex reports.	Web based access after single server or distributed installation of the Cognos BI Server.
Query Studio	Web-based interface used to create reports.	Web-based interface in which packages published through Framework Manager can be opened and metadata can be used to generate ad hoc queries and quickly view data in a simple manner. Similar to Report Studio but intended for more naïve users.	Web-based access after single server or distributed installation of the Cognos BI Server.
Analysis Studio	Web-based interface used to slice and dice multi-dimensional data sources like cubes.	Web-based interface in which dimensionally modeled packages and cubes published through Framework Manager can be opened and metadata can be used to slice and dice data to achieve ROLAP.	Web-based access after single server or distributed installation of the Cognos BI Server.

Component name	Component type	Use case	Access type
Event Studio	Web-based interface used to define events which can act as triggers to various pre-defined actions.	Web-based interface in which packages published through Framework Manager can be opened and metadata can be used to crated conditions and triggers to automate pre-defined actions based on the events.	Web-based access after single server or distributed installation of the Cognos BI Server.

Integrating IBM Cognos TM1 with IBM Cognos 8 BI

Before proceeding with the actual steps of the recipe, we will take a note of the following integration considerations:

▶ The measured Dimension in the TM1 Cube needs to be explicitly identified.

▶ The Data Source needs to be created in IBM Cognos Connection which points to the TM1 Cube. New Data Source can also be created from IBM Cognos Framework Manager, but for the sake of simplicity we will be creating that from IBM Cognos Connection itself.

▶ The created Data Source is used in IBM Cognos Framework Manager Model to create a Metadata Package and publish to IBM Cognos Connection.

▶ Metadata Package can be used to create reports, generate queries, slice and dice, or event management using one of the designer studios available in IBM Cognos BI.

We will focus on each of the above steps in this recipe, where we will be using one of the Cubes created as part of demodata TM1 Server application and we will be using the Cube as a Data Source in the IBM Cognos BI layer.

Getting ready

Ensure that the TM1 Admin Server service is started and demodata TM1 Server is running. We should have IBM Cognos 8 BI Server running and IBM Cognos 8 Framework Manager installed.

How to do it...

1. Open the TM1 Architect and right-click on the **Sales_Plan** Cube.

2. Click on **Properties**. In the **Measures Dimension** box, click on **Sales_Plan_Measures** and then for **Time Dimension** click on **Months**.

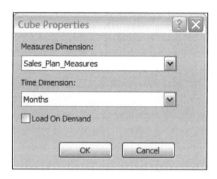

3. Note that the preceding step is compulsory if we want to use the Cube as a Data Source for the BI layer. We need to explicitly define a measures dimension and a time dimension.

4. Click on **OK** and minimize the TM1 Architect, keep the server running.

5. Now from the Start menu, open IBM Cognos **Framework Manager,** which is desktop-based tool used to create metadata models.

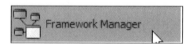

6. Create a new project from IBM Cognos 8 Framework Manager.

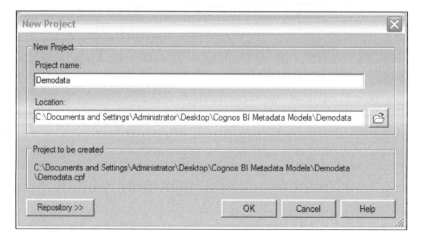

7. Enter the **Project name** as **Demodata** and provide the **Location** where the model file will be located. Note that each project generates a `.cpf` file which can be opened in the IBM Cognos Framework Manager.

8. Provide valid user credentials so that IBM Cognos Framework Manager can link to a running IBM Cognos BI Server setup. Users and roles are defined by IBM Cognos BI admin user. Choose **English** as the authoring language when the **Select Language** list comes up. This will open the **Metadata Wizard - Select Metadata Source**.
    We use the **Metadata Wizard** to create a new Data Source or point to an existing Data Source.

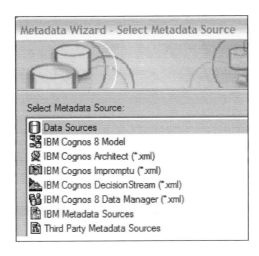

9. In the **Metadata Wizard** make sure that **Data Sources** is selected and click on the **Next** button.

10. In the next screen, click on the **New** button ▭ New... ▭ to create a new Data Source by the name of **TM1_Demodata_Sales_Plan**.

11. This will open a **New data source** wizard, where we need to specify the name of the Data Source.

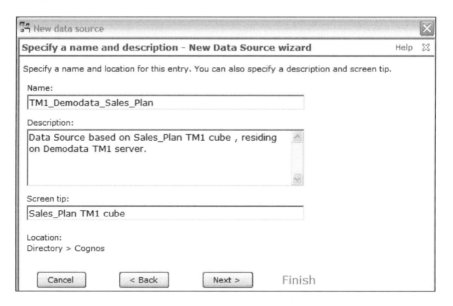

12. On next screen, it will ask for the Data Source **Type** for which we will specify **TM1** from the drop-down, as we want to create a new Data Source based on the TM1 Cube **Sales_Data**.

13. On the next screen specify the connection parameters. For **Administration Host** we can specify a name or localhost, depending on the name of the server. In our case, we have specified name of the server as **ankitgar**, hence we are using an actual name instead of a localhost. In the case of TM1 sitting on another server within the network, we will provide the IP address or name of the host in UNC format.

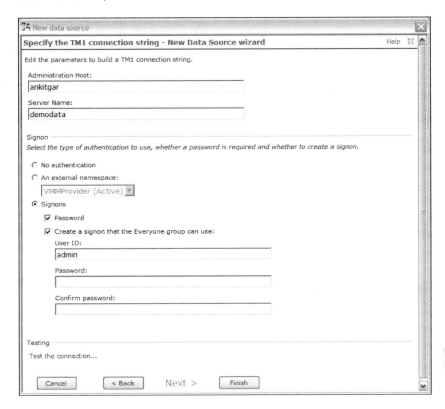

14. Test the connection to test whether the connection to the TM1 Cube is successful.

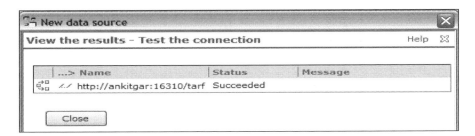

15. Click on **Close** and proceed. Click on the **Finish** button to complete the creation of the Data Source.

16. The new Data Source is created on the Cognos 8 Server and now can be used by anyone with valid privileges given by the admin user. It's just a connection to the **Sales_Plan** TM1 Cube which now can be used to create metadata models and, hence, reports and queries perform the various functions suggested in the preceding sections.

17. Now it will return to **Metadata Wizard** as shown, with the new Data Source appearing with the list of already created Data Sources.

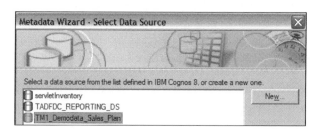

18. Click on the newly created Data Source and on the **Next** button.

19. It will display all available Cubes on the DemoData TM1 Server, the machine name being the server name (localhost/ankitgar).

20. Click on the **Sales_Plan** cube and then on **Next**.

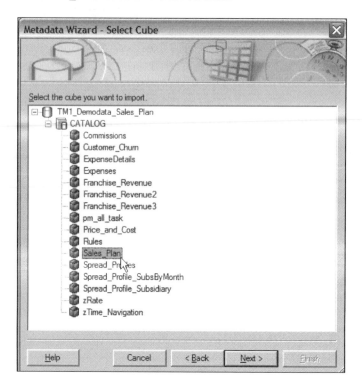

21. The next screen allows users to **Select Locales**. We don't have any such considerations so go ahead by clicking on the **Next** button.

22. Uncheck **Create the default package** checkbox and click on the **Finish** button.

23. This will now open the Cube in the IBM Cognos Framework Manager Tool. We will now create a new metadata package which will include the Cube. We will then publish it onto the IBM Cognos Connection.

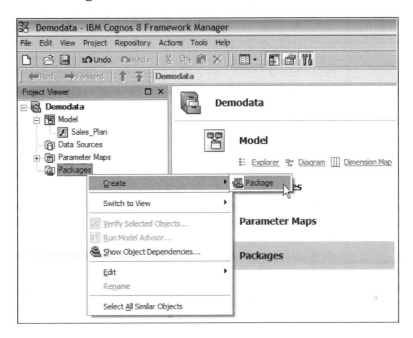

24. Right-click on the **Packages** icon and in the **Create Package** wizard provide a **Name** to create a new package, by name of **TM1_Demodata_Sale_Plan**. The **Create Package** wizard pops up when we right-click on **Packages**, click on **Create | Package**.

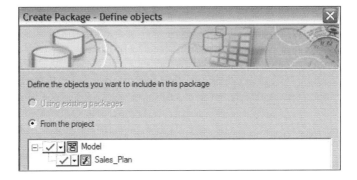

25. Now we have created the **TM1_Demodata_Sales_Plan** package and want to publish it on the IBM Cognos BI Server so that it is available to users to work with reports and the package.

26. In the **Publish Wizard**, uncheck the checkbox **Enable model versioning**, which is used to maintain different versions of the same model. Click on the **Next** button.

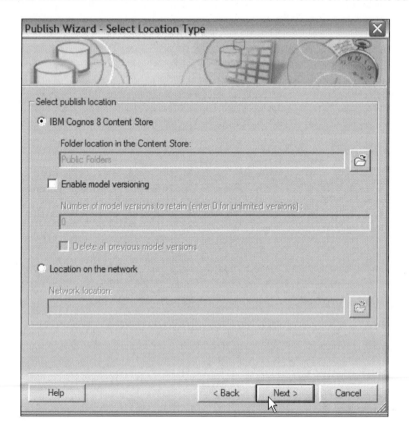

27. In the next screen, define the security on the metadata package if applicable. In our case we will not specify any additional package level security and so click on the **Next** button.

28. Publish the package by accepting the default parameters and click on the **Publish** button.

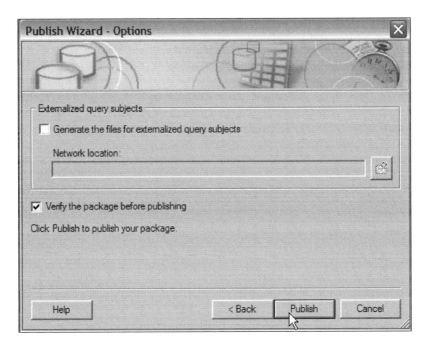

29. So, now we have successfully published the package to the IBM Cognos Connection on the IBM Cognos BI server. Click on **Finish** and save the model.

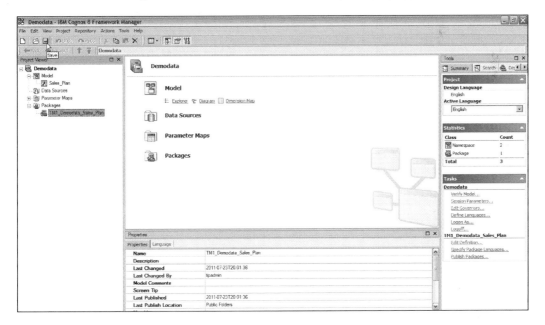

In the IBM Cognos Framework Manager Tool we can only access the Cubes, we cannot edit them.

30. Now open the IBM Cognos Connection page by clicking on the URL to access the IBM Cognos BI Server. In general, installations have URLs in the following format `http://<machine_name>/cognos8`.

31. This is provided by IBM Cognos admin, once installation of IBM Cognos BI Server is done and security has been set up. The IBM Cognos Framework Manager tool is then configured to talk to the IBM Cognos BI Server through IBM Cognos Configuration, which is desktop-based and contains connection parameters to the IBM Cognos BI Server.

32. We will be using a similar IBM Cognos 8 setup; however, configuration details have been skipped and we will directly focus on using the newly published package and making use of it.

33. Log on to the IBM Cognos Connection by clicking on the URL. Provide login credentials and we are now able to view all the published packages, along with our **TM1_Demodata_Sales_Plan** package based on a TM1 Cube.

 We are accessing this through a supported web browser as suggested in the IBM Cognos 8 BI documentation. In this recipe we are using IE, but other supported browsers can also be used in a similar fashion.

34. Now click on the **TM1_Demodata_Sales_Plan** package and then click on the **Launch** menu.

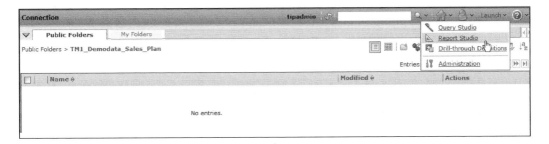

35. The menu displays a list of available designer studios available. Here **Query Studio** and **Report Studio** are available to us. Depending on security privileges, we may be given access to one or more studios. Here, for our users, **Analysis Studio** and **Event Studio** are not visible and hence not available to us. We will try opening the package in **Report Studio** and create a report from it.

36. Select the **Report Studio** option and a pop up will open the studio, wherein the report can be authored based on the package and on our case based on the TM1 **Sales_Plan** cube.

 IBM Cognos BI does not have a write-back facility to the database and hence data cannot be updated to the Cube through the BI layer. It can just be read based on what is written through TM1.

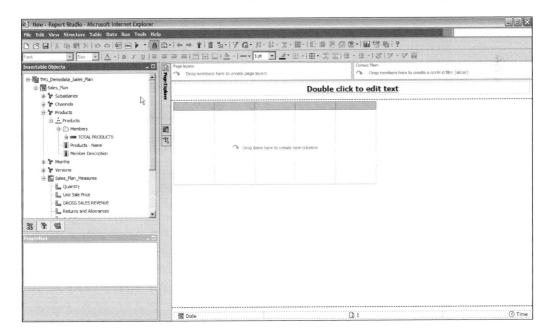

37. In the **Report Studio**, the left-hand side pane, **Insertable Objects**, shows up the package we have just published, which has objects from the **Sales_Plan** TM1 Cube. Items can be dragged and dropped onto the right-hand side authoring pane to create the report. Report can be then executed and saved on the server.

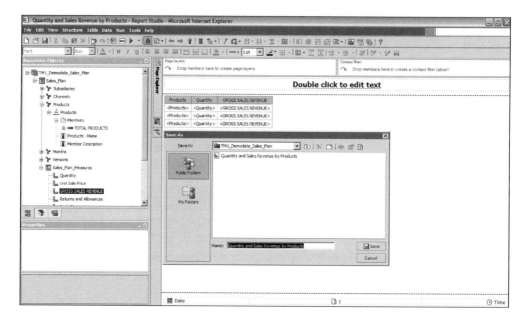

38. Reports can be saved to the server, from which they can be accessed by business users on an ad hoc fashion or can be scheduled to be executed at specific time intervals and distributed to users through e-mail in different formats.

39. The preceding screenshot shows up the newly created and saved report on the IBM Cognos BI Server. As and when we make changes to the data in the **Sales_Plan** Cube, these will be reflected in the report in real time.

How it works...

In this recipe, we have seen how we can use TM1 Cubes as Data Sources to create reports in IBM Cognos BI. Report authoring in IBM Cognos BI, and using various features according to different business use cases, is altogether a different subject of discussion and is out of the scope of this book. Here, the intention is to show how IBM Cognos TM1 and the IBM Cognos BI layer talk to each other. Detailed discussions on authoring reports in IBM Cognos BI can be found in the *IBM Cognos 8 BI Cookbook* by Packt Publishing.

TM1 Cubes can also be used in IBM Cognos Enterprise Planning applications in a similar fashion. Detail discussions on the IBM Cognos Enterprise Planning tool can be found in the *IBM Cognos Enterprise Planning Guide* by Packt Publishing.

Index

Thank you for buying
IBM Cognos TM1 Cookbook

About Packt Publishing

Packt, pronounced 'packed', published its first book "*Mastering phpMyAdmin for Effective MySQL Management*" in April 2004 and subsequently continued to specialize in publishing highly focused books on specific technologies and solutions.

Our books and publications share the experiences of your fellow IT professionals in adapting and customizing today's systems, applications, and frameworks. Our solution-based books give you the knowledge and power to customize the software and technologies you're using to get the job done. Packt books are more specific and less general than the IT books you have seen in the past. Our unique business model allows us to bring you more focused information, giving you more of what you need to know, and less of what you don't.

Packt is a modern, yet unique publishing company, which focuses on producing quality, cutting-edge books for communities of developers, administrators, and newbies alike. For more information, please visit our website: www.PacktPub.com.

About Packt Enterprise

In 2010, Packt launched two new brands, Packt Enterprise and Packt Open Source, in order to continue its focus on specialization. This book is part of the Packt Enterprise brand, home to books published on enterprise software – software created by major vendors, including (but not limited to) IBM, Microsoft and Oracle, often for use in other corporations. Its titles will offer information relevant to a range of users of this software, including administrators, developers, architects, and end users.

Writing for Packt

We welcome all inquiries from people who are interested in authoring. Book proposals should be sent to author@packtpub.com. If your book idea is still at an early stage and you would like to discuss it first before writing a formal book proposal, contact us; one of our commissioning editors will get in touch with you.

We're not just looking for published authors; if you have strong technical skills but no writing experience, our experienced editors can help you develop a writing career, or simply get some additional reward for your expertise.

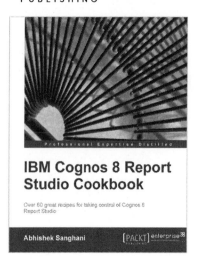

IBM Cognos 8 Report Studio Cookbook

ISBN: 978-1-849680-34-9   Paperback: 252 pages

Over 80 great recipes for taking control of IBM Cognos 8 Report Studio

1. Learn advanced techniques to produce real-life reports that meet business demands

2. Tricks and hacks for speedy and effortless report development and to overcome tool-based limitations

3. Peek into the best practices used in industry and discern ways to work like a pro

4. Part of Packt's Cookbook series-each recipe is a carefully organized sequence of instructions to complete the task as efficiently as possible

IBM Cognos 8 Planning

ISBN: 978-1-847196-84-2   Paperback: 424 pages

Engineer a clear-cut strategy for achieving best-in-class results using IBM Cognos 8 Planning

1. Build and deploy effective planning models using Cognos 8 Planning

2. Filled with ideas and techniques for designing planning models

3. Ample screenshots and clear explanations to facilitate learning

4. Written for first-time developers focusing on what is important to the beginner

5. A step-by-step approach that will help you strengthen your understanding of all the major concepts

Please check **www.PacktPub.com** for information on our titles

IBM Lotus Notes and Domino 8.5.1

ISBN: 978-1-847199-28-7   Paperback: 336 pages

Upgrade your system and embrace the exciting new features of the IBM Lotus Notes and Domino 8.5.1 platform

1. Upgrade to the latest version of Lotus Notes and Domino

2. Understand the new features and put them to work in your business

3. Thoroughly covers Domino Attachment Object Service (DAOS), Domino Configuration Tuner (DCT), and iNotes

4. Packed with expert tips and useful screenshots

IBM WebSphere Application Server v7.0 Security

ISBN: 978-1-84968-148-3   Paperback: 312 pages

Secure your IBM WebSphere applications with Java EE and JAAS security standards

1. Discover the salient and new security features offered by WebSphere Application Server version 7.0 to create secure installations

2. Explore and learn how to secure Application Servers, Java Applications, and EJB Applications along with setting up user authentication and authorization

3. With the help of extensive hands-on exercises and mini-projects, explore the various aspects needed to produce secure IBM WebSphere Application Server Network Deployment v7.0 infrastructures

Please check **www.PacktPub.com** for information on our titles

Printed in Great Britain
by Amazon.co.uk, Ltd.,
Marston Gate.